D0025573

FRENCH PAINTING

BETWEEN THE PAST AND THE PRESENT

PRINCETON MONOGRAPHS

IN ART AND ARCHAEOLOGY

XXVII

PUBLISHED FOR THE

DEPARTMENT OF ART AND ARCHAEOLOGY

PRINCETON UNIVERSITY

FRENCH PAINTING

BETWEEN THE PAST AND THE PRESENT

ARTISTS, CRITICS, AND TRADITIONS,

FROM 1848 TO 1870

BY JOSEPH C. SLOANE

PRINCETON, NEW JERSEY
PRINCETON UNIVERSITY PRESS

COPYRIGHT, 1951, PRINCETON UNIVERSITY PRESS

ALL RIGHTS RESERVED
LC Card: 72-11943
ISBN: 0-691-00306-8 (PAPERBACK EDN.)
ISBN: 0-691-03817-1 (HARDCOVER EDN.)

FIRST PRINCETON PAPERBACK EDITION, 1973

SECOND HARDCOVER PRINTING, 1973

THIS BOOK IS SOLD SUBJECT TO THE CONDITION THAT IT
SHALL NOT, BY WAY OF TRADE, BE LENT, RESOLD, HIRED
OUT, OR OTHERWISE DISPOSED OF WITHOUT THE PUBLISHER'S
CONSENT, IN ANY FORM OF BINDING OR COVER OTHER THAN
THAT IN WHICH IT IS PUBLISHED.

PRINTED IN THE UNITED STATES OF AMERICA
BY PRINCETON UNIVERSITY PRESS AT PRINCETON, NEW JERSEY

To M. M. S.

PREFACE

ALTHOUGH many volumes have been written about French painting in the nineteenth century, certain aspects of the subject have not as yet been sufficiently investigated. Among these are the critical reactions to the paintings of the middle of the century, and the more general connection between art and the broader intellectual interests of the time. The amount of material available as evidence is extremely large, and it may be only after a number of studies have been made that the true nature of this period will become known. If the present book contributes to that end, it will have amply served its purpose.

Some of the material contained in Part One has already been published in "The Tradition of Figure Painting and Concepts of Modern Art in France from 1845 to 1870" which appeared in the *Journal of Aesthetics and Art Criticism,* September, 1948, and is reused here by kind permission of the American Society for Aesthetics. These parts have, however, been revised and much expanded.

The author wishes to express his gratitude for the award of the Hodder Fellowship by the Special Program in the Humanities of Princeton University which made the research and writing of the book possible. He is also more than grateful to Professor Earl Baldwin Smith of Princeton for many hours of invaluable counsel and criticism. Thanks are also extended to Professor George Boas of the Johns Hopkins and Professor Jean Seznec of Oxford for help and advice when they were most needed, and to Miss Margot Cutter of Princeton University Press for her assistance in preparing the manuscript. Mr. Ian Fraser of the American Library in Paris did so much to make the collection of the proper illustrations possible that the writer will be long in his debt, and the cooperation of the staff of the Frick Art Reference Library was also much appreciated. To numerous other colleagues and friends who were patient enough to listen and kind enough to suggest, he gives grateful acknowledgment. Lastly he wishes to express his appreciation of the leave of absence granted by Bryn Mawr College without which the completion of the study would have been long delayed.

J. C. S.

Bryn Mawr, Pennsylvania
June, 1950

PREFACE TO THE SECOND PRINTING

IN coming back once more to the ideas contained in the original printing of this book, it is clear that the mind of the author, at least, has not changed about them in the intervening years. The book was intended to open the way to a more tolerant study of the French painters of the mid-nineteenth century and to suggest that there were valuable approaches to the art of the period which had not yet been explored. The interpretation of this most complex century had, by the 1940's, tended to crystallize into a set of judgments which precluded the reception of many useful and significant insights into what had actually taken place. The artists worth considering had been too firmly separated from the artists *not* worth considering (Thomas Couture, for example) so that an almost stifling odor of sanctity hung about those selected while an equally oppressive smell of death hung over everyone else.

The book was an attempt to break this mold, to insist that there was much yet to be discovered before we could assume that the evidence was all in or that we knew all we needed to know. While it is true that no shattering reversal of opinion has taken place in the past thirteen years, it is also true that we now are beginning to get a far better view of the art of the century as a whole than we had before. If the present study still has a usefulness in this expanded scholarship, it is a pleasure to bring it forward once more in a new and less expensive format.

The book has not been outdated by subsequent research; it is simply an earlier essay in a field now more fully mapped. A distinguished editor said of it before the first printing that it was a moral book, and this was not an age that was kind to moral writing. If it has survived in spite of this, the author is particularly pleased because the loss of moral opinions from humane studies has been a tragedy. Scientific method as a tool for the examination of the central truths about painting or any other medium is highly imperfect.

Modern art, as most of its advanced practitioners and critics agree, is in serious disarray, and part of the difficulty may stem from a fairly general abandonment of value judgments such as were troubling keen minds a hundred years ago when the present volume closes. These difficulties are with us still, a fact which may make timely this exposition of some of them.

J. C. S.

Chapel Hill, North Carolina
January, 1973

CONTENTS

ILLUSTRATIONS

The pictures are arranged in chronological groups designed to give the reader an idea of the order in which the majority of them came to the attention of the critics and the public. Paintings which were shown at the Salons are marked with an asterisk (*), and are included under the year of exhibition rather than that of creation where the two are not the same. A few whose dates are uncertain have been included in an appropriate group. Titles have been kept in French, and the ones used are those most commonly employed by the critics; for this reason they may vary somewhat from those in common usage today. The *Patrouille turque* by Decamps may not be the one exhibited in the Salon of 1831. All pictures in oil unless otherwise indicated.

FRENCH PAINTING

BETWEEN THE PAST AND THE PRESENT

INTRODUCTION

THE purpose of the following account of certain ideas and events connected with the history of French painting in the middle years of the last century is to examine a crucial historical moment when the art of France, as well as that of Europe generally, was passing from the well-charted waters of tradition into the hitherto untraveled channels of modern expression; it was, in truth, a period lying between the past and the present. Before it, tradition was still in control, albeit with waning force; when it ended, the authority of the past was broken, leaving the modern movement well founded and flourishing. For reasons which will be advanced presently, we shall here be concerned only with subject matter and the attitudes taken toward it, attitudes revealed not only in the paintings themselves, but in the critical commentary upon them. The standards used by both artists and critics in judging the worth of a theme or the handling of it will sometimes be found to differ from those in common use today. But such differences are illuminating, for they furnish important information about the social and intellectual environment in which art was being produced, and even fresh insight into our understanding of the pictures themselves. The question of the relative value of these norms of a hundred years ago and more recent ones must be resolved by each individual for himself, but however he may decide, the comparison should not be without interest.

The descriptive terms employed in a discussion of this kind are, it must be remembered, relative rather than absolute; in certain cases exact definition is virtually impossible. Realism, for example, is never complete in any painting. If it were, the result would be the subject over again rather than an interpretation of it; and beyond a rather vague limit, the more perfect the illusion of reality, the less the picture is a work of art at all. Such a term must be regarded as indicating an emphasis, a degree, rather than a total exemplification. Other words like romanticism, classicism, and traditionalism are to be understood in the light of similar reservations. The artistic ideas and movements of the time were not separate entities in themselves, but tendencies which stressed certain aspects of artistic creation at the expense of others deemed of less value. As will be seen later, the same individual often held views which in some absolute sense would seem to be contradictory, but which in the atmosphere of change and uncertainty then prevailing might easily exist side by side. The thought of a society, as well as of an individual, is seldom, if ever, entirely logical.

In plan, the study is divided into two parts, both of which deal primarily with subject matter rather than style, for it is with the transformation of the thinking about the former that this book is concerned. The material covered in both parts is briefly outlined here so that questions which may arise but are not answered in the first, can be held in abeyance until their discussion in the second.

Part One deals with the various theories held by leading individual critics or by several writers in common. These are considered apart from the paintings to which they were applied so that the reader may become familiar with their general nature and essential premises. Some of them were derived from actual examples, either from the past or from current production, while others were the result of a broader interest in the state of society as a whole and the place which art might, or should, occupy in it. In other words, these ideas were in some cases deductive and in others, didactic, though the effect of the latter on the course of art is problematical. Space is lacking in which to discuss their origins and gradual evolution up to the time when they were applied to the work of the mid-nineteenth century, for most were of a considerable antiquity and had interesting, if complex, histories. It is to be hoped that the reader will have some previous familiarity with many of them, and that the significance of the others will be apparent from the use to which they were put.

Considered thus, apart from specific examples, these theories can, if we like, be applied to any painter whatever, and the same artist be made to appear in different lights depending, as it were, on the color of the lens through which he is being viewed. In this manner, the painters of a hundred years ago appeared good, bad, and indifferent to the critics according to their various points of view. The primary intention here is to make these attitudes as clear as possible. Anyone previously acquainted with the art of the period will inevitably compare them with his own standards and find himself sometimes impatient with them, sometimes in violent disagreement. But a plea is made for a fair hearing. In some cases, the failures and defects of these judgments will be painfully apparent, and an effort will be made to underline them. In other cases, however, the old judgments may seem in certain ways superior to the ones to which we have been accustomed. An understanding of them requires an open mind and a willingness to listen to ideas of another day that are based on premises somewhat different from our own. Enough quotations have been included to allow the reader to form his own opinion, and he may sense that there is room for a reappraisal of some of our commonly accepted criteria. It was this awareness that first led the author to attempt the present study.

It will be observed that the material in this section falls into a kind of pattern; one might almost call it a progression, were it not for the fact that this word implies a time sequence which is not actually present. What we are dealing with here is the shift from a traditional attitude to a more modern one, and this change is marked by stages each more or less distinct from the others, albeit overlapping in the sense that all existed at roughly the same time.

The first of these stages is the extreme conservative position which holds that art can build successfully only on the past, that "literary" values are an essential element in great art, and that the main function of style is to make those values clear and effective for the observer. In this view, subjects should be drawn from sources such as the antique or the Bible, with exceptions in favor of other great literary themes and important historical events. In its debased form, it came to include all sorts of anecdotes, contemporary battles, events, official functions and the like, or even exotic scenes of a rather grandiose but unhistorical nature.

The next stage, which includes the idealistic aspect of positivism, we will call the humanitarian. It divests itself of the past, of kings and heroes, gods and saints, and turns to man himself as he is in his present condition. This attitude is essentially sympathetic to man as subject matter for art, and at the same time analytical in the sense of desiring a penetration of human nature profound enough to lead to a new ideal based upon man as he is, rather than on some ideal projection of him in terms of imaginary or historical supermen. In one way it is traditional too, for although it rejects the trappings of the past and its iconography, it hopes for a new symbolism and a new idealism to replace the ones now considered outworn. As will be seen later, it was beset by one fatal weakness, namely, the virtual impossibility of abstracting any fixed and universal symbols out of a society undergoing a very rapid and fundamental transformation. The "modernism" of this position lay in the fact that its subjects were to be drawn directly from life and its attention devoted to man in his contemporary status.

The next, the so-called realistic, stage was a movement closely allied in the thinking of the time to the scientific side of positivism, and, at least subconsciously, to the tenets of materialism and science in their emphasis upon quantitative rather than qualitative conclusions. Here man is really an object of interest by virtue of his existence as a fact, the most interesting of all objects perhaps, but not essentially different from trees, clothes, or the sky. This view was as anxious to get rid of the past as the other, but chiefly for the purpose of having a new look at the world minus the blinders imposed by tradition and custom, rather than for any desired elevation of common persons into a new position of eminence. From this angle, the mind, soul, and emotions of any man represented in a picture were of comparatively little consequence; the thing to do was to look at kinds of men and kinds of things in a way which had hitherto been prohibited. It is far from easy to define what was the exact meaning of the term "realism," since the critics themselves were not too clear on the point, but in one important respect it unquestionably referred to the practice of choosing new subjects drawn from life represented in an unusually direct manner. The technique by which this was done was of less moment, as will be explained later.

Finally, there is the view that the object is no longer something which has its own rights, as it were, but is significant chiefly in terms of the artist's feelings, or reactions to it. In art of this kind, human beings are not so much studied with a view to revealing their inner nature or suggesting the possibilities of the mind and soul in any general way, nor are they taken at their face value for the interest there is in looking at them as types or examples of the many fascinating things the world contains. They are seen as bases, starting points, for artistic presentations of form, color, light, design and the like, and as subjective revelations of the artist's own temperament, interests, and reactions to his own experience—experience not so much of his intellect or spiritual life, as of his eyes. The sources often remain fixed in the realm of contemporary fact, but the end product exists largely in the sensitivity of the artist himself.

These four stages of criticism reflected a transformation of art itself, but unless they are understood for what they were, unless one is familiar with the variety of attitudes which formed the basis for contemporary reviews, the reactions to specific works will seem haphazard and confusing. It is not uncommon today for biographers to list the statements made about various artists, but they are usually arranged under the simple categories of favorable or unfavorable, and since these same painters have now achieved the status of masters, the unfavorable comments are likely to be regarded as stupid, whereas they are often extremely acute if considered in the light of the intellectual climate of their time. Whether this climate was healthier than our own or not is naturally an entirely different question.

In Part Two, the artists themselves are discussed—partly in the light of their own views, partly through the eyes of the critics who judged them, and partly in the sense of a general evaluation of their progress toward novel forms and the aptness of contemporary efforts to describe this motion. This section is not intended to be a history of the painting of the time; nor does it intend to give a biographical account of the men who played the important roles. It attempts rather to describe those aspects of the artists' work, and the ideas relative to them, which were involved in the formation of modern attitudes toward the function of subject matter in painting. This is the more difficult part of the book, for anyone familiar with this art will have already formed his own judgments about its nature and the expressive intentions of the painters concerned, and it will be a question as to whether these should, or should not, be modified in the light of more contemporary opinion. Were the critics of those days as keen as our own? Were they prevented from making accurate appraisals by their nearness to the artistic events which they were attempting to understand and evaluate? No final answers to these questions need be offered, for the reader will draw his own conclusions; but taking the critical output as a whole, it may be suggested that what was lost through a lack of perspective, was gained through a surer knowledge of the environment and a closer acquaintance with the artists themselves. If we are prepared to set any real store by the opinions currently expressed in regard to the art of our own times, we should, presumably, be willing to concede a similar respect for these earlier observers. Since their criteria differ from some of ours, the temptation is only too strong to accuse them of not being properly equipped for their job, but the temptation should be resisted.

The reader must be warned at the very outset that most of the writers discussed believed honestly that subject matter was of the utmost importance, that art was intended to convey certain concepts which we might describe as "literary," concepts without which painting, in their estimation, could never be truly great. This belief was severely shaken by the rapid change taking place everywhere in society, but uncertainty should not be confused with stupidity or lack of intelligence—those were indeed difficult times. The famous phrase, *ut pictura poesis*, ("as is painting, so is poetry"), was applied well on into these days, affecting the entire outlook on art; and if we today do not hold to this notion, if we believe that "literary" art is, by definition, inferior, then at least we show how great a change has come over criticism in a little more than a hundred years. The problem becomes more difficult the moment we attempt to decide whether one of these positions is better than the other. If we maintain, as some have done, that the proper experience of art is principally confined to the pleasurable reactions obtained from harmonious relations of line, form, and color; if we insist with Maurice Denis that "a picture—before being a battle horse, a nude woman, or some anecdote—is *essentially* a plane surface covered with colors assembled in a certain order," then we are going to have trouble with a proper evaluation of Michelangelo's Sistine Ceiling, which was patently far more than this, even though we find a perfect explanation for our enjoyment of a work by Matisse, who has not concerned himself with equivalent problems of human destiny. On the other hand, if we hold to the notion that art's chief purpose is the idealization of nature and the holding of the mirror of virtue up to imperfect man—that is, if we concentrate on the subject rather than the form of the work—we will be hard pressed to find adequate words of praise for Matisse, and are apt to think much too highly of the art of Hippolyte Flandrin. It is, clearly, a dilemma, and the critics of the mid-nineteenth century, like ourselves, were on the horns of it. The majority of them, however, did not hesitate to take sides. With the exception of a few men who were prepared to abandon traditional subject matter (or any other of a similar nature) in favor of a fresh individuality of expression and technique as described hereafter, most of the writers we shall discuss leaned toward a belief in the necessity for a subject with moral or traditional significance. Other subjects were admissible, but inferior. To the degree to which any modern reader puts his faith in the current idea that a work of art is essentially a new object in itself to be admired and judged entirely upon its own inner merits without reference to the world of common visual experience (or its extension in myth, religion, or legend), to that extent he will find this material uncongenial and its authors in error. He must, however, guard against too rigid an application of this theory to the great art of the past, for if all "literary" elements be ruled out, say, of the art of Giotto, what is left will be something obviously less than its total effectiveness upon the beholder, whether it be strictly aesthetic or not. If there is a mixture, it would seem to be hardly worth the trouble to extricate the one in the hope of being able to ignore the other, or enjoy them separately at different times. Conversely, a person who allows himself to be overly persuaded by the eloquence of a Delécluze or a Thoré will soon discover that he has lost the power to enjoy any of the art after Delacroix and Millet, and that is a patent absurdity.

This is not the place to argue the aesthetic problems involved in the relation of form to subject, or to decide the relative merits of the arguments in favor of an art of essentially formal content and effect as against that which has some sort of definite moral intent. It is, however, impossible to be completely objective, and one's preferences and convictions will out in spite of the best of intentions. It must then be admitted that the present writer has a firm belief that both subject matter, in the traditional or conceptual sense, and the formal sensuous aspect of the work may well have a place in the final product, and that in the case of the very greatest art of all, the two are inextricably combined into a whole more effective than either would be alone. It is a truism, of course, that trivial and insincere meanings are far worse than no ulterior significance at all, but this is not to say that when such meanings involve the deepest spiritual desires of mankind they are still a hindrance to the proper enjoyment of the work. It can further be said that purely abstract art in which no real object is recognizable, if it be skillfully and harmoniously contrived, is superior to a work which, in spite of a minute and technically adept technique, never rises above the level of counterfeiting an anecdote from life, either real or imaginary. It is fair to say that the concern of the critics with whom we shall be dealing was not primarily with art in general, but with the heights to which it might conceivably reach. They were not content merely to enjoy any well painted and visually agreeable object presented for their inspection, though they did enjoy many such, but were basically concerned with the mainsprings of "great" art, the loftiest reaches to which it *might* attain under the proper conditions.

Perhaps there is some significance in the fact that there was a traditional category of "great" painting. It may seem ridiculous to suppose that anyone can deliberately set out to achieve greatness, and surely there were almost none among the painters of the time who had any aptitude for it. Yet one cannot help admiring the idea in the abstract, for what it meant was that the artist set himself the problem of dealing effectively in pictorial form with what was imagined to be the most important and difficult side of human nature: its nobility and its capacity to rise above itself. Idealism is not in itself unworthy, but it was unhappily tarnished by the fumbling efforts of incompetent minds to express it in terms which had lost the largest part of their validity. To strive for spiritual significance was quite legitimate when the attempt was honest, but the times seemed to condemn such lofty aims to dry failure. The remembered greatness of the past was an unfortunate criterion, but it was all that was available to illustrate the concept. The critical literature of the time is strewn with examples of settlements for something less, and yet it was always done with regret. Rightly or wrongly the critics believed the observer could expect certain standards of the artist, and they also felt they had a place in formulating them. If this ever was their privilege, it has been surrendered since.

It is inevitable that style will be more emphasized where interest in content is secondary, but when people are enthusiastically concerned with what a picture is about, they tend to regard style as the means by which the final dramatic or spiritual effect is well or poorly achieved, rather than as a separate basis for analysis. If critical appraisal is to rest on the quality of the idea which the picture conveys, then such matters as pose, facial expression, composition, light effects, and so on, will be considered not in any abstract sense but in relation to the effect they have upon the theme itself. It is, for instance, conceivable that a design of great abstract beauty might be applied to a scene of the Crucifixion so as to render the significance of that moment virtually null and void, but the picture, as a composition, would still be highly pleasurable to the eye. Since the criticism of the years prior to the advent of an essentially modern style was inclined to think in terms of realization of theme, it was natural that it should be somewhat less expert in the discussion of style. If to this fact be added the scorn—in itself, often well founded—with which we now regard many of the subjects exhibited, the criticism is occasionally likely to seem silly if not worse. But there is a danger here: the ultimate basis on which the criticism rests should not be confused with the object to which it is applied. A humanitarian attitude applied to the art of Rembrandt will yield important results, but applied to the work of a small-minded academic genre painter it will seem ridiculous. The period thus presents the frequent paradox of a theory noble in its abstract form and downright stupid in its application to individual pictures. Possibly these writers should never have attempted to erect the fine critical structures they did, since they largely lacked proven examples on which to use them in their own day; but it would have been hard to ask them to keep still just because the art they saw didn't measure up to the hopes they had for it.

These experts were therefore less capable in the field of style, and as a result have not been widely read except by specialists once style became the preponderant issue, or at least once the interest in theme became different from their own. But we are confining our discussion to a particular period, and the focus of the argument will be subject matter, and the ways in which it was regarded. To borrow a phrase from the period itself, we shall be speaking of that part of painting which speaks more to the mind than the eye. If some of the conclusions to be drawn from such a discussion are negative, they do not necessarily lose their value on that account.

A word should, perhaps, be said about the adjective "literary" as applied to art. Fixed definitions of this term are not numerous, but we generally understand by it a picture or statue which tells a story. Delaroche's well-known *Les Enfants d'Edward IV* (*The Princes in the Tower*) is a fair example of what is meant. In almost photographic detail we see the grim walls of the prison, and the terrified boys and little dog starting up at the first faint sound of the jailor's feet as he comes to bring their unhappy lives to a tragic conclusion. If we are susceptible to this kind of thing, our scalp tingles with dread and our eyes become moist at the thought of so sad and unmerited a fate. All this is well and good, but the line which divides it historically from something of quite a different sort is extremely hard to draw. Are we to say, on this basis, that Poussin's *Les Bergers de l'Arcadie*—which tells a subtler but far more involved story—is also "literary"? Is the Joshua Roll to be similarly classified? Or Carpaccio's *Legend of St. Ursula*? Is the term applicable to any picture which "tells" any story? Does it mean that if the same subject or event can also be described in words, that is the criterion for its use? Most people would not care to go so far, but they may have a hard time in saying just how far they do go. In the opinion of this writer it would be better not to use the term at all. Essentially, there lies behind any written or painted version of an event—whether real or imaginary—the event itself, expressed, if one may say so, in neither form. Possibly it is the artist's misfortune that in describing what he has done we have to use symbols which are, primarily, not his modes of expression but those of the writer, the man who may be trying to express the scene too, and in the symbols that are rightfully his. In spite of the fact that it is too much of a counterfeit of reality, it is hard to say that any words can truly reproduce the effect which the Delaroche picture has upon the observer; this can only be obtained by *seeing* it. The task of the critic is thus, in a

9

way, hazardous to start with, unless the person whom he is addressing knows the picture at first hand. It is true that he finds it easier to describe a picture which does depict an anecdote, for he can retell the anecdote in his own words—as Gautier did—or comment in understandable fashion on the way the artist has handled the action, the emotion, the setting, and similar matters where his words have a parallel (but not identical) competence. But when the matter turns to visual effects, that part of the picture which must be seen, the reactions to which are essentially visual and not verbal, he has far more difficulty. One has a certain sympathy for the attention which writers on art in earlier years gave to the subject—as long as that was something about which extended comment was possible—for they felt less sure of themselves when it came to discussions of the harmony of forms or value relationships. Possibly some of the trouble the public has today in making sense out of a good deal of the writing on abstract art is a result of the fact that the author must put into words what cannot be expressed verbally. A comparison of the commentary on Picasso's *Guernica* with that evoked by Delacroix's *La Liberté sur les barricades* would be instructive.

The critics of the mid-century, writing at a time when traditional subjects had become so out of date as to be generally boring, were thus forced to practice their own art on uncongenial or inadequate examples. In the cases where genius still dealt with such themes—Ingres and Delacroix, for example—they had something solid enough to work on, but these opportunities were all too rare. When, on the other hand, they came to pass judgment on subjects that were not dramatic, ideal, or moral (in the best sense of that term), they naturally found them wanting. A later age ceased to expect something else, with the result that its eyes were slowly opened to the exciting spectacle of an essentially different, yet engrossing, approach; but these critics were no longer able to make demands on the painter and had to cease asserting their claim to a share in the formulation of the principles according to which art was to be produced. Their new task was the difficult one of reeducating, both themselves and the public, in order to understand what the artist was doing, to feel as he felt, and grasp the significance of complex, even secret, expressions of his personality. This was by no means easy unless they were fortunate enough to share and sympathize with the drives that had led the painter to create.

The present study is confined to developments in France, partly to keep the inquiry within reasonable bounds, but more particularly because France was the center of these developments and the movements outside her borders were far less decisive. The English contribution to modern landscape had been made largely in the early part of the century (except for Turner's later influence on the Impressionists) and Pre-Raphaelitism remained chiefly an English phenomenon. The French humanitarians did not base themselves on Ruskin or even refer to him, and other English critics, with the exception of Gilbert Hamerton, need not be considered during these critical years. Modern French art certainly was not decisively influenced, in the developments with which we are concerned, by what was going on across the Channel.

The German schools were more significant, but the cold intellectualism of Kaul-

bach, Cornelius, and Overbeck had its native counterpart in Chenavard, and represented a side issue at best. "Realism" flourished in Munich and Düsseldorf, but it was
not essentially different from similar forms occurring in France. Later the art of northern Europe made a distinct contribution to contemporary developments, both in
painting itself and through the influence of Richard Wagner, but this occurred after
our period was over. The French may have had a painfully nationalistic idea of the
supremacy of their own school, but it was justified, though not in exactly the way that
most of the critics imagined. Paris did indeed become the artistic capital of the world,
sharing ideas and influences common to other parts of Europe, but distilling from
them the essential elements of a new painting which was later to become international.

In the process, however, these elements and the controversies by which they were
established were colored by the native character of French thought. This character
can, perhaps, be described as a desire for rational order and clarity controlled by taste.
The intellectual, social, and artistic results were not as carefully integrated or as struc-
tural as those of the Greeks, nor was the rationality scientific; its products were rather
practical, measured, human systems tested and adapted until they fitted the requirements of the French mind and then subtly transformed by taste into something quite
perfect and complete. So true was this that the forms thus developed tended to become
static and conservative for the reason that any further alteration would spoil them for
minds which delighted in their careful symmetry. French society of the later seventeenth century witnessed the most complete expression of this mental habit in nearly
all phases of life, but long after the splendor of Louis XIV and his heirs had been swept
away, the memory and the manner of thinking remained.

Since it was not calculated to produce flexible systems, this attitude resisted change,
but where change occurred anyway, it came to the fore immediately to check and control the results. In its severe political form it was gradually defeated by a long series
of revolutions and reforms—the monarchical principle eventually succumbed to
democracy—but in such fields as those of art and criticism it remained an active force,
dominant in conservative quarters and latent in progressive ones. When the concepts
of rational clarity were finally overthrown by the triumph of individualism in the
field of subject matter, they turned up almost immediately to guide and control the
new interest in formal problems. In theme, Cézanne was far from Poussin, but in his
feeling for organization he was very close. In the pages which follow, the reader is asked
to bear this French passion for clarity in mind, to remember it when he finds the shell
of an idea being fought for long after the substance within has dried up, and to think
of it when, in the midst of violent attacks on tradition, the progressives continue to
paint with a clarity and restraint which is, as usual, controlled by an almost faultless
taste.

PART ONE. THEORY

I. SURVEY OF THE PERIOD

"IT IS true that the great tradition has been lost, and that the new one has not been made." This significant sentence appears in Charles Baudelaire's review of the Paris Salon of 1846.[1] He was speaking of figure painting which had been traditionally regarded as the most important of all subjects in the hierarchy of types regularly employed by earlier French critics. The situation to which he was calling attention was very apparent in the art of the time and was to have a strong effect upon the later history of painting in general. Its true meaning and importance can be made clear by an examination of the twenty-two years from the Revolution of 1848 to the outbreak of the Franco-Prussian War in 1870.

Many of the ideas about painting which were current under the Second Empire had been put forward earlier, as writers became more and more concerned with the problem of an art which would be appropriate to the times, while the painters strove for an elusive originality and a proper place in a bourgeois world. The art and ideas of the immediately preceding period, from the establishment of romanticism to the revolution which removed Louis Philippe from the throne of France, have been discussed by Léon Rosenthal in his book, *Du Romantisme au réalisme*,[2] but although the year 1848, which marks the end of his study, was indeed a sort of climax, as he points out, it by no means brought to an end the discussion of the immediate future of art, nor had any truly modern art appeared, except in landscape.[3] On the contrary, the arguments were continued with increasing vigor, partly as a result of a certain conservative reaction immediately thereafter, and partly because of the sudden and startling appearance of what adverse criticism sometimes referred to as "the cult of the ugly" (Fig. 23).[4] Rosenthal's analysis of the diverse and conflicting trends in painting during this earlier period shows that although there had been experimentation and variety, no strongly-rooted style made its appearance in the field of figure painting, and theories about a new art had little nourishment in the works themselves. The period after the close of his book actually witnessed the appearance of what was, basically, a genuine modern art, and thus the contemporary writing takes on a greater significance than the criticism in the preceding years. The new painting imposed a severe test upon the commentators who had to recognize and evaluate it in its earliest phase.[5]

[1] Charles Baudelaire, "Salon de 1846," in *Curiosités esthétiques, Oeuvres complètes* (ed. Crépet), Paris, 1923, p. 196. Hereafter all references to the Salons will mean those held in Paris unless otherwise stated.

[2] Paris, 1914. For even earlier statements of some of these ideas, see Rosenthal, *La Peinture romantique*, Paris, 1900.

[3] As will be seen later, landscape had already become essentially "modern" in the work of men like Corot, Rousseau, Daubigny, and the group generally associated with them. See below, Chap. IX. From the point of view of subject matter neither Delacroix nor Ingres were "modern," as will be explained later.

[4] That is, realism.

[5] The characteristics of modern art as they are exemplified in content are discussed at the end of Chap. VIII. In a time sense, all art of a progressive (i.e. nonacademic) nature produced after this formative period will be referred to as modern. The last hundred years cover its existence to date.

Since the foundation of the Academy in the seventeenth century (to go no farther back), writing about art had been primarily concerned with subject matter, the relation of pictorial or sculptural content to that of other media, the means by which it might be most effectively treated, and other considerations of a similar nature; that is, it was rational in character. Of all subjects, man, especially in his more spiritual and moral aspects, had been easily the most important.[6] Pictures dealing with such themes were classed as "history painting," and even though the actual examples grew increasingly mediocre, this type remained at the top of the list of possible subjects. Toward the end of the eighteenth and the beginning of the nineteenth centuries, however, a growing number of writers turned to somewhat different views, Mme. de Staël even going so far as to say that "Those who don't love painting very much in itself, attach great importance to the subjects of pictures."[7] Such statements, of course, indicated a radical reversal of the previously accepted notions, which had been widely shared by artists themselves,[8] about art as one of the greatest instruments for the moral and spiritual betterment of man. The whole traditional concept of the ideal was threatened by new attitudes which were more concerned with emotional reactions, individualism, contemporaneity, progress, and the importance of painting as such.[9] Nevertheless, the old hierarchy which set "la peinture d'histoire" at the pinnacle of artistic achievement, and landscape and still-life at the foot, was too deeply rooted to be easily overthrown, and it remained generally in force until after the middle of the century.[10] It may be suggested here that it required a wide readjustment in the thinking about the whole of society and mankind to bring this about, a readjustment which affected many phases of life in addition to the arts.

During the first half of the century, the two greatest figure painters in France both believed in this tradition, a fact duly noted by contemporary critics. Baudelaire, for example, in spite of his admiration for Delacroix, could not fail to notice that his subjects were not modern (Fig. 8), and his brilliant appreciation for the quality of Ingres'

[6] Cf. Poussin: "The grand manner consists of four things: subject-matter or theme, thought, structure, and style."

"The first thing that, as the foundation of all others, is required, is that the subject-matter shall be grand, as are battles, heroic actions, and divine things. . . . Those who elect mean subjects take refuge in them because of the weakness of their talents." From Poussin's *Observations on Painting*, here quoted from R. Goldwater and M. Treves, *Artists on Art*, N.Y., 1945, p. 155.

[7] Mme. de Staël, *De l'Allemagne* (ed. Charpentier), Paris, 1886, p. 406.

[8] The formulation of the principles on which ideas about the grand manner and history painting were founded were, at least in France, primarily the work of practicing artists. Critics adopted and extended them, but they were

basing themselves not only on an examination of the works produced in this mode but also on what the painters had actually set forth as precepts.

[9] See Stendhal's description of a modern ideal as set forth in Chap. XIX of his *Histoire de la peinture en Italie*, Vol. II. This personage would be endowed with a lively wit, charming features, a sparkling eye, much gaiety and feeling, a svelte figure and the agile appearance of youth. "We have nothing to do," he said, "with antique virtues" (*Histoire*, ed. Arbelet, Paris, 1924, Vol. II, p. 115).

[10] Rosenthal points out that there was a considerable upsurge of traditionalism in nearly all its forms during the years from 1830 to 1848 (Rosenthal, *Du romantisme, passim*, but esp. Chaps. IV, VI, VIII).

style did not extend to his themes (Fig. 12).[11] The less famous painters of both liberal and conservative groups were also content to paint inside the broad confines of the old concepts of the nature and function of subject matter.[12] At the end of the period, however, antitraditionalism was common, if not actually universal, among the younger progressives who made it clear that history painting was not for them. As already suggested, the new spirit in art was indicative of a different idea of man's place in the world. Instead of being the superior person of the classic tradition or the creature of God, he was now an object, in many ways like other objects, and though he was presumably still the most interesting of these, he was shorn of much of his erstwhile grandeur and pathos. The Emperor Napoleon in Ingres' ceiling for the Hôtel de Ville (Fig. 33) was an essentially different person from the unfortunate Maximilian in the famous painting by Manet (Fig. 79).

What then did Baudelaire and other critics mean by "the great tradition"? An exact definition is hard to give, since the term, and others like it (including "history painting"), were loosely and variously used. In its narrower meaning it referred to the art of Italy from Raphael on,[13] reinforced by a devotion to the supposed principles of ancient art—chiefly Roman. At its broadest, it was the whole inheritance of western European painting, and included the great Spanish masters, Rubens, Rembrandt, and even the minor Dutchmen.[14] Dürer and Holbein were grudgingly admitted near the end, and by the middle of the century, Ingres and Delacroix were widely regarded as being the latest, perhaps the last, exponents of it.[15] In one aspect or another, it furnished the criteria for comparison and judgment of contemporary work, and when that work departed radically from it, as will be described later, the traditionally-minded critics, though far from speechless, found themselves hard put to it to discuss it intelligently. It is certain that whatever else the great tradition may have signified, it was

[11] See below, Chap. VII.

[12] Cf. Rosenthal, *op.cit., passim*. However, it is important to distinguish between certain narrow traditions such as those of the École or the Institut, and the broader European tradition which included the great masters of all countries since the beginning of the Renaissance. During the July Monarchy, French painters were increasingly influenced by the latter. For a most stimulating discussion of the influence of tradition, see André Malraux, *Psychologie de l'art*, Vol. I, *Le Musée imaginaire*, Geneva, 1947. He says (p. 53) that romanticism was not so much opposed to "a broad classicism as to a narrow neo-classicism."

[13] This would be the Ingres' view, though it may be recalled that in his early years he was attacked as being "Gothic" as a result of his taste for Raphael in his earlier and more Peruginesque manner.

[14] Meissonier, one of the most successful painters of the century was admiringly compared to the minor Dutch masters. Rosenthal, *op.cit.*, p. 380, mentions the popularity of Dutch art in the period before 1848.

[15] Cf. Baudelaire on Delacroix in 1846: "It is on account of this entirely modern and new quality [his melancholy] that Delacroix is the latest expression of progress in art. Heir of the great tradition, that is to say the amplitude, nobility, and pomp in composition, and worthy successor of the old masters, he has more mastery than they of grief, passion, and gesture. . . . Take away Delacroix and the great chain of history is broken and falls to the ground" (Baudelaire, *Curiosités esthétiques* [ed. Lévy], Paris, 1885, p. 116). This passage is interesting as showing Baudelaire's interest in Delacroix as both a modern and a traditionalist. For further discussion on this point see Chap. VII. Ingres' relation to the tradition was, of course, even more obvious.

vitally concerned with subject matter and man's nature as exemplified pictorially. It should be remembered that the controversies over the art of the two leaders was, at bottom, a stylistic one, while those which raged around Courbet were chiefly concerned with subject—his style was praised by some of his bitterest opponents.[16] Romanticism as embodied in the art of Delacroix played an important part in the development of the modern movement, a role which cannot be described here, but in the opinion of the time, the revolution he effected did not run counter to the broader tradition of content, whereas Courbet's "insurrection" was an outright attack on it.

Historically considered, the period with which we are dealing was one of conflicting social forces somewhat concealed under the deceptively tranquil exterior of the Second Empire. Paris, the focal point of French life, was not alone in experiencing an unease which had not been allayed by the swift establishment of an authoritarian régime hard on the heels of revolution. It was felt all over Europe, and today, a hundred years later, the world is still experiencing reverberations from the shots fired behind many a barricade across the continent.[17] Society was changing, as it does, convulsively, and 1848 was a major upheaval. Doubt and perplexity were widespread:

It [the nineteenth century] is a composite of heterogeneous elements which attract each other in order to annihilate themselves as far as possible. Today the human spirit is at once religious and sceptical; it goes to church and it traditionally loves Voltaire; it is monarchical with an afterthought of the republic; it is republican with secret inclinations for monarchy; it is moral without too great a horror of vice; it is perverse without too much hatred for virtue.[18]

A similar uncertainty appears in a good deal of the other writing of the time, and the number of different views as to what should be done was an index of the difficulty of the problems society faced. Materialism and progress coupled with an increasing faith in science were the concepts by which some hoped to inaugurate a new era of human well-being, but to others they seemed to deprive the world of its values and to reduce man to the level of an automaton.[19]

[16] Maxime du Camp put it as follows in his review of the Salon of 1857: "M. Courbet . . . paints *materially* in a way in which no one has painted in France for a long time. . . . But it is not enough; in his case the hand has an inconceivable cleverness, but he lacks soul completely . . ." (Maxime du Camp, *Le Salon de 1857*, Paris, 1857, p. 101).

[17] For a good account of the general social and political movements of the period, see R. C. Binkley, *Realism and Nationalism 1852-1871*, N.Y., 1935. The passages dealing with the art of the time are, however, not entirely supported by the evidence, as for instance in the following generalization (p. 46): "The salon, as it was kept pure of radical influences, remained dull; the pictures hung by the jury conformed to official canons of taste, but remained without influence on art history." As will be seen from the present essay, this is not a correct picture of the Salons during the period.

[18] Étienne Malpertuy, *Histoire de la société française au XVIIIᵉ et au XIXᵉ siècle*, Paris, 1854, pp. 330-331. Malpertuy's distaste for democracy, which he finds too strenuous, was apparently shared by Delacroix. In a letter to George Sand dated May 28, 1848, after quoting someone to the effect that liberty mixed with danger is preferable to a peaceable servitude, he says: "I have come, alas! to the contrary opinion, considering above all that this liberty bought with battles is not truly liberty . . ." (*Correspondance générale de Eugène Delacroix*, publ. by André Joubin, Paris, 1936, Vol. II, p. 350).

[19] The literature on this subject is too extensive and involved to be entered into here,

This uneasiness had been growing steadily since the early years of the century, and was to be found in the world of art as well as elsewhere. Many artists and critics were deeply disappointed by the failure of the revolution of 1848, which they had hoped meant a new day for art as well as society generally, but instead had only resulted in the reestablishment of restrictions on thought and expression which they had believed ended forever.[20] The feeling that there was something seriously wrong with painting, and beyond that, with society itself, persisted. But there was little agreement on the exact nature of the difficulty or how it might be corrected.[21]

Today it is not hard to see why this should have been so, for society was indeed changing, and art was changing with it. The names of Delacroix and Ingres stood out clearly above all the rest just as the Goncourts said in a summary of the art world about 1840: "All the young painters (*toute la jeune peinture*) turned toward those two men whose two names were the two cries of the war of art."[22] But after them? As has already been mentioned, their work by this time was no longer new; the critic and the conscientious Salon visitor knew perfectly what to expect in each new work. And yet, in spite of this familiarity, in spite of the undeniable fact that what was original in their art had been revealed many years before and had not been significantly amplified since, they continued to dominate the field without serious rivals.[23] A host of able figure painters practiced in the years before the middle of the century, but their contributions to contemporary art appeared small by comparison, and seem even smaller now. It was true that a most important revolution had occurred in the field of landscape, but this was still considered an inferior type.[24] Many critics, even among the

---

but mention may be made of the introduction to Ernest's Renan's *L'Avenir de la science* and Samuel Butler's *Erewhon*. Renan's book was written about 1849 but not published until 1890 at which time he wrote a preface to it in which he looked back upon his ideas of almost a half-century earlier: . . . "I say it frankly. I cannot conceive how, without the old dreams, one will rebuild the foundations of a noble and happy life" (Ernest Renan, *L'Avenir de la science*, Paris, 1890, p. xviii). The whole problem of the moral bases of modern society is becoming increasingly important. Cf. Lecomte du Noüy, *The Road to Reason*, N.Y., 1949, and other recent works on the same theme.

[20] See, for example, the account of the plight of the liberals after 1848 as given in Albert Guérard, *Art for Art's Sake*, N.Y., 1936, Chap. IV.

[21] The degree to which this feeling was widespread in the art world can be gathered from the following partial list of artists and critics who commented on it: Astruc, Bougot, Burty, Castagnary, Challemel-Lacour, Champfleury, Chenavard, Chesneau, Courbet, Delaborde, Delacroix, Delécluze, de Mercey, Doll-

fuss, Du Camp, Dumas, Hamerton, Ingres, Loudun, Petroz, Proudhon, Silvestre, Taine, Thoré (W. Bürger), the Goncourts, and Zola. The gloomiest of all was apparently the philosopher-painter Chenavard, who believed that not only art but the whole world was in a decline. See below, Chap. XIII. This pessimism among men of art was already well founded in the 'thirties (see Rosenthal, *Du romantisme*, pp. 345ff.).

[22] Edmond and Jules de Goncourt, *Manette Salomon* (ed. Charpentier), Paris, 1910, p. 16. This famous novel on the art life of Paris was first published in 1867.

[23] As early as 1838, DeLaunay wrote in *L'Artiste*: "Today what are Messieurs Champmartin, Decamps, E. Delacroix, E. Deveria, Gigoux, Paul Huet, Roqueplan, and so many others? Just what they were ten years ago, minus fire, minus youth" (quoted in Rosenthal, *Du romantisme*, p. 171). The eclecticisms of the lesser men were borrowed from the wide inheritance of European art which Malraux calls "the old museum."

[24] See below Chap. IX.

very conservative ones, agreed that it was here that the "modern" school had been most successful, but most of them also implied that this fact merely underlined the gravity of the plight into which art as a whole had fallen. Only a very few, like Castagnary, could feel that this development was both proper and hopeful; that for art, man and nature could be on an equal footing.[25]

As the years passed, leaving the supremacy of the two older leaders unchallenged, thoughtful men naturally began to wonder who the new masters were to be who would, or could, succeed to their positions. It was a vexing problem, for although the aspirants were numerous, they all seemed to lack the originality and power which would have to be the hallmark of their greatness. Several artists like Decamps (Fig. 6) and Horace Vernet (Fig. 14) enjoyed high reputations during their lifetimes, but opinion was almost unanimous in denying them the final accolade of equality with the very best.

At the Salon of 1850-51 the figure of Gustave Courbet burst upon the scene with a violence which seems somewhat extraordinary to those accustomed to the transcendant boldness of more modern art but was quite understandable in a period of weakening assurance as to the exact postion of art in a changing society.[26] The *Enterrement à Ornans* (Fig. 23) and the *Casseurs de pierres* (Fig. 24) furnished ample opportunity for the exercise of all shades of critical opinion, but not many were convinced that they really might be the forerunners of a new "grand manner" brought forth by the needs of a new age. Even among the truly original talents of those years, Courbet stood rather alone, and was apparently the only artist generally regarded as presenting a serious threat to the figure tradition. Daumier, as will be seen later, was widely known and admired for his lithographs, but these were not thought of as being equivalent to major painting, and his oils were seldom exhibited and were known chiefly to his friends and admirers. Millet was bitterly attacked by the extreme right, but generally speaking he was not paired with Courbet, nor did he ever become the focus of such universal controversy.[27] After 1848, Corot turned more and more to figure painting, but he had been labeled as a landscapist, and his work in this new direction was largely ignored. On the eminence of notoriety, Courbet stood by himself.

By 1860, his more revolutionary days were over, and he began to receive considerable sums from the sale of landscapes, hunting scenes, and rather academic studies of the nude, but the few greatly disputed pictures remained in the mind of the times, forming an important part of the foundation for the painting of the *avant-garde* in the decade before the war with Germany.[28] In the 'sixties, Manet succeeded him as the butt

[25] See Chap. II, note 36, in regard to the common use of graded types of subject.

[26] Courbet had been exhibiting for several years; his *Après dînée à Ornans* was even bought by Charles Blanc for the state in 1849. The pictures mentioned here, however, seemed startlingly different to the public and critics of 1851. See below, Chap. xv.

[27] See below, Chap. xiv. Because of the imag-

inative and symbolic qualities in his art he was far more acceptable to conservative minds.

[28] Duranty, one of the ardent champions of this group, wrote in 1876: "The origins of these efforts, the first manifestations of these temperaments are to be found starting from the studio of Courbet . . ." (Ed. Duranty, *La Nouvelle peinture* [new ed. by Marcel Guérin], Paris, 1946, p. 32). He goes on to list the other

of the conservative jibes—a sure sign of his originality—and carried the transformation of art still further to a point where it can be considered essentially modern. These two, along with the group from the Café Guerbois,[29] the landscapists,[30] and one or two others, achieved a type of expression which for the first time in the century made their pictures a truly complete product of their time.[31] At first its form was understood by only a very few outside the artists' immediate circle, which was quite natural. The eagerly awaited modern movement had at last appeared, but quite outside the sphere of history painting or any traditional extension of it; it ignored the hierarchy of subjects and dealt neither with man's moral nature nor with the ideal as the past had known it. Indeed, it cared very little for subject matter at all.[32] Small wonder, then, that not many recognized it for what it was, and those who failed need not be held up to scorn now that the passage of time has made the whole development reasonably plain. It was too much to expect that they should have immediately thrown off the habit of thought which had been handed down from all the great ages of the past they admired. The great tradition had fallen on evil days, and most said so with vigor, but they did not feel it necessary on that account to throw overboard all the principles on which that tradition was based, and they could not help believing that an art which failed to pay attention to such principles was bound to be inferior—more so, perhaps, than the admittedly mediocre attempts of the traditional artists.

The ideas which have made humanity live for many centuries are slow to vanish, even when their reign has ended, for paganism, despite the arrival of a new religion and a new civilization, still lives in our arts, our customs, our habits, and the names of the abolished gods continue to designate our months and days. Today art has at its disposal only dead ideas and formulas which no longer correspond to its needs. From this [comes] this uneasiness, this vagueness, this diffusion, this facility for passing from one extreme to another, this eclecticism, and this cosmopolitanism, this traveling in all possible worlds which leads from the Byzantine to the daguerreotype, from a far-fetched mannerism to a deliberate brutality. It is well known that something must be done,—but what?[33]

That was indeed the question. The years seem to have proved the worthy conservatives wrong, for much that was beautiful, new, and important came from those very

---

precursors of the movement, including Ingres and Millet. The presence of Ingres may be explained on the basis of Degas' admiration for him. See below, Chap. xix.

[29] That is, the so-called Impressionists. The confusion resulting from the use of this term to describe this group of artists as well as to refer to a manner of painting practiced in its most extreme form by Monet, makes its clear use very difficult. Degas is hard to equate with Sisley.

[30] Chief among these in the estimation of the period would be Corot, Rousseau, Daubigny, Diaz, Français, and Chintreuil. Later Jongkind and Boudin received some favorable attention, but the Barbizon painters seem to have re-

mained dominant to the end of the period.

[31] The transformation in landscape was, of course, an earlier development.

[32] Cf. Malraux, who declares flatly that during Manet's career painting not only renounced subjects, but also the world of which the imagination had been the preferred means of expression, a world beyond what the eye alone enjoyed. It was no longer concerned with the sublime or the transcendant. "What," he says, "became of a painting which no longer imitated, no longer imagined, and no longer transfigured? Painting." (Malraux, *Musée imaginaire*, p. 74). See below, *passim*.

[33] Th. Gautier, "De l'art moderne," in *L'Artiste*, 5e série, Vol. x (1853), pp. 135ff.

modes which they despised and attacked; yet it may still turn out that there was a degree of justice in their insistence on the necessity for moral significance and human dignity in any painting to which the word "great" was to be applied.[34] The tragedy for them was the fact that events had apparently made such art impossible, and the results of modest talents attempting this impossibility were naturally doomed to failure. If the art of Delacroix may be considered as one of the last examples of what they admired,[35] his views on the subject, as expressed in a letter to Alexandre Dumas in 1859, have a certain pertinence:

You are right in complaining of the trend of the arts. Formerly we looked to the heights. Happy was he who could reach them! I fear that the stature of the fighters today doesn't even allow them to have such a thought. Their little narrow truth isn't that of the masters. They search dully with a microscope. Farewell to the great brush, farewell to the great effects of theatrical passion![36]

[34] Cf. Francis Henry Taylor, "Modern Art and the Dignity of Man," *Atlantic Monthly*, Dec. 1948, pp. 30-36.

[35] This, of course, was after the battle over his art was over except for a few like Delécluze who would never admit that he was among the very great of the age. Naturally the conservatives did not like him as well as they did Ingres, but even though their admission of his importance was grudging, it was made, and virtually everyone saw his connection with the great tradition.

[36] Delacroix, *Correspondance*, Vol. IV, p. 97.

II. THE GENERAL NATURE OF THE CRITICISM

SO MUCH was written about the arts during this period that one can form a very clear picture of the interest they aroused, of the effort expended in an attempt to understand them, and of the wide variety of opinions held concerning their past history, their present condition, and their future development.[1] Of all the arts, painting undoubtedly attracted the greatest attention, particularly the work of contemporary artists. At no previous period in history had there been so vast an army of critics concerned with this subject, and never before had so large an audience been addressed. On the part of the critics, the quality of writing ranged from some of the most perceptive analysis ever written, to the fatuous presentation of shoddy clichés; on the part of the readers the interest varied from cheap judgments about the reigning Salon favorites to a sincere and developed interest in a form of expression which had always been dear to the French heart and mind. That the artistic fare which the painters provided was generally mediocre, entirely failed to dampen the enthusiasm with which each new Salon was awaited.

This large body of writing was called forth by a volume of production which was also without parallel. In the opening section of his review of the Salon of 1850, Delécluze gives some interesting statistics about the growth of the number of pictures exhibited: 707 in 1806 as opposed to 5,180 in 1848; and also as to the number of artists participating: 303 in 1810 against 1,664 in 1850. He notes that while the pictures have increased more than sevenfold and the exhibitors fivefold, the number of "presumed celebrities," as he wryly calls them, has only risen from 21 to 42.[2] The task of the critic

---

[1] The bibliography of Salon criticism is badly in need of accurate compilation. So far as the author is aware, no complete, or even reasonably complete, publication of it is in existence. The late Maurice Tourneux made a good beginning with his *Salons et expositions d'art à Paris*, Paris, 1919, but it is very far from exhaustive. A. Tabarant has a lengthy bibliography in the back of *La Vie artistique au temps de Baudelaire* which contains many titles of Salon reviews, but is not complete either. The author's list of reviewers' names for these twenty-two years alone exceeds two hundred and thirty, and the actual Salons themselves run to several hundred more. The labor involved in assembling such a bibliography would be prodigious, as the articles are scattered through hundreds of journals many of which were of a most ephemeral nature and others provincial and hard to find. A large percentage of this material is practically valueless, but there may well be writers now forgotten whose ideas could profitably be studied anew. In the present work the author makes no claim to having examined even a majority of the total, but no critic who appears to have had any very considerable reputation in his own day has gone entirely unconsulted. There are doubtless omissions which a later and more detailed study will be able to rectify, but it is hoped that they will be found to be among the less important men.

It is unfortunate that in a number of cases the writings of some of the better-known critics have not been carefully listed either. The material contributed to various journals by men like Gautier and Houssaye was very considerable, but if there are definitive bibliographies of it, the author has not been able to find them with a reasonable search. It may, therefore, be said that at least a selective list of the critical writing on art in the nineteenth century would be of the utmost usefulness to scholars in this field.

[2] E.-J. Delécluze, *Exposition des artistes vivants*, Paris, 1851, pp. 6-7. To the modern eye, the number of forty-two still seems to be extremely high.

faced with this unwieldy object of his professional function was formidable indeed, and one can hardly wonder that good work, particularly by new men, often went unnoticed. The tireless patience exhibited by reviewers like Gautier, who hated to omit any word of praise he thought due even the humblest practitioners, is not only commendable, it is nearly incredible.[3] The opposite reaction to this appalling multiplicity was to discuss only a baker's dozen and leave the rest of the mass alone. Baudelaire and Zola may stand as examples of this extreme.[4] Modern art was born, as it were, in the midst of a multitude and in the presence of a host of witnesses, but those who were responsible for it, and those who recognized it at birth formed a very minute part of the total assemblage. And yet this mass of art and the generalities of a prolix criticism reveal many of the most important groundswells in the artistic thinking and practice of the time. Against their slower movement, the related but more vivid action of the few influential men is quite distinct.

The number of critics is too great (over two hundred and thirty at the very least) to deal with every one even if they all deserved mention, which they do not, so the majority will serve as a background, a sort of chorus for the more prominent parts spoken by the few. Of the total group, a surprisingly small percentage were art critics and nothing else. If the men like Charles Blanc, Georges Lafenestre, and Paul Challemel-Lacour[5] who held official positions in the Ministry of Fine Arts or other governmental offices are ruled out, the list becomes very short indeed. Even Théophile Thoré (W. Bürger) was active in political affairs for many years before he turned his entire attention to the history and criticism of art.[6] The number of positions available, the prestige of an official status, and the opportunity for close and interesting association with art and artists drew many intelligent men with critical ambitions into the government service, though, as will be seen later, they had to be of a somewhat conservative turn of mind in order to qualify, since the government of Louis Napoleon had very definite ideas on the subject of the proper kind of art for the nation.[7] In France, political figures occasionally wrote on matters artistic, a practice which went back at least as far as Guizot's famous Salon of 1810,[8] and continued intermittently thereafter—a performance which seems most remarkable to Americans who are accustomed to less

[3] Cf. Gautier's credo as a critic quoted on p. 33 and again on p. 86.

[4] In his review of the Exposition Universelle of 1855, Baudelaire confines himself to discussing Ingres, Delacroix, and Courbet. Zola, in 1866, speaks of Manet, Monet, Ribot, Vollon, Bonvin, Roybet, Courbet, and Millet. Due to his difficulties resulting from the eulogy of Manet he had to cut the review short, but the only other people whom he really wished to discuss at any length were Corot, Daubigny, and Pissarro. A select list out of hundreds of exhibitors!

[5] Very brief notices about all the critics mentioned in this book have been listed in the Appendix. Some of these writers were not sufficiently famous to be listed in the usual biographical sources and information about their lives and work is often difficult to find.

[6] See Appendix.

[7] See below, pp. 43ff.

[8] M. Guizot, *Études sur les beaux-arts en général*, Paris, 1860. The first essay is entitled: "De l'état des beaux-arts en France et du Salon de 1810." This was a pretty conservative effort extolling the virtues of painting founded on sculptural principles. Its fame was doubtless due more to the author than the substance. Thiers also wrote art criticism.

astute judgments on art from their own politicians.[9] Not infrequently a successful career in artistic journalism was the road to official appointment. Many inspectors, librarians, bureau chiefs, and curators in the government service continued to write articles and books which, taken as a whole, constitute an impressive body of critical and historical material.[10]

The greater part of the published commentary on contemporary art came from the men (and women)[11] writing for the innumerable papers and journals with which France was flooded.[12] They exhibited an astonishing diversity of interest, discussing history, politics, drama, music, and the arts with equal facility, and, in addition, often producing novels, poetry and plays of their own. Arsène Houssaye, Paul de Saint-Victor, Champfleury, Paul Lacroix—to name only a few—were truly "men of letters" in the broadest sense. Théophile Gautier, in addition to his literary renown, was possibly the most highly regarded critic of the day,[13] and Baudelaire was unquestionably one of the most brilliant. In the opinion of these "journalists," art was closely allied to a wide sphere of human affairs and could, furthermore, be discussed intelligently without devoting a lifetime to its study. There were, of course, many who were genuinely unqualified to give the pronouncements which fell so glibly from their pens, and the student is puzzled by the large number of names signed to only one or two Salon reviews which often cannot be further identified but which, at the time,

[9] Cf. President Truman and "fried egg" art.

[10] A few examples may be mentioned: Chas. Blanc, who was twice Director of Beaux-Arts, wrote several books of which the most important was his *Histoire des peintres de toutes les écoles* (finished in 1875). Frédéric de Mercey held a variety of government offices including that of chief of the Beaux-Arts Division in the Ministry of State. His *Études sur les beaux-arts* appeared in 1857. Georges Lafenestre, who wrote several books on Italian art, was attached to the Ministry of Beaux-Arts in 1870, eventually becoming Associate Curator of Painting in the Louvre (1886), etc. Théophile Silvestre, whose *Histoire des artistes vivants* is so frequently referred to in this book, after performing several artistic missions for the government was made an Inspector-General of Beaux-Arts. The list could be lengthened considerably.

[11] Such as Comtesse d'Agoult who wrote under the pseudonym of Daniel Stern, and Mme. Noémi Cadiot who signed herself Claude Vignon.

[12] According to Henri Avanel, in the years from 1848 to 1851 alone there were 789 political papers and journals plus 400 on other subjects (Henri Avanel, *Histoire de la presse française depuis 1789 jusqu'à nos jours*, Paris, 1900).

[13] This judgment was by no means unanimous, however. A conservative like Hache could list him with Paul de Saint Victor and Charles Blanc as one of the three great critics of the day, and Baudelaire admired him for rather different reasons, but there were some who felt differently, like Eugène Loudun: "A quick reputation has been made for M. Chassériau. M. Théophile Gautier, who is a literary pupil and would not exist if M. Victor Hugo had never lived, has fallen completely in love with M. Chassériau, himself a pupil in painting who would be nothing without M. E. Delacroix. These two imitators understand each other. The result of ten years of publicity and exaggerated eulogies is that today [he] has not made one step of progress." (See E. Hache, *Les Merveilles de l'art et de l'industrie. Antiquité, moyen age, Renaissance, temps modernes. Salon de 1869*, Paris 1869 [text by E. Hache], p. 232; Chas. Baudelaire, *Curiosités* [ed. Lévy], p. 8 under "Salon de 1845" and *L'Art romantique* [ed. Lévy], Paris, 1885, p. 182; Eugène Loudun, *Le Salon de 1852*, Paris, 1852, p. 18.) Georges Lafenestre was one of his warmest defenders (*Artistes et amateurs*, Paris, n.d., chap. on Gautier).

were apparently acceptable to harassed editors looking for someone to write the year's Salon. The only virtue possessed by most of these is a rather masterly use of the cliché.

Even a number of philosophers, historians, and social theorists, who were primarily concerned with other matters, devoted earnest attention to art in its contemporary manifestations and their opinions often had wide influence on the thinking of others more regularly devoted to the discussion of the subject.[14] Pierre-Joseph Proudhon, for instance, was unable to stay away from it, even though he confessed to complete professional ignorance. The title of his famous book, *Du Principe de l'art et de sa destination sociale*,[15] shows that his interest lay in the connection between art and a broad complex of social questions, and he was by no means the only one to have such a concern.[16]

Nor were artists themselves silent about what was being done; a considerable bibliography of their writings could be assembled. Actually, a number of critics were, or had been, painters: Delaborde, de Mercey, Astruc, Nadar, Galimard, and Privat, for example, while artists of considerable prominence recorded their ideas on their own work and that of the times at some length. The articles, journal, and letters of Delacroix are well known; Couture published his famous *Entretiens*,[17] and Courbet signed his name to several statements of his belief.[18] Such material as this can be further amplified by consulting the quoted statements of painters as recorded by friends, biographers, and so on.[19]

Several of the most prominent literary men who concerned themselves with criticism were at least competent amateurs, such as Jules de Goncourt who was an etcher of some ability,[20] and in their youth it was Zola, rather than his friend Cézanne, who won the prizes in drawing.[21] But more important is the fact that these poet- or novelist-critics were creative artists themselves, albeit in a different medium. They knew the difficulties of creation and expression, the nature of inspiration, the hard limits imposed by form, and though there were those who felt that this sharing of similar but not identical artistic experience was bad for both painting and criticism,[22] it must be admitted that in certain ways they had a special insight into the painters' problems.

[14] See below, Chap. v.

[15] Written in 1863 but not complete even at the time of Proudhon's death in 1865. The balance of the volume as printed was assembled from his notes. The edition used here is that of Bouglé and Moysset, Paris, 1939.

[16] See below, Chap. v.

[17] Thos. Couture, *Méthode et entretiens d'atelier*, Paris, 1868.

[18] The question of the authorship of these has been raised. Fontainas believes that he had his friends help him with the actual writing (A. Fontainas, *Courbet*, Paris, 1921, p. 37). They undoubtedly expressed his ideas fairly accurately, even if he wasn't actually responsible for the text.

[19] Cf. the volumes now appearing under the direction of Pierre Courthion: *Collection. Les Grands artistes vus par eux-mêmes et par leurs amis* (Geneva) and books like Hans Graber's *Edouard Manet nach eigenen und fremden Zeugnissen*, Basle, 1941.

[20] Philippe Burty, the critic and connoisseur, published them in 1876 (*Les Eaux-fortes de Jules de Goncourt*).

[21] John Rewald, *Cézanne et Zola*, Paris, 1936, p. 9.

[22] Ernest Chesneau, for example, said later in his *Education of the Artist* (London, 1886), that much of the confusion prevailing in this period resulted from the fact that "writers gave a language to art and did it badly" (p. 34). Fernand Desnoyers blamed the critics for injecting too much philosophy into art so that

Several important conclusions can be drawn from this brief survey of the men who wrote the criticism presently to be examined. In the first place, the universality of interest and the range of informed opinion on the part of many of the more interesting writers make their views on art particularly interesting from the point of view of the relation of that art to the social scheme as a whole. They felt the pressures, the uncertainties, the problems of the time in many different fields, and were deeply interested in their effect upon painting. Art, for most of them, was not created in a void, nor did it drop silently and mysteriously from above; it was a form of human and social expression which was bound up with the needs and aspirations of men as much as anything else they did. They, as critics, were affected by these forces and they believed, with some justice, that the artists were too.

This leads to the second conclusion, which is that the customary gap which is believed to exist between the creator and the observer—i.e. the critic—is not much in evidence during this period. Too many critics were artists themselves for anyone to claim that they did not know whereof they spoke. Nor did the artist-critics form a homogeneous group against the nonartist-critics. The fact seems to be that the groupings were formed along the lines of commonly shared ideas and beliefs. The commentary of a second-rate academic painter like Galimard[23] is indistinguishable from that of an inferior academic critic who had never put brush to canvas. The Goncourts and Zola, who were at least mainly literary in their interests, shared an understanding of the art of Manet with Gonzague Privat who was primarily a painter.[24] To be sure, the artists were mainly rather inarticulate and preferred to paint their convictions rather than talk about them, but it is safe to assert that for every important painter there was more than one critic who understood quite clearly what he was driving at. It is incorrect to believe that the more radical men were not understood in their own day, though it is, of course, true that the public as a whole and the *majority* of critics did not. How could they be expected to? A radical alteration of the bases on which painting rested was taking place, led by a few unusual people with ideas that were not only original but difficult to grasp[25] and quite unappealing to many types of minds.[26] The bourgeois undoubtedly had bad

---

the observer was expected to read it rather than see it (Fernand Desnoyers, *Salon des refusés. La Peinture en 1863*, pp. 9-10). See also the brief discussion of "literary" painting given in the Preface. Georges Lafenestre made Gautier out to be almost a painter himself (Lafenestre, *Artistes et amateurs*, p. 131).

[23] Auguste Galimard, *Examen du Salon de 1849*, Paris, 1849. Galimard exhibited a *Vièrge aux douleurs* and a *Christ* in this same show.

[24] Privat exhibited a portrait in the Salon of 1869 which received this comment from Ernest Hache: "In the female portrait offered us by M. Privat there is a healthy and powerful impression which well marks his promising début" (E. Hache, *Les Merveilles de l'art*, p.

259). The author has seen no reproductions of Privat's work. Thieme-Becker lists him as a painter of portraits, genre, and landscape. See below, Chap. XVII for his criticism of Manet.

[25] It may be that they were really too simple, for the appreciation of the art of Manet rested on a rather direct and instinctive reaction to harmonious colors and contours rather than an involved intellectual analysis. The traditional Frenchman wanted something on which he could exercise his reason.

[26] It might be mentioned in passing that there are people today who prefer the art of tradition to the more modern forms, and such persons need not be harshly judged for that reason alone.

artistic manners, and so did many of the critics who were prepared to tell them only what they wanted to hear, but as things then were, it would have been a miracle if they had behaved differently. The historical problem in evaluating this critical material is to pair off the right painters with the right authors, and to analyze fairly the reasons for opposition. The divergences occurred between the critics of one persuasion and the artists of another, not between all artists and all critics. In addition, some writers urged certain courses of action upon the painters which the latter either could not follow or were not interested in following. Only if the intelligent observer has no place in art at all can the ideas of such men be considered irrelevant and immaterial. Conversely, the painters were quite within their rights in paying no attention, and in many cases they would not have been able to follow these suggestions even if they had wanted to, since the times were not ripe for it. All of which is to say that the connection between what was written and what was done was often very close, and when it was not, the differences were instructive.

Reference has already been made to the vast amount of material published on art at this time. Numerous books were printed and articles on every conceivable aspect of the subject poured forth in profusion. Some journals like *L'Artiste* and *Le Gazette des beaux-arts* were devoted to nothing else,[27] while others of a more general nature like *La Revue des deux mondes* or *La Revue européenne*, carried a considerable amount of material of this kind. It was common for many papers to print at least short reviews of the Salons, which were always important events in any year in which they occurred.[28] Accounts of sales, notices on the death of distinguished painters, critiques of recently completed mural commissions, discussions of aesthetic and historical problems, appraisals of the art and exhibitions of other countries, descriptions of important works in progress, comments on exhibitions other than the Salons, summaries of the current state of different kinds of art—all these kept the amateur informed of anything and everything that was going on.

For the student of contemporary ideas about the art of the day, the Salon review is particularly basic reading. It was here that the current output was continuously examined as a whole, and here that more general ideas were freely discussed. These latter were covered in separate articles in some cases, or even in books,[29] but for some of the best critics the Salon was *the* form in which their ideas were put forth.

The reason for this importance is clear. In spite of certain lapses, exclusions, and abstentions, the Salon exhibitions afforded an unparalleled opportunity for seeing what

[27] *L'Artiste* published material on all the arts as well as a considerable amount of poetry and other noncritical literature. For a time during this period it even had material on fashions. The brilliance of the list of contributors to this journal was extraordinary.

[28] Salons were held in the following years during this period: 1848, 1849, 1850-51, 1852, 1853, 1855 (Exposition Universelle), 1857, 1859, 1861, 1863 (also Salon des Refusés), 1864, 1865, 1866, 1867 (both a Salon and the Exposition Universelle), 1868, 1869, 1870. For information on the composition of the juries, etc., see C. H. Stranahan, *A History of French Painting*, N.Y., 1888, Chap. VII.

[29] This was particularly true of philosophical, aesthetic and social ideas which were put forward by men who were not essentially critics by profession. Proudhon, Taine, Bougot, and Milsand may serve as examples. The influence of books such as theirs can often be traced in the reviews themselves.

was being done by nearly every painter of consequence in the country, and seeing it all at the same time and place. Artists of every kind wanted their work to be shown since the Salon was the gateway to recognition, and all but a very few managed to exhibit a good deal of the very best of their paintings. After 1870, the Salons became far less interesting since the better men were inclined to stay away,[30] with the ultimate result that the word has become almost synonymous with mediocrity, but such was certainly not the case earlier. The regular shows were augmented twice in this period by the universal expositions of 1855 and 1867, both of which afforded opportunities for comparing the art of France with that of the rest of Europe and even America. The retrospective character of the exhibition in 1855 gave critics a particularly good chance to summarize the progress, or lack of it, made during the first half of the century.

The Salons were enormous and confusing, but they were also very valuable and nearly always furnished adequate grounds for a fair judgment as to the general state of art.[31] Indeed, they lay at the very center of an understanding of the trends of the period, and the fact that they were often mismanaged, poorly mounted, savagely restricted, and full of a great deal of very bad art leavened by a modicum of something better, does not seriously impair their importance—the more so since the energetic critics were not averse to going around and having a look at pictures which had been excluded, and giving some account of them as well,[32] thus enlarging the scope of their review, as it were, to include what had stupidly been omitted by the juries.[33]

[30] One of the chief reasons for the abstention of the progressives after 1870 was the constant rejection of much of their work by the juries. Cf. Manet's preface to his private exhibition of 1867 quoted below, p. 182.

[31] The decline of the importance of the Salons after 1870 has led to the erroneous impression that they were never of real importance. Actually the reverse was true and nearly all artists, good or bad, exhibited in them as frequently as possible. Daumier was somewhat of an exception, and Ingres felt himself in a strong enough position to abstain when he felt like it, but this was not the case generally. Recognition came from showing there, and from recognition came commissions and a livelihood. One great success in the Salon could make a man's fortune almost overnight, and it was there that the artist introduced himself to the buying public. Private shows and studio viewings were not usually successful during this period. Government prizes were useful as were also government commissions, and the way to both led at least partly through these exhibitions. Aside from small exhibits put on by dealers, there were virtually no other shows where the artist could display his wares before a large audience, and all attempts on the part of the artists to set up an exhibition scheme of their own seem to have been ineffectual until a later date. (There was a great deal of agitation in this direction during the 'forties.)

One of the scholarly tasks which must some day be done if the nineteenth century is to be fully understood is a careful and painstaking analysis of the Salons, all other means of exhibition, the operations of dealers including prices, the rules and regulations for exhibitors, juries, and awards with all their numerous modifications, the various plans for improving the recognized evils of the current practices in these matters, and the exact nature of official and private patronage. When these facts have been carefully gathered and discussed, the exact economic status of the artist will be much clearer than it is now, and important light will be thrown on certain developments which are now imperfectly grasped.

[32] The most outstanding example was probably Zola's review of the Salon of 1866 in which he devoted most of his attention to Manet who had been refused admission (E. Zola, "Mon Salon" in *Mes haines* [ed. Charpentier], Paris, 1895, pp. 287ff.).

[33] The problems raised by the iniquities of the juries were discussed year after year and at great length by many critics.

Published either as articles (often serially) or as separate books, the reviews took a variety of forms, some of which were quite stereotyped.[34] The simplest was a reprint of the official catalogue expanded to include critical comment in small type underneath the works considered worthy of mention and designed as a pocket companion for the visitor which would let him know when to pause and when not to bother, and what attitude to assume in front of the more controversial pictures.[35] Others were mainly an opportunity for the author to express his views on art as such at greater or less length. The majority of the reviews were something of a combination of the two types: certain general remarks forming an introduction, followed by a more detailed analysis of the work of the artists considered worthy of mention. A division into sections was customary, sometimes by alphabetical groups, frequently according to the hierarchy of subjects or some particular variant of it more in agreement with the author's per-

[34] A rather interesting terminology was employed to classify artists, movements, methods of treatment, etc. A few of them may be mentioned as typical:

le style — In the mouths of the conservatives this did not mean style in general, but in its traditional sense, as applied to "great art." It implied a high degree of finish or completeness, careful handling of form, and some suggestion of grandeur and ideality in the general presentation.

fantaisiste — A painter (like Diaz, to whom it was often applied) who paints what might be described as imaginative genre, especially with a classical flavor.

ethnographe — A painter concerned with the exact depiction of specific locales, either foreign or domestic, with respect not so much to landscape as to the habits, customs, etc., of the inhabitants.

orientaliste — A painter drawing his themes from Africa or the Near East. Occasionally they went further afield but not often.

paysanneries — Paintings of the life of rustic folk. Distinct from landscape.

ouvrier — A painter like Courbet who had a powerful manner of painting but was not of the first rank, usually because of a lack of imagination.

science — A term used to describe that part of painting which exhibited the artist's capacity in a technical sense.

animalier — A painter of animals. (Troyon).

Pompéistes and Néo-Grecs — These terms were applied to men like Gérôme and his pupils, describing an art which was classical, highly finished, archaeologically realistic, and rather anecdotal in character. Ingres' *Stratonice* was thought to be the parent of this type of painting (Fig. 12).

la grande peinture — This was the traditional type of painting dealing with heroic or religious themes and regarded as having an elevated moral import. In a somewhat strict usage it was equated with *la peinture d'histoire*.

[35] See, for example, the *Catalogue complet de Salon 1846 annoté par A. H. Delaunay*, Paris, 1846, which was simply a reprint of the official catalogue with a sentence or two of comment under the name of the artist. Apparently some people needed a shorter guide, or else the critics didn't always have too much time, for one small brochure was entitled: *Dernier jour de l'Exposition de 1865. Revue galopante au Salon*, A.-J. Lorentz, Paris, 1865. This brief effort was dedicated, interestingly enough, to the students of the École des Beaux-Arts.

sonal beliefs.[36] Painting was usually considered first, then drawings, water colors, pastel and engraving, followed by sculpture and architecture,[37] all categories except painting being rather briefly discussed. Special types of Salon review such as the comical or satirical type made famous by Gill, Cham, and Nadar,[38] or the etched "Letters" with marginal illustrations done by A. P. Martial[39] appear along with the more formal reviews, most of which were unillustrated. It was just as well that they were not, for the etchings, engravings, and lithographs done as illustrations were, for the most part, travesties on the originals.[40] Besides, everyone went to the Salon to see for himself.

As might be expected, most of the reviews were little more than a string of trite appreciations of artists already well known, with a judicious mixture of adverse comment and paternal advice thrown in to convince the reader of the qualifications of the critic to pass judgment. In the case of novel talents, the safest recourse for the inferior critic was usually a declaration that the paintings in question were obviously inimical to the best interests of art and an abrupt consignment of the offending examples to limbo. Zacharie Astruc even suggested in his *Salon of 1859* that there were those who waited until everyone else had spoken up, read the results, and then published a composite. This may well have been close to the truth in many cases, though he alludes to an even more underhanded practice, that of coming up behind the people in front of a picture and noting down what they are saying![41] The stupidities of these cheap criticisms cannot be denied, and they unfortunately were read by many people, including the unhappy artists at whom they were directed. Ernest Chesneau, who was at times a brilliant analyst of the faults of French art and taste, described the stylistic basis of this stiff and inflexible attitude:

The means of art are fiction (and not illusion). Between the artist and the spectator there exists an unconscious preliminary agreement which permits the former to show, and the

[36] The hierarchy referred to had fallen on somewhat evil days by this time and there was a steady stream of complaints to the effect that it was getting extremely hard to know in what category a picture really belonged. Roughly speaking, it ran as follows: History Painting (which included religious, historical, and classical subjects), Genre and Portraiture, Landscape, and Still Life. Some put portraiture next to history painting, others put it lower. Military painting was regarded by some writers as coming under the heading of history painting. As the glossary given in note 34 shows, there were more and more special classifications added as time went on.

[37] Not all categories were always included. In the case of serial publication of the review, the different sections were sometimes divided among different critics, one man taking painting, another sculpture, and another architecture.

[38] Examples: Gill, *Salon pour rire, 1864; Nadar jury au Salon de 1853*, etc.

[39] A pseudonym for Martial Potémont. The etchings with which these are illustrated are far above the general level of reproductions available at the time in other publications. The plate of Courbet's *Remise des chevreuils* from the *Salon de 1866* is almost photographically perfect. It is interesting that in this year Potémont included Monet among the painters whose work was "above all eulogy."

[40] *L'Artiste* was particularly proud of its plates but most of them seem pretty poor in quality and scarcely gave a good impression of the actual appearance of the picture. One publication, *L'Autographe au Salon*, got many of the exhibiting artists to do sketches of their pictures and reproduced these in a rather disorderly format.

[41] Zacharie Astruc, *Les 14 stations du Salon 1859*, Paris, 1859, pp. 124ff.

latter to recognize, on a plane surface which the hand will cover, the relief of bodies or the perspective of land fading to the horizon. Among naturally artistic people, such as the Italians of the sixteenth century, this convention was universally recognized. Art could vary its processes infinitely—it would always be understood. Each transformation, each extension applied to representational signs found immediate intelligent attention. The contrary must be said of France. We need the slow education of practice by means of the engravings which decorate our apartments, by the idle visits to the annual exhibitions, by chance meetings, and notwithstanding all that, a strong spiritual eagerness is necessary before we can adopt a leading aesthetic fiction, that of the fashionable school. As though exhausted with such effort, the reason for which does not seem to us well demonstrated, if another fiction appears with claims on our respect, we close our eyes, and so long as it lasts, we declare it false or ridiculous, we refuse it the right of existence.[42]

Chesneau was explaining the lack of understanding which greeted the art of Delacroix, but his meaning is broader still and applied to subject matter as well.[43] The inferior critics, therefore, supply us with information as to the general run of uninspired conservative artistic thinking, since that was the line of least resistance and the clichés for more modern forms had not yet been hallowed in those early days; but beyond that they have little value.

The conservatives were not alone, however, in having a set of standards against which they could measure individual painters and their works. The humanitarian liberals had their own, and so, later on, did the advocates of pure painting[44] and others. The possession of a system was not always considered necessary for good criticism, however, as was shown by the respect in which Théophile Silvestre was held by his contemporaries even though his famous book was lacking in any fixed theoretical basis, a major defect in the eyes of Barbey d'Aurevilly who admired him greatly.[45] In some instances these *a priori* grounds for judgment are truly extraordinary, an example being a review of the Salon of 1845 by D. Laverdant in *La Phalange*, a Fourierist paper,[46] where the pictures are divided into two main groups: "happy" and "unhappy," and the author is pleased to report an increase in the total number of happy works.

[42] Ernest Chesneau, "Le Mouvement moderne en peinture. Delacroix," *Revue européenne*, Vol. XVIII, 1861, p. 511. (The articles of this series were later published in book form: *La Peinture française au dix-neuvième siècle: les chefs d'école*, Paris, 1862.) This discussion of the art of Delacroix ranks among the very best in the bibliography on this painter.

[43] In spite of this description of the inflexibility of the French artistic mind, Chesneau had a good deal of trouble himself when it came to the new talents of the modern movement.

[44] See below, Chaps. V-VIII.

[45] Barbey d'Aurevilly, *Les Oeuvres et les hommes. Sensations d'art*, Paris, 1887, pp. 31ff. (Since the author says that Silvestre's book has "just been published," this piece would seem to have been written soon after 1866.) Barbey thought Silvestre the greatest critic of the time but reproaches him for a lack of general ideas on which to hang his remarks. Some critics made a great display of impartiality and disdained any kind of *a priori* position. But cf. Baudelaire's Salon of 1846 where, under the title "A quoi bon la critique?" he says that any critic to be effective must take sides and be "passioné" (Chas. Baudelaire, *Curiosités* [ed. Lévy], p. 82).

[46] D. Laverdant, *La Mission de l'art et du role des artistes. Salon de 1845* (extracts from *La Phalange, revue de la science sociale*). This extraordinary little work contains a very full statement of what might be termed the Fourierist aesthetic, a strong plea to the artist to join the great social crusade.

When honestly and thoughtfully applied, however, principles such as those used by Castagnary in his famous Salon of 1857, or by Baudelaire, Zola, Delécluze, Thoré, and several others as a means of making some sense out of a chaotic situation had great merit (even though some were not finally approved by the course of events) for they raised standards against which art could be compared, and in the process showed what was actually happening not only to painting itself, but also to the thinking about it. Strangely enough, some of the most incorrect, or rather unfruitful, ideas are of the most interest, although in a rather negative sense.[47]

It was often in the attempt to apply these principles to the actual works themselves that the critics came to disaster. Gautier, for example, when speaking of art in general was frequently very acute, and appeared to see with considerable clarity the forces which were changing art, but when he came to speak of the painters themselves, he disliked some of the best, like Millet, and praised to the skies the art of men so obscure that their names, outside of his pages, have virtually disappeared. The catholicity of his taste was admitted: "We have often been accused of indulgence," he wrote, "it is a reproach which we accept. Criticism, according to us, ought to be rather a commentary on beauties than a search for faults. . . ."[48] And yet it is hard to forgive him for teaching so many eager readers to like so much second- and third-rate stuff. It must be admitted, however, in the light of the many apparent mistakes made by even the most enlightened critics, that the correct and absolute interpretation of contemporary paintings lies beyond the powers of all but the clairvoyant. The thoughtful men did the best they could, which was often excellent, and nearly always both interesting and provocative. It is all too easy to condemn their opinions from the vantage point of time.

One is, of course, entitled to inquire what these men thought their function was, and what effect they actually had on the production of the painters and the taste of the public.[49] The answers to these questions are difficult, if not impossible, because there was such a diversity of belief about the first point, and a lack of evidence as to results in regard to the last two. Certain it is that many writers spoke condescendingly to the artists in the manner of indulgent parents or crabbed schoolmasters—or even worse—and it must have required a colossal egotism on their part to believe that the artists would listen attentively and strive to do better according to their instructions. Some painters declared flatly that the only effect of criticism was on prices, which tended

[47] This is particularly true of the humanitarian position presently to be discussed.

[48] Th. Gautier, in an untitled introduction to Vol. III, 6e série, of *L'Artiste*, 1856-57, p. 4.

[49] The problem of the general function of criticism is far too complex to be gone into here. Opinions about it, as might be supposed, differed. Some rather trenchant remarks on the subject were made by M. H. Dumesnil in *Le Salon de 1859*, Paris, 1859: "It must be admitted that we are in better possession of the rhetoric of art than art itself, and our civilization is being dragged into other currents: that of science which sparkles, to the honor of our century, with an extraordinary brightness, and above all that of material interests.

"Criticism has little power today over the direction and tendencies of art, it is seldom that anyone listens, even when, by chance, it gives good advice. . . . Nevertheless it has a role in the affairs of our times . . . its duty is to place itself, as much as possible, in the *artist's position and simply give his opinion*" (pp. 2-3; italics mine).

to fluctuate somewhat in accordance with the press an individual received, yet it is also true that some artists like Millet and Manet were sustained in their struggle against misunderstanding by the sympathy and insight of those who saw what they were after and gave encouragement.

That the critics succeeded in elevating the general taste, or in initiating the public into the real problems and joys of artistic understanding is doubtful, the more so because there was so much uncertainty as to just what was good and what wasn't. Gautier tried to get everyone to like almost everything, and Baudelaire thought he made some progress, but it is hard to say for sure. Chesneau, who was well aware of the difficulties, wrote very earnestly of the necessity of lifting people to the level of fine art rather than bringing art down to them, but it is probable that few heard him.[50] And yet it is indisputable that people were interested in art and flocked to the Salons in great numbers. They eagerly awaited the news of the latest success or scandal at the show and apparently relied on the critics to tell them about their favorites as well as the butts of popular ridicule. The Salon was a great national event; it was enjoyed as a sort of festival. A few went with a view to purchase, but far more because they could look without having to buy. If Daumier is to be believed, it was visited by all classes and all ages, and consequently received an attention in the press commensurate with the interest taken in it. It is inconceivable that so many papers would have given space to it or so many writers engaged to tell about it, if it had not been of very real interest to great numbers of people. The depressing thing, apparently, was that this interest was so badly directed, with the result that the populace praised the worst and abhorred the best, though a suspicion arises to the effect that any really original artist must have had at least a few admirers.

At all events, there was a demand for comment and discussion which the press met by printing both in great quantity. Some critics must have written primarily to state their own views creatively, probably without much regard for ulterior purpose or educational effect, and in the case of the best among them, this was reason enough. If they did have purposes in mind, they would presumably include a desire to support publicly the art of which they approved, to speak to those who were interested in listening, to satisfy themselves as to the meaning of what they saw and liked (or didn't like), and to put their taste and experience at the service of the public and their own friends among the artists. To their great credit it can be recorded that there was probably never a time when more good sense and clear analysis (mixed with a certain amount of dross, to be sure) was written by an age about an art which it was seeing for the first time—that is, its own.

[50] The whole tenor of the first part of his book, *The Education of the Artist*, is to the general effect that both the artist and the observer in the modern age need to be educated to a point where they can both paint and enjoy a profound spiritual art. If this does not happen, painting will become devoid of ideas and the property of a few people specially trained to enjoy it and talk about it.

III. THE CONSERVATIVES AND THE GOVERNMENT

AS HAS been mentioned earlier, ideas as to the nature of a "modern" art had been developing before the end of the eighteenth century—ideas concerned with individualism, contemporaneity, revolt against tradition, and the determining effect of environment—but these had, naturally, been paralleled by theories that clung to other concepts, more hallowed by time, which were believed by many to be universal and therefore just as applicable to the present as to any previous age. Consequently the expressed opinions of the period with which this study deals can be divided into two classes: one, which held that a revitalization of traditional modes of French painting was the only solution; and a second, which claimed that the social order in the process of formation would produce a new art to accompany it, and that a definite break with the past was unavoidable. Of the latter group, some were primarily concerned with what ought to happen, while others, in a more objective vein, tried to imagine what would be forthcoming as a necessary result of past history and contemporary developments.

Without attempting to outline a whole aesthetic or establish the limits of a philosophy, the conservative position must be discussed. In one way it represented the challenge of the past to the present, and in another it was the foil for the arguments and practices which eventually created what we think of as modern art. When it is applied to the arts of antiquity and later periods we are inclined to agree with much of what it believed, but as a guide to the art of our own times, there is a strong feeling that it should be cast out altogether. The problem involved, of course, far exceeds the limits of artistic controversy, and in time it transcends the limits of our period by hundreds of years, but, as we shall see, its fate in the brief span of our discussion was of an unusual importance for the later history of painting.

The quarrel between the "ancients and the moderns" was by no means new in the nineteenth century. As Bury points out in his study of the idea of progress,[1] the notion that society was degenerating from a never-to-be-forgotten magnificence achieved in antiquity (or possibly the Renaissance as well) was actively challenged in the early seventeenth century by a contrary view which held that society was actually improving. The moderns were, at first, in the minority, but as time passed and the concept of human progress began to capture the imagination and mind of the west, they became dominant, and, at the last, the ancients were forced to fight a losing rearguard action, the sad plight in which we find them in the middle of the nineteenth century.

As not infrequently happens, the argument became somewhat oversimplified, and tended to boil down to the simple question of whether the past or the present was the more admirable, and to exclude either compromise or a more measured view of the merits and defects of each. Progress, as an idea, has one fatal weakness: the lack of any

[1] John Bagnell Bury, *The Idea of Progress*, London, 1921.

sure knowledge of the end toward which it is moving. Movement for its own sake without sure anticipation of some worthy destination may be exciting, but it is not reassuring nor spiritually satisfying. If the goal is known, and is admirable, then there is no excuse for not being as near it as the passage of time and human effort allow; under these conditions to be wedded to the past in any important respect is both stupid and morally indefensible. On the other hand, if we do not know where we are going, if the ultimate destination—and even the means of moving toward it—are in reasonable doubt, it is permissible to hold to the idea that people of previous ages may have been closer to it than we, or at least that they were striving toward a different aim which may have been as valid and compelling as ours. The dilemma posed by the idea of progress has not as yet been solved, and the crushing defeat of the ancients may not have been altogether just. For this reason, if no other, it is pertinent to inquire into their beliefs as held in our period.

If progressivism makes a fetish of modernity, if it assigns positive value to things just because they are recent, then conservatism may be said to do the exact opposite by making the past the only true seat of value and prizing only that which is old. The cautious observer of these opposites must come to the conclusion that there is some merit in each and total truth in neither, however unsatisfactory such a compromise may seem when the lines between the two have been as sharply drawn as they were in the development of modern society. Common sense tells us that everything new and recent is not good, but it is equally plain that if only that which is past is valuable, we might as well give up the struggle and die quietly, unnourished by the hope of improvement or the excitement which comes from life itself. A better course would be to attempt to carry forward from what has gone by the things which seem to have enduring value, and replace those whose usefulness is over, or which have been proven false, by new ones fashioned from more recent experience. Yet in battle, one must take sides or keep still, and even though it was clear by the middle of the last century that the moderns were in possession of the field, the conservatives fought on stubbornly. Much of what they professed to believe was not worth defending, but some of it was, and still is, valuable to man if he really cares to know what sort of a creature he is.

Whatever the reader may personally believe to have been the proper side in this controversy, the traditionalists felt that the great epochs of the past formed the soil from which any great modern art must grow; the art of the great masters, to change the metaphor, constituted a tree whose newest leaves must be firmly attached to the branches and trunk which had been growing for centuries. Creativity and originality were judged largely in terms of previous performance, a habit which, in the eclecticism of the years before 1848, led to a great deal of confusion between the pastiche and the truly novel, of which latter there was very little indeed.[2] Different critics used various masters as models for comparison with contemporary painting—Raphael, the Greeks, Rembrandt, and so on—while others were content with any similarity to some painter who only needed to be safely dead and reasonably honored by time. The lesson they

[2] Cf. Rosenthal, *Du romantisme*, especially Chap. IX.

tried to teach was that since the artists of former times had been content to build on their own schools and predecessors, those of the present should do likewise.[3] The occasional suspicion that there was little foundation left was unsettling, but it did not seem to invalidate the theory.

Beyond reverence for the past, the conservative view maintained that art must be concerned with beauty (as opposed to ugliness) and with an ideal;[4] that is, with an idea of perfection which only the artist could supply in concrete form. The thinking on these matters was often hazy and uncertain, but there was an underlying conviction that the world should not be accepted as it was, but as it should appear recast in a more heroic mould. This was the classic notion of history painting, but by the middle of the century it had become rather scarce in practice except for mural work,[5] and been replaced by the battle piece (and other "official" events) in which a detailed realism was employed to show the world not as it was generally but as it was, or had been, under certain very specific circumstances (Fig. 14). In the case of the orientalists a similar realism was often employed to transport the beholder to scenes considered more exotic than those available to the average Parisian. The ideal became debased to a form of sickly perfection in which finish was confused with beauty and anecdote with thought or spirituality (Fig. 11). However deplorable much of this art was, the traditionalists wanted art to continue to present man as a noble being, a character in some significant way more important than the observer himself, and most of the best ones were, for that reason, very guarded in their praise of Vernet, Meissonier, and Delaroche, the masters of the "juste milieu" and the popular favorites. These writers knew what they wanted, even if they were not able to find it anywhere on the walls or in the studios, a situation which accounted for no little bit of the current pessimism about the future.

[3] In his account of the Salon of 1855, Delécluze said (for probably the hundredth time) that what was needed was not to be modern but to deal in new ways with the old ideas "which have been current since the origin of civilization." From this practice comes "the habitual use of reason," a use which is very dear to the author's heart (E.-J. Delécluze, *Les Beaux-arts dans les deux mondes en 1855*, Paris, 1856, p. 303). For an excellent study of this fine but stiff-necked character, see Robert Baschet, *E.-J. Delécluze témoin de son temps*, Paris, 1942. For all his prejudices, he was an intelligent man.

[4] Statements of various kinds about the ideal are, of course, numerous among the conservatives. A fair example of their position is the following from Charles Blanc's review of the Salon of '67: "How great is the part which education plays in the talent artists have, whatever one may say! The art of idealizing the true, of simplifying the spectacles of nature and dignifying them by bringing them together in a strong unity; this superior art which we call style is not an infused grace, an innate faculty. One teaches it when one is a master, and one learns it to become one" (Chas. Blanc, in *Les Artistes de mon temps*, Paris, 1876, p. 469).

[5] There were a great number of these commissions during the first two-thirds of the century. The careers of Ingres, Delacroix, Chassériau, Flandrin, Chenavard, and Puvis de Chavannes (to name some of the more important executants) were closely bound up with these large-scale compositions. Murals constituted the most important branch of non-Salon art. Cf. Gautier's review of the Salon of 1857, in which he says that the absence of history painting in the galleries is due solely to the fact that it is all on the walls of public buildings (Th. Gautier, "Le Salon de 1857," in *L'Artiste*, 7e série, Vol. 1, 1857, p. 189).

To put it a little differently, the traditional position held that art had a moral or spiritual function, that it should deal with man in terms of the highest mental qualities which he possessed.[6] This must not be interpreted as meaning that they wanted art to preach, to tell the ignorant how to behave, or to hold a mirror up to virtue. It was rather a belief that in ways peculiar to itself—ways which neither literature nor music nor any other art form could exactly match—painting could communicate something to man which was greater and finer than anything he could find in the world around him, and that this communication was not only beneficial, it was the highest function of the art. The misfortune was that the terms which had been used for this purpose, namely the classical and Christian epics, overlaid with more recent literature about mediaeval and other periods, did not now appear to be valid thematic sources.[7] The conservatives were, in a sense, desperate; they refused to give up the idea that art should continue to explore man's spiritual nature, but the symbolic conventions which had been employed for this purpose in the past were no longer available.[8]

They may be criticized on the grounds that the very artists whom they professed to admire did not actually believe in these lofty ends. This was partly true; Veronese was hardly as devout as Giotto, and Perugino may have been an atheist, but even in cases where classicism and religion had been used merely as a support for expressions of stylistic beauty or spectacles of richness and pictorial splendor, the nature of man as

[6] Cf. Henri Delaborde's remark to the effect that up to now artists have been bound together by the joint possession of moral intentions: "All of them, to the extent of their power and the class of their talent proposed above all to translate with their brush either a profound thought or an ingenious idea" (Henri Delaborde, *Mélanges sur l'art contemporain*, Paris, 1866, p. 68, under heading "Le Salon de 1853").

[7] The decline in potency of such themes was no new phenomenon. In the middle of the eighteenth century, La Font de St. Yenne complained of the sad state of painting which no longer dealt with great truths as in the days of Colbert. Even religious themes had become "boring" (La Font de St. Yenne, *L'Ombre du grand Colbert, le Louvre, et la ville de Paris, dialogue. Réflexions sur quelques causes de l'état présent de la peinture en France*, Paris, 1752, p. xxviii and p. 218). The Comte de Caylus was similarly worried about the plight of great painting. For the earlier nineteenth century, see Rosenthal, *Du romantisme*; for academic art in the eighteenth century, see J. Locquin, *La Peinture d'histoire en France de 1747 à 1785*, Paris, 1912.

[8] The art of the great tradition was in a large measure symbolic and had been predicated on a foreknowledge on the part of the observer of the subjects dealt with. By the mid-nineteenth century these subjects as well as their meanings were unknown to many people who now constituted the art public. It is significant that explanations of all pictures concerned with any literary, classical, or religious theme were given in small type in the official catalogue so that their meaning could be ascertained on the spot. Even the people who did have the requisite foreknowledge were not necessarily interested in them, especially if they believed that they were no longer applicable to modern life. Thoré attacked this outworn symbolism very directly: "It is between these two languages, these two arts, that all literary and artistic schools have alternated for the past three centuries. In our West, there are actually but two forms, each of which expresses a partial idea—the catholic allegory and the pagan, equally impenetrable to 'strangers' and equally indifferent to the modern spirit of the peoples who still use them" (Th. Thoré, *Salons de T. Thoré. 1844, '45, '46, '47, '48*, Paris, 1868, pp. xxi-xxii of the Preface; this preface was written at the time of the publication of the collected Salons and is signed with his pseudonym, W. Bürger).

a superior being was implicit.[9] Even the humanitarians like Thoré, however tired they were of the trappings of the past, and however anxious to achieve a new art for the future, still wanted something in which man would appear, as he had formerly, to be an admirable, thoughtful, sensitive creature, a person whose real nature was not apparent on the outside, but could only be understood imaginatively. Both the traditionalist conservatives and the progressive champions of "an art for man" were in agreement on the necessity for this imaginative insight.[10] As will be seen later, it was this seeming lack of imagination on the part of Courbet (Fig. 41) which they felt kept him in a different class from Millet (Fig. 27), and really constituted the essential difference between the two.[11] Millet, in their eyes, was a man of such imagination that he raised the humble peasant almost to epic proportions; Courbet just looked at him sharply.[12]

Among more reactionary critics the notion of style itself was bound up with the idea of what the great subject was, or should be—even to a ridiculous extent: "M. Curzon possesses the feeling for style in the highest degree, and expresses it by placing antique figures near a Roman ruin."[13] Inanities of this sort furnished the revolutionaries with a target too large to be missed. It was, in fact, the poverty of an art adhering to the past and the incapacity of ordinary critics which contributed greatly to the success of the modern movement, and in the process of winning the battle, it tended to discard the genuine virtues of all art of moral import as well.

Nowadays it may seem a heresy to have attacked the bases on which the new art was to arise, and yet it would be wrong to suppose that it was only a blind lashing out at the new in favor of the old. Delécluze, the great champion of Ingres and the severe critic of Delacroix, complained bitterly about new ideas (the fascination of the sketch as opposed to the "finished" work of art was the immediate object of his wrath) but in damning it, he showed that he had a certain insight into its true nature. The following passage, quoted from his revue of the Salon of 1850, is unusually perceptive. He said that the new concept of painting,

. . . [believed] that the true artist should only obey his instinct and his fantasy [i.e. imagination]; that graduated and severe studies are only harmful to the development of genius; that every artist can be sufficient unto himself and should learn what he needs to know by his own experience; that he is considered to have his own poetics (*poétique*), style, and way of doing things without embarrassing himself with what others have thought and done; that everything which resembles a school and by that tends toward a certain unity of principle, is destructive of individual genius, and finally that art is only an exercise, made easy, of the faculty of reproducing on the canvas, without choice, reflection and criticism, the images

[9] This is roughly what Malraux means by "the fiction." See Malraux, *Le Musée imaginaire*, pp. 96ff.

[10] Cf. T. Thoré, *Salons de W. Bürger*, Vol. II, p. 14, "Le Salon de 1864."

[11] Imagination was, of course, the mental quality which transformed the world of appearances into the world of art. The realists seemed to them to be just giving the external world right back again, and to pick the least attractive aspects of it to reproduce.

[12] See below Chaps. v, vi, xiv, and xv.

[13] Léon Lagrange, "Le Salon de 1864," in *Gazette des beaux-arts*, Vol. xvii, 1864, p. 13.

and ideas—however coarse they may be—which come into the mind through the intermediary of the senses.[14]

All these ideas he regarded as "monstrous errors," but he knew what they were, and being a rational Frenchman, condemned them roundly.

It is not within the scope of this essay to attempt an explanation of the causes of the unhappy state of history painting, since we are here dealing only with the current nature of these ideas and their relation to actual practice, but no discussion of the conservative position would be complete without a brief mention of some of the reasons which the critics themselves felt were responsible for it. Certain of these were shared by the progressives, who differed mainly in regard to solutions.[15] Most of them seem to be symptoms rather than causes, such as general observations to the effect that painters were abandoning the true principles on which all great art should be based.[16] This was doubtless true enough but can hardly be classed as an explanation. Perhaps a little nearer to the real difficulty was the claim that religion and the lore of antiquity had somehow ceased to be related to modern times, but here again one asks for a deeper reason.[17]

Others felt that the support of the government had been inadequate and even bungling,[18] a matter which will be discussed presently in more detail. Another suggestion was that the trouble was primarily due to a lack of education in the meaning and understanding of art on the part of both the painters and the public.[19] A few laid the blame at the door of society itself which through its own confusion and uncertainty had become, as it were, artistically derailed, and so hoped that reestablishment of security and cultural continuity would bring back the days when men could look naturally to the eternal values of the past.[20]

[14] E.-J. Delécluze, *Exposition des artistes vivants, 1850*, Paris, 1851, pp. 102-103. It may be that these evil traits in current French art seemed to him to have rushed into the vacuum left by the departure of any powerful central guiding ideas behind the grand style. This situation, he believed, had been evident as early as 1810 (E.-J. Delécluze, *Louis David, son école et son temps*, Paris, 1855 [written in 1835], pp. 324ff.).

[15] I.e.: What could be done to rescue art from its state of apparent decline?

[16] Alexandre Dumas put it this way in 1859: "Why these successive failings among the new generations? Why this forgetfulness of the holy mission? Why this kind of negation of man, this scorn for poetry, this culpable apostasy of history, this disdain for the great pages, this love for little leaflets, this rage of Elzevirs?" (A. Dumas, *L'Art et les artistes contemporains au Salon de 1859*, Paris, 1859). He blames this on the men "charged with directing the public taste" (pp. 4-5).

[17] Cf. Thoré as quoted above, note 8.

[18] See below, pp. 43ff.

[19] This was Ernest Chesneau's thesis in *The Education of the Artist*.

[20] In an article signed "Wallon," published in *L'Artiste*, this cultural failure is emphasized: "Thus it is with our century; it no longer sees anything but the exterior beauties of art; it has only an artificial intellectual life. But that ancient faith, that immense faith from which the beautiful drew its existence and its form, that faith which inspires the great artist with great thoughts has not been with us for a long time, and art has fled with it" (Wallon, "De la symbolique des arts," in *L'Artiste*, 4e série, Vol. VIII, 1847, p. 226). The humanitarians, who were usually social liberals, were more prone to lay the blame on society than the conservatives, who were likely to be in greater agreement with the government. It was not always advisable to criticize the social situation during the Second Empire. See the discussion of the governmental attitude which follows.

Nearly all these criticisms of the current state of art stemmed from the fact that what was essentially the Cartesian mode of thought, that way of thinking which had been implicit in the structure of French society during her great years under Louis XIV and had persisted in many quarters during the following two centuries, was now over-thrown by a later system less concerned with rigid principles, first causes, and eternal rational truths. This Cartesianism was accompanied in the minds of many people by certain established and hallowed concepts deriving from the great classic and Christian epics. But many of the changes which led to the formation of the social world as we know it today were quite antithetical to all three of these sets of standards, or ways of conceiving man's place in the cosmos. Democracy, for example, was far more fluid and, for the French at least, far more uncertain than monarchy, while science was moving away from the Newtonian ideas of the changeless operation of natural law expressed in mathematical certainties toward a more exciting but less secure position which stressed the relationships between things. Evolutionary concepts and positivism allowed results to change leaving only the principles which governed them to remain as constants.

One might say that the same shift was occurring in art criticism, and among creative painters as well. The traditional analyses of art history had produced a set of rather fixed principles for the guidance of the artist, which if they did not go back to God himself, were at least supposed to have the sanction of the ancients and the great masters of the Renaissance. The modern view, on the other hand, denied the validity of this entire structure, conceived the individual to be more important than any norm or ideal, and turned directly to life and nature from whose impact on the self new pictorial forms were to be developed. If things were not eternal in the fields of natural science or politics, there was no more reason why they should be so in art.

But art had always been thought of as having an intimate connection with moral law and the spiritual aspirations of mankind. In these fields the changes ushering in our era were even more disturbing, for where there were other scientific systems to replace the outworn Newtonian scheme, and other political systems to serve in the place left vacant by the decline of the monarchical principle, there were no moral substitutes for the spiritual heritage which was being done away with. Sociology, at least as Comte envisaged it, was supposed to fill the void, and natural science was ex-pected to inaugurate a spiritual improvement by ameliorating man's environment, but it is doubtful if this is what actually happened, and in any case, the signs of a general social rebirth were slow in putting in an appearance, and often contradictory when they did appear. Conscience won a freedom it had never known, the benefits of society were gradually extended to more and more people, but the price was a heavy one: the surrender of moral certainty and the loneliness of spiritual individualism. Even if the future ideals of society had been clearly apparent from the start, it is ques-tionable whether the artist would have been any better off, for they were not likely to be embodied in any epic form; they were not going to be personifiable. The discovery of anesthesia eased the physical suffering of countless thousands, but the artist was

41

never able to celebrate the fact in fitting terms. Modern patterns of social behavior evolved quickly enough and were suited at once to the requirements of an industrial and materialistic age, but in the traditional sense, they were scarcely spiritual. If men were to improve, they were going to do so via the laboratory and the statistical table rather than by a comparison of themselves individually with a transcendent ideal which was conceived to be common to them all. The expression of such an ideal had been the true goal of the great art of the past; the difficult challenge which had been faced, if not mastered, by all those who ever attempted the form. In the future, either a new ideology accompanied by a new symbolism would have to be forthcoming, or the days of "great" art were over. This was a momentous fact, and the second alternative was one which certain types of minds could only contemplate with genuine horror. It is small wonder that some of them hoped, mistakenly, that the forces which seemed to be shaping society into its new form would be short-lived, or else would be radically modified until they assumed a character less antagonistic to their own cherished opinions.

Whatever their detailed reasons were, all the conservatives wanted a greatness for the present to rival that of the past whose glorious examples were hanging on the walls of the museums. This was not to be, at least not in the form they expected, for the fulfillment of their desires would have required a turning back of the clock of history, an impossible retrogression.

One of the difficulties encountered in an effort to make a fair statement of the conservative case at the time of this study is the unhappy fact that there were very few real minds among those who made a show of professing it. In its driest and most artificial form, the ideas of which it was composed could be had for very little trouble, and since it was some portion of them which constituted the intellectual stock-in-trade of the larger part of the art-going public, a ready and admiring audience was awaiting both paintings and pronouncements neatly framed in them. But in the hands of men like Delécluze, Blanc, Chesneau, Mantz, and a few others, it had a validity and persuasiveness which usually avoided the painful rigidity of less temperate reviewers like the Vicomte Delaborde: ". . . the spectacle which is presented by the Salon of 1853 will leave no doubt in the mind of anyone about the regrettable results of individual caprices, and—what is even more vexatious—about the materialist tendencies of contemporary painting."[21] This, of course, was mainly a blast at Courbet, but it showed the reactionary in action. There was, however, a certain majesty in the remarks of as distinguished a scholar and so ardent a lover of art as Charles Blanc, when, at the very end of the period (1869), he wrote:

When we observed, when we said that French painting was falling into decadence because the progress made by our artists in inferior classes [of art] was being accomplished at the expense of great art, we were not the only one to notice it and to say it; and that which proves that our view was not the isolated one of a peevish mind, is the fact that the govern-

[21] Henri Delaborde, *Mélanges sur l'art contemporain*, p. 68.

ment, itself confessing this decadence, instituted the extraordinary prize of one hundred thousand francs to raise the level of art.[22]

The reference to great art, the use of the government opinion as confirmation, the idea that inferior types have been developed at the expense of something finer—all these are of the essence of traditionalism. Blanc, of course, represented a rather unusual case, for he had been an ardent republican as early as 1841, and had been made Director of the Beaux-Arts in '48, both of which facts would ordinarily mark him as a liberal.[23] But by 1859 he was founding the *Gazette des beaux-arts*, which was certainly no organ of the *avant-garde*, and by 1868 he was elected to the Academy. For all of his devotion to the past, he had an eye, and three years before the date of the passage just quoted, gave a very warm appreciation of "this majestic [grand] portrait of Camille" by Monet (Fig. 77), to whom should go a certificate for "picturesque life." In his lexicon, this was high praise. Like the best of this group, he knew painting when he saw it, but he was unable to see it except from the standpoint of the past, and there lay the difficulty.

It would not be profitable to analyze the opinions of this group more fully, since they are, for the most part, reasonably homogeneous, but mention must be made of one other aspect of conservatism: the one which had to do with the state. It may be observed historically that France had taken the lead in the establishment of a close bond between art and the state in the seventeenth century. Richelieu, and later Colbert, had seen clearly the advantages which would accrue to the government from such an association, and Le Brun had seen what power it would place in the hands of the artists. At a time when the structure upon which the great tradition was founded was beginning to be weakened by profound social and intellectual changes, it was suddenly strengthened by being made a part of the greater majesty which was the property of the state. The ideas of moral grandeur which attached to the person of the king and his government were extended, in part, to apply to the art which was, so to speak, at their service. Irrespective of the quality of the results produced, a certain nobility was conferred upon any art which was related to these governmental ideals. Nationalism, love for France herself,[24] respect for authority vested in the ruling power, and a desire to root the greatness of France deep in the past were all factors contributing to the undeniable strength of the academic system. It is significant that, in spite of a great deal of very mediocre art produced by the academicians in the two hundred years following its establishment, the system itself—along with various later ramifications of it—survived every political upheaval to which the nation was subjected, and these were both numerous and important.[25] The history of French academism cannot be entered into here, but

---

[22] Chas. Blanc, *Les Artistes de mon temps*, Paris, 1876, chapter on Chenavard, p. 191.

[23] Many of the more progressive critics were republicans, i.e. of the left.

[24] The chauvinism of French criticism under the Second Empire is painfully marked, especially at the time of the great exposition of 1855.

[25] These would include the French Revolution, the Napoleonic period, the Bourbon restoration, the July Monarchy, the revolution of 1848, the Coup d'État of 1851, the events of 1870-71, and the final establishment of the Third Republic.

its inherent and tenacious strength should not be ignored.[26] The idea that the state had a definite function in relation to the arts, and that, conversely, art had a responsibility to the state, became so firmly fixed in the social structure of the country that it was able to persist long after the art which presumably expressed the suitable notions of ideality, grandeur, and morality had become dry, anachronistic, and a definite impediment to the healthy growth of more contemporary forms. Respect for government, as government, has a conservative influence, and this influence affected the state's outlook on art whether the form of it was monarchical, imperial, or democratic.

The growth of society put an ever greater strain upon the rather creaky machinery of artistic exploitation of national virtue, and by the nineteenth century such art was mainly a habit without any actual support from society itself. The innermost sanctum of this official conservatism was really not the government but the membership of the Institute, a group whose artistic ineptness did nothing to help an already desperate situation. Though their fame was supposed to be conferred by France herself, they usually did the crowning themselves, becoming a close and bigoted clique of almost petrified talent.[27] It is a common error to identify them with the government, but the fact is that the two were not infrequently in quite violent opposition, and their actions were in many ways very different.[28] There was hardly a critic—or artist either—of any worth at all who did not consider their painting very near the bottom of the entire current output, and their nefarious influence on the Salon juries is too well known to require discussion.

Although the administration frequently disassociated itself from the conservative extremes of the Institute, there is no denying that the regular governmental agencies were animated by ideas coming from a point well to the right of center. Under Louis Napoleon, the administration supported traditionalism with great earnestness. His ministers were only too anxious to preserve the connection between the grandeur of "great art" and that of a great state which had been so magnificently established by Louis XIV. The official attitude was made abundantly plain in the speeches delivered at the time of the award of the medals and other honors in the Salons. Those of 1852 and 1857 may serve as examples.[29] In 1852, particularly, the creation of the Empire

[26] More studies are needed in this field of the excellent quality of Jean Locquin's *La Peinture d'histoire en France de 1747 à 1785*.

[27] See Stranahan, *History of French Painting*, pp. 130ff., 191.

[28] The case of Delacroix is revealing in this regard. In spite of the obvious disparity between his art and the precepts supported by the Academicians, he received a very large number of important governmental commissions. Had the award of these been in the hands of the *Institut* it would have been a different story.

[29] Cf. Eleanor Spencer, "The Academic Point of View in the Second Empire," in *Courbet and the Naturalistic Movement*, ed. G. Boas, Baltimore, 1938. The endeavors of the government to support an art of its liking are excellently described. There was a general return to a more conservative attitude about the Salons after the excessive freedom of the famous show in 1848. In spite of certain liberalizing moves on the part of the Ministry of Fine Arts, the official position underwent little change during this period. This whole volume is most valuable for a study of the art of the mid-century.

was so recent that the Minister of the Interior, the Duc de Persigny, felt a heavy responsibility for underlining the relation of state and art:

If a government which has its origin, its very principle, in the poetic feeling of the masses, should disdain the cult of the arts for that of material things, it would be false to the conditions of its existence and would misunderstand the genius of the country. Indeed, it is not in France that the arts need fear the industrial and commercial tendencies of modern civilization. Whatever may be the mode of activity of our society, nothing can weaken the chivalrous and artistic side of the national character. . . . What then is necessary for the arts to prosper among a people eminently artistic and chivalrous? A single thing; a government which has its roots in the depths of the nation, its strength and its future in the popular faith. . . .[30]

Art in the grand manner would flourish as a result of the solicitude of the state; the people had a natural flair for the finest in art, which was to be aided and abetted by the power of government.[31] In view of the results achieved, this may appear to have been overly optimistic, but there were many who believed it.

M. Fould, the Minister of State who gave the address in 1857, expressed the same attitude in even more positive form.

In fact, when one considers the actual Exposition in its entirety, or when one compares it to preceding expositions, one will be forced to recognize that few of them have gathered together as many works of real merit, and revealed to France as great a number of new talents.[32] These new talents are the hope of the future. Faithful to the traditions of their illustrious masters, they will know how to bind themselves perseveringly to those serious studies without which the happiest genius remains sterile or wanders astray; they will know how to prefer the solid and durable pleasures of the true glory to the ephemeral satisfactions which are given by a too easy success; they will know that sometimes it is necessary to resist the public taste, and that art is very near to losing itself when, abandoning the high and pure regions of the beautiful, and the traditional paths of the great masters to follow the teachings of the new school of realism, it seeks for nothing more than a servile imitation of the least poetic and elevated offerings of nature. . . .[33]

The worst sin of all is "that deplorable tendency to put art at the service of fashion or the caprices of the day."[34] A great many noble themes are available:

Poetry, morals, religion, history—those divine sources which inspired the masters are not dried up for their successors, and at no time has France furnished more ample material for the chisel and the brush of her artists. How many great things just from the beginning of the reign! How many touching and sublime themes. . . .[35]

Painting must not be at the services of the "caprices" of the day, but it can and should lend its support to the administration.

[30] Catalogue, *Salon de 1853*, p. 8. The speeches and awards were published at the beginning of the catalogue of the following Salon.

[31] For reasons of propaganda the government had to assume that the popular taste was good, which it clearly was not.

[32] The really new talents, unfortunately, were precisely the ones of which the government did not approve.

[33] Catalogue, *Salon de 1859*, pp. viii-ix. The indirect reference here is to Courbet's *Demoiselles au bord de la Seine*.

[34] *Ibid.*, p. ix.

[35] *Ibid.*, p. ix. Note the reference to the contemporary milieu. This "modern" concept was often shared, when it seemed advisable, by the conservative wing.

It was also true, of course, that the government was not only clothed in the supposed majesty of the traditional past, but was made up of men who were essentially bourgeois themselves and were equipped with the taste common to that class at that time. This was also conservative and not too well informed, alternating between personal preference and ideas as to what the best art should be. Since these officials often had public moneys at their disposal for the purchase of pictures by the state, their taste had a very direct bearing on the general situation; so much so that some reactionary painters seem to have been able to gain a living by this means alone. With very few exceptions, the work of the more revolutionary painters was not thus supported, a fact which added more fuel to the artists' dislike of both the government and the bourgeoisie.

It would be a mistake to dismiss these official remarks too lightly, for the history of French art shows that the artist was, at heart, a Frenchman too, and the important painters of all persuasions longed wholeheartedly for the recognition of the official world of art—and not entirely from mercenary motives either. Delacroix might be bitterly disappointed at his failure to be elected to the Academy,[36] but he continued to exhibit in the Salons year after year and to give much time to service on its juries;[37] and though Courbet haughtily refused the Legion of Honor in 1870, the next year he found himself "up to his neck" in the political world of art.[38] Eventually, however, the conservative official attitude became so oppressive that a clean break between the government's art bureaus and the progressive wing became a necessity.[39]

The criticism of the period is filled with bitter and resentful attacks on the manner in which the government was discharging its obligations toward the artists and the people;[40] innumerable suggestions were made for reforming the whole system from

[36] Delacroix, *Correspondence*, Vol. III, p. v. Joubin notes that it took eight failures before he was admitted in 1857 to the chair left vacant by the death of Delaroche. Delacroix was a very proud man, which makes this all the more remarkable. The letters, calls, and entreaties necessary to propose oneself for a seat constituted a very humbling experience, and the members were scarcely painters whose work he admired. Alexandre Dumas wrote of him: "Delacroix, a man of wit, of science, and of an imagination which has only one oddity— that of obstinately wanting to be the colleague of M. Picot and M. Abel de Pujol, and who, happily—at least so we hope—will not be that" (*Journal of Eugène Delacroix*, trans. by Walter Pach, N.Y., 1937, note 62, pp. 350-351).

[37] He was apparently well thought of in this capacity by his fellow artists. In 1848 when the exhibitors elected the jury, Delacroix received the third largest number of votes—five behind Ingres and twenty-seven behind Léon Cogniet. For some years he was never lower than fourth in the voting.

[38] Cf. C. Léger, *Gustave Courbet*, Paris, 1929, pp. 158ff.

[39] The official position seems eventually to have hardened into a stupid prejudice.

[40] Note, for example, Castagnary's outburst in the review of the Salon of 1868: "Thus M. de Nieuwerkerke, Superintendant of Fine Arts will be overcome in the struggle he has long been waging in the name of authority. When, on the day following the second of December, thinking of the inroads already made by naturalism, he cried out before the full assembly of artists that 'the mission of the state is to discourage the false vocations and false talents which obstruct all avenues,' he did not know that a few years would suffice to reduce his pretentions to nothing, and that these 'false vocations and false talents' were precisely the ones which would end by gaining the balance of public opinion.

"What good it is to him now to have wished to create an official aesthetic, and to have

the schools to the juries, but very few questioned the general advisability of govern-mental support, or quarreled with its ultimate aims. In other words, the remarks just quoted had a broad foundation in the thinking of many independent critics and amateurs; what they wanted was correction, not abolition.

Amid the low caliber of the paintings, the growing lack of an informed (i.e. tradi-tional) taste, and the incapacity of the government to improve matters, the position of the conservative was far from hopeful. Maxime du Camp, reviewing the Salon of 1861, found it dull in the extreme and was moved to state with devastating, if mistaken, finality that in the ten years of its existence, the Empire had not produced a single work destined to survive.[41] At the close of his melancholy reflections he inquired if all hope for French art must then be abandoned. His answer, put forth without any great conviction, suggested that a painter would arise who would love art,

who has reflected on what it ought to be and has led his curiosity and his studies among the modern masters and the old masters, who slowly disengages his originality by hard work, who moves forward courageously toward the higher end . . . and who one day or another will appear to found the French school of the second half of the nineteenth century, for that of the first half has fallen into imbecility.[42]

Some sort of revival of the great tradition in a new and powerful form was the best that this group could see for the future, but they had no clear idea about how it might be accomplished.

---

posed the principle that the arts are made for the splendor of thrones? Not a one of the men whom he has taken in his powerful hand and raised one by one onto a pedestal is left standing. . . " (J. A. Castagnary, "Le Salon de 1868," in *Salons*, Paris, 1892, p. 252. All references to these *Salons* are from Vol. 1).

[41] Maxime Du Camp, *Le Salon de 1861*, Paris, 1861, p. 4.

[42] *Ibid.*, p. 197.

IV. NEUTRAL VIEWS

CERTAIN critics, while admitting that concessions would have to be made to the changing times, took a rather neutral view, declining to attempt detailed predictions for the future or to abandon the past entirely. Théophile Silvestre's *Histoire des artistes vivants* is perhaps the outstanding example of the writing of this kind.[1] In an earlier chapter mention was made of the fact that he was criticized for not establishing a system of ideas as a framework for his discussion of the men of the day whom he considered important,[2] but in a sense it was his relative neutrality which makes his judgments so interesting today. His choice of painters is rather unusual: Horace Vernet, Ingres, Delacroix, Chenavard, Decamps, Diaz, Corot, and Courbet,[3] yet for each his perception is keen and his criticism nearly always just. Diaz and Vernet seem of minor importance today, and Chenavard has been almost entirely forgotten except in Lyon,[4] but at the time the book was written they were all men of either great or unusual reputations, and constituted a fair choice among the better painters.

He was not entirely persuaded of the greatness of Ingres, about whom he said: "M. Ingres has nothing in common with us, he is a Chinese painter wandering astray, in the nineteenth century, in the ruins of Athens."[5] Though this is a somewhat inaccurate description one cannot fail to see exactly what he meant. He continues: "To follow the perfection of form by design and mutilate the design by color is the fatal task of M. Ingres."[6] On the other hand, he knew the art of Delacroix as thoroughly as Baudelaire (whom he admired),[7] and found there a greatness equal to that of the past; in fact, he refers to him as "perhaps the last of the great family."[8] He is equally penetrating on Courbet:

Here is one who, in seven years, has alone made more noise in the city than twenty celebrities would know how to, assisted by their noisy followers. Some regard him as the robust and vivacious personification of a new art, like a new Caravaggio who battles imagination to the profit of reality. . . . Others take him for a sort of rag-picker of art, spearing the truth in the mud of the streets after having confiscated and thrown in his basket the last tatters of the romantic school of 1830 and the wigs of the Academy; the fanatics have placed him at a single bound above all the artists of our time, and he himself swears with resolute faith that he will shortly efface all modern works from the memory of the century. Most people . . . disdain him.[9]

. . . One must recognize in him, under penalty of injustice, at one and the same time a painter full of force, originality, and extravagance, who, by the value of temperament, ambition reacting against the past and the triviality of its tastes, often throws himself, head lowered, into ridicule, and compromises solid qualities which no one can seriously contest.[10]

The chapter devoted to Chenavard pays careful attention to the depth and eccentricity of that remarkable man, and shows an ability, which was peculiarly Silvestre's own, to

---

[1] Théophile Silvestre, *Histoire des artistes vivants, français et étrangers. Études d'après nature*, Paris, 1856.

[2] See Chap. II, p. 32 and note 45.

[3] Also discussed are the sculptors Barye, Préault, and Rude.

[4] Paul Chenavard will be the subject of a monograph by the author in the near future.

[5] Silvestre, *op.cit.*, p. 33.   [6] *Ibid.*, p. 21.

[7] *Ibid.*, p. 46.   [8] *Ibid.*, p. 75.

[9] *Ibid.*, p. 241.   [10] *Ibid.*, p. 242.

analyze what an artist's performance was really worth, irrespective of the sides generally taken in the heated battles then raging. But he stays away from the future. Realism is good as far as it goes, but it is too narrow and makes the fatal mistake of ruling out imagination. History and the Bible have not been exhausted and they are for all people of all time, the present included.[11]

It does not seem to me to be demanding too much of the artist to ask of him a tendency toward civilization, morality, a significant expression. . . . A painter of worth is not, doubtless, condemned, under pain of a lack of interest, to a program of precise utility, to reproduce anecdotes of morality in action, the great scenes of history in magic lantern or Diorama subjects, finally to draw pamphlets and allegories from nature, but to whom will he speak and what will he be able to say without passion and purpose?[12]

The dilemma was plain; the answer to it was left to others.

Such an answer was attempted by Ernest Chesneau, a firm, if erratic, believer in the nobility of art and an informed student of the present difficulties. Only fifteen years old at the opening of this period, he became a protégé of the great Nieuwerkerke[13] and was for many years on the staff of the Louvre. His writing begins in the early 'sixties and continues down to his publication, in 1886, of the summary of his years of thought on the state of art during his lifetime.[14] It is permissible to use it here since on internal evidence it can be seen to be mostly conceived prior to 1870, and, like most conservatives, Chesneau's ideas remained quite constant from the beginning. As early as 1861, in a series of articles on "The Modern Movement in Painting" which appeared in the *Revue européenne*,[15] he was willing to accord excellence, but not greatness, to an art for art's sake. The finest artists of the past have attempted, he said, "to express the infinite by the finite," and they "give way to a . . . need for interior exaltation [which is] limited in expression like everything human, but limitless in their hearts."[16] Such great men are rare:

. . . below them at various levels, must be placed those spirits who, cutting themselves off from the idea, seek in nature only the immediate beauty of the elements, the beings which vivify it. They are endowed with exquisite organs, it is true, but ideal culture is lacking in them and finds them indifferent. Nevertheless they have a role, and it is a great enough one

---

[11] *Ibid.*, pp. 275-276.   [12] *Ibid.*, p. 13.

[13] Alfred Emilien, Comte de Nieuwerkerke was one of the most imposing artistic figures of the age. A sculptor by profession, he made his debut in the Salon of 1843 and exhibited at intervals thereafter until the 'sixties. But his reputation was made in official circles where, after being made a Chevalier of the Legion of Honor in 1848, he rose very rapidly. In 1849 he was appointed Director-General of the museums of France and later occupied the post of Superintendent of Fine Arts which was created for him by Napoleon III, in whose favor he most definitely was. He was showered with official honors during the Second Empire, and yet, in spite of a certain snobbishness

resulting from his wealth and position, he seems to have had the interests of art very much at heart, at least according to his own standards. The conservative critics like Houssaye seem to have had a high regard for him, and he was at least partly responsible for the artistic reforms which were attempted in 1863. It was he who purportedly took Courbet to lunch before the opening of the Exposition Universelle of 1855 in an attempt to get him to behave in a more orthodox manner as regards his painting.

[14] E. Chesneau, *The Education of the Artist.*

[15] See above, Chap. II, note 42.

[16] Chesneau, *op.cit.*, in *Revue européenne*, Vol. XIII, 1861, pp. 140-141.

to satisfy a lofty ambition: that of revealing natural beauties, initiating souls through the senses. The road, whose side paths only they have traveled over, will be traversed by others whom they awakened, others who will prolong it and occupy its whole width . . . but in the rigorous meaning of the word, they are not great artists.[17]

The art of "picturesque fantasy" as begun by Watteau and Chardin is delightful, but "it is the result of an art which no longer has anything to say or no longer knows how to say anything great; which, without moral basis, seeks to seduce the senses and not satisfy the soul; a formula with no inward echo."[18]

Chesneau suffered from indecision, a common ailment of the period, so he was unable to reconcile the taste for realism with an opposite urge toward idealism. The present could not be ignored, but the past was vital too; and so on through a lengthy discussion of the evils of present art forms which is curiously interlarded with an obvious pleasure in them.[19] He never lost the belief that "great painting" in the traditional sense was not really worn out, and yet he said that realism was really the proper mode for the French.[20] In the 'sixties he could not honestly see what the progressive group was driving at—his account of the Salon des Refusés is disappointing[21]—but later he admired them in his own way and even said that Manet's people were really more than just people, they were the successors of the Medeas and Bacchuses of the past (Fig. 70).[22] He took a keen delight in the art of Moreau because it was both classical and at the same time intensely personal—imaginative in a modern sense (Fig. 71).[23] He believed both in the grand manner and in being modern, but when he thought about it, he found that one canceled out the other.

The nineteenth century surely affords no better example of the intelligent mind set adrift by sweeping change. And yet there is much that is valuable here, for it is in the very statement of his uncertainties that the nature of the questions troubling the times can be seen, and he knew them all. He was deeply preoccupied with the intensely difficult problem of realigning art and society, a problem which, he felt, had become acute.[24] Art had left the people behind, for it had become the property of a clique who claimed to be the only ones to understand it.[25] Furthermore, the development of a new materialistic society had neglected the question of the place which it should assign to

---

[17] *Ibid.*, p. 141.   [18] *Ibid.*, p. 143.

[19] This seems particularly evident in his two little volumes entitled *L'Art et les artistes modernes en France et en Angleterre*, Paris, 1864, and *Les Nations rivales dans l'art*, Paris, 1869. He condemns Manet for not being able to draw but admires his audacity. Whistler caught his eye in the Salon des Refusés even though Chesneau felt compelled to describe his *Dame blanche* as "bizarre." He thought the return to realism, while not a proper end in itself, was a healthy sign for the French had always had a flair for it, etc. His ideas about really advanced art at this time may, perhaps, be summed up by his phrase: "Better a thousand times this insensate exaltation than the

mortal quiet of the satisfied" (*Les Nations rivales*, p. 345).

[20] Chesneau, *L'Art et les artistes modernes*, pp. 3ff.

[21] *Ibid.*, pp. 187ff.

[22] Chesneau, *The Education of the Artist*, p. 36.

[23] *Ibid.*, pp. 165ff. For Chesneau, a person who could be as imaginative as Moreau with material which, in other hands, was stale and dry, was essentially modern. He had, in this critic's opinion, the supreme poetical pictorial imagination of the contemporary school. See below, Chap. XVI.

[24] *Ibid.*, Introduction p. xiii, and *passim*.

[25] *Ibid.*, pp. 6, 10, and elsewhere.

the arts. The successful bourgeois class mistrusted the career of an artist and saw to it that its sons did not enter it, thus cutting off any influx of more cultivated people from the ranks of those who were doing the creating.[26] The majority of painters were poorly educated, some were even illiterate,[27] and so how could they understand their times enough to get at the heart and essence of them? In some passages he even came close to the position of the humanitarians. Speaking of the art of decoration and ornament he says:

Does art play no greater part in life than this? Are we to ask of it no more than that it should be a joy to our ears and to our eyes? Must we be satisfied to regard a masterpiece of architecture or music as nothing more than a vehicle of pleasurable suggestions and incitement to the senses? Or rather, has not each of these arts a definite function in the concerted efforts which humanity keeps astir in the hope of solving, or at any rate of formulating, the problems that distract the mind? In short, is art strictly limited and conditioned by purely physical and sensuous phenomena? Has it no place in the moral life?[28]

He believes, for all his doubts, that it has; and the way to put it there is by means of education. The unlettered artist must be taught enough so that he can evaluate the world in meaningful terms; the bourgeoisie must be educated to a place where it will lose its mistrust of art and thus contribute to the ranks of the artists a group of men who have had the advantages that only a first rate education can give. If the artists are really informed, we will eventually get an art which can deal as importantly with the life around us as Rembrandt did, or Gericault, in the *Radeau de la Méduse* (Fig. 10).[29] But again he wavers—on the one hand modern life shows us little that is heroic and yet, on the other, the past is not contemporary—and he and the reader are both left unsatisfied.

It cannot be too greatly regretted that the artists of the present day seem to be shut up—walled up, in a special and very narrow round of conceptions and opinions. They devote themselves wholly to the practice of their craft, and never seem to think of anything beyond the technique of their respective arts. Everything like a general view, or any collation of the various modes of intellectual energy, lie outside their ken; the older the artist, the narrower the horizon. . . .[30]

All of which may have been very true, but who was to help the artists out of the quandary? Chesneau did not have the solution even for himself, and it seems more than doubtful if education, however excellent, can ever give to art a new symbolism until society has prepared it outside the classroom. And when it is in existence, the artists will know it before the teachers.

[26] *Ibid.*, p. 67; see also pp. 8ff.

[27] *Ibid.*, p. 77.

[28] *Ibid.*, p. 3. He specifically warns the reader against confusing ends and means in art: "The end of art is the interpretation of the soul of man, with all its emotions and feelings, its sorrows, joys, and doubts, its passions, its enthusiasms, its loves and hatreds, its heart-sickness and hopes, its knowledge of what is present and real, its aspirations above and beyond it—the soul in its entirety, as completely as the conditions of each art will allow, and without any limitation but those set by these conditions" (p. 21).

[29] *Ibid.*, pp. 234-235.

[30] *Ibid.*, p. 88.

The critical dilemma posed by the conflicting claims of idealism and realism is also unmistakably apparent in an important essay on art criticism by Bougot, published in 1875.[31] The date of the book falls somewhat beyond the limits of this study, but internal evidence again shows, as in the case of Chesneau's even later work, that the material for it was gathered during the Second Empire. The author believes that a modern ideal which is tied closely to the circumstances of contemporary civilization will fail since it will lack universality and thus be soon out of date.[32] However, it is a difficult matter to infuse the events of the past with a vitality and interest which will make them acceptable to men in the middle of the nineteenth century. People who can steep themselves in history may be able to enjoy its scenes and its truths as vividly as Chesneau suggested,[33] but this will not be the answer for most men in spite of the success which Delacroix achieved. Unable to accept an historical approach (Chesneau himself had a hard time with it, as we have just seen), Bougot is equally unconvinced of the virtues of a modern idealism arising from the contemporary milieu of positivists like Comte or the humanitarians like Thoré and Castagnary. Art must serve an escapist function, he declared, and this will be impossible if it is eternally connected with the facts of material existence.[34] Furthermore, the artists of the past who have been great were not so because they were the most accurate reflections of the ages in which they lived, and Taine's concept of the "personnage regnant" is rejected as far as art is concerned.[35] Having thus found himself dissatisfied with both the past and the present, Bougot has no other solution to offer than the rather weak one of an art devoted to an ideal so general and so basic that it will appeal to all ages, past as well as present.[36]

Enough has now been said of the difficulties which faced those writers who had more or less faith in the greatness of the past. They were hemmed about by a series of situations so difficult that solutions to them must well have seemed impossible. The art which endeavored to embody their principles was admittedly very poor; even if it had been far better, the chances were that the public would have cared no more for it, since most people did not fundamentally understand the past nor were spiritually moved by it. These critics knew that art must somehow get back into phase with society, but if it accomplished this at the expense of its moral value, the victory would be a hollow one. And what signs were there that society intended to produce its own moral symbols? Such things, as Chesneau saw, came very slowly—the epic was for the past, prose was for the present.[37] And finally, the values by which men lived seemed to be changing; man was not to be the same creature in the eye of science and a mechanically operated world as he had been formerly. The choice before the contemporary analysts was thus a truly formidable one: they could either hold on to

[31] A. Bougot, *Essai sur la critique d'art,* Paris, 1875.

[32] *Ibid.,* pp. 357ff.

[33] *Ibid.,* p. 354. Of course, Chesneau himself wasn't able to make up his mind entirely between the claims of the past with its great themes and the present with its greater vividness.

[34] *Ibid.,* pp. 359-360.

[35] *Ibid.,* pp. 358ff. For Taine see Chap. v.

[36] *Ibid.,* pp. 372-373.

[37] E. Chesneau, "Le Mouvement moderne," *Revue européenne,* Vol. XVIII, 1861, pp. 489ff.

what they thought was indispensable for great art and become anachronisms along with it, forced to praise works of whose mediocrity they were well aware, or they could give up all such ideas, change their spots, so to speak, and welcome a new form which appeared to be uninterested in the nobility of man, fascinated only by the world of daily fact or the reaches of the individual imagination, and expressed in artistic terms which seemed to them to be blatant, unfinished, unstudied, and contrary to all technical propriety. Theirs was indeed a difficult lot.

V. POSITIVISTS AND HUMANITARIANS

THE most interesting ideas as to the probable future of painting are to be found among the men who were willing, even eager, to make a break with the past, and having done so, to find a satisfying solution in terms of the present itself. These views fell into three loose groups. The first held that society, in some fashion, would automatically produce an art suitable to its character, though the exact nature of that art might not yet be clear; or that it would specifically produce new ideals accompanied by a new and effective symbolism to replace those no longer usable.[1] The second group claimed that art should become merely a frank exposition of nature and the social scene as they were, i.e. that painting should shift to contemporary subjects which would not be arranged in any hierarchy of importance, adopting a rather bold and direct attitude toward them, and leaving ideal beauty and morality to fend for themselves.[2] The last group felt this to be a sterile and unsatisfying approach; it believed that modern art would spring chiefly from the artist's personality, that subject matter would be not only neutral in the traditional sense, but relatively less important, while temperament, individuality, and originality assumed primary significance.[3] In this view, art was to be very largely an end in itself, with a strong emphasis on technique, albeit of a kind vastly different from that understood by the conservatives. All of these writers were united in the belief that any real return to the greatness or mental habits of the past was unthinkable in the near future. They undertook an earnest search for a way out of the same dilemma that upset their less daring colleagues, namely: what should be done when the progress of society interrupts the stream of an artistic tradition and dries up some of its most important sources? One of the bywords of the day was "Il faut être de son temps";[4] but it might have been phrased: "Comment être de son temps?"

Negatively, all three were opposed to tradition, to the past as anything but a stylistic source (and that only within limits which certainly excluded the pastiche), to academism as it was then practiced, to the clichés of traditional criticism, and to most of the governmental arrangements for art education and exhibition. They were further united by an active interest in contemporaneity, in the individual, either alone or as a participant in the larger social effort, and in nature as man finds it. On matters pertaining to morality, idealism, materialism, science, the relation of art to literature, and the degree of subjectivity desirable in art, there was far less agreement.[5] It must be borne in mind that by devoting their energies to the problem of how to be modern,

---

[1] The writings of men like Comte, Taine, Proudhon, Thoré, and Castagnary fall in this classification and will be the chief writers discussed.

[2] These were the so-called realists and included Champfleury, Duranty, and Desnoyers.

[3] Zola and the Goncourts are the chief names, but others may also be included. See below, Chaps. VII and VIII. Baudelaire might, in some ways, be included also.

[4] This phrase was used as early as 1828 by Émile Deschamps in *La Préface des études françaises et étrangères* (ed. Henri Giraud), Paris, 1923. Cf. George Boas, "Il Faut être de son temps," *Journal of Aesthetics and Art Criticism*, Vol. 1, 1941, No. 1, pp. 52-65.

[5] Compare Baudelaire's hatred of progress and mechanical works generally with Comte's and Taine's faith in positivism and mechanistic doctrines.

they came more sharply in contact with such concepts as those of scientific determinism, progress, and socialism, than did those who were trying to escape these things via the eternal principles of ages gone by. As a result, the impact of these concepts on criticism is most evident among the progressives.

The American and French Revolutions were indices of a growing awareness on the part of society of the importance of a portion of the population hitherto largely at the mercy of the traditional ruling classes. Indeed, one of the unique features of western culture in recent times has been the fact that theoretically the needs of all the people have been taken into serious consideration in the planning of the state. Ironically, at the very moment when liberty, equality, and fraternity were being proclaimed as the broad rights of all, the less economically fortunate members of the body politic were being forced into misery and servitude by the growth of industrialism, the concentration of capital, and the development of a new credit structure. This is not the place to describe the nature of social theory in the late eighteenth and nineteenth centuries, but it was generally evident that the idea of progress, which was becoming a major intellectual force, was being earnestly applied to the question of the status of the lower classes, and that to the believers in it, the future would be a great age in which all humanity, rather than a small section of it, would lead a full and rewarding existence. Society was not static, it was in motion, and man had it in his power to direct that motion toward desirable ends if he could understand and control the laws which governed it.

These laws, like those of other phenomena, were held to be the concern of science, and the confidence in this field of endeavor was increasing as rapidly as the discoveries for which it was responsible. In its methods and techniques man seemed to have developed a tool which, if properly used, could solve all problems and eventually bring the world to a state bordering on perfection. It was entirely natural that science should be called in to investigate the social condition of man as well as his material environment and physiological structure, and all of the leading social theories of the early nineteenth century were strongly influenced by it. Comte even went so far as to maintain that sociology, the "science" of human relationships, was not only the most important of all, but would, when properly understood, lead to the very goal of progress itself, the entirely harmonious society. It was in terms of these two great concepts that the future of humanity was considered, and those who put their trust in them felt that the spiritual regeneration of mankind would follow inevitably upon the scientific solution of his material problems; he could be saved, as it were, by external applications without the need of any inner spiritual rebirth.

If, in the opinion of many people, man's future rested upon these two great bases, it was natural that their influence should be apparent in the different fields of activity with which those persons were concerned, and the arts were no exception. The writing on this subject makes frequent reference to such concepts as the operation of laws, the moral significance of representational forms, the need for a new symbolism devoted to the needs and aspirations of all men, and the uselessness of traditional ideals which were conceived of as being the property of a privileged minority.[6] The major socialists included art in their schemes for a new order and assigned important functions to the artist in the necessary struggle to bring them about, a responsibility which the artists for the most part declined to accept, and which certain critics attacked bitterly as being a betrayal and misconception of the true function of the arts. But there were others, able writers such as Thoré and Castagnary, who espoused the cause of social liberalism and called upon the painters to do their part in its promotion. While not accepting the traditional ideas as to the nature of great art, they still believed that painting had a moral purpose which would be nourished by the emergent ideals of democracy, social justice, and progress; ideals which could and should replace those of the Christian and classical systems. The scientific aspect of the matter, however, was of less interest since it was far more difficult to apply, and seemed to be rather inhuman and antagonistic to imagination. Taine was willing to believe that art was only a rather automatic and mechanical product of forces operating as determinants in a rather neutral fashion, but his views do not seem to have had as wide an appeal among the socially-conscious critics as did the humanitarian position. Although liberal social thought had little effect upon actual creation, the attempt to apply it was a significant aspect of the times in which modern art was being formed.

Among the philosophers of the nineteenth century, there were few who had a more pervasive influence than Auguste Comte. His ideas seem to have spread in various ways and forms into nearly every corner of thought, and to have had a popular interest and acceptance of the most unusual sort. From the appearance of his *Cours de philosophie positive* in 1842 down to the present day, his view of the laws of relatedness and his emphasis upon the study of the way things behave rather than the way they originated, have had a most marked effect upon the development of modern ideas in many fields. Like most important systems, his was not absorbed in its entirety, but rather in parts, some here, some there, and, at times, in rather contradictory fashion. Science adopted his ideas of the relativity of knowledge, which finally put an end to the doctrines of absolute scientific truth as the seventeenth century had known them, while the supremacy of the supposed scientific attitude became ever more widely accepted among the people as a whole, becoming a veritable object of faith.[7] As Chesneau said, "Scientific philosophy tends to make science the law of moral life, as it is of physical life"—a very clear reference to positivism.[8] Zola remarked: "The movement of the age is certainly realist, or rather, positivist,"[9] and many others saw the imprint of Comte's mind upon the times as a whole. He intended his laws to be the basis for the entire fabric of culture (art included), in which science and philosophy

[6] See Jean-G. Lossier, *Le Rôle sociale de l'art selon Proudhon*, Paris, 1937, Chap. II. The author is considerably indebted to this able summary of ideas about "social" art. For "l'art pour l'art," see below, Chap. VIII.

[7] Cf. Lecomte du Noüy, *The Road to Reason, passim.*

[8] Chesneau, *Education*, Introduction, p. xiii.

[9] É. Zola, *Mes haines* (ed. M. Le Blond), Paris, 1866, p. 226, under the heading, "Les réalistes au Salon."

would have to be reformed in line with new principles, after which an age would dawn wherein harmony would be universal.[10]

The direct influence of positivism was felt not only on science, but also on artistic theory, and though its effect was mainly amoral, i.e. materialistic, in principle, it was highly ethical, containing a moral plan which included a definite and important place which should be occupied by the arts in the society of the future.

Comte believed that moral speculation had been in error since it had been based on interior observation; once it had been turned outward and placed on a proper scientific footing, it would be valuable once more:

We have seen that the most advanced part of the human race has exhausted the theological and metaphysical life, and is now at the threshold of the fully positive life, the elements of which are all prepared, and only awaiting their coordination to form a new social system, more homogeneous and more stable than mankind has hitherto had any experience of. . . .

Again, this last fulfillment of the intellectual evolution necessarily favors the ascendancy of the spirit of generality, and therefore the sentiment of duty, which is by its nature closely connected with it, so as naturally to induce moral regeneration.[11]

In this ingenious manner was science established as the guide to the moral life. The concept of duty which he mentions here appears elsewhere at this time, not only in the work of Proudhon, but also in that of the humanitarian critics generally, but it cannot be said to have captured the interest of many artists.

The bright optimism of this view of a world whose salvation only awaited the formulation of a proper science to deal with it, was shared to an extent by Ernest Renan, who wrote, but did not publish, his famous *L'Avenir de la science* in 1849. In it, the superior quality of the future is insured by the promise of inevitable progress. For Renan, as for Comte, science was man's hope; its clear eye would see the answers hitherto clouded by the unrealistic dogmas of the past. But although the advances made by this great intellectual implement soon staggered the world, the moral development which was supposed to accompany them lagged badly. This was already apparent before the end of the century, for when Renan wrote the preface to his great work shortly before the end of the century, the picture was much darker:

. . . Human destiny has become more obscure than ever. What is serious is that we do not see for the future, excepting a return to credulity, a means of giving humanity a catechism acceptable henceforth. It is possible, then, that the ruin of idealistic beliefs is destined to follow the destruction of supernatural beliefs, and that a real abasement of human morality dates from the day it saw the reality of things.[12]

[10] *The Positive Philosophy of Auguste Comte*, trans. by Harriet Martineau, London, 1896, Vol. III, pp. 300ff.

[11] *Ibid.*, pp. 311-312.

[12] E. Renan, *L'Avenir de la science*, Paris, 1890, Preface, p. xviii. Renan's doubts were both somber and severe: "These variations [i.e. in the direction of socialism, nationalism, etc.] are caused by the uncertainty of our ideas about the end to be gained and the ulterior fate of humanity [p. xvi]. . . . It can be that the whole human development is of no more consequence than the moss or lichen which gathers round any moist surface. For us, however, man's history preserves its primacy, since humanity alone, so far as we know, creates the conscience of the universe [p. xiii]."

Science, as Lecomte du Noüy has pointed out, is essentially a quantitative rather than a qualitative inquiry,[13] and in one sense it may be said that modern times completed a shift in art from the latter to the former, a shift which had been in gradual preparation since the seventeenth century. It was then that genre, portraiture, and landscape first came into full flower, forms of subject which were comparatively little concerned with the requirements imposed by "great" art. In the eighteenth century, Chardin and Watteau possessed possibly the finest pictorial talent of any artists in Europe, but in traditional terms, they were painters of an inferior mode and did not deal with the ideas involved in the expression of "historical" subject matter. Moral judgments were not at the heart of the problems they solved, and when, in the middle of the next century, the great tradition finally passed from the scene, painting had virtually abandoned qualitative expression of human values, turning instead to nature as such seen through the temperament of an individual. It would be wrong to maintain that Comte was finally responsible for this change; as we have seen, it had been taking place slowly for two centuries or more, but there is little doubt that he expressed attitudes which were, in simpler form, common to many people—even to the age itself. Much of this aspect of the transformation of subject matter was doubtless unconscious, instinctive almost,[14] but the similarity between the popular positivist attitude and the materialism of much of the art at the beginning of the modern movement is striking.[15] When Renan speaks of giving humanity a "catechism," he means, of course, an effective symbolism, and it may be recalled that the Symbolist movement in literature and art was in its full swing at the time the preface was written (1890).

To return to the use which Comte made of the arts, it is apparent that they occupied a very important position in his plans for the world. Although the artist would, like everyone else, live under the domination of laws and reason, and would be subordinated to the prevailing social "solidarity," art would nevertheless be a powerful force in helping men to arrive at a finer and higher development. The confidence with which he viewed the artistic future was virtually boundless:

> In order to sing the prodigies of man, his conquest of nature, the marvels of sociability, the true aesthetic genius will find above all from now on, under the active impulse of the positive spirit, a fruitful source of new and powerful inspirations, susceptible to a popularity never before equaled, because they will be in full harmony either with the noble instinct of our fundamental superiority or the ensemble of our rational convictions.[16]

Comte's philosophy left a deep impression upon the art criticism of the period, promising as it did that out of the very confusion of the present would arise a new art

[13] Du Noüy, *op.cit.*, the last chapter. Speaking of developments of the last hundred years or so, he says: "Human reason, and above all rationalism, have inherited the prestige that was formerly the appendage of the priest and, in the light of this apotheosis, *the apparent death of moral tradition passes almost unnoticed*" (p. 218, italics mine).

[14] The attacks upon what was left of the tradition which presumably embodied these outworn moral opinions were, however, both vocal and bitter.

[15] Cf. Zola's equation of realism and positivism. The context was entirely artistic in the article quoted. (See note 9 above.)

[16] A. Comte, *Cours de philosophie positive*, Paris, 1842, Vol. VI, p. 882.

to celebrate the wonders of society in terms which would be clear and moving to every-one. This emergence was to be the result of the same forces which would produce the new science and the new industry, but it was not to be a purely neutral or negative product, for it had a high social purpose: "Thus all truly philosophic spirits can now understand that the occurrence of the universal reorganization will spontaneously procure for modern art at one and the same time an inexhaustible nourishment, through the general spectacle of human marvels, and an eminent social destiny to make the final economy better appreciated."[17] "One can affirm," he said, "that this new life will soon find an uninterrupted idealization,"[18] and the fundamental purpose of the aesthetic life must always be to "charm and improve the lowest as well as the most elevated beings by raising the former and soothing the latter."[19] This cheerful picture of the future of art, for all its positivism, was still strongly tinged with the traditional concept of art as a moral force, though the nature of the exact means by which it was to fulfill this high purpose was not made evident. There was, in fact, a definite dichotomy in this philosophy; on the one side was a cogent defense and exposition of a modern determinism, and on the other, an idealism which was actually elevated to the status of a religious cult.[20]

The materialism and mechanism of the age had a strong appeal for another writer whose opinions on art were widely read and discussed during this period. This man was the eminent historian, Hippolyte Taine. He founded his aesthetic on the premise that art was the rather automatic or mechanical product of "race," "milieu," and "moment."[21] It was natural that ideas which tied art so closely to the operation of entirely contemporary forces should have interested critics who were themselves fascinated by the new interest in the world of actual visible phenomena. This matter will be discussed later in this book,[22] but it may be mentioned here that it was quite

---

[17] *Ibid.*, p. 882.

[18] *Ibid.*, p. 878.   [19] *Ibid.*, p. 876.

[20] This development apparently occurred toward the end of his life.

[21] The question of whether or not Taine based himself to any great degree upon Comte is difficult to answer. The general emphasis upon relativity and the operation of positive laws as artistic determinants would seem to make the connection obvious. Yet Taine himself maintained that his masters were Jouffroy and Hegel (see Victor Giraud, *Essai sur Taine*, Paris, 1909, p. 71 and note 1). D. D. Rosca felt so strongly on this subject that he wrote a lengthy treatise entitled: *L'Influence de Hegel sur Taine théoricien de la connaissance et de l'art* (Paris, 1928), of which Part IV of Chapter III is entirely taken up with a denial of the fact that Taine was a Comtian; but at the very end he says that, at least in part, Taine misunderstood Hegel, and that the identity of his views with those of the German philosopher was, in a sense, illusory. The point is not of sufficient importance to this discussion to warrant a more extended examination of it, but it can be said that there are authorities who maintain the opposite view: F. Brunetière, *Discours de combat*, Paris, 1916, pp. 223ff. (not a pure positivism as Comte enunciated it, but a "debased" version formulated by Littré); L. Venturi, *History of Art Criticism*, N.Y., 1936, p. 229 ("From the positivistic philosophy of Comte, Taine drew the idea of the ambient . . ."); and K. E. Gilbert and H. Kuhn, *A History of Aesthetics*, N.Y., 1939, p. 479. In any event, there was obviously more than a superficial similarity between the two, and both were expressing the confidence of the age in scientific explanations of many phenomena which had hitherto not been regarded as susceptible to them.

[22] See below pp. 73ff.

natural for Émile Zola, one of the leaders of the later naturalist movement in literature, to devote a chapter of *Mes haines* to an account of Taine's views.[23]

The great historian explained art as a phenomenon resulting from the operation of external forces: "The work of art is determined by an aggregate which is the general state of mind and surrounding manners."[24] The ideal, in his opinion, is not perfection of beauty but conformity to an idea, for purposes of effectiveness or clarity.[25] The moral tone which is so evident in Comte is largely omitted, but a similar determinism resulting from the operation of natural principles is very apparent. Laws are a marked characteristic of his explanations and art flourishes or withers in accordance with "moral temperatures," the "force of the public mind" and similar factors which bear a close analogy to those of the evolutionary scientific system proposed by the founder of positivism.

In Taine's view, the social milieu was, therefore, the final determinant in the production of works of art. At the bottom was a general situation which produced attitudes and feelings among the people; these eventually grouped themselves around a single person who displayed them in concentrated form and thus became the "personnage regnant." This person the artists were to present to the public, either by representing his character or by addressing themselves to him.[26] To Taine, the new world was to be one governed by laws and forces over which the individual would have little power. In this connection it may be valuable to recall certain observations made by Hegel thirty years before.[27] The ideals of modern times, he said, were so close to the everyday practices of men (actually they were just the virtues of daily life) that they were confined in scale to the stature of the ordinary individual. The grandeur of the ideals which had once been associated with positions of great eminence such as kingship were thus lacking. Kings and judges were now merely parts of a social structure which defined them and their virtues as well; the people looked askance at any expression of individuality which exceeded the bounds set for them by society. The world, in short, had no more use for the heroic individual on any universal scale; he, and his moral stature, must be cut down to a size which fitted more easily into the general pattern of things. For Hegel, it would appear that the office, not the person, had become the symbol, and it was only in more private pursuits that unlimited originality was still permissible.[28]

[23] É. Zola, "M. Taine, artiste," in *Mes haines* (ed. Le Blond), pp. 157-178.

[24] H. Taine, *Lectures on Art*, trans. by John Durand, N.Y., 1875, Vol. I, p. 157. These lectures were delivered in the winter of 1864-65 before the students of the École des Beaux-Arts.

[25] *Ibid.*, "The Ideal in Art," Vol. I, p. 180.

[26] *Ibid.*, Vol. I, p. 159. Bougot attacked this figure vigorously because he believed that the history of art did not support the hypothesis. Cf. Baudelaire's "dandy."

[27] Hegel, *The Philosophy of Fine Art* (trans. by E. P. B. Osmaston from the collected edition of 1835), Vol. I, London, 1920, pp. 259ff.

[28] It might be suggested from a reading of these interesting ideas that the traditional individual is the person who acts upon his environment, changes it, and by so doing is superior to it, while the modern counterpart must express his individuality inwardly, the only direction in which he has real freedom. This would be in agreement with an interpretation of modern art as being essentially private and personal as opposed to the traditional view which asserted that it had a moral force and function, thus making the artist an individual who operated on his environment and

In other words, environment was now so powerful that individualism, in its heroic sense, had largely succumbed to it.

Speaking to his art students, Taine was nearly as optimistic as the author of positivism, and for similar reasons:

You have observed that each situation produces a certain state of mind followed by a corresponding class of works of art. That is why every new situation must produce a new state of mind and consequently a new class of works; and therefore why the social medium of the present day, now in the course of formation, ought to produce its own works like the social mediums that have gone before it. . . . Accordingly it need not be said in these days that art is exhausted. It is true that certain schools no longer exist and can no longer be revived; that certain arts languish, and that the future upon which we are entering does not promise to furnish the aliment that these require. But art itself, which is the faculty of perceiving and expressing the leading character of objects, is as enduring as the civilization of which it is the best and earliest fruit. What its forms will be, and which of the five great arts will provide the vehicle of expression of future sentiment, we are not called upon to decide; we have the right to affirm that new forms will arise, and an appropriate mould be found in which to cast them. We have only to open our eyes to see a change going on in the condition of men, and consequently in their minds, so profound, so universal, and so rapid that no other century has witnessed the like of it.[29]

He goes on to say that the enormously swift developments in the fields of science, communication, trade, and the like are spreading everywhere and "man is cultivating his intellectual faculties and ameliorating his social condition. . . . Such renewal of minds and things brings along with it a renewal of art."[30] Taine saw clearly that art must change as everything else was changing, but he did not bother, or was unable, to tell the students before him what this art would be like, or how they might find their way to it. The artist would seem to be only a predetermined product of social conditions rather than any sort of active agent helping, as the humanitarians hoped he would do, to lead men to a better life. It was dangerous to suggest, as he did, that the social setting was almost the entire determinant of the course which modern art must actually take, but in a negative sense he can be said to have made plain which ways it could *not* go, and to that extent he was proven right.

Comments on this attitude appear from time to time in the criticism of the period. Charles Dollfuss, the original editor of the *Revue germanique*, in an article on modern art written in 1864, agreed with Taine, but objected that his theory did not explain intelligence, genius, and uniqueness.[31] Some others, while admitting the justice of the idea, became a little impatient at the slowness with which this social control became fruitful. Jules Claretie said somewhat later: "I am astonished that in an age when, for example, railroads have been created, artists have not been found—modern Ghirlandaios or Carpaccios—to cover a whole station with frescoes, and poets to sing of

---

was presumed to have an effect on it. This line of speculation might well be pursued further.

[29] Taine, *op.cit.*, pp. 162-164.

[30] *Ibid.*, p. 164.

[31] Charles Dollfuss, "L'art moderne," *Revue germanique*, Vol. XXXI, No. 2, 1864, p. 245.

these inventions.[32] Gautier, in fact, had begun to complain along these lines as far back as 1848.[33] Zola, who was favorably impressed by Taine's views, found it hard to accept a theory so causal and positivistic that it left no room for the triumphant individual in whom he believed so wholeheartedly, and implied that, as a man, Taine was unhappy over the actual results and implications of his ideas in actual practice—caught, so to speak, between the need for personal liberty and the regimentation of the scientific laws in which he professed to believe.[34]

More complete acceptance of positivism is found in one of the few books written during the period on the subject of art criticism itself. The author, Pierre Petroz, finds that realism is a step in the right direction in an age of artistic confusion when the "new ideas are far from being precise and definite,"[35] but the realists have to do much more than merely draw their inspiration from the world of fact. He refers to them as "more or less unconscious empiricists" and says that they are "separated, or nearly so, from all theological or metaphysical bonds; they attach themselves to no general doctrine of any value."[36] They believe that by this means they are securely protected against being deceived and harboring "vain illusions," but the situation is not as simple as that:

In fact it is not sufficient to contemplate reality, to love it, in order to have a healthy, serious, elevated aesthetic conception. One must also know, at least roughly, the laws which govern it from a point of view as much physical as moral, that is to say, one must not be ignorant of the conditions of existence of beings and things, the rules which govern the spontaneous manifestations of feelings and passions, the normal development of the life individual and the life collective. Artists will not have such ideas, exact and precise, until the day when a general, positive, systematic doctrine will be universally accepted, and that day has not yet come.[37]

The references to rules, laws, and a "positive systematic doctrine" show the source of this position. Petroz professed to see the outlines of this doctrine, but, unhappily, he neglects to say what they are.

The confident prediction that the new society would of necessity produce a new art was not enough to satisfy everyone; its actual form and the factors which would be decisive in its formation became the object of general speculation. Comte, for all his positivism and faith in science as the future savior of society, saw art as a moral force

---

[32] Jules Claretie, *Peintres et sculpteurs contemporains*, Paris, 1882. Again this is one of those later works the substance of which was obviously formed in the period of this book. The story of the idea of murals in railroad stations would make an amusing study in itself, for it had an interesting history in the middle years of the century. Stations being entirely modern and "popular," what better place for the new art which was to sing the glories of the new mechanical age?

[33] Th. Gautier, "Du beau antique et du beau moderne," first published in *L'Événement*, Aug. 8, 1848. Here quoted from *Souvenirs de théâtre, d'art, et de critique* (ed. Charpentier), Paris, 1883, p. 203.

[34] Zola, *Mes haines* (ed. Le Blond), p. 173.

[35] Pierre Petroz, *L'Art et la critique en France depuis 1822*, Paris, 1875, Introduction, p. iii. The book was actually written prior to 1870.

[36] *Ibid.*, pp. 335ff.   [37] *Ibid.*, p. 338.

and believed that the artist had a duty to perform in the betterment of the human condition.

This idea was shared by a group of men whom it is convenient to call humanitarians, that is, the critics who believed in progress and were devoted to the idea that art must be for all men, not just the rich alone, and that it must seek its strength in the common power and nobility of mankind rather than in the exposition of difficult themes which only scholars could understand. For them, common people were as fine and noble as the heroes of antiquity, and could be deeply moved and even exalted by an art which was honestly devoted to their aspirations expressed in intelligible terms. The past had had its symbols—the mediaeval Christian and the Renaissance humanist had felt the strength of them—but it was now time for the world to supply a fresh set in which men could believe anew, a set which would furnish the iconography of a modern art. It was essentially this which Thoré was calling for when he demanded of the artists the creation of an "art for man."[38] Chesneau had pointed out that to expect such epic results in contemporary art was a vain hope,[39] but Thoré, Proudhon, and Castagnary did not share his pessimism. In all the critical writing of the mid-century, there is no more stirring, and perhaps no more tragic, plea for art than this one. The artists, however, could not provide what society was not prepared to furnish; it was unfair to expect them to, even though Millet did make a sincere attempt, not at the request of the critics, but as a result of a similar faith in common people.[40]

The humanitarians, like the conservatives, were in search of an idealism centered upon the figure of man himself, but this time the concept was different. He was not to be the superior being of former times, but a commoner whose nature was as spiritual and essentially noble as that of the saints and heroes of the past, an inhabitant of the present and a worthy object of the artist's greatest powers. This position went beyond the limits of thinking about art alone,[41] for political liberalism, and even socialism, were implicit in it, not infrequently combined with anticlericalism and antimonarchism:

Religious painting and historical or heroic painting have become gradually enfeebled to the same extent that theocracy and monarchy, to which they refer, have become weakened; their elimination, almost complete today, leads to the absolute domination of genre, landscape, portraiture which exalt individualism: in art, as in society, man is becoming more and more man.[42]

---

[38] Th. Thoré, *Salons de T. Thoré*, Preface, p. ix. The preface, as noted before, is signed with his pseudonym of W. Bürger. A surprising number of people who knew the writing of "both" did not know their identity.

[39] Chesneau, "Le Mouvement moderne," p. 489 (Vol. XVIII of *Revue européenne*).

[40] "But, to tell the truth, the peasant subjects suit my temperament best; for I must confess, even if you think me a socialist, that the human side of art is what touches me most. . ." (from a letter from Millet to Alfred Sensier, here quoted from *Jean-François Millet*, by Alfred Sensier, trans. by Helena de Kay, Boston, 1881, p. 93).

[41] Even the conservative position saw art as a human activity closely related to other social functions and duties of mankind.

[42] J. A. Castagnary, "Le Salon de 1857," *Salons 1857-1870*, Paris, 1892 (Vol. 1 of two), p. 7. Note the leveling out of subject matter with a new emphasis on themes previously considered of lesser importance. Nature began to be less a background for man and more some-

Nature and man, landscape, portraiture, genre—there is the whole future of art. Is there not more than enough there to surpass and conquer the ancients? . . . The theory which I have just put forward tends to establish the fact that art, by a motion proper to it, is modifying itself at the same moment in its subject and in its object; in its subject in that the traditional spirit is being little by little blotted out before the free inspiration of the individual; in its object by the fact that the interpretation of man and nature are being slowly substituted for divine myths and historical epics.[43]

Art has beauty and not an idea as its object. But through beauty it must make people love that which is true, that which is just, that which is fruitful for the development of man. . . . Everything which expresses, in thoughtful form, a profound characteristic of man or nature, encloses the ideal since it leads to reflection on the essential points of life.[44]

Formerly art was made for gods and princes. Perhaps the time has come to make an ART FOR MAN.[45]

From these quotations it can be gathered that man and nature (on a more equal footing than formerly) were to be the themes of the future, and that much that was wonderful could be expected from them. The individual in the modern sense was coming into his own; men would rejoice to see *themselves* at last after an overexposure to the sights of history and the summit of Olympus.[46]

Théophile Thoré, the brilliant critic and art historian, was probably the most respected adherent to this position. He had begun his Salons in the 'thirties and had also established a reputation as a liberal by his political journalism and his part in the revolutions of 1830 and 1848.[47] For all of his interest in the modern, in the new place of man in art, he was not unalterably opposed to the past as such, though his interests lay quite naturally with the Dutch more than other schools.[48] But man "did not exist in the arts of former times—of yesterday, and it still remains to invent him."[49] There were, of course, exceptions: Caravaggio, Valentin, Velasquez, the Le Nain, Chardin, the Dutch, and especially Rembrandt; but "nevertheless all that has been considered up to now as 'little' painting—genre painting."[50] What is important now "is to break the old prison of the double symbol [i.e. the classic and Christian], to emerge from the Babel of confused tongues, and create, by virtue of common thought, a common language as well. . . ."[51] Once art has achieved a language which all can understand, it will create new allegories, fables and the like, which will be understandable to every-

thing of equal interest: the two are, in one sense, fused—i.e. man is essentially a part of nature. This will be discussed further below.

[43] *Ibid.*, p. 11.

[44] T. Thoré, "Le Salon de 1864," *Salons de W. Bürger 1861-1868*, Preface by T. Thoré, Paris, 1870, Vol. II, p. 14.

[45] T. Thoré, *Salons de T. Thoré*, Preface, p. ix.

[46] There is a certain feeling of delight in natural things in much of this writing which is reminiscent of the fresh pleasure in the world characteristic of the early Renaissance.

[47] See biographical notice in Appendix.

[48] Thoré was one of the most distinguished of the earlier French art historians, his work on Vermeer being particularly well known. See H. Marguery, "Un Pionnier de l'histoire de l'art: Thoré-Bürger," *Gazette des beaux-arts*, 5th per., Vol. XI, 1925, Part I, pp. 229-245; Part II, pp. 295-311, 367-380.

[49] Thoré, *Salons de T. Thoré*, p. xxvi.

[50] *Ibid.*, pp. xxxiv-xxxv.

[51] *Ibid.*, p. xxxix. This whole preface is an interesting discussion of traditional symbolism and its inadequacy for the present.

one.[52] The sad state of things at present cannot be blamed on the artists: "it is not their fault if philosophy and thought have been proscribed by bourgeois society,"[53] and though unity and the brotherhood of man will eventually follow the present period of uncertainty, society doesn't know it as yet. "Society itself," he said in 1861, "to consider it from the aspect of its public morality, hasn't the air of understanding very well where it is going. It has lost all basis in the past, and scarcely guessing the future, abandons itself to chance, without faith and seemingly without hope."[54] Until society settles down, the new art cannot appear. In the meantime, the artist can do no better than go to man and nature and look at them anew.[55] "The progress of contemporary art consists, then, in translating into harmonious form the irresistible feeling which draws the world toward unity."[56] This was surely a difficult program!

It must be observed that what was loosely referred to as "realism"[57] was far from being the final solution to the problem as Thoré saw it; at best it was a stop-gap to be used only until the greater art of man should be achieved by a more stable society. On the other hand, individualism based on direct natural reactions was not the answer either. He unquestionably approved of individuality: "the more the individual mark is impressed on a work of art, the stronger the master."[58] But art must contribute to the brotherhood of man, it must devote itself to the search for the human ideal, the new language which all would understand. He criticized Manet for attaching no importance to the humanity of his subjects, for making no differentiation in his treatment of animate and inanimate objects.[59] For the humanitarians, any form of naturalism (or "realism") which lacked moral intent was not really satisfactory. Millet, whom Thoré had "discovered" as an able artist in 1844, received very high praise, for he could elevate the peasant to a type and make a living symbol out of a common man (Fig. 27), but even he was not quite his ideal painter.[60] In the Salon of 1861 he remarks that Courbet and Millet are the two master painters of the show and will have a secure place in the future, but neither of them will ever reach the greatest heights. His chief enthusiasm is thus tinged with disappointment.

In 1863 the humanitarian ideal found its most controversial spokesman in the person of the social philosopher P.-J. Proudhon, whose extraordinary book *Du principe de l'art et de sa destination sociale* was written that year. Originally intended as a brief commentary on *Le Retour de la conférence* by Courbet (Fig. 58), it was later expanded

---

[52] *Ibid.*, p. xi.

[53] *Ibid.*, "Le Salon de 1845," p. 105.

[54] W. Bürger, "Le Salon de 1861," *Revue germanique*, Vol. xv, No. 2, 1861, p. 253.

[55] *Ibid.*, p. 254. This, of course, was the basis of his interest in "realism" of which he did not entirely approve.

[56] W. Bürger, "Des tendences de l'art au XIXe siècle," *Revue universelle des arts*, Vol. I, Apr.-Sept. 1855, p. 85. There seems to be a good deal of Comtian influence in Thoré's ideas, but the idea of the great unity toward which society is moving apparently came from

Joseph de Maistre (*ibid.*, p. 84).

[57] See below, Chap. VI.

[58] W. Bürger, "De la beauté dans les arts," *Revue universelle des arts*, Vol. III, Apr.-Sept. 1856, p. 194.

[59] T. Thoré, *Salons de W. Bürger*, Vol. II, p. 531.

[60] It is a little difficult to say just why this was. It may have been that in spite of his enormous admiration for the work of a man who was really the only important humanitarian painter of the day, he found him a little narrow, too restricted in scope.

into a treatise on art generally, though it was still unfinished at the time of his death in 1865.[61] It aroused no little comment and antagonism, possibly because the author was both hated and feared by many Frenchmen who reacted violently to such of his maxims as the famous: "Property is theft." The reviews of the Salon of 1865, which contained Courbet's portrait of him, show a variety of interesting attitudes toward both man and book. A conservative like Challemel-Lacour moves from the picture, which is "seriously painted" but "neither true, beautiful, nor agreeable," to the treatise which, he believes, will not do much for the fame of either of them, and as he warms to his subject he finds that Proudhon was "mad," "feverish," etc., and seems to have been rather afraid of him.[62] Zola, of course, made the most devastating attack of all in *Mes haines*,[63] and the sum of these criticisms was so successful that the book promptly fell into a sort of oblivion from which it has never been entirely rescued. It was not even included in the first *Oeuvres complètes* published between 1866 and 1883.[64]

But not everyone was as antagonistic. Castagnary, the greatest, perhaps, of the defenders of Courbet, was under the influence of Proudhon's views on art as early as 1857, and Eugène Spuller says, in the introduction to the collected *Salons*, that "his masters, if he had any, were Michelet and P.-J. Proudhon."[65] Thoré himself, in the Salon of '65, has a most interesting comment on the philosopher's famous definition of art as being an "idealistic representation of nature and ourselves with a view to the physical and moral improvement of our species."[66] The idea is good but it goes too far, for the artist is not a didactic moralist, but one who makes beauty available to others, an act which is his means of producing the true and the just. Thus Thoré finds that although art, science, and morality do not have the same object, they do arrive at the same result, namely, this same physical and moral perfection of our species. The difference in the two views is just what would be expected between a social philosopher of Proudhon's type and a trained critic and art historian with social interests.

The author of *Du principe* admits candidly at the outset that he does not know anything about the technique of art or the criticism of its more painterly aspects (a fatal admission for his opponents like Barbey d'Aurevilly, Philip Hamerton, and

[61] P.-J. Proudhon, *Du principe de l'art et de sa destination sociale* (Oeuvres complètes, new ed. by C. Bouglé and H. Moysset; int. and notes by Jules L. Puech), Paris, 1938. There is some question as to the degree of collaboration with Courbet. The latter wrote to his father to this effect and said that the book was to be a sort of introduction to an exhibition of his work to be shown in England (P. Courthion, *Gustave Courbet*, Paris, 1931, p. 42). From Proudhon's letters it is at least certain that Courbet asked him to write something about his picture (*Le Retour de la conférence*). From this grew a full-sized book (see

Du principe, Introduction, pp. 1-3).

[62] P. Challemel-Lacour, "Salon de 1865," *Revue germanique*, Vol. XXXIV, No. 1, 1865, p. 95.

[63] Zola, *Mes haines*, "Proudhon et Courbet."

[64] P.-J. Proudhon, *Oeuvres complètes*, ed. Marpon and Flammarion, Paris, 1866-83, 35 vols.

[65] J. Castagnary, *Salons*, Preface, p. v. His published remarks on the subject of the social purpose of art were, of course, earlier than Proudhon's book.

[66] T. Thoré, "Le Salon de 1865," *Salons de W. Bürger*, Vol. II, p. 176.

Zola), but asserts his right to speak about it as a social phenomenon.[67] Interested as he was in the ferment of ideas about progress, justice, and the lot of the common people, he could not refrain from discussing them in the field of art as well. Like Comte and Taine, he is certain that the arts rest upon, and are responsive to, laws and principles, and these are intimately related to the nature of man himself.[68] The "axis" of the human spirit is formed by the two concepts of "conscience and knowledge" or "justice and truth."[69] It is mainly with the first of these pairs that art is concerned. Men have a special faculty for the arts, and the proper object of this faculty is the ideal, which will, therefore, be the future mainspring of artistic creation.[70] His definition of it is uncommonly classical: "The ideal is all that which conforms to the idea," and he continues: "the idea is the typical, specific, generic notion which the spirit forms of a thing, an abstraction of all materiality."[71] But this ideal is not an isolated object of contemplation, nor is it sufficient unto itself; quite the contrary. The basic point in the book is that in art the ideal has a function: the improvement of the world.[72] The artist "is called to cooperate in the creation of the social world, a continuation of the natural world."[73] The task of the painter is thus to extract the essence of materiality and use it for the betterment of his fellow man. The trouble with the art of the day is that it has lost touch with this essence, that is, with the collective feeling, consciousness, and intuition of the time. Being cut off from this reality, it wanders astray, and the artist finds himself a lonely man "shooting at random," deprived of the support of his fellows.[74] It is, in short, "l'art pour l'art."

Since he was an anarchist, Proudhon believed in the innate and collective goodness of mankind, a goodness which it was the artist's duty to bring forth: "The artist's role, having for its end the arousing in us, through the vision of the ideal, a moral sensibility, feelings of dignity, and 'delicatesse,' is an auxiliary one."[75] Obeying no law but his own better nature, he must put himself at the service of society and must contribute his share to the common effort.[76] He must be an integral part of a unified order and must find his freedom, as well as his ideals, within it. In troubled times, such as then prevailed, he will find it hard to discover the collective conscience and make use of it, but try he must. "For art to become more rational, I mean that it should learn to express the aspirations of the epoch itself as it expressed the intuitions of the primitive era; that it should seize ideas, assimilate them; that it put itself in harmony with the universal movement, that it penetrate it."[77]

---

[67] Proudhon, op.cit., pp. 47ff. Cf. P. G. Hamerton, *Painting in France after the Decline of Classicism*, London, 1869, p. 18; also J. Barbey d'Aurevilly, *Les Oeuvres et les hommes. Sensations d'art*, pp. 1ff. This essay seems to have been written shortly after 1869. Proudhon's most serious mistake was to attempt an historical analysis of the art of the past, about which he was largely ignorant.

[68] Proudhon, op.cit., pp. 52ff.

[69] *Ibid.*, p. 185.

[70] *Ibid.*, p. 59.   [71] *Ibid.*, p. 62.

[72] *Ibid.*, pp. 64ff.   [73] *Ibid.*, p. 64.

[74] *Ibid.*, pp. 271-272. Cf. Rosenthal on the loneliness of the "revolutionaries" of 1815-1830 (Rosenthal, *La Peinture romantique*, pp. 65ff.).

[75] Proudhon, op.cit., p. 68.

[76] *Ibid.*, pp. 257-258. This idea is implicit in much of the argument of the book.

[77] *Ibid.*, pp. 158-159.

From these rather abstract theories, Proudhon turns to the art of Courbet as an illustration of them in actual practice, and professes to see there, at least in germ, the new ideals and the new artistic revelation of society. In a discussion of *Le Retour de la conférence* (Fig. 58), he believes that the painter attempted to show

... the radical incapacity of religious discipline to maintain in the priest the severe virtue which is demanded of him; that moral perfection sought by faith, by works of devotion, by the contemplation of a mystic ideal is reduced to gross failures, and that the priest who sins is the victim of his profession far more than he is a hypocrite or an apostate.[78]

This, of course, was some distance away from Courbet's intention of making a sort of peasant's jibe at the venality of the clergy.[79] He was incapable of thinking in the complex and elevated terms which were ascribed to him, a fact which the philosopher actually had to admit: "Courbet, more artist than philosopher, has not thought all that I have found [in him]: it is all simple. Assuredly he has not conceived his subject of the *Curés* [i.e. *Le Retour de la conférence*] with the force which I see in it and which I point out. ... But, admitting that what I have thought I saw in these figures may be an illusion on my part, the thought exists; and since art has value only through its effects, I do not hesitate to interpret it in my own way."[80] Yet Proudhon felt that an art which did no more than show the people as they really were was the starting point for an art of the future which would be "critical," that is, it would undertake the analysis of society for the betterment of mankind and would thus point the way to the ideal.[81] In spite, therefore, of all his elaborate critique of Courbet's pictures and the subtle motives and ideas he found therein, he actually regarded them as only the precursors of the art he really wanted. The arrival of this art would not be immediate: "the summit of art, this peak to which all artists should aspire, is still far from us; so far that it will take generations to create the types or models, the clever observers to discover them, and a public to recognize and understand them."[82] It was significant that Courbet was the only precursor of such a movement whom he could find, though he confessed that he did not know all the work of Millet and said that he also might be on the right road.

It was mentioned earlier that Proudhon had had a certain influence on the views of Jules Antoine Castagnary, unquestionably one of the most interesting of the critics of the period.[83] This is undeniably true, even though Castagnary's thought is not as clear and logical as that of the socialist from whom he got so many ideas. As a young man he wrote a review of the Salon of 1857 which attracted immediate attention and indicated clearly that art was not to be considered apart from social affairs but rather as an integral part of them. Very near the beginning occurs the following passage: "In this book only the Fine Arts are dealt with. But by virtue of what has just been said,

[78] *Ibid.*, p. 212.
[79] This was almost the last of such pictures in Courbet's *oeuvre*, only the *Aumône d'un mendiant* was later (1868). With the *Paysans de Flagey revenant d'une foire* and the *Casseurs de pierres* they seem to have formed a sort of highway series.
[80] *Ibid.*, p. 221.
[81] *Ibid.*, pp. 171, 232, and elsewhere.
[82] *Ibid.*, p. 241.
[83] See above, p. 66.

to deny or affirm as regards art is to argue and conclude not only about Aesthetics, but also about Religion, Philosophy, Morality, Politics and the rest: the part is as great as the whole."[84] Of all the reviewers of the day, he was the one who stated his premises most clearly and tried to be the most rigorous in holding the practice of art up to them. He went on to review the great shows for over twenty years, but the clue to his approach to them all is to be discerned in the very first one: a heartfelt passion for an art at the service of mankind. Freedom is at last at hand, in art as elsewhere, and he makes man say: "Beside the divine Eden from which I have been chased forth, I will construct a new Eden which I will populate myself. I will place at the entrance Progress, invisible sentinel; I will put a flaming sword in his hand and I will say to God: 'You will not enter!' "[85] Allowing for a certain flamboyancy on the part of a twenty-seven-year-old critic, it is still a clear enough indication of the impossibility, which all the humanitarians felt, of carrying on in the great religious tradition of the past.[86] In a previous quotation from this same source,[87] we saw that the classical part of the tradition was equally vain for the present. The debris of religion having been cleared away and history renounced, man and nature remain—and they are everything. "It is by working tirelessly for the exaltation of your being, and in consequence for the apotheosis of man, that you will justify the morality of art."[88] One is a little staggered by the vehemence of this cry for a new dispensation and the readiness with which the author casts into the discard all that the past had thought and felt about the nobility of the human race in favor of a new man who was apparently somewhere about waiting to be discovered, but who had hitherto been oppressed and kept in seclusion. This is the more astonishing in view of the recent disaster of the democratic movement after the revolution of 1848,[89] but can be explained on the basis of a general and continuing liberal fervor. To the true believer in social progress, the failure of the Second Republic was but a temporary reverse, and there was bright promise for the future once men had affairs in the right hands.

Nature, both human and otherwise, became the yardstick by which man's advance toward self-fulfillment was to be judged, even though a long period of study and experiment would be necessary before he really understood his own potentialities or those of the world about him.[90] Eleven years later, in 1869, Castagnary still felt very much the same way, which prevented him from following the change from "realism," which he admired, to the more subjective form of naturalism which succeeded it. He either failed to understand its aims or did not approve of them, for in 1869 he thought

[84] Castagnary, "Philosophie au Salon de 1857," *Salons*, p. 2. This was first published in *Le Présent*, then republished separately by Poulet-Malassis. The title is indicative of the author's bent.

[85] *Ibid.*, p. 6.

[86] The antireligious sentiment of the French republicans of this period is interesting. Castagnary's views here are not dissimilar in many ways from the ideas which underlay Chena-

vard's great scheme for the decoration of the Panthéon (see below, Chap. XII).

[87] See above, p. 63.

[88] Castagnary, *Salons*, p. 10.

[89] Cf. Guérard, *Art for Art's Sake*, Chap. IV. The rather oppressive atmosphere of the Second Empire was at least conducive to rebellious sentiments of this sort.

[90] Castagnary, *op.cit.*, pp. 47-48.

Manet more "bizarre" than "powerful" and felt that although he based his art on nature, "he neglects to give it as an aim the interpretation of life itself" (Fig. 84).[91] This necessity for a deep understanding of humanity was not at issue in the case of landscape, and his praise for the group headed by Rousseau, Corot, and Daubigny was unstinted (Fig. 39). They had solved the problem to his satisfaction as far as nature was concerned, but the matter of man himself was apparently more difficult.

At first he was somewhat reserved about Courbet, for although his art grasped the externals, "his spiritualism is not sufficiently exalted so that he arrives at a consideration of forms and groups as condensations of the universal soul and pursues the latter under the shape of the former. However that may be, his landscapes surely do not lack value" (Fig. 25).[92] There is apparent here the same distinction between the painting of the figure and that of nonhuman nature which was noted above. But as the years went by, he came to give Courbet a full measure of appreciation. Mentioning the painter's famous dictum about translating the customs, ideas, and appearances of his time, he says: "For my part I know of no more elevated [statement] and I doubt that the great masters of all times ever proposed any other."[93] If Courbet was less of an idealist in human affairs than he had seemed at first, Castagnary did not upbraid him for it, but settled for what he did have—a great power over the presentation of the common scene. "The Velasquez of the people" was what he called him.

Millet, naturally enough, was his other favorite, but he did not pair him with Courbet, as, indeed, very few critics did (Fig. 44).[94]

What essentially distinguishes M. Millet is the fact that, in painting his peasants, he does not seek to portray personages, to study expressions, to set passions in motion. He has understood that where intellectual development is nil, where consciousness is indistinct and confused, the diversity of physiognomies becomes indifferent. . . . He generalizes brusquely, passes over individualities, and arrives at one bound at the typical character of the race, seeking to differentiate it only by the different situations into which he leads it. Possibly with this violent foregone conclusion he will always make the same woman and the same man, the same sky and the same landscape; but what does it matter if the austere rigidity, the slow strong pace, the somber grandeur of these populations of the soil . . . are found in their entirety in the humble scenes which he sets before our eyes?[95]

Since Castagnary displays the limits of the humanitarian position most clearly, we may conclude this chapter with a few quotations which sum it up, revealing both its strength and its fatal weakness. He is inquiring into the origins of the new school of objective naturalism and asks:

Whence comes it? It has issued from the very depths of modern rationalism. It springs from our philosophy which, by replacing man in the society from which the psychologists have removed him, has made social life the principal object of our research from now on.[96] It springs from our ethics which, by substituting the imperative notion of justice for the

---

[91] Castagnary, "Salon de 1869," *Salons*, p. 364.

[92] *Ibid.*, p. 26, under "Philosphie au Salon de 1857."

[93] *Ibid.*, p. 148, "Salon de 1863."

[94] *Ibid.*, p. 151. Also, see below, Chap. XIV.

[95] *Ibid.*, p. 76, "Salon de 1859." It would seem that Millet was really closer to his ideal, but he liked Courbet's work better.

[96] This sentence has a very Comtian tinge.

vague law of love, has established the connection of men to each other and lighted the problem of destiny with a new illumination. It springs from our politics which, by posing the
equality of individuals as a principle and the equation of conditions as a desideratum, has
caused false hierarchies and lying distinctions to disappear from the spirit.[97]

"Naturalism" as he calls it, has knit up the broken bond between man and nature—
so far only in the life of the fields; the life of the city being still in reserve[98]—and it has
done something else. Castagnary believed that the artist had been displaced in society,
that he was no longer in the position he had once occupied in human affairs, but now
the new school "by replacing the artist at the center of his times with a mission to
reflect on them, determines the true usefulness of art, consequently its morality."[99]

Landscape painters "have, in this century, done the greatest thing given men to do,
they have brought about a revolution";[100] but their achievement is not enough:

To have nature complete, and "being" in all its forms, one must turn to society itself;
show man, woman, and child in the diverse conditions of their existence; run over the whole
scale from the laborer to the sailor, from the herdsman to the soldier, from the judge to the
legislator; study at every step, under the double light of drawing and color, the alterations
or embellishments of the human face; indicate the essence of temperaments, mark the impress of passions; unfold at the same moment the misery which debases and the opulence
which deforms; exalt work and condemn laziness; paint, finally, in its physical and moral
form, through all the situations which incessantly modify now one and now the other, this
fragment of creation which believers call a lump of clay, and which we, who are more
religious, have learned to call man and humanity.[101]

This is the new person who replaces the saints and heroes, in him lies the hope of the
future, and he is the one the artists must study, understand, and exalt by sifting away
the dross and making his true nature stand revealed. Art must take an active guiding
hand as well as showing what mankind really is. It was a noble idea and a natural
outgrowth of the liberal spirit of the times, but how much easier it was to suggest than
to embody in plastic form! Castagnary himself was sometimes quite genuinely confused
when he came to apply the theory to the actual instance.[102] Rembrandts or Daumiers
were few and far between, and rare indeed was the painter who had Balzac's gift for
making the monumental out of the trivial. Even more important was the fact that
artists like Millet and Courbet, on whom Castagnary and the others pinned their
hopes (albeit with some reservations), had not been so kindly treated by society that
they were likely to be inclined to sing its praises in any universal sense. Millet's peasants

[97] *Ibid.*, p. 140, "Salon de 1863."
[98] *Ibid.*, p. 105. The idea that the new painting had done well by "rural life" but had so
far kept that of the city "in reserve," was not
confined to Castagnary. Millet and Breton (in
the opinion of a number of critics) plus Courbet had done very well by the peasantry. Who
would do as much for the Parisian? Daumier
and Gavarni—even Guys—had presented such
characters with great power but not in painting; that is, they were regarded as graphic

artists, or, in the case of Guys, as an artist-
reporter. For a fuller discussion, see below,
Chap. XII, and also Chap. VII for Baudelaire's
estimate of Guys.
[99] *Ibid.*, p. 106.
[100] J. A. Castagnary, "Salon de 1868" under
L'Art in *Le Bilan de l'année 1868*, p. 305.
[101] Castagnary, "Salon de 1863," *Salons*,
p. 146.
[102] See below, p. 163.

were his friends whom he loved and understood, but that could scarcely be said of the Parisians, and the same held true for Courbet and the worthy folk of Ornans. As it turned out, no one appeared to apply the humanitarian ideal to the painting of the city dweller, a phenomenon the cause of which may have been suggested by Thoré (Fig. 73):

Courbet, judging that the times were difficult, and that assuredly military men and princes constitute that which is most beautiful in painting, has refrained from risking his menagerie of outlaws. It is true that there have never been so many stones broken in Paris, but he has understood that interest centers on those who have them broken rather than on those who do the breaking. He has, therefore, thrown himself back on the stags and foxes, against whom one cannot profess antipathy.[108]

Later on, the man of the city *was* celebrated, but in a different fashion, by Manet, Degas, Renoir, and Toulouse Lautrec.

[108] T. Thoré, *Salons de W. Bürger*, "Salon de 1861," p. 36.

VI. OBJECTIVE NATURALISTS

THE journal *Réalisme*, founded in 1856 by Edmund Duranty and other friends of Champfleury, lasted for six issues and then suspended publication.[1] This brief existence was in a way symptomatic of the "realist" movement as such, in spite of the fact that the term had been used earlier and was certainly widely current much later. The span of pictorial "realism," at least what Champfleury meant by the term, was not actually in excess of seventeen years, from the exhibition of Courbet's *Après dînée à Ornans* in 1849 (Fig. 20) to the appearance of Thoré's famous epitaph: "Who would believe that the great success of the Salon of 1866, a unanimous success, belongs to Courbet! Well, my dear friend, your business is done, accomplished—ended. Your brave days are over. Here you are accepted, medaled, decorated, glorified, embalmed" (Fig. 74).[2] In all fairness, it must be stated that Courbet *was* the "realistic" movement in painting, just as Delacroix had been the romantic movement twenty or thirty years earlier. If Courbet, or someone very much like him, had never lived, there might never have been the controversy over the idea of truth to nature even though the same terms were used to describe Millet, Jules Breton, Ribot, and several others of greater or less consequence. It is difficult, therefore, to discuss the theory attached to Courbet's art without the art itself, but this may be more profitably examined in the second section of this book. However, in the minds of many people, the name of Champfleury was bound so closely with that of the painter that the two were considered to be the opposite sides of the same coin,[3] and his views, along with those who felt as he did, can thus be examined somewhat in the abstract so long as we bear in mind that they apply chiefly to the work of one man.

Much has been written on the subject of "realism" in general, most of it being devoted to literature, and involving the discussion of a large part of the letters of the nineteenth century.[4] Attempts at definition are abundant, but their very profusion makes clear interpretation in any specific instance difficult. An exhaustive analysis of the tendency to use the natural world as a direct source of artistic inspiration, which is the basis of the term in its pictorial applications, lies well beyond the scope of the present book, but some discussion of it cannot be avoided, for "realism"—whatever it was—was central in the critical writing with which we are concerned.

The age, as we have already seen, was one of rapid change, of unsettled social ideas, and of considerable intellectual experiment and uncertainty. Realism was, in various ways, quite closely associated with several of these aspects, and consequently the opinions as to just what it was were inevitably varied themselves. Some writers made realism almost equal to materialism or positivism, others thought it a form of socialistic

[1] From Nov. 15, 1856 to April 15, 1857 (Duranty, *La Nouvelle peinture. À propos du groupe d'artistes qui expose dans les galleries Durand-Ruel*, Paris, 1876; new ed., foreword and notes by Marcel Guérin, Paris, 1946, p. 9).

[2] T. Thoré, *Salons de W. Bürger*, Vol. II, p. 276 (Salon, '66). Cf. E. Bouvier, *La Bataille réaliste*, Paris, n.d., Chap. VII.

[3] Cf. Bouvier, *passim*.

[4] Cf., for example, René Dumesnil, *Le Réalisme*, Paris, 1936.

thinking, still others considered it merely antitraditionalism. Desnoyers said that any artist who saw clearly and sincerely was a realist, and so it went.[5] The passage of time has not cleared the air, for any modern eye can see that a painter like Delaroche was, in some ways, very realistic indeed, but his work was never linked in his own day with what Courbet was doing. Ingres himself was realistic to a degree, but if this was so, how could Millet be described by the same adjective? Philosophically, one may speak of realism as opposed to nominalism, but when the critics of the middle of the century used the word "realism," what they meant was actually a sort of nominalism. Nor is the solution to be found by introducing the term "naturalism," as a good number of writers did.[6] Some meant by this word what their colleagues meant by the other, and where a distinction was implied, it was by no means clear. Most of the authors with whom we are dealing left the understanding of their terminology up to the reader, expecting him to get the sense of it from the context and the pictures to which it was being applied. This is of scant help today in a general discussion where more inclusive meanings are essential.

Several careful attempts have been made to bring a degree of order out of this chaos. Du Val, in his study of the use of the term "realism" in *La Revue des deux mondes*,[7] finds that it was used there by Gustave Planche as early as 1835 to describe that type of art which attempted to reproduce nature more or less exactly in the sense of its physical or external appearance, and this was its general meaning thereafter. However, this definition is not very helpful, for if the term was used in such a way thirteen years before the appearance of Courbet's "new" manner, what was so unusual about what he was doing? Du Val claims that its use was more prominent in *art* criticism in the decade before 1850,[8] a view which is supported by Bouvier's analysis of the ideas of Champfleury, which were clearly a result of his contact with the art of his friend from Ornans.[9] But, wherever it may have originated, and however inexact and confusing it was, the term became a part of the regular coinage of art criticism, associated with a variety of others such as "the real," "reality," "the true," "imitation," "the cult of the ugly," and so on.

In spite of the information available on the subject, the problem is not readily resolved, and it seems necessary to supply specific terms suitable to the present discus-

[5] F. Desnoyers, article on realism in *L'Artiste*, 5e série, Vol. XVI, 1855-56, p. 197.

[6] This was especially common in the 'sixties.

[7] Thaddeus Ernest Du Val, Jr., *The Subject of Realism in the Revue des Deux-Mondes (1831-1865)*, Philadelphia, 1936, p. 17. For a more general discussion of the reaction to realism, see Bernard Weinberg, *French Realism: The Critical Reaction, 1830-1870*, N.Y., 1937, Chap. IV, and elsewhere. See also, E. B. O. Borgerhoff, "*Réalisme* and Kindred Words: Their Use as Terms of Literary Criticism in the First Half of the Nineteenth Century,"

P.M.L.A., Vol. LIII, 1938, pp. 837-843.

[8] Du Val, *op.cit.*, p. 23. In his discussion of the difference between realism and naturalism, the author makes a "scientific" interest characteristic of the latter and its chief distinction from the former. This may have been entirely true in literature, but was certainly not the case in art prior, at least, to Impressionism (see Du Val, p. 9). The book contains interesting material on the relation to realism of liberalism, socialism, etc., as seen through the eyes of the conservative writers for this journal.

[9] Bouvier, *op.cit.*, pp. 222ff.

sion.[10] Such terms must fulfill two main functions: to furnish a name other than "realism" which can conveniently be applied to the art of Courbet and the theories connected with it, and to make a reasonably clear distinction between this art and that of Manet and others which, although similar, was sufficiently different so that the same label applied to both only makes the confusion worse.

To describe Courbet, the phrase "objective naturalism" will be used, and the reader is asked to understand that this is roughly equivalent to "realism," but only when applied to his art and the opinions of his supporters. If any generalization can be attempted, it would be to the effect that painting of this kind looked at nature for the sake of looking at it; an art, as the phrase went, of *nature naturante*—of nature being nature. The observer, in this case, was to learn from the artist's presentation much about the world around him that was new and fascinating. The second term, which describes a different phase of this interest in nature, will be called "pure painting." It implies a shift in interest, in emphasis, from the object (i.e. nature) to the artist, so that the picture, while still dealing with *nature naturante*, is really an expression of the artist's own sensitivity and individuality of conception. Zola's famous phrase about art being "a corner of creation seen through a temperament"[11] is exactly descriptive of pure painting. In a work of art there are, he says, two elements: the first is the real one which is nature, and is the same for all eyes to see; the second is the variable—man's individuality—which is the more important.[12] It will thus be seen that the difference between the two terms lies in the relative importance of nature as it "really" looks and the expressive, "temperamental" handling of what is observed. When the former is dominant, the picture is a work of objective naturalism (i.e. "realism"); when the latter is decisive in the final effect, it is a piece of pure painting. The distinction is not intended to be final or absolute—such definitions in art never are—but it will, perhaps, serve to explain why Courbet was admired by the realist critics but was far less attractive to the Goncourts. The former were willing to accept painting which represented the world, as it seemed to them, on its own grounds; the latter wanted the world only on their own personal terms, or the personal terms of someone else with whose sensations and reactions they were in sympathy. As will be described later, nature had been accepted on more or less objective terms in landscape long before it was so accepted in figure painting, a fact which has considerable significance for an understanding of the artistic developments of the time.[13]

Jules Husson, who signed himself Champfleury, was the leading spokesman for objective naturalism as a critical position in the arts. As previously mentioned, Courbet's painting acted as a sort of catalyst to crystallize his views, which did not take clear form prior to 1848 although he had been exposed to ideas about literary realism much earlier. The attraction between the mind of the one and the art of the other was strong enough so that Champfleury was led to pick out *La Nuit classique de*

[10] The terms here described are only intended to be of use in the present discussion.
[11] É. Zola, *Mes haines* (ed. Charpentier), p. 25.
[12] *Ibid.*, p. 281, "Le Moment artistique."
[13] See below, Chap. IX.

Walpurgis[14] from among the thousands of canvases exhibited in the unwieldy show of that year, and he took it upon himself to inform the public that its author was "a great painter."[15] From that time forward this enthusiasm was the painter's chief critical support until Champfleury's ardor cooled sometime after 1857, the final break between the two men occurring in 1865. It is noteworthy that after 1857, Courbet largely gave up his more "outrageous" subjects and turned to safer and more profitable themes.[16]

In the late 'forties, Champfleury joined the group that met at the Brasserie Andler where he listened to the pronouncements of the painter with great attention.[17] In 1851 appeared his critique of the *Enterrement* (Fig. 23), a powerful statement of the new naturalist credo which bestowed on the new painting such adjectives as "serious and earnest, ironic and brutal, sincere and full of poetry."[18] By 1855, at the time of Courbet's show, the tide was in full swing, realism was a word on every tongue, and an interesting series of articles appeared in *L'Artiste*.

The general tenor of the reviews in this famous journal was conservative in the 'forties and 'fifties. Clément de Ris and Arsène Houssaye were responsible for a good many of them,[19] and though they did not stand with the most extreme right, they looked askance at much of the new. Millet received a favorable notice in 1851,[20] but in the same account of the Salon, De Ris thought that the *Enterrement* was so awful that he declined to discuss it at all.[21] Earlier, in the first flush of democratic enthusiasm aroused by the events of '48, Houssaye had delivered himself of a curious exhortation to the peasantry—"Au peuple des campagnes"—in which he told them to be of good cheer for he was one of them, referred to the "holy communion of work," and assured them that the Republic would do them justice.[22] This apparently did not last very long as an editorial policy, for the sentiments expressed soon thereafter were not such as to jar the sensibilities of the government of Louis Napoleon. The direction of the journal was, however, not so narrow as to preclude other points of view. Gautier wrote in the midst of the uproar:

Why has Courbet been passed over in silence? [This was apropos of the official awards.] He has been an event at the Salon; with his defects, for which we have upbraided him briskly, he mixes superior qualities with an incontestable originality; he shakes the public

---

[14] This picture is no longer visible since the *Lutteurs*, exhibited in the Salon of 1853, was painted over it.

[15] Quoted in Bouvier, *La Bataille réaliste*, p. 233. It appeared originally in *Le Pamphlet*, Sept. 28, 1848.

[16] This matter is examined in some detail in Chap. xv.

[17] According to Bouvier, the group included Bonvin, Chenavard, Castagnary, Préault, Duranty, Desnoyers, and others (*op.cit.*, p. 235). Apparently Courbet declaimed his views at some length and with great vigor. It seems, however, that he couldn't make a formal

speech, nor write with any skill.

[18] Champfleury, "Courbet," *Grandes figures d'hier et d'aujourd'hui*, in *Oeuvres illustrées de Champfleury*, Paris, 1861, pp. 231ff.

[19] In the light of this general attitude, Houssaye's interesting letter supporting Monet and Renoir is of great interest. See below, p. 202.

[20] Clément de Ris, "Le Salon de 1851," *L'Artiste*, 5e série, Vol. v, 1851, p. 6. The famous *Semeur* is described as energetic and full of movement.

[21] *Ibid.*, p. 34.

[22] A. Houssaye, "Au peuple des campagnes," *L'Artiste*, 5e série, Vol. i, 1848, pp. 49ff.

and the critics; he has his enthusiasts and his detractors—he should have been given a first class medal like M. Antigna.[23]

In 1855, the Salon review was entrusted to Charles Perrier who apparently represented the editorial views of the paper, and who promised his readers a special section at the very end in which he would deal separately with the art of Courbet.[24] Before he got around to it, Champfleury published a short piece entitled: "Du Réalisme. Lettre à Madame Sand." This was a ringing defense of Courbet in which he took the part of those who said of the artist's work: "It is an incredible audacity, it is the overthrow of all institutions by means of the jury, it is the direct appeal to the public, it is liberty."[25] Realism, he says, is the word used to attack all originality and he claims that there has been nothing like the *Enterrement* since David's *Mort de Marat*.

In the same issue appeared the following notice: "We have often published the fact that *L'Artiste* is a free rostrum where the editor-in-chief allows all those who have a feeling for art to speak, whatever their heresies may be. This explains the manifesto of M. Champfleury about Courbet."[26] Shortly after this, Perrier came out with a vigorous rebuttal in which he defined realism, as he saw it in Courbet, as "a system of painting which consists in exalting and exaggerating one of the real sides of nature— I speak of matter—to the detriment of another no less real, which is the spirit."[27] Needless to say, there was no editorial notice after this contribution.

But the matter did not rest there. In December, Fernand Desnoyers published a personal declaration of faith in "realism" which is one of the best statements of it to appear in print: "Realism is the true painting of objects. . . . The word *realist* has only been employed to distinguish the sincere, clear-sighted artist from the creature who persists, through good faith or bad, in seeing things through colored glasses. . . . Realism, while not being an apology for the ugly or the evil, has the right to represent what exists and what one sees." He claims for painting and literature the same right "which mirrors have" and concludes by saying, "Enfin, le Realisme vient!"[28] The reference to mirrors—unselective devices for reflecting anything set before them—is significant, for it implies that this art accepts one subject as readily as another, that there is no inherent difference in importance which the artist must observe, and that the old hierarchy of themes is flatly rejected. The art of objective naturalism thus put in place one of the essential pieces in the framework of the new art: the neutrality of subject matter.[29]

---

[23] Th. Gautier in a short notice on the Salon awards, *L'Artiste*, 5e série, Vol. VI, 1851, p. 118. From what the author has seen of the art of M. Antigna, this coupling of names is another example of the erratic (or overinclusive) nature of this critic's taste.

[24] Chas. Perrier, "L'Art à l'Exposition Universelle," *L'Artiste*, 5e série, Vols. XV and XVI. The review ran in many installments beginning on p. 15 of Vol. XV. The mention of Courbet is on p. 134.

[25] *L'Artiste*, 5e série, Vol. XVI, 1855-56, pp.

1ff. In this letter he refers to a statement by Proudhon in his *Philosophie du progrès* (1853) apropos of Courbet's *Baigneuses* (Fig. 32): "Any figure, ugly or beautiful, can fulfill the aim of art."

[26] *L'Artiste*, 5e série, Vol. XVI, p. 28.

[27] Chas. Perrier, "Du réalisme. Lettre à M. Le Directeur de *L'Artiste*," *ibid.*, p. 85.

[28] Fernand Desnoyers, "Du réalisme," *ibid.*, pp. 197ff.

[29] By neutrality, the author means that the various available subjects for artists were no

The articles in *L'Artiste* set forth, in a small compass, the general nature of the controversy. Why, asks Desnoyers, has there been such a row?

Because Realism says to people: we have always been Greeks, Romans, Englishmen, Germans, Spaniards, etc., let's be ourselves for a little while, even if we are ugly. Let us write, let us paint only what is, or at least, what we see, what we know, what we have lived. Let us have neither masters nor pupils! A singular school, isn't it?—where there are no masters, no pupils, and whose only principles are independence, sincerity, individualism![30]

In its pure form, objective naturalism differed very markedly from the position taken by the humanitarians. It has already been pointed out that Proudhon was forced to inject his views into the art of Courbet,[31] that Castagnary really gave up his earlier idealism about this art in favor of a belief that it was a step in the right direction.[32] To the believers in a new social ideal, objective naturalism was basically inadequate since it did not get at the core of the problem; it was important only as showing that the past could be got rid of and the way cleared for something new. But as long as Courbet exercised to the full his forceful vision of things seen, he was quite satisfactory to Champfleury, Desnoyers, Duranty, and their friends, who did not ask as much as their more socially-minded colleagues. A whole new morality was not required, just honesty toward the world of fact: "Logically it would be more worthwhile to paint the lower classes first, in which the sincerity of feelings, actions, and words is more in evidence than in high society."[33] Humanitarianism included a social order of which painting was a vital part; objective naturalism was only a useful and exciting way of looking at life, an open window looking out on man and nature.

A gentle, but firm, summary of the quality of such naturalism occurs at the end of Sainte-Beuve's discussion of Champfleury's book on the Le Nain.[34] The great critic did not often concern himself with matters artistic,[35] but he had an acute, wide-ranging interest, and his comment is worth listening to, even though he, somewhat like Proudhon, disclaimed any technical knowledge of the subject:

---

longer considered to have any order of relative importance, and also that they had no obvious significance in a moral or didactic sense. Cf. the quotation from Castagnary on p. 63. When the world is seen quantitatively, qualitative standards tend to decline in importance. It has always seemed to the author that there was a certain significance in the anecdote related by Vollard. He was sitting to Cézanne for his portrait on a very flimsy stand which collapsed when the subject became sleepy and let his head fall to one side. The artist's immediate comment was: "You wretch! You've spoiled the pose. Do I have to tell you again you must sit like an apple? Does an apple move?" The equation was really more than one of pose (A. Vollard, *Paul Cézanne. His Life and Art*, N.Y., 1926, p. 121).

[30] Desnoyers, *op.cit.*, p. 200.

[31] See above, p. 68.

[32] That is, that while the world was preparing itself for the great future which lay before it, any art which focused attention in the general direction of man and nature was doing a good thing. This may account, in part, for Castagnary's praise of several artists who painted the right kind of theme even though the quality left much to be desired.

[33] Champfleury, *Le Réalisme*, Paris, 1857, pp. 10ff.

[34] Sainte-Beuve, *Nouveaux lundis*, 2nd rev. ed., Paris, 1872, Vol. IV, pp. 116-139 (Monday, Jan. 5, 1863).

[35] In a rather lengthy notice on the life of Delécluze he shows an admirable understanding of the strengths and weaknesses of that austere critic, but he did not write very extensively on the fine arts (see *Nouveaux lundis*, Vol. III, 1870, pp. 77-124; written in August, 1862).

Reality, you are the foundation of life, and as such, even in your asperities, even in your harshness, you interest serious minds, you have a charm for them. And yet, in the long run and all alone, you will end by gradually repelling [them], by surfeiting them; you are too often dull, common, and tiresome. It is surely enough to meet you at every step in life[36]—in Art, at least, while finding and feeling you always present or nearby, one wants to have to do with something else. Yes, at every moment you need to be renewed, refreshed, to be heightened at some point, at the risk of being stifling and perhaps annoying through being too ordinary. At the least, you must possess and add to your merits this imitative genius—so perfect, so animated, so fine that it becomes, in its turn, something like a creation and a magic; this marvelous use of the means and processes of art which, without sprawling and making itself apparent, breathes or sparkles in each detail as in the whole. In a word, you need style.

If possible, you further need *feeling*, a sympathetic side, a moral beam which penetrates and comes to light you up through some chink or opening: otherwise you soon leave us cold, indifferent, and, men that we are, since we carry ourselves about everywhere and never leave ourselves, we are bored with not finding our part and place in you.

While being observed and respected, you also need, and that is the finest triumph, a certain something which fulfills and completes you, which corrects without falsifying you, which exalts you without making you lose contact with the earth, which gives you all possible spirit without ceasing to appear natural for a moment, which leaves you recognizable to all, but more luminous, more charming, more beautiful than ordinarily in life—in short, you need what is called the *ideal*.[37]

For Sainte-Beuve, nature as such was insufficient, however vital it was as the basic element of experience. Among the somewhat conservative critics, this "certain something" which reality lacked was variously described, but invariably missed in the art of Courbet and those whom they associated with him.[38] Whether it was called the ideal, imagination, or social purpose, it had to do with some universal control, some ordering of matter in terms of human values and aspirations. The void left by this exclusion was easily filled for some people by a delight in the organization and form of the picture itself as well as its revelation of the personality of the artist as an individual, but it was a form of pleasure which was difficult, if not impossible, for men thus far nourished by tradition to adopt.

The distinction between objective naturalism and an "art for man" was not only felt by the humanitarians, but also by more neutral observers like Clément de Ris, who was an advocate of neither position. In the 'fifties, he found the art of Courbet very hard to take,[39] but at the same time he had warm praise for the imaginative sympathy with which Millet approached the life of the peasant. Further, although he was no believer in "art for art's sake," he could, and did, give great credit to Courbet's "painterly" abilities.[40] When, as Thoré said,[41] the painter from Ornans gave up his wild ways and "fell back on the stags and foxes," he became a success at once in the

---

[36] Cf. Bougot's remarks to the effect that in art one must get away from life as it is to another world (*Essai sur la critique d'art*, pp. 359-360).

[37] Sainte-Beuve, *Nouveaux lundis*, Vol. IV, pp. 137-138.

[38] Men such as Ribot and Antigna.

[39] Cf. his review of the Salon of 1851 in *L'Artiste*, 5e série, Vol. VI, p. 34.

[40] De Ris, "Salon de 1853," *L'Artiste*, 5e série, Vol. X, p. 131.

[41] See above, p. 72.

very quarters where he had recently been despised, even though he may not have been regarded as a "great" painter in the traditional meaning of the term.[42]

If, therefore, the work of this man was the true touchstone for the quality of objective naturalism in painting, and if the support he received from the "realist" critics actually constitutes the body of appropriate theory—two assumptions which seem to be borne out by the evidence—then we may conclude that "realism," in its most provocative (or irritant) form, did not last long after 1857; that it was by no means identical with humanitarianism; and that it was likewise different from a more subjective type expressed in the art of Manet and defended by the Goncourts and Zola.[43] And yet, brief and narrow as it may have been, it was of crucial importance. It constituted a declaration of war on the past, a reassertion of the power of the individual equal to that achieved earlier by Delacroix, and was a most vivid demonstration of the fact that for some people, at least, man was no longer either divine or heroic, but just something to paint for the interest there was in him as the inhabitant of a world hitherto very imperfectly known, but now coming into new focus under the influence of science, industry, progress, and a host of associated ideas whose full import was not yet understood. The humanitarians wanted to help shape this world; the so-called realists were content to try to look it squarely in the eye.

[42] Even Maxime Du Camp, who had heaped scorn upon him earlier ("we deal only with art, we have nothing to do with M. Courbet," 1855), now found him at least "a very clever worker," and thought the *Remise des chevreuils* was almost good (Maxime Du Camp, *Les Beaux-arts à l'Exposition Universelle, et aux Salons de 1863, 1864, 1865, 1866, 1867*, Paris, n.d., pp. 219ff., "Le Salon de 1866"). The next year he says he is one of the best landscapists in France but should stay away from the figure (*ibid.*, p. 344).

[43] See below, Chap. VIII.

VII. BAUDELAIRE AND GAUTIER

THE foregoing classification of certain modes of thought about art, and the association of certain names with those modes, naturally has only a relative value. Men of the skill and learning of the critics here discussed do not fit altogether neatly into any system; and yet ideas were shared, positions taken, opinions set down in print which must somehow be set in order if the times are to be understood. At the very best, however, certain figures will always escape classification: such is Charles Baudelaire, possibly the most acute, and certainly the most difficult to understand fully, of all the critics of the middle of the century.

By the flickering brilliance of this unusual mind, one can see many of the ideas which were later incorporated into both the theory and practice of art, some of them original, some of them borrowed,[1] some unique with him, others shared by many of his contemporaries. The importance of the individual, the necessity for imagination, freedom of technique, a sensitivity to pictorial effect, a correspondence between the sensations of the various bodily organs, the emotional effect of color, the need for a truly modern art, the importance of an almost morbidly refined perception, a hatred for things mechanical[2]—these and other facets of his many-sided intelligence flash out from the pages of his writings on art, but they are sometimes hard to hold steady for a longer look, and almost impossible to simplify into a coordinated whole.

Two things, at least, seem clear: in his own way, and by rather devious methods, he was concerned for a number of years with the problem of a wholly modern art including the ideas which it should embody; and he was never able to find an artist who entirely satisfied his requirements. He postulates an imaginary figure, "the painter of modern life," attempts from time to time to make his hero, Delacroix, into the painter of the age without quite succeeding, and finally, after rejecting the candidacy of Courbet, comes to rest with a long and interesting appreciation of the art of Constantin Guys. For Baudelaire, as for most of the other critics, the object of his search was a figure painter, for though landscape was certainly one of the fields in which the art of the future was being prepared, man's fate in society was of the greatest concern to thinking people of the day, and what was needed above all were the painters to set him down, noble or not, against the background of the life he was going to have to live, apparently deprived of the solace of orthodox religion and the inspiration of the classical ages.

In his real critical debut, the Salon of 1845, Baudelaire approaches the subject directly after complaining of the lack of novelty, invention, and ideas in the art he has been observing: "And yet we are surrounded by the heroism of modern life—our true feelings stifle us enough so that we should know them. Neither colors nor subjects are lacking for epics."[3] But there is no painter

---

[1] See M. Gilman, "Baudelaire and Stendhal," *P.M.L.A.*, 1939, pp. 288-296.

[2] Baudelaire, *Curiosités* (ed. Lévy), pp. 258ff., "Le Salon de 1859."

[3] This and the following quotation are from "Le Salon de 1845," *Curiosités* (ed. Crépet), 1923, p. 77.

. . . who will know how to tear out of actual life its epic side, and make us see and understand with color or drawing, how grand we are in our neckties and varnished boots![4] . . . May the true seekers next year be able to give us that singular joy of celebrating the arrival of the new!

This might almost be taken as a plea to Delacroix to turn to modern life, since the references here, as well as in other Salons, to drawing and color are inspired by his enthusiasm for the master's handling of those very means of expression. Earlier in this same review he had said, "M. Delacroix is decidedly the most original painter of ancient and modern times,"[5] but the great man was nearly fifty and his style had been well established fifteen years earlier. Baudelaire's hero among the artists might well be the most original in the century, but he was not *new*, nor was he interested in the contemporary scene, a fact which explains the plea for an artist yet unknown who could celebrate the present in fitting manner.[6] In the review of the following year, he included a section entitled "De l'héroisme de la vie moderne," in which he defends modern man in his black suit and white tie as a suitable subject.[7] Contemporary themes are usually restricted to public functions, military victories and the like, but there is another, a private nobility both in the elegant life of society and in the underworld beneath it.[8] The example offered is that of a minister defending himself eloquently on the floor of the Chamber of Deputies, but, in his enthusiasm, Baudelaire does not realize that this could not be an acceptable symbolism nor a universal ideal—his minister would be an object of respect only to the members of his own party, not, unfortunately, to men generally.[9] The almost mystic significance he attaches to the drab clothing of the bourgeois is symptomatic of that highly personal symbolism which marks so much of his poetry, and which had so great an effect on the Symbolist movement toward the end of the century. "What is pure art according to the modern conception?" he asks, "It is to create a suggestive magic containing both the object and the subject, the world exterior to the artist and the artist himself."[10] As Raymond has said, in his work "the object and the subject absorb one another."[11] For all of his brilliant

[4] The problem of an epic style based upon the dull and close-fitting masculine costume of the day had been discussed by a number of critics. See, for example, Quatremère de Quincy, *Essai sur l'idéal dans ses applications pratiques aux oeuvres de l'imitation propre des arts de dessin*, Paris, 1837, p. 314 and generally in latter part of the essay.

[5] Baudelaire, *Curiosités* (ed. Lévy), p. 5.

[6] The distinction between Delacroix as the greatest of modern (i.e. contemporary) painters and a painter (still unfound) of modern life must be kept clear. He was definitely the former in Baudelaire's opinion, but not the latter. See also Chesneau's explanation of why Delacroix could not paint contemporary subjects (Chesneau, "Le Mouvement moderne," *Revue européenne*, Vol. xviii, 1861, pp. 480ff.).

[7] Baudelaire, *Curiosités* (ed. Crépet), pp. 196ff.

[8] Cf. Castagnary (*Le Bilan de l'année 1868*, p. 355), who said that the new art was still on the private level and is not sure whether or not events are preparing for a "public life" which will furnish the great modern subject matter. It would seem that art continued on the private level for some time.

[9] Baudelaire, *op.cit.*, p. 199, "Salon de 1846." The nobility to be found in society, which is mentioned here, is expanded more fully when he later discusses the "dandy" as a type and as a symbol. (See *Le Peintre de la vie moderne* [1863] as trans. by P. G. Konody in *The Painter of Victorian Life*, N.Y., 1930.)

[10] Baudelaire, "L'Art philosophique," *L'Art romantique* (ed. Lévy), Paris, 1885, p. 127.

[11] Marcel Raymond, *De Baudelaire au surréalisme*, Paris, 1933, p. 24.

penetration into the appearance of the world about him, the effective symbols which he found were so highly individual that they could never be the basis for any universal repertory such as the humanitarians were seeking, nor did he probably intend them to be.

He was fascinated by the real world as well as by the imaginary one of the mind, as his interest in the brilliant group of caricaturists bears witness. He admired Lami, Gavarni, and especially Daumier, because they had the eyes to penetrate society and extract meaning from it, but gifted as they were, their art was still caricature and not, therefore, on the same plane or scale as the art of Delacroix.[12] He believed that Daumier was the finest of them all, as indeed he was, but he qualified his esteem by calling him "a great caricaturist . . . a *special* artist belonging to the illustrious family of masters."[13] Strangely enough, in his search for the truly modern he finally settled for something which was very close to caricature, and quite far from Delacroix: the art of Constantin Guys.

Courbet, the most obviously new talent of the 'fifties, was a friend for several years,[14] but even the amazing strength and the revolutionary quality of his work were unable to satisfy the critic's conditions. In his account of the Exposition Universelle of 1855, Courbet is compared to Ingres, a juxtaposition which would scarcely have occurred to a less original mind. Ingres is found to be out of tune with the times: "he immolates himself on the altar of those faculties which he sincerely believes to be the grandest and most important." In the following passage Courbet is ruled out as the artist of the future—and objective naturalism along with him:

However enormous the paradox may appear, it is in this that he [Ingres] approaches a young painter whose remarkable beginnings have recently been produced with the appearance of an insurrection. M. Courbet, also, is a powerful workman, a savage and patient will; and the results he has obtained, results which for some spirits already have more charm than those of the grand master of the Raphaelesque tradition, due, no doubt, to their positive solidity and their loving cynicism, have, like those latter ones, this which is singular: they exhibit a sectarian spirit, a killer of abilities. Politics, literature—these also produce these vigorous temperaments, these protestants, these antisupernaturalists, whose only legitimacy is a spirit of reaction which is sometimes wholesome. The providence which rules the affairs of painting, gives them for accomplices all those whom the predominant adverse idea has left bored or oppressed. But the difference is that the heroic sacrifice which M. Ingres makes in honor of tradition and the Raphaelesque idea of the beautiful, M. Courbet accomplishes to the profit of nature—exterior, positive, immediate. In their war against the imagination they obey different incentives, and two inverse fanaticisms lead them to the same immolation.[15]

[12] Baudelaire, *Curiosités* (ed. Aubry), Paris, 1946, pp. 397, 408.

[13] *Ibid.*, p. 409.

[14] The friendship broke up for a variety of reasons, but in the passage quoted below there is still a feeling of respect. Much more actively critical was a fragmentary article recently discovered by M. Crépet. It was written in the same year and was intended as a blistering attack on the painter and also on Champfleury. For some reason it was never published. (See Baudelaire, *Juvenilia* [ed. Crépet], Paris, 1939, p. 579 and M. Gilman, *Baudelaire the Critic*, N.Y., 1943, p. 90.)

[15] Baudelaire, "Exposition Universelle de 1855," *Curiosités* (ed. Crépet), p. 234.

Courbet is thus merely a revolutionary, a champion of a narrow cause whose appeal is largely that of its reaction against more common outlooks, and there is no true future in his art. "Eugène Delacroix," he wrote, "will never be found in the company of that crowd of vulgar artists and writers who, in their limited intelligence, take refuge behind the vague and obscure word 'realism.' "[16] Objective naturalism was certainly not the mode for a man who called imagination "the queen of faculties"—and then gave it his own personal twist: "It is the imagination which has taught man the moral sense of color, contour, sound, and perfume."[17]

In the same article that compared Courbet and Ingres, Baudelaire discusses the women in Delacroix's pictures—Ophelia, Desdemona, Marguerite, the Virgin—who all seem to be carrying some secret grief, and he remarks that the artist seems to be the best endowed for expressing the nature of the modern woman "in her heroic manifestation, in the infernal sense or the divine."[18] But Delacroix didn't paint such women as they were to be found in Paris, nor the scenes in which they moved. The greatest painter of the century, the man with a modern soul who spoke to the feelings through line and color, the giant among the pigmies—all this he was, but "*the* painter of modern life" he was not. To the poet, he belonged, in important respects, to the past, to the great tradition, to the finest masters in history whose fellow he was: "Delacroix's work sometimes seems to me a kind of remembrance of the greatness and native passion of the universal man."[19] So the search continued.

In 1863, four years before his death, there appeared a series of pieces on the work of Guys which were gathered together to form an essay entitled "The Painter of Modern Life."[20] This artist was formerly a member of the staff of the *London Illustrated News*, and his pictures (Fig. 50) were swift sketches of contemporary life ranging from the military caste and the world of fashion all the way down to the inhabitants of the less attractive Parisian bordellos. At first, Baudelaire classes him with the other graphic artists—Gavarni, Daumier, and the others—which was in itself high praise, but it becomes evident as he proceeds that he is really prepared to lavish all his feeling for an art of the world in which he was living upon the somewhat slight talents of this favorite. Deprived of contemporaneity in the subjects of his idol's pictures, repelled by the lack of elegance and imagination in Courbet, and at a loss for any other considerable figure on whom to pin his eagerness,[21] he elevated Guys to a position which

[16] Baudelaire, *Eugène Delacroix, His Life and Work*, N.Y., 1947, p. 20.

[17] Baudelaire, "Salon de 1859," *Curiosités* (ed. Lévy), p. 265.

[18] Baudelaire, "Exposition Universelle de 1855," *Curiosités* (ed. Crépet), p. 248.

[19] Baudelaire, "L'Oeuvre et la vie d'Eugène Delacroix," *L'Art romantique* (ed. Lévy), p. 6.

[20] See note 9, p. 82.

[21] Baudelaire was, of course, a friend and supporter of Manet (see below, Chaps. XVII, XVIII). In a letter to his friend, dated May 11, 1865, he said, among other things intended to cheer up the discouraged painter, "and you, you are only the first, in the decrepitude of your art," by which he meant that although painting was not in very good shape generally, Manet was the best there was. Further on in the same letter, Baudelaire quotes several people as saying that his friend's art has defects but there is an "irresistible charm" in it, an opinion which agrees with his own. His enthusiasm, while genuine enough, was restrained (Baudelaire, *Lettres 1841-1866*, Paris, 1907, pp. 435-436).

he must have realized was not entirely in keeping with the pictures themselves. The artist had a fine command of line and wash, a penetrating eye for costume, for uniforms, for the poses of men and women in the various activities which he records, for the action of horses and the strange elegance of the carriages of the period, but his figures are often out of scale and awkward, their faces expressionless (Baudelaire to the contrary), and the concepts as a whole are slight, however charming they may be. The critic, however, sees in him the man of the world combined with that strange aloof figure of pride, snobbery, and cold self-sufficiency: the dandy, a creature so essentially modern that he had long fascinated Baudelaire.[22] Guys, he thinks, has seized the flavor of life, has been able to catch it on the wing, as it were, and in the process lose none of its charm and grace. Gone from this critique are all the deeper virtues which had been so skillfully described in the analyses of Delacroix, Courbet, and the rest; what remains is a fervent admiration for a man who could fix on paper the modernity Baudelaire felt must always accompany any true beauty.[23] This was what had been lacking before, and in choosing Guys he was willing to surrender much of the other part of beauty—its more eternal or universal qualities. But "M.G.," as he is referred to in the articles, was surely no man to "tear out of actual life its epic side"; he was only a charming and tasteful sketcher of the scenes of war and society.

It was mentioned earlier that the objective phase of naturalism was succeeded by a more subjective one,[24] and in this change the influence of Baudelaire was certainly felt. Both in his poetry and in his criticism there is a strong current of inwardness, of subjectivism, which is most characteristic. In his mind it is one of the essential elements of romanticism, an artistic attitude which he carried forward while at the same time transforming it into something quite different from its earlier form. "Romanticism is not precisely in the choice of subjects nor exact truth, but in the manner of feeling," he wrote in 1846. "Who says romanticism says modern art—that is to say, intimacy, spirituality, color, aspiration toward the infinite, expressed by all the means the arts contain."[25] In speaking of color he blends sight and sound and describes it in terms of harmony and melody: "I do not know if some analogist has solidly established a complete gamut of colors and feelings"; and he recalls a quotation from Hoffman about music, "which I find to be an analogy and in intimate reunion between colors, sounds, and perfumes."[26] In 1859, while comparing the imaginative painter to the "realist," he makes the former say "I want to illuminate things with my spirit and project the reflection on other spirits."[27] So strong is this feeling that he takes the

[22] Konody, *The Painter of Victorian Life*, pp. 35-58, 127-135.

[23] *Ibid.*, p. 94.

[24] See above, pp. 21, 75.

[25] Baudelaire, "Le Salon de 1846," *Curiosités* (ed. Lévy), pp. 85-86.

[26] *Ibid.*, pp. 92-93. The quotation is apparently in Hoffman's own words.

[27] "Le Salon de 1859," *Curiosités* (ed. Lévy), p. 275. His remarks on realism here are interesting. He believes there are two great divisions among painters, of which one is the imaginative type, and another, "which calls itself *realistic*, a word with a double meaning whose sense has not been exactly determined and which we will call *positivist* in order to make its error more evident. [It] says 'I want to represent things as they are, or better, as they would be if I did not exist.' The universe without man. The other, the imaginative [divi-

landscapists to task for being too literal: "Thus they open a window, and the whole space included in the frame of it, trees, sky, and house, take on for them the value of a poem ready-made."[28] But any kind of obvious or philosophical meaning draws his fire as well: "Instead of simply extracting the natural poetry from his subject, M. Millet wants at all costs to add something else. In their monotonous ugliness, all these little pariahs have a melancholy and Raphaelesque pretentiousness."[29] Chenavard (Fig. 36), the mysterious philosopher-painter and friend of Delacroix, is discussed at length in a special essay on "Philosophic Art" at the end of which the author concludes that Chenavard "is a great decadent spirit, and will remain as a monstrous sign of the times."[30] If a subjective approach to pictorial sources in nature and a transcendent individuality are common to many artists after the middle of the century, the contribution of Baudelaire in that direction was not inconsiderable.

Another of the unclassifiables is Théophile Gautier. There was probably no other critic whose pronouncements on art carried as much weight as his, none who was so widely, even reverently, esteemed. Today he seems not to deserve so high a rank among his contemporaries, a judgment concerned solely with his remarks about painting and not intended to reflect upon the rest of his literary effort. At times he was marvelously apt in his judgments—the little article in *L'Artiste* quoted above is of the highest quality[31]—but he was so uneven, he lavished praise so indiscriminately on art of merit and art of almost none, that one wonders how one person could have said all that he did. In a single Salon ('47), he could say of Gérôme's *Combat des Coqs* (Fig. 11) that it exhibited "a rare elegance and an exquisite distinction" and then go on to remark: "A singular talent, that of M. Corot: he has an eye without a hand, he sees like a consummate artist and paints like a child between whose thumb and first finger one puts a brush for the first time. . . ." But lest feelings be hurt, he adds, "Oh well! all that doesn't keep M. Corot from being a great landscapist."[32]

His contemporaries observed the catholicity of his tastes. In an article in *L'Artiste* in 1849, an anonymous character signing himself simply "an artist who did not exhibit," attempts a review of the reviewers and sums Gautier up by saying that he flattered everybody.[33] There seems to be a degree of truth in this, for the great man himself admitted that he had often been accused of indulgence, but defended himself by saying: "We are a poet and not a judge. To study a work, understand it, express it with the means of our art, that is what has always been our aim. *We love to put beside a picture a page in which the painter's theme is taken up by the writer.*"[34] This, it would seem, was the clue both to his method and to his success in his own day.

---

sion] says 'I want to illumine things with my spirit and project the reflection on other spirits'" (p. 275).

[28] *Ibid.*, p. 326.   [29] *Ibid.*, p. 327.

[30] Baudelaire, "L'Art philosophique," *L'Art romantique* (ed. Lévy), p. 135. This essay was never finished and exists only in an abbreviated form.

[31] See above, p. 21.

[32] Th. Gautier, *Salon de 1847*, Paris, 1847, pp. 25, 176.

[33] *L'Artiste*, 5e série, Vol. III, 1849, p. 176, "Salon de 1849. Critique de la critique."

[34] Th. Gautier, *L'Artiste*, 6e série, Vol. III, 1856-1857, p. 4 (Italics mine). This credo would seem to constitute a sort of nineteenth

The critic of those years had to do the best he could without any illustrations of the pictures, or if he had them, in the form of feeble lithographs or etchings, they were of little use in conveying an idea of the quality of the work in question. Gautier was undoubtedly very skilled in the painting of "word pictures" and the reader of his Salons could get an idea of what any given picture was like as seen through Gautier's eyes—not analyzed, but reproduced, as it were, in a totally different medium.[35] That what the reader got was really a picture by Gautier rather than the artist, did not make the reading any the less delightful; but now that the photograph can supply at least a vivid idea of the subject and the way it is handled dramatically, which was what interested Gautier the most, the value of such word pictures has diminished greatly. Not caring to take any very clear stand on the issues which racked more partisan critics, preferring a rather magisterial approbation of almost everyone, there is not a great deal left once his account of the theme has lost its interest, replaced by the picture itself. It must be added, in all fairness, that not infrequently Gautier's picture was far more interesting than the original. Perhaps the warmest tribute paid to him came from his friend and disciple, Baudelaire, who said that he had brought up a whole generation of Frenchmen to love art—the art of all times and all places.[36]

---

century version of the idea of *ut pictura poesis*, that painting and "poetry" are but slightly different having more in common than we would now believe. When painting gave up being "about" things, this type of criticism was inevitably doomed.

[35] It is interesting that Baudelaire, who called him "the perfect man of letters" (and was himself a far better art critic), thought of him as a great expounder of "the beautiful" of all countries, and described the skill with which he understood the wonders of the current British school: "Lanseer, whose beasts have eyes full of thought," etc. His loyalty seems to have gotten the better of his own good judgment (Baudelaire, "Théophile Gautier," *L'Art romantique* [ed. Lévy], pp. 180-183).

[36] Baudelaire, *op.cit.*, p. 182.

VIII. PURE PAINTING

THE discussion of these last two critics leads to the difficult matter of what some have called "art for art's sake." This phrase was in fairly common use during the period, but, as was so often the case, its meaning was not always made entirely clear. In the main it seems to have referred to an emphasis on technique, that is, on painting as such, with much less attention to meaning, moral content, ideality and similar elements of traditional art. More recently, it has been rather neatly described as any form of art which has the mere creation of beauty as its end and is otherwise intentionally useless.[1] The ideas behind it were set forth in some detail in Gautier's preface to *Mademoiselle de Maupin*, and Baudelaire's *Fleurs du mal* is considered to be an almost perfect example.[2] But the problem is not easily solved, for a hundred years ago the term was also used to describe the work of the meticulously realistic artists, the painters of the *juste milieu*. It is hard to equate the symbolic poetry of Baudelaire with the finicky exactitude of a Delaroche or a Vernet. What was meant, apparently, was that these painters were too preoccupied with their craft and not enough with what they were saying, and it seems probable that the literary application of the term was not identical with its artistic usage.

In order to avoid argument over the term, and in an attempt to discuss only that art which was important for the development of modern forms, the phrase "pure painting" will be used. It will be recalled that this label describes painting which is essentially intended to delight the eye, in which the artist is more important than his subject, in which content is primarily only a basis on which formal or painterly effects can be established, which has little or nothing to do with moral or intellectual judgments, which regards a wide variety of themes as of equal interest, and in which the individual artist's concept of beauty and his personal reactions are the main reasons for the existence of the picture. Space does not permit a discussion of the original sources from which this theory of art was developed, but it was already of critical interest before this period opens, and for a long time thereafter. The dissociation of painting from any art of ideas was discussed by the Goncourts in the preface to their review of the Salon of 1855:

> Is it not rather its [i.e. painting's] destiny and its fortune to delight the eyes, to be the material animation of a thing, the representation of something for and by the senses, and not to aspire too much beyond the recreation of the optic nerve? Is not painting rather a materialist art, vivifying form by color, incapable, by the intentions of drawing, of vivifying the inner, moral, spiritual part of the creature?[3]

Baudelaire, even earlier, had said much the same: "Painting is only interesting by virtue of color and form, it does not resemble poetry except insofar as the latter

---

[1] Albert Guérard, *Art for Art's Sake*, N.Y., 1936, p. xvii. For the French aspect of this subject see A. Cassagne, *La Théorie de l'art pour l'art en France chez les derniers romantiques et les premiers réalistes*, Paris, 1906.

[2] Guérard, *op.cit.*, pp. 48, 59.

[3] E. and J. de Goncourt, *Préfaces et manifestes littéraires*, Paris (Charpentier), 1888, p. 244.

awakens ideas of painting in the reader."[4] On the side of individualism, Zola said, "In art I am a curious person who has no great rules, who leans willingly toward works of art provided they are the strong expression of an individual; I admire and I love only unique creations which, in a fine manner, affirm a human aptitude or feeling."[5] In these different statements the core of the idea of pure painting can be seen without the necessity of a final definition. It was seldom found in any complete form, but as a tendency it is quite readily noticeable.

Possibly the most direct statement in support of this view to appear during our period was in a little volume on Ruskin written in 1864 by a somewhat obscure critic named J. Milsand. *L'Esthétique anglaise. Étude sur M. John Ruskin* was a rather tart analysis of the Englishman's ideas, especially his views on the moral purposes of art which the author finds faulty in the extreme. Milsand's remarks should really be read in their entirety, but the following passage will give a fair idea of the tone:

Almost like Wordsworth, I will say that facts belong to science, to art belong feelings; all that which gives us an understanding of a thing is prose, all that which gives an impression is poetry. In other words, we approach science when we seek to free ourselves from our own personal emotions in order to conceive what objects are outside ourselves; we move toward poetry and art when our emotion gets the upper hand and gives us primarily the awareness of the moving forces of our own nature which things have set in motion. . . . If we descend into the depths of our souls . . . we will see very quickly that that which makes us artists . . . consists precisely in escaping the domain of our intelligence, in becoming a man who no longer judges, who no longer perceives things by the ideas which his spirit forms of them, but who has only an awareness of a disturbance, a rapture which cannot be explained. . . .[6]

Traditionalism as well as objective naturalism are both ruled out in favor of a total concentration on individual emotion and sensory reaction, and the artist is set forth as being essentially anti-intellectual. The influence of this essay was apparently not great, but the ideas which it contains are both interesting and advanced for their time.

Gautier and Baudelaire are frequently cited as being exponents of art for art's sake, but it is legitimate to inquire whether this was as true of their art criticism as of their other writings. In the case of the former it is only partially so, at least during the period of our discussion. No ardent believer in it, no worshipper at the shrine of beauty for its own sake, could have written, as Gautier did, a long and detailed exposition of Chenavard's cartoons for the Panthéon, a series of entirely didactic pictures drily executed in grisaille. But this entire project so fascinated him that he devoted one of his longest critical articles to it, and gave every evidence of a complete and sympathetic understanding of its involved and highly philosophical content.[7] Indeed, his criticism throughout is marked by a keen interest in the subjects of the pictures, even in in-

---

[4] Baudelaire, *Curiosités* (ed. Lévy), p. 166, "Le Salon de 1846."

[5] É. Zola, "M. H. Taine, artiste," in *Mes haines* (ed. Le Blond), p. 172.

[6] Paris, 1864, pp. 123-124.

[7] Th. Gautier, "Le Panthéon. Peintures murales," *L'Art moderne*, Paris (Lévy), 1856, pp. 1-94. It was first written in September 1848, very shortly after Chenavard received the commission.

stances where the quality of the work was very low.[8] As late as 1869 he denied that "la grande peinture" was in decadence as everyone else was claiming; it was just not being exhibited at the Salons.[9] His influence on others—the Goncourts, for example—may have been in the direction of an art for art's sake, but his own reactions to pictures were more general and included praise for almost every type.

In the case of Baudelaire, the connection seems to be more easily established, but again a description of him as only a lover of pure art is misleading. His poetry is surely free from conventional morality; he plunges deeply into a personal world of sensations and iridescent symbols drawn from his imagination. But there is another side which is far more objective, more rational, and very patently concerned with real life.[10] That this aspect of his mind is colored by the other, does not alter the fact that a good deal of his art criticism is extremely rational; in analysis, his subjectivism gives way to a clear, precise, and objective dissection of the problem, only the conclusions remaining highly personal. What he saw in Delacroix was what many of the *avant-garde* saw too; he realized what Manet was after, and encouraged him to withstand the attacks of the philistines who made the painter's life almost unbearable.[11] He rejected the art of Courbet since it was unimaginative (a *sine qua non* for him), and classed Chenavard as a "decadent" even though he was intellectually interested in the artist's purposes.[12]

The art of Manet and the men who were grouped around him had a strong flavor of pure painting. Their subjects were drawn from the world as it was, and were presented with a certain directness which showed that the artist was entirely willing to accept them as he found them—unidealized and unheroic. But what he was not prepared to accept, was their external appearance either as it had been rendered according to the various traditional systems, or as a strict attention to the common experience of them would dictate.[13] Realism was ready to take the world on its own terms to a great extent, that is, the terms of the general experience of it, but the pure painters accepted it only on their own. Nature became for them something which could be exploited for purposes of their own individuality, and this change was of great importance.[14] By insisting on their personal ways of seeing and by obstinately refusing to

[8] Cf. his lengthy description of Baudry's *Charlotte Corday* in *Abécédaire du Salon de 1861*, Paris, 1861, p. 21.

[9] Th. Gautier, "Le Salon de 1869," *Tableaux à la plume*, Paris (Charpentier), 1880, p. 277. His real failure to understand what Manet was doing was another sign that, at least in art criticism, he was not a particularly strong friend of pure art. See below, Chaps. XVII, XVIII.

[10] Had Baudelaire's mind been, so to speak, entirely subjective and emotional, he would never have been as brilliant a critic as he was. His thought was not consistent from first to last, but his insight was extraordinary and his articles were often models of lucidity. For his stature in this field, see M. Gilman, *Baudelaire the Critic*.

[11] Cf. Chap. VII, note 21.

[12] Baudelaire, "L'Art philosophique," *L'Art romantique* (ed. Lévy), p. 135.

[13] Manet quarreled with Couture over a difference in their ways of seeing things, each having an equal right to his own view. It would seem that Manet did not see exactly as nonartists saw either; in short, he saw as Manet saw, and that was a personal matter. He seems to have spent much time, study, and effort, in perfecting this individual vision.

[14] Malraux suggests the very interesting idea that the originality of this new art was not primarily a way of seeing, but "the search through the forms for an interior schema which then takes, or does not take, the form of objects, but of which the objects are only

accept the ways which custom had made natural, they inevitably alienated the majority of the critics who not only failed to understand how they could see things in such ways, but were further annoyed by what they considered to be the same absence of imagination in respect to *subject* which had bothered them in the art of Courbet.[15] To understand Manet properly it was necessary first to understand the painter, and then to appreciate his use of tone, contour, color, and the rest on *his* terms; but what most of the critics wanted, of course, were paintings that expressed not private reactions (visual or otherwise) but the aspects of things familiar to everyone. For the best of them, the quality of genius lay in the depth, wisdom, and originality with which these acceptable and comprehensible objects were treated. Some were quite prepared to include contemporary themes so long as they were dealt with in this fashion, but insisted that the painter must speak to *them*, that he had, as it were, a duty toward the observer. The progressive group, however, associating this attitude with the horrors of contemporary popular art, vigorously denied all such assumptions. This rejection was proven to be justified, for the art which even the best of their antagonists wanted was, in the current state of society, impossible. A new or refreshed idealism, expressed imaginatively, was out of the question.

The objective naturalism of Courbet with its powerful frontal attack on an enfeebled tradition was responsible for a reappraisal of what art could be in modern times, and served as an inspiration to the generation which was actually to achieve the transition to newer and more stimulating forms. The finicky realisms of the academic genre painters against which they were reacting were leading art toward a perfectionism, a form of "art for art's sake," which was almost mechanical in its accuracy. In the hands of uninspired but highly trained artists, imitation rather than creation was being set up as a goal, and this was clearly a path leading to disaster.

The danger inherent in such attempts to counterfeit reality was underlined by the rapid development of photography.[16] The camera became popular with astonishing rapidity because it seemed to be a marvelously quick and inexpensive way to do what many of the academic painters were doing "by hand." In one sense, the photograph was the quintessence of realism, for it was a relatively nonhuman recorder of what the eye saw, untroubled, in the process of reproduction, by any interference from the mind.

---

the expression" (Malraux, *Musée imaginaire*, p. 79). In the sense that the object is regarded as being important only for what the artist's individuality will do to it, this is true, but it was also a way of observing, for it is well known that we see only what we are interested in seeing. A doctor and an artist looking at the same fat man will see quite different things with different meanings attached to them.

[15] Eugène Loudun's review of the Exposition Universelle of 1855 is a fair example: "What M. Courbet is looking for is the representation of people as they are, as ugly and as gross as he encounters them; in fact, the commoner

they are the more he is attracted to the painting of them, it is one reason more; but everything is at the end of his brush, there is nothing generous, nothing lofty, nothing moral in the head which guides his hand; he invents nothing, has no imagination; he only has craft, he is only a workman in painting as others are in furniture and shoes" (Eugène Loudun, *Exposition Universelle des beaux- arts. Le Salon de 1855*, Paris, 1855, p. 140).

[16] The process was first given to the French public in 1839. The expansion of the photographic industry in the next twenty years was phenomenal.

Later, the photographer's control over the camera as an artistic instrument established the technique as an art in itself, but in the early years it was its mechanical ability to represent with the greatest accuracy which was the source of its fascination; the average untrained observer, then as always, got a very real pleasure in sheer recognition. As Gisèle Freund has pointed out,[17] it was this fact which made it so acceptable to the bourgeois, the more so since its products were infinitely cheap in comparison with the high cost of an artist's handiwork.

As will be seen presently, this new medium was a direct threat to those artists who were merely producing involved and finished technical imitations at the other end of the scale from pure art in which temperament and formal considerations were the chief factors. By contrast and analogy, therefore, it served to reveal how wide the gap actually was between conservative and progressive practice in this period. The men, both artists and critics, who really knew what painting was, and what it could and should do, were not in the least concerned about the camera for they didn't see it as a rival at all, but a sort of sister art which might in time have a very fruitful development. Delacroix, the greatest of the traditionalists, was actually very much interested in it, believing that it could be of great assistance to the painter as a sort of ultrarapid sketching medium,[18] and many of the new generation, Degas for example, made extensive use of it without in any sense surrendering their own individuality or creative independence. Nadar, who was a caricaturist himself, turned to photography, but it in no way affected his artistic judgment as a critic.[19]

Until a great deal more is known about the exact influence of the camera on the development of nineteenth century art, it will be dangerous to make too many generalizations, but it would seem that it may have aided the progressives by revealing the weakness of the popular art which they were combatting so vigorously. Delaroche's reaction to it at first was one of fright: "Painting is dead from this day on";[20] and Paul de St. Victor was equally worried twenty years later: "Photography ruins art, it prostitutes taste and vision, it discourages the engraver whose slow and careful tool cannot fight against its dexterity and its legerdemain contrivances."[21] The rising reputation of

[17] Gisèle Freund, *La Photographie en France au dix-neuvième siècle*, Paris, 1936, p. 7, and elsewhere. The author is very much indebted to this fascinating book in the discussion which follows. There is also much useful information on this aspect of nineteenth century photography in Erich Stenger's *The History of Photography*, trans. by E. Epstean, Easton, 1939. See also the excellent publications of Beaumont Newhall.

[18] Delacroix was a member of the Société Héliographique (Freund, *op.cit.*, p. 74). He saw in it a "precious auxiliary" for art but it was not art itself since the spirit and not the external appearance of things was the basic element. The idea that it was a separate art in its own right took hold slowly but surely. A lawsuit to settle the question occurred in 1862

(Freund, p. 130). A group of artists drew up a statement to the effect that it was not, but Delacroix refused to sign.

[19] Felix Tournachon, the author of *Nadar jury au Salon* previously cited in connection with Courbet. A large number of artists and literary figures sat for him.

[20] Stenger, *op.cit.*, p. 182. "The beautiful execution of the photographic picture is an achievement surpassing any other kind of presentation." He recovered very rapidly, though, for in the same year he told Louis Arago that it was a "boon" for the artist (Stenger, p. 74).

[21] *Ibid.*, p. 184. Engraving was apparently valued more as a reproductive process than as an original graphic art in its own right (Cf. Ph. Burty, "Exposition de la Société Française de Photographie," *Gazette des beaux-arts*, Vol.

the popular photographers, who were making large sums of money out of a brisk trade in portraits and genre scenes for bourgeois patrons, very soon led to the challenge direct: i.e. whether photography couldn't do what the artists were doing, and do it just as well at much less expense. The following passage from Disderi's *L'Art de la photographie* of 1862, is significant in many ways, not the least of which is the list of artists with whom the author feels he can compete:

In an immense studio, perfectly fitted out, could not the photographer, master of all light effects, by means of shades and reflectors, supplied with backgrounds of all sorts, decorations, accessories, costumes, with intelligent properly dressed models, could he not compose genre pictures, historical scenes? Could he not seek feeling like Scheffer, style like M. Ingres? Might he not deal with history like Paul Delaroche in his picture of *La Mort du Duc de Guise?*[22]

"Style like M. Ingres" was out of the question, but the rest of the claim was not too wide of the mark.

It might be thought that the camera menaced the realism of the Champfleury type, and it is possible that it did serve to shorten its life, although the objective naturalists felt that no mechanical contrivance could really grasp the essence of reality. The fact is, however, that in 1855 the attendance at Courbet's show, so prominently labeled "Realism," was very meager whereas the galleries exhibiting the photographs were thronged.[23] There was no doubt that the people were interested in some kinds of realism, and had there been no photograph, the artistic form might conceivably have lasted longer. This is not to say that Courbet's painting was in direct competition; far from it. However objective his friends may have said his work was, it was always essentially painterly. But that part of their doctrine concerned with seeing the world unflinchingly in all its imperfection and ugliness may easily have been undermined by the advent of a process which did exactly that. The reasons for the very short existence of the full objective naturalist theory are not entirely plain, but this may have been a contributing factor.

It is possible that the photograph actually performed a service for modern art in siphoning off part of the interest in a straight fidelity to nature into another medium altogether. But although it was far removed from certain ideas behind pure painting, in another way it was very close to an important characteristic marking the new art from the beginning—that is, complete neutrality toward content. Since photography was still essentially mechanical, it could not idealize successfully, nor could it imagine or interpret in the sense understood by painters.[24] Objectivity was inherent in it, and

---

II, 1859, pp. 209-221). By 1867 he was saying that the photograph indicated the close and inevitable end of the art of engraving (Burty, "La Gravure et la photographie," *Gazette des beaux-arts*, Vol. XXIII, 1867, pp. 252-271).

[22] Freund, *op.cit.*, pp. 95-96.

[23] *Ibid.*, p. 105.

[24] The efforts to overcome this handicap by photographing expression on the models'

faces were essentially ludicrous. The Disderi plan came to nought. Freund makes it plain that in the early years the photographers borrowed as many of the painter's tricks as they could adapt to the new medium. The lack of ability to idealize via the photograph was emphasized by a law passed in 1850 forbidding the sale of photographs of nudes (Freund, *op.cit.*, p. 132).

its products had some of the cool imperturbability of science itself. At the same time, a lack of interest in human welfare as a theme for art was becoming increasingly apparent in the progressive branch of French painting. The rise of landscape, the nature of objective naturalism, and the final equation of importance among all subjects have already been mentioned, and though the development was in no way the result of the mechanical objectivity of the camera, the two were parallel in their lack of spiritual concern over the object.

In painting, the trend may be partly explained by the reaction in certain quarters to the collapse of liberalism after 1848, and a distaste for the ethics of the bourgeoisie which seemed everywhere triumphant.[25] This unmoral attitude is apparent in Gautier's introduction to *Mademoiselle de Maupin* cited above,[26] while for Baudelaire the most essentially modern figure was the dandy whose glacial calm lent an air of superiority to a frame of mind which was, presumably, not much interested in anything.[27] Since the disappointed liberals felt that religion and the classical virtues—at least in art—were dead, and found the social codes of business both crass and philistine, there was scarcely any other moral system they could adopt other than a socialistic one. But here the idea of art at the service of society was so repulsive that it could not even be seriously considered. As Zola said in reply to Proudhon, "We [the artists] are not at the service of anybody, and we refuse to enter yours."[28] The Goncourts round out the position by saying, "To ask a work of art to serve something, is almost to have the ideas of the man who had the *Naufrage de la Méduse* (Fig. 10) made into a clock picture with the face in the sail."[29] The only thing for the artist to do was to make his own decisions, express his own individuality, and let matters take their course. Neutrality in regard to subject was common to both objective naturalism and pure painting, but in the case of the former it was intentionally unbiased in somewhat the same fashion as scientific inquiry, whereas in the latter it was chiefly the result of a lack of interest in moral questions and a distaste for most of the art which dealt with them. In some instances, a definite antagonism to ordinary morality served to upset this indifference, turning neutrality into a definite satanism. The work of Félicien Rops was possibly the outstanding example in the field of art, and it was not uncommon in literature as well.[30]

If pure painting is characteristic of much modern art, the work of Manet can well

[25] Cf. Guérard, *Art for Art's Sake*, Chap. IV, and R. C. Binkley, *Realism and Nationalism*, p. 1.

[26] "The great pretence of morality which reigns nowadays would be very funny, were it not very wearisome" (Th. Gautier, *Mademoiselle de Maupin*, trans. by F. C. DeSumichrast, N.Y., 1900, Preface, p. 47).

[27] "The dandy aspires to insensibility" (quoted from Konody, *The Painter of Victorian Life*, p. 47). Baudelaire was fascinated by the idea of a character which was at once the center of society and completely independent of it.

[28] Zola, *Mes haines* (ed. Charpentier), 1895, p. 27. The whole paragraph is an excellent statement of the pure painter's position.

[29] E. and J. de Goncourt, *Idées et sensations*, Paris (Charpentier), 1877, p. 232. (The book was written in 1866.)

[30] "Rops is the only true artist . . . I have found in Belgium," Baudelaire, letter to Manet, May 11, 1865, in *Lettres 1841-1866*, Paris (Mercure de France), 1907, p. 435.

serve as an introduction to it, while the criticism he received will illustrate the manner in which it was received at the time. As will be seen later, the greater part of this criticism was adverse, but there were several important critics who defended both the painter and the type of art which came from his brush. Baudelaire and Zola were the most famous, but Astruc, Privat, and the Goncourts spoke in his favor and seemed to understand quite clearly what he was doing.

The Goncourt brothers were particularly important in this respect, for although they seem not to have written a great deal about his work at the time,[31] they were in a large measure responsible for the creation of a critical environment in which it could be appreciated at its true worth.[32] They undoubtedly shared some of Baudelaire's feeling for an art individually created and enjoyed for its own sake and no other, for they wrote in their *Journal*: "It is indeed curious that it should be the four men the least tainted by any trade, by any industrialism, the four pens vowed most completely to art, who have been arraigned on the benches of the correctional police: Baudelaire, Flaubert, and ourselves."[33] Gautier also may have influenced them, but whatever the background of their opinions, by the early 'fifties "they were adepts of the doctrine of *l'art pour l'art.*"[34] In their review of the Salon of 1852, they state their partisanship of realism "but not realism sought exclusively in the ugly."[35] Objective naturalism was not for them; Courbet remained in disgrace as late as '67: "Nothing, nothing, and nothing in this show of Courbet's . . . the ugly then, always the ugly, and the bourgeois ugliness, ugliness without its great character, without the beauty of ugliness."[36] The art of ideas in a traditional sense fared no better, for they rejected any notion that painting was a book, a "painted language of thought," and asserted that it was rather a delight to the eye with a function of "vivifying form by color."[37] What they were looking for was, as Sabatier says, "an expressive realism, idealistic in the sense of the quintessential, a realism seen from the artist's perspective."[38] In *Manette Salomon* (1867) they pointed out that the art of the hero Coriolis—who was, in a sense, their mouthpiece—was not well received in 1855 because of a kind of conspiracy not to appreciate "the new realism which he brought, a realism sought outside the stupidity of the daguerreotype, outside the charlatanry of the ugly, a realism which strove to draw contemporary style

[31] Sabatier, in his *Esthétique des Goncourts* (Paris, 1920, p. 536), gives the impression that it was considerable, but the present author is unable to find it in material to which he has had access. There is no mention of Manet in the *Journals* during this period. In actual practice, the taste of the brothers was erratic, to say the least. Their admiration for De Nittis is a little hard to understand, but in such highly personal reactions as theirs, consistency is not necessarily to be expected.

[32] See below, Chaps. XVII, XVIII. There were a number of critics who understood and admired his work in the 'sixties.

[33] P. Sabatier, *op.cit.*, pp. 77-78. Quoted

from the *Journals*, Vol. I, p. 358.

[34] Sabatier, *op.cit.*, p. 68. The phrase is Sabatier's. It means something akin to "pure painting." It would seem to be more valid in regard to their artistic views than those of Gautier.

[35] E. and J. de Goncourt, *Études d'art*, Paris, n.d., p. 8, "Le Salon de 1852."

[36] E. and J. de Goncourt, *Journal des Goncourt*, Paris (Charpentier), 1891, Vol. III (1866-70), p. 164. The entry is for Sept. 18, 1867.

[37] In the preface to "La Peinture à l'exposition de 1855," *Préfaces et manifestes littéraires*, pp. 243-244.

[38] Sabatier, *op.cit.*, p. 437.

from the typical form—selected and expressive of contemporary images."[39] Objective naturalism was to be transformed by the artist's sensitivity into something which was ideal, not in a moral sense, but in terms of style. Painting was to renounce rules and traditions, it was to be the product of the individual temperament, and though a certain interest in matters social, or even moral, was not ruled out, it was never to be the chief purpose of the work.[40] Their search for subtle essences of personal interpretation, for nuances perceptible only to the sensitive eye, led them to a taste for an oddly assorted group among the painters of the day: Rops, Degas, Raffaelli, Moreau (whom they noticed as early as 1852), Decamps (they approved of orientalists who showed imagination) and de Nittis, and finally to the conclusion that landscape was, after all, the type par excellence for moderns.[41] In the graphic arts they admired Daumier, but most of all their good friend Gavarni to whose life and work they devoted an extended study.[42] Something of what Baudelaire saw in Guys—the man who saw the essence of contemporary life—they found in Gavarni. Like themselves he was "aristocratic," and to a degree pessimistic, observing the world with an even candour and wry wit. The very diversity of their artistic enthusiasms, and the lack of any "system" in their taste, are both prophetic of a later critical tendency to praise and enjoy the amazingly varied output of western art of more recent years.

The most powerful voice raised in defense of the art of Manet was that of Émile Zola. "It seems," he said, "that I am the first to praise M. Manet unrestrainedly,"[43] and although this was not entirely true, he aroused a critical storm of far greater proportions than had been stirred up by the earlier notices of Gautier, Astruc, and Privat. He had the insight to see that something new and important was going on, and that the earlier revolution caused by the realist episode was now succeeded by a different one which, although it owed much to what had happened in the 'fifties, was different and represented a further advance away from traditional principles. For all that he referred to the painter from Ornans as "mon Courbet,"[44] he included him among "the fallen ones" in 1866, reproaching him for not keeping up to the high level of his work of the previous decade.[45] Realism was not the only issue, or even the most important; actually temperament was the thing.[46] Since nature did not change, the seat of value had to lie in man's reaction to it.[47] In objective naturalism he saw little room for this individualism since nature was dominant, not the painter.[48] Courbet's naturalism of

[39] E. and J. de Goncourt, *Manette Salomon* (Charpentier), 1910, p. 331.

[40] Sabatier, *op.cit.*, pp. 364ff.

[41] Goncourts, *Études*, pp. 167ff.

[42] E. and J. de Goncourt, *Gavarni, l'homme et l'oeuvre*, Paris (Charpentier), 1896.

[43] Zola, *Mes haines* (ed. Le Blond), p. 218, "Mon Salon." In the sense that he was the first to find *nothing* wrong with Manet, this may have been true. Gautier's favorable notice of '61 was now out of the question in the light of what he had said later. See also Astruc's remarks in 1863, quoted on p. 192.

[44] *Ibid.* (ed. Charpentier, 1895), p. 34.

[45] *Ibid.* (Charpentier), p. 310.

[46] *Ibid.*, p. 300.

[47] *Ibid.*, p. 281.

[48] *Ibid.*, p. 224. Here he objects to Taine's system on the grounds that where natural laws and environment control everything, where is the place for the individual? But he wants a basis in the real world: "Painting dreams is children's and women's sport, men are charged with painting realities" (*ibid.*, p. 300).

the 'fifties was, for him, chiefly an expression of individuality, and this Zola admired, but Manet, the man whose temperament more obviously *transformed* this same nature, was superior: "He [Manet] treats figure paintings as it is permitted in the schools to treat still-life; I mean that he groups the figures before him, somewhat haphazardly, and that he has no other desire than to fix them on the canvas as he sees them, with lively contrasts which they make by separating themselves from each other."[49] The artist was a sort of visual analyst, and is compared to a scientist in this respect.[50] Zola has, in fact, been described as having a certain "scientific" bent as evidenced, for example, by his preface to the second edition of *Thérèse Raquin* (1868),[51] but at this stage in his career it would seem that in painting, the subjective side was of greater interest. His pleasure in the art of Pissarro is founded on exactly the same individual basis: "Here the originality is profoundly human . . . it resides in the temperament of the painter himself."[52] Courbet, he felt, had deserted the cause in the 'sixties,[53] and Manet was the new hero along with his friends of the Café Guerbois. His views constitute a further proof of the short life of objective naturalism.

Although it is probable that Zola was influenced by the Goncourts (who certainly affected his literary ideas), his bolder and more pugnacious criticism does not carry the same air of acute sensitivity to emotional stimuli carried to almost unhealthy extremes.[54] In his attack on the entire philosophical position of "social art" which has already been mentioned ("your communality and your equality nauseate us"),[55] he praised Courbet for reasons almost exactly opposite to those advanced by Proudhon. The definition of art as a means toward the moral and physical betterment of mankind is replaced by another: "A work of art is a corner of creation seen through a temperament."[56] He sets the artist free: free of social obligations, free of moral compulsions, free to be himself, a self which the public can accept or reject as it likes:

> I am an artist, and I give you my flesh and blood, my heart and thought. I put myself naked before you, I give myself up good or bad. If you wish to be instructed, look at me, applaud or hiss, let my example be an encouragement or a lesson. What more do you want of me?[57]

Zola sees the artist as a creature apart, a being whose thoughts are "absolute," who leaps to perfection in one bound and attains the ideal in his dreams.[58] His indifference to public opinion in any form and the equality of goodness and badness are both instructive.

If Zola's words were at all prophetic of the future course of art and criticism, and they seem to have been, then here was the *coup de grâce* to the traditional view of the artist as a man speaking in a tongue which people not only can understand rationally,

---

[49] *Ibid.*, p. 346.   [50] *Ibid.*, pp. 346-347.

[51] "Above all else, my aim has been scientific." Here quoted from Fernand Doucet, *L'Esthétique d'Émile Zola et son application à la critique*, The Hague, 1923, p. 140.

[52] Zola, *Mes haines* (Charpentier), p. 320.

[53] *Ibid.*, p. 313.

[54] Zola did not actually meet the Goncourts until 1868. *Germinie Lacerteux* (1865) apparently had a great effect on his thinking. Cf. Sabatier, *op.cit.*, p. 552.

[55] Zola, *Mes haines* (Charpentier), p. 27.

[56] *Ibid.*, p. 25.

[57] *Ibid.*, pp. 25-26.   [58] *Ibid.*, pp. 39-40.

but by understanding, be delighted, uplifted, and spiritually moved. It also puts an end to the optimistic view that the artist is going to use his gifts to help society emerge from a state of confusion and trouble. He becomes a complete entity in himself, responsible only to his own soul and art, disdaining the approval or censure of the nonartist. His lonely state, deplored by Proudhon, is here made into a virtue of the highest order. Zola's artist was, in truth, of his age, but in 1866 he was born too soon.

The vigor and boldness of these opinions caused a storm almost as intense as that which had sprung up over the paintings themselves. The author had to leave the staff of *L'Événement* for the time being as a result of the outrage which he had committed against the sensibilities of the French public,[59] although *L'Artiste*, with a bravery similar to that which had allowed the earlier piece by Champfleury, printed his views toward the end of the year over another editorial disclaimer.[60] Even Théodore Duret, the future historian of the *avant-garde*, was not yet as enthusiastic as this, for in 1867 he takes a somewhat condescending attitude toward the much abused artist and says that though he has merit, he has erred in starting to paint before he really has mastered the manner of doing it.[61] The two critics are in agreement, however, on the broader principles: "the superior painter is yet one who, at the same time in which he succeeds in fixing a personal emotion on the canvas, finds that he has an original style with which to express it."[62] The early individualists were martyred for this devotion to their own sensitivity, but it was their creed and could not be surrendered however fierce the storm.

By 1870 the main outlines of the new theory about the nature and purpose of painting were clear enough, even though they were as yet the property of a very few people. The very boldness of the steps necessary to establish such an art prevented all but the most sympathetic eyes from seeing that it was actually the only possible solution to the problems of which nearly everyone was aware. The courage necessary to abandon the safety of the practices of the past and endure ridicule and poverty for the sake of being the honest and devoted exponents of pure art and personal expressiveness was great indeed, and won for these artists an heroic place in the history of art. Their freshness and vigor, which were in such sharp contrast to the palid charms of the traditionalists, eventually obtained the acclaim of the entire artistic world and the few early voices lifted in behalf of their revolutionary attitude gradually swelled to a great chorus of approval. This is not the place to give an account of the later formulations of modern theory which eventually found a place for a more varied and difficult artistic output

[59] The public was most infuriated because Zola chose to speak principally of an artist who had been excluded from the Salon entirely. See below, chapters on Manet.

[60] É. Zola, "Une nouvelle manière en peinture. Édouard Manet," *L'Artiste*, 8e série, Vol. XIII, 1866, pp. 43-64. (At this time the title of this journal was *Revue du XIXe siècle*. The bound volumes are, however, numbered consecutively in spite of this temporary change of name.) The notice said: "*La Revue du XIXe Siècle* has its doctrines but it also has its free tribune to which it invites the expression of all opinions on art. That is why it prints this bold study" (p. 43).

[61] Théodore Duret, *Les Peintres français en 1867*, Paris, 1867, p. 108. Duret devotes a whole chapter to Manet.

[62] *Ibid.*, p. 23.

than the west had ever seen before, but the foregoing account shows how those formulations were made possible. When the artist had cut himself off from the past with its gods and saints, when he had declared his allegiance to himself and his own age, when he had made it plain that the subject was not important except as a basis for the picture which could be made from it, when all objects whether living or not were demonstrated to be of equal interest, when artistic excellence was to be judged on the degree of individuality exhibited rather than the moral or dramatic interpretation offered, when the physically ugly was as beautiful as the handsome, when art had been readjusted to the conditions of a new and changing social scene, when moral responsibility had been rejected—when all this had been accomplished, and not before, then the way to modern art lay open. These alterations were of momentous importance, not only for the new liberty and vitality which they brought to painting, but also for the concepts of humanitarianism and idealism which they left behind.[63]

It must not be assumed from this that the art which abandoned the traditional spiritual bases for creation was, by that fact, inferior. On the contrary, having relieved itself of the dead weight of outworn and apparently unsuitable ideas inherited from a vastly different past, it promptly sprang up full of new vigor and produced such interesting and compelling results that that which was left behind was not only not missed, it came to be regarded as having been a hindrance.

If, however, art was here reflecting a similar ammorality on the part of society as a whole, then there was a deeper problem involved which men could ignore or leave unsolved at their peril. This was the problem—to state it in only one of many possible ways—of progress unregulated by some cogent form of moral idealism. We shall return to this matter in the last chapter of the book.

[63] Before leaving the topic of pure painting, special mention may be made of a book published during this period which contains interesting ideas on the subject, namely Rodolphe Töpffer's *Réflexions et menus propos d'un peintre genevois* (Paris, 1848), which appeared two years after the author's death. It is a rather sprightly essay on aesthetics which, as Albert Aubert remarks in the preface, is mainly made up of digressions. In one of these (Book 5, Chap. xxiv), the author vehemently attacks the doctrine of "art for art's sake," condemning it on the grounds of a lack of those qualities of thought, morality, and spiritual beauty which are essential to fine art, a position which was traditional enough, especially in view of his obvious sympathy for the idea of *ut pictura poesis* discussed in an earlier chapter (Book 4, Chap. IX). But in his appreciation of the qualities inherent in the art of children, and in his claim that a sketch or simple drawing can produce vivid impressions of the beautiful—that is, that completeness, as such, is not necessary to a work of art—he is essentially modern. Art, he says, does not have to be particularly imitative since representations of natural objects are only signs, and the experience of the beautiful comes, not from the object, but its transformation into the sign (Book 6, Chap. xxiii). (For an account of the influence of this book, see M. Schapiro, "Courbet and Popular Imagery," *Journal of the Warburg and Courtauld Institutes*, Vol. IV, 1941, pp. 178-179.)

IX. LANDSCAPE

LANDSCAPE offered both artists and critics a relief from the dilemma imposed by the changes in the social world. The painting of nature, or scenery, could be all things to all men, and so the bitter antagonisms which arose over ideas about man himself were notably absent in the discussion of the work of the great "paysagistes." Basically, the difference in the way the two forms were received lay in a distinction between two worlds: that of human activity, and that of nature. The former seemed to be in a state of flux, while the latter, except as affected by man's enterprise, appeared changeless, eternal, and offered a charming escape from the press of affairs. The ferment of social ideas, the growth of industrial populations, and concentration of great wealth, the changes in modes of living caused by applied science—these and other related factors were imparting a certain urgency to the life of the individual without anyone's being too sure what was going to come of it all, or seeing very clearly what kind of a society would emerge when things had settled down, but nature remained beyond the reach of this turmoil. To many, she seemed both well ordered and serene by comparison; Castagnary went so far as to maintain that the revival of French landscape was a direct result of the fact that society, disgusted with itself, sought the quiet calm of the fields and woods as an escape.[1] His comment on a picture by Jeanron, *La Pose du télégraphe électrique dans les rochers du Cap Gris-Nez* (1857), is a classic example of the reaction of an intelligent humanitarian critic to the intrusion, in art, of commercial activity upon natural beauty: "[The picture] is a firm and vigorous landscape which merits but a single reproach, but an essential one. Why the electric telegraph? What does it signify, I do not say in this canvas, but in any canvas? What is there in common between this thread of brass, this industrial, useful product, and landscape, the refinement and expression of the beautiful in nature? It is evidently nonsense. If landscape admitted threads, they could only be gossamer ones."[2] The Goncourts displayed a somewhat similar attitude when they explained the triumph of this form of art on the grounds that after man has abused and violated nature in a physical sense, his spirit turns to her again in art.[3]

But in spite of a certain interest in landscape, most people remained predominantly bound up in their own affairs, and thus naturally took a more vivid interest in what others thought of their social position, customs, appearance, moral standards, ways of earning money, and, indeed, in the whole structure of the society to which they belonged. For this reason they were particularly sensitive to paintings dealing with such matters in which they were, in a sense, reflected.[4] Whether this reflection was

[1] Castagnary, *Salons*, p. 17, "Le Salon de 1857."

[2] *Ibid.*, p. 59.

[3] Goncourts, *Études d'art*, p. 177, "La Peinture à l'Exposition de 1855."

[4] The reaction to Courbet's *Enterrement à Ornans* was an excellent example. The worthy folk who had posed for it were rather staggered to learn what brutes they were in the eyes of the Parisians. Even Champfleury, who thought it a great picture, referred to it as the "masterpiece of the ugly" and said it wasn't the painter's fault if provincial life made people so grotesque. It took a bold man to

direct, or only by implication, they looked to see whether it was distorted or not, or rather, to decide whether it was sufficiently idealized to render its contemplation pleasurable. In such pictures as these, they sensed a comment by the artist either on themselves or mankind in general.[5] The choice of subject, the class to which the characters belonged, the manner in which they were presented, the details which were included or omitted, the ugliness or beauty of the faces—all these seemed to add up to an opinion about the social state of affairs, even though this might not have been the conscious purpose of the artist. In the case of certain painters, this presumed opinion expressed in the picture could not fail to antagonize many observers.[6] A part, at least, of the opposition to Courbet's pictures, and the suspicion of socialism attached to them, was the result of reading into them such judgments upon society, which may or may not have been actually present.[7] Far more agreeable, therefore, was that art whose comment, real or implied, was connected with persons from other lands or distant times about whom anyone was free to hold whatever opinions he chose.[8] An artist who elected to paint the personages of his own environment had to count on arousing the preferences and prejudices which individuals entertain about themselves and others, and take his chances on the results. As subjects for art, the dead and the distant were far safer than the living and the near.

In the case of landscape, on the other hand, man was involved mainly through his feelings as he projected himself into the scene and enjoyed it much as he would the countryside if he were actually in it. When actually represented in its midst, he was rather a part of the whole than a superior creature, as Duret observed in his review of French painting in 1867:

I come now to an examination of the group of painters in which the truest and most marked individuality of the modern French school resides, the group of painters who depict inanimate nature, landscape; or, if they paint animals and man himself, do not separate them in their pictures from the exterior world in which they are placed, but, on the contrary, bind them intimately to it, and thus reproduce scenes in which the actors and the theater complete each other, and the one is explained by the other.[9]

---

attempt the same kind of honesty in regard to the Paris public itself, which was, presumably, not much handsomer (Champfleury, *Grandes figures d'hier et d'aujour-d'hui*, Paris, 1861, p. 242).

[5] The adverse reactions to the *Homme à la houe*—who was a noble figure in Millet's eyes—included the following: "*L'Homme à la houe* exceeds the limits of ugliness and even those of truth. . . . This man is affected with idiocy. . . . He makes you sick to look at him" (C. de Sault, *Essais de critique d'art. Salon de 1863*, Paris, 1864, pp. 100-101). Thoré actually said that Courbet's art was regarded as being critical of the ruling class (*Salons de W. Bürger*, Vol. I, p. 417, "Le Salon de 1863").

[6] Millet and Courbet were not alone, for Manet received equally harsh judgments on this score. The *Olympia* portrayed a type only too well known to many of the worthy bourgeois visiting the Salon.

[7] The extent of Courbet's actual support of socialism is a somewhat debatable point in spite of his friendship for Proudhon.

[8] Delaroche, Meissonier, Vernet, and the orientalists dealt with subjects in which such touchy matters as the present state of society (except perhaps in its officially successful guise) were not at issue, and their contemporary popularity is well known.

[9] Duret, *Les Peintres français en 1867*, p. 21.

Not all landscapes were regarded as suitable. Courbet was occasionally criticized for representing the harsh and treeless aspect of his native countryside (Fig. 29),[10] and even Rousseau was censured for painting a nature too wild and harsh for perfect enjoyment. But these were minor in comparison to the general approbation accorded an art which was taking a fresh look at sky, trees, hills, and water. For the majority of critics this was an enjoyable and healthy development, but to show nature more nearly as she looked was a far different matter from doing the same thing for human beings. Landscape furnished an imaginative outlet, an escape from worldly sordidness, but the painting of contemporary people engaged in their daily affairs was no escape whatever, and often served instead as a reminder of things more pleasantly left forgotten.[11] If the seamy side of existence was to be exhibited at all, it must either be made attractive through the addition of beauty or sentiment,[12] or else dealt with satirically as by the great caricaturists. The painter of landscape was under no such compulsion, for the presentation of a twisted oak did not involve the *amour-propre* of the beholder as did the rough body of Millet's *Semeur* (Fig. 27) or the fleshy magnitude of Courbet's *Baigneuses* (Fig. 32). The distinction was a fundamental one and explains, for example, why Thoré admired Chintreuil's experiments with light, but found Manet's *Bain* (*Le Déjeuner sur l'herbe*, Fig. 59) "to be of a highly improper taste."[13]

The origins of modern French landscape have usually been associated, correctly, with the work of Corot, Rousseau, Daubigny, Diaz, and their friends. In spite of the fact that they were a distinctly diverse group when considered as personalities, they shared a love for nature in its actual rather than its imaginary forms, and saw it as the individuals they were, rather than through the eyes of tradition. This is not to say that Corot was uninfluenced by Claude, or that Rousseau got nothing from Ruysdael, or that none of them were influenced by the English, but their work as a whole was fresh, original, and comparatively free from the stylistic stereotypes that had dominated this form of art since the seventeenth century.

To explain the appearance of this particular group at just this time is no easy matter. It was, of course, true that a strong tide of interest in nature and man's personal relation to it had set in during the eighteenth century, a tide which was deepened and directed by the thought and writings of Jean Jacques Rousseau. He did much to enrich man's capacity to feel and to be emotionally moved by the sight of mountains, streams, fields, and sky. It would be hard to deny that the great developments in the art of landscape around the turn of the century were not in some measure due to a new awareness of nature which he had planted in men's minds, just as some of the

[10] Eugène Loudun, *Le Salon de 1852*, p. 8. Apropos of *Les Demoiselles de village*, he says: "One cannot imagine an uglier, more barren, more disagreeable landscape."

[11] Cf. Bougot, *Essai sur la critique d'art*, pp. 359-360. People have to escape from their daily lives.

[12] Breton's popularity with the conservative critics is instructive; see below, Chap. XIV.

[13] T. Thoré, *Salons de W. Bürger*, Vol. I, pp. 425, 427, section IV of the review of the Salon of 1863 called "Le Salon des reprouvés." He gave Chintreuil a good notice in 1861 and again in 1864. This painter could well be re-studied.

quality of Wordsworth's poetry can be traced to the same source. The new conception of scenery which he set forth became so widely influential that it would be logical to see its influence in the work of water-colorists like Girtin and Cotman as well as in the great sketches of Constable. It is customary to say that this freshness of vision came later to the French, but it is a significant fact that the painter Valenciennes, a classical landscapist of the purest dye, painted studies in Italy in the 'eighties which have a clarity and vividness recalling the early Roman work of Corot.

The new naturalism seems to have appeared first in sketches, in informal private pictures rather than the completed canvases meant for public inspection. It was so with Valenciennes, and even truer of Constable, whose finest work is to be found there rather than in his larger and more finished canvases. Corot also seems at his best when he is informal and painting largely for his own satisfaction. Eventually this type of casual and apparently sketchy landscape triumphed over the other more meticulous form by virtue of its greater spontaneity and liveliness, for it carried a more intense effect of natural appearance.

Strangely enough, although literary romanticism was marked by a strong interest in scenery, especially of the wilder sort, it was not characteristic of French romantic painting. In Germany, Caspar David Friedrich delighted in rugged peaks, lonely forests, and cold moonlight, but Gros, Géricault, and the great Delacroix himself paid very little attention to them, nor did such lesser figures as Boulanger, the Deverias, and Ary Scheffer. On the other hand, none of the leading Barbizon artists were closely associated with the literary romantic circle, and Corot, the most important, was notoriously aloof from general movements of this sort throughout his life. Yet, in a way, they too were romantics, at least in the sense that they found their emotional satisfactions through close contact, almost identification, with the world of nature. Essentially, they were painters of feelings, not ideas, whose sensations were aroused by direct experience with the earth and sky. Their delight was too spontaneous and natural to ever become doctrinaire. They left little theory for the guidance of those who came after, and if the results achieved, especially in the case of Rousseau, gave a rather startling impression of reality, that reality sprang from a whole-hearted admiration for natural prospects from which human passion and strife were excluded rather than from any materialistic interest in things as they really are. This individual interest in nature, a romantic trait if you like, was quite a different matter from the current scientific enthusiasm for it expressed through the new biology and the emergent theory of evolution.

It must be remembered, too, that the tradition in landscape was less firmly established than in the field of figure painting, and thus a transformation could be effected with less violent opposition. The neoclassicism of David had been only incidentally concerned with it, and the stylistic modes of Claude and Poussin on the one hand, and the Dutch on the other, had retained their dominance more through habit than by the application of principles deeply seated in a complex of ideas about the true nature of man.

The Barbizon artists were, naturally, treated with indifference or even hostility in some quarters, but this was due less to the fact that they were developing a type of landscape unencumbered by classical theory than to the originality with which their scenes were painted. To the die-hards of the Institute, who largely controlled the juries, originality in any form was dangerous, irrespective of what was involved. They saw to it that Rousseau was refused time and again,[14] and although Corot was accepted quite regularly, his canvases were placed so as to attract very little attention. The public appears to have been quite apathetic to these changes and the art which revealed them—a significant circumstance, for it proved that neither the public nor the critics who spoke for it regarded such pictures as a challenge to them or their way of life, something which could hardly be said of objective naturalism. The theory of classical landscape, which is not easily grasped, had probably been beyond them in the first place, so the new form may not even have seemed very different from the old. It was rather slowly, therefore, that it dawned on any considerable number of people that an important development had occurred, and as the new version became familiar, a few began to buy examples for their homes. The critics came to the artists' support quite early, and though they were never able to give Chintreuil the success they thought he deserved,[15] by the 'sixties they had established Corot, Rousseau, and Daubigny as authentic masters.

This change eventually left landscape in a position of equality with other types of subject matter formerly considered superior. Castagnary claimed even more than equality; he said that Troyon and Millet were the painters "who have made landscape the most important branch of the art of our times. . . . And that is why the roles are reversed today, why that which was formerly the lowest [now] occupies the first rank, why that which was at the summit now scarcely exists except in name."[16] But this was a stronger statement than most critics were at first willing to make: "Without claiming the first rank for landscape," said the more conservative Chesneau, "by analogy we can be convinced that in the future, contemporary French landscape will be the least contested claim to fame of our school of painting"[17]—a view which summed up the feeling of a good many others. The work in this field was the best that was being done anywhere, but the type was still considered by many to be an inferior one all the same. Looking for worth, the critics were willing to accept it where they could find it, but such art was definitely not the supreme excellence of which painting was capable. De Sault, reviewing the Salon of 1863, remarked rather unfairly that this form "best supports mediocrity," by which she meant that it was easier to do a picture of hills and clouds than it was to portray the passions of the human soul in a convincing manner. She continued: "Without having the rank and merit of great painting, it permits art

[14] This amounted almost to persecution in the 'forties.

[15] He finally got a medal in 1867.

[16] Castagnary, *Salons*, p. 72, "Le Salon de 1859." It is somewhat curious that he here makes Millet and Troyon the painters respon-

sible for the new importance of landscape. Nearly everyone else felt that Millet was a figure painter and Troyon was possibly the leading "animalier" of the day.

[17] E. Chesneau, *L'Art et les artistes modernes en France et en Angleterre*, pp. 198-199. *1864*

to become popular without vulgarizing itself through overtures to bad taste."[18] Even Baudelaire shared this prevalent view: "I will confess with all the world that the modern school of landscape is singularly strong and clever; but in this triumph, this predominance of an inferior type, in this silly cult of nature unpurified, unexplained by imagination, I see an evident sign of a general decline."[19] It would seem that the attitude toward landscape was somehow determined by the attitude toward the painting of the human form, for as long as the latter was all-important, the former could never rise above its inferior status. Eugène Loudun, a somewhat arrogant critic, offered a rather ingenious explanation for the growing esteem in which it was held:

> In our days landscape has achieved an importance and a development hitherto unknown. . . . We no longer look inward at ourselves, we turn our attention outward; the same is true in art, and to the extent that we forget how to portray the feelings of men, we become more skillful at representing inert nature, matter, and the brute. Our landscape school is superior, in its way, to our history painters.[20]

As the years went by and the fate of history painting became increasingly apparent to everyone, the hierarchy which had been created to glorify it became anachronistic. It was hard for the critics to go on singing the praises of an art form the current examples of which were so obviously dry and lifeless. Merit eventually won its own recognition, and if it had to be noted in forms which tradition said were of lesser value, so much the worse for tradition. The passages already quoted show the reluctance with which the believers in a more heroic art accepted the undeniable excellence of landscape, and exactly the same attitude was to be found in regard to genre, the mode in which the other part of the new movement was being expressed.[21] Since genius was traditionally associated with great art and great art alone, these new forms, however brilliant and original, could only exhibit talent. Fairly typical is the opinion of such a conservative as Maxime du Camp, who wrote in his Salon of 1857:

> Before beginning the examination of the works with which we will be occupied, it is well to say a word about a general symptom which leaps to the eyes of even the least clairvoyant. Apparently the search for the beautiful and the ideal, the aspiration toward a superior nature, the understanding of that living part which God has put in all things are vanishing, giving place to an extraordinary material cleverness; technique dominates art; the brain grows dim while the hand, agile and sure of itself, acquires, deepens, and puts to use the most difficult processes.[22]

[18] C. de Sault, *Essais*, pp. 142-143.
[19] Baudelaire, *Curiosités* (ed. Lévy), p. 326.
[20] E. Loudun, *Le Salon de 1855*, p. 156.
[21] As the old categories became more and more difficult to recognize, the language of the lesser critics becomes more and more confused. Albert de la Fizelière, describing Jules Breton, said: "There is a man who has entered great art at one shot. He has made himself the historian of agricultural labors" (Fizelière, *A-Z ou le Salon en miniature*, Paris, 1861, p. 15). This shows as clearly as any one quotation

could what had happened to ideas about the great tradition.

[22] Maxime Du Camp, *Le Salon de 1857*, Paris, n.d., p. 5. The word translated as "technique" in the quotation, is "métier" in the original. It signifies skill in handling the medium of paint; talent, therefore, rather than any kind of genius. It is probable that Du Camp is here referring both to *trompe-oeil* imitation and broader naturalism like Courbet's.

Albert de la Fizelière likewise declined to accept the new scale of values, but took a more optimistic view in 1861: "Genre painting, adopting the principles formulated by the landscape schools, in its turn enters on this fertile path at the end of which modern art must infallibly find the new form of historic and religious art."[23]

Thus modernism, if this term may be used to convey the idea of an art drawn directly from the times in which it is produced, appeared first in the humble field of landscape.[24] A return to nature as a source of inspiration was one of the basic ideas of the whole progressive current in criticism, and just such a return had been achieved by Corot, Rousseau, and their fellows. In fact, this approach became nearly universal among the landscapists as early as the 'forties, but it took far longer for a similar movement to gain great momentum among the figure painters.[25] In 1864 Castagnary is still hoping that now that landscape has triumphed, *tomorrow* art will enter the cities and deal with social customs. He is so disgusted with the figure painters that he fears the great revolution will never occur there at all, and the only evidence of the change will have to be found in an art which, though natural, is not human in his sense of the term.[26] Although his particular brand of naturalism never did become popular among artists, the turn away from tradition toward nature was eventually accomplished in the field of figure painting, but the upheaval necessary to effect it was far more deep-seated and severe, since a great deal more of human custom, prejudice, and thought was at stake. Man clung tenaciously to his illusions about himself.

[23] Fizelière, *op.cit.*, p. 5.
[24] I.e. "humble" in the traditional sense.
[25] The development in landscape occurred in the years from 1830 to 1848, but, as Rosenthal makes clear, figure painting was badly becalmed, as far as new developments were concerned, for the duration of the period he describes (Rosenthal, *Du romantisme au réalisme, passim*).
[26] Castagnary, *Salons*, p. 205, "Le Salon de 1864." For all his love of landscape, it was never entirely satisfying for him.

PART TWO. PRACTICE

X. FROM IDEAS TO PAINTING

IN Part One the main critical attitudes of the period following the year 1848 were set forth.[1] Many of them had originated in the quite remote past, others in the years immediately preceding, but in the majority of cases their embodiment in actual artistic practice did not occur earlier than the period of our discussion. The art of Courbet, Millet, Manet, and the others presently to be discussed, formed the transition from a subject matter largely controlled by traditional thinking to one whose characteristics may properly be called modern. The criticism accompanying this art, thus far considered largely in the abstract, was not, of course, intended to exist in a vacuum; it was designed to apply directly to contemporary activity. Unless the general honesty of these writers is to be called into question, we must believe that they sincerely intended to find out where art was going and why, as well as to outline the best courses for it to pursue. They looked closely and patiently at vast numbers of pictures, talked with innumerable artists, visited their studios, and searched their own minds for explanations of problems and trends which they found both interesting and difficult.[2] They were nearly all taking some active part in the life of the changing social order of the middle of the century, and many of them attempted to see how such external forces as science and materialism were going to influence artistic activity. Whether the critic believed he was addressing the artist as a sort of advisor, or was speaking to the more or less uninformed spectator, is relatively immaterial; the important thing is that he was passing a contemporary judgment on the art of his fellows, and in the process was making plain the climate in which that art was being produced.[3] It is not necessary to decide here whether the critics led the artists or trailed behind them. There were probably instances of both kinds. Our purpose is to see what people

[1] The reader is referred to the Preface where the plan of the book is discussed. It seems advisable to touch again upon certain of the points raised earlier before entering into the account of the reception accorded the paintings themselves.

[2] By no means all of these are discussed in the present study. One of the most interesting is the matter of the sketch versus the "finished" work of art. This was one of the aspects of Delacroix's art which troubled the conservatives who regarded such bold brushwork as a sign that the artist's thought was not fully rounded. Corot was also accused of what might be called "sketchism," and this was one of the charges leveled at Manet. The idea that painting should show evident signs of passion or verve in its final form was abhorrent to those who regarded the art as being something capable of perfection. The critic who signed herself De Sault made a specific point of this in her review of the Salon of 1863. She quotes from a letter by Courbet appearing in the *Chronique des arts*, June 7, 1863, as follows: "My dear friend, at Saintonge I have made seventy or eighty sketches, or paintings only begun, of which two are at the Salon. But the picture of the *Curés* is the one which has the most significance on all counts and is the only one I wanted to show." De Sault takes offence at the idea that the artist should deliberately send unfinished pictures to the Salon and regards it as a direct abuse of his privilege (Courbet was, and had been, *hors concours*) (C. de Sault, *Essais*, pp. 95ff.). In those early days the latitude for technical experiment was far narrower than in the present century. One cannot help wondering what would have happened if a collage of newspaper, sand, and cardboard had been submitted.

[3] See Chapter II on the critic's purposes.

then living thought about this work, what the artists believed they were doing, and how the two sets of ideas appear when taken together. What follows, therefore, will not be a history of French painting of the period, but rather a study of what certain artists did, in the light of the critical opinions of the time and in comparison to certain traditional theories against which they were reacting.

The verdicts reached about them did not always coincide with those of later years, but it must not be assumed for that reason that these conclusions were unintelligent.[4] In the broad view of social history, we may be said to be living in the same age, even though the last hundred years have emphasized some aspects of life which the citizens of the Second Empire thought of lesser importance, and we must realize that they were, in a special way, much closer to the past than we. If this period was one which made a decisive break with tradition, and that is the contention of this study of it, then the artists, and the men who studied what they were doing, were in its shadow to a far greater extent than is the case today. It might even be said that we may have lost the capacity for a full understanding of some characteristics of that tradition almost altogether, or if we have not, we can usually know them only intellectually or scientifically, not emotionally. The modern student of the arts is vastly better acquainted with the meaning and history of the painting of previous epochs, but it is doubtful if he can *feel* it as well or be so deeply moved as his forebears were. We believe, very naturally, that the study and criticism of art have progressed along with everything else, and consequently incline to the view that our opinions on these matters are superior, but one may at least admit that the better writers of this earlier time are very persuasive, and be tempted to draw certain comparisons between their views and ours which are not always to the advantage of the latter. The painters with whom we will be dealing were, for the most part, the fathers of the modern movement, and that is one reason why they have been admired, sometimes extravagantly. It might seem that criticism of them ill befitted the citizens of the world which they were among the first to understand, but the commentary of their own time ought not to be judged entirely on this basis, for men then living didn't know exactly what the future held, and there was much which these critics had received from the past that they were loath to give up until they knew they had to. It proved, eventually, that this was a real necessity, and the artists and writers who were acute enough to see it before the rest of society was able to, deserve high praise. What is not necessary, is to assert that the change into the modern era was *in every respect* a change for the better.

Anyone examining these developments today is thus faced with the difficult task of trying to see fairly what was thought and done a hundred years ago. The problem of what is, or was, going on in the artist's mind in the creation of any picture arises at once to plague the analyst whose own thoughts are necessarily different; partly because he is a nonartist, and partly because his environment is not the same. The best that

---

[4] In one fairly recent book, adverse comments are listed under the simple heading of "sottises," which may be variously translated as: "foolishness," "stupidity," "nonsense," "stupid blunder," or "insult."

can be done is to observe what was said and painted with as few prejudices as possible, and then attempt an exposition of the social and intellectual climate in which the painters were working. The elapsed time since then may not even yet be sufficient to allow a really accurate appraisal. Are we now able to form a clear idea of the true worth of the personal humanitarianism of Millet, or the mystical egalitarianism of Chenavard who believed that world fraternization was a symptom of the decay of society? Do we know what Manet was thinking when he painted the *Exécution de Maximilien?* All we really know for certain is what others thought at the time (and since), what the artists said, and what appears to be present in their pictures. But there is much to be learned from this contemporary reaction, and for that reason a study of it is well justified. Parts of it seem archaic, parts are stupid, parts are both thoughtful and penetrating, and the latter are not entirely made up of the statements of the supporters of the progressive masters.

All the artists of the period cannot be included in this survey; to do so would be impossible and unrewarding. A choice has been made on the basis of those kinds of painting which most clearly illustrated the problems and developments that occurred in subject matter and the attitudes toward it during these twenty-two years. Some of the examples illustrate positions which were later carried forward, others were failures and had little or no consequences, but any age is known as much for what it rejects as for what it accepts. We come, then, to the account of certain important acceptances and interesting rejections.

XI. INGRES, DELACROIX, AND THE
OLDER GENERATION

AT the risk of some repetition, it will be necessary first to inquire briefly into the ideas of the leading artists of the generation which preceded the revolution inaugurated by the art of Courbet. As we have seen, there were two whose reputations far outshone all the rest: Ingres, clothed in the majesty of his cold formality, and Delacroix, firing the imagination with his color and the passion of his brushwork. For all the arguments which had centered upon their two styles, they were quite similar in regard to their attitudes toward the art of the past, though Delacroix had a more inclusive taste than his rival.[1] Leaving aside what the critics thought about them, each regarded himself as an extension of the great tradition into the present, and both believed that the future of "great" art in France could not lie outside tradition. In the history of style, they have been justly considered as the forerunners of much modern art, exerting a strong influence on many of the masters of the latter part of the century, but a similar claim can scarcely be made for them with respect to subject matter and their attitudes toward it.

Ingres, as is well known, made constant references to the importance of studying nature, but with a very special interpretation.[2] In spite of the realism of much of his own work (such as in his drapery or the famous portrait of M. Bertin) he did not mean naturalism as it was understood by Courbet or Champfleury.[3] As he put it, there is a "great difference between the art of reproducing in a picture the characteristic aspects of nature which one has selected beforehand, and the talent which consists in simply copying carefully on the canvas 'the man one has had come and pose.' "[4] He rejected the idea that there was any need for a "modern" art, for that of the past was certainly good enough still (Fig. 12):

There are not two arts, there is only one. It is the one founded on eternal and natural beauty. Those who seek elsewhere are mistaken, and in the most fatal manner. What do these pretended artists mean who preach the discovery of the "new"? Is there anything new? Everything has been done, everything has been found. Our task is not to invent, but to continue, and we have enough to do in using, after the example of the masters, these innumerable types which nature constantly offers us, in interpreting them with all our heart's sincerity, in ennobling them by that pure, firm style without which no work is beautiful. . . .[5]

[1] His journal and letters as well as his published articles show how wide was his interest and how keen his insight into many kinds of painting.

[2] "It is in nature that one can find that beauty which is the great object of painting; it is there that one must seek it and nowhere else. . . . The principal and most important part of painting is to know which are the most beautiful and most suited to that art of the things which nature has produced so that one can make a choice among them according

to taste and the manner of the ancients" (Ingres, *Écrits sur l'art*, Preface by Raymond Cogniat, Paris [?], 1947, p. 35).

[3] The difference lay in large part in the matter of *choice*: "You realists who want nature alone and without choice . . ." (*ibid.*, p. 31).

[4] *Ibid.*, p. 15.

[5] *Ibid.*, p. 39. An interesting, if belated, example of the idea of decay so earnestly debated in the controversy between the ancients and the moderns from the seventeenth century on.

In this significant passage his ideas on both style and content are made abundantly clear. It was a negative attitude, but at least it was succinct.

Stylistic analysis of the art of the later century has revealed how much such men as Degas and Renoir owed to Ingres, but if his own words are to be believed, he would have thought their art of a very inferior kind. In the passages quoted we find that objective realism can never rise above the level of "talent," beauty in nature is eternal and in no sense confined to some particular or transitory example, artists are not to try to think up something new to fit modern times, but are to continue with the guaranteed past, and though they are to observe nature, they must not fail to "ennoble" her before they are finished (Fig. 33). It was Ingres who wanted the *Radeau de la Méduse* (Fig. 10) removed from the Louvre so that it might "no longer corrupt the taste of the public who must be solely accustomed to that which is beautiful!"[6] In 1857 he called Paris "that thankless country, given over to the most violent and absurd anarchy of the arts without hope of a return."[7] It is very doubtful if the use to which his mastery of line was later put, or the subjects to which it was applied, would have seemed, in his eyes, anything less than vulgar. From the point of view of content, of general artistic attitude, there was a wide gulf between his views and modern theory as it was finally evolved.[8]

He was, of course, the darling of the more extreme conservatives, a living proof of the justice of their position, a norm by which other arts could be easily measured, and equally easily damned, although, unfortunately, there was only one of him. To Delécluze, he summed up all the essential grandeur and purity of style which was the only fitting accompaniment to the lofty ideals of *la grande peinture*, but more than that, he furnished the grounds on which Delacroix could be accused of corrupting the taste of the young,[9] and naturalist art could be described as one in which "the people have no names, no fame: whose insignificant subjects are drawn from the humblest, even the commonest, of private lives, and which, in short, has no luster which can arouse admiration, respect or pleasure, a kind of painting supremely boring when it is not revolting...."[10] To use Ingres as a model had the virtue of simplifying judgments, but

---

[6] *Ibid.*, pp. 53-54.   [7] *Ibid.*, p. 79.

[8] "Art lives on high thoughts and noble passions" (*ibid.*, p. 29).

[9] Delécluze, *Les Beaux-arts dans les deux mondes*, p. 199. "I will not be so unjust as to accuse this painter [Delacroix], still very young [i.e. in 1822 and 1824] of having sought intentionally and resolutely to change completely the principles on which painting had reposed since Leonardo da Vinci—and even since antiquity—but what is certain and an historical fact is the sudden instantaneous revolution which those two works [i.e. *Dante et Vergile* and *Les Massacres de Scio*] produced in the ideas of those men still young and entering upon the career of art. In place of the *beauti-*

ful, which up until then had been the goal one proposed to reach, was substituted truth without selection which sought to elevate the insignificant by the piquant contrast of the ugly."

[10] Delécluze, *Exposition des artistes vivants. 1850*, Paris, 1851, p. 244. This was a propos of a little volume he had come across called *La Foi nouvelle dans l'art* (anonymous). The association of objective naturalism with socialism was involved, and the latter particularly aroused his wrath. But in spite of his intellectual opposition to any art embodying either or both of these ideas, he saw quite distinctly what was up: "That which seems to tend toward some sort of development, in short, the

it had the defect of leading to an almost complete antagonism toward any progressive form of painting. His defenders were unlikely to imagine that his style alone could be useful.

In spite of the undisputed eminence of his position in the world of art, Ingres was not immune from criticism leveled at those very qualities which Delécluze and the others admired so much.[11] The humanitarians were not inclined to give him any very great ovation and Champfleury made all manner of fun of his peculiarities, particularly his habit of bursting into tears on very little provocation.[12] But whether or not the critics were favorable, they recognized his unique position and the distance which separated him from any of his pupils or followers, like Flandrin, or Amaury-Duval whom we have to thank for a most revealing portrait of the master.[13] The Neo-Greeks (Gérôme, Fig. 11), or the academics (Cabanel, Fig. 57, or Baudry, Fig. 56)[14] were evidence enough that what he could do within the narrow formality of the classic-Renaissance tradition skillfully blended with direct observation, was quite beyond the grasp of its more ordinary practitioners, even though his own thematic treatment was sometimes dry and lifeless as in the celebrated *Stratonice*.[15] An able mediocrity was the best they could achieve, perfect enough but deadly dull.[16]

Delacroix was a more complex figure, and any brief summary of his ideas is certain to do an injustice to his brilliant, if somewhat uncertain, mind. The evidence, how-

---

new effort in this exposition has been attempted by the author of the *Enterrement à Ornus* [the name was misspelled in the catalogue] in which the artist seems to be devoting himself to proving that the choice of a thought, of a subject and of people; that the composition of a scene and the search for beautiful and agreeable forms which up until now have been thought to be essential conditions for art, are for him, on the contrary, entirely indifferent, and that any idea, any subject, and any natural appearance suffices for the painter from the moment he has the ability to render this naturalness, whatever it may be, with truth and energy." This is so accurate a description of Courbet's art, including both its good points and its bad ones, that one is astonished, the more so since this was its first really important appearance. (The passage is from the *Exposition*, p. 243.) Delécluze included in his little book a summary of the critical reactions to Courbet's paintings of that Salon.

[11] Cf. Castagnary's bold attack in his very first Salon: "This fellow (bonhomme) who has never had either inventiveness or style, who has owed his fame to bad canvases and has preserved it by bad ceilings, who has gone astray all his life and who, today, at the end of his resources makes childish paintings; this

fellow, I say, has been admirable every time he came to a portrait . . ." (Castagnary, *Salons*, p. 43, "Philosophie au Salon de 1857").

[12] "With the tears which M. Ingres has shed during his life one could put on a water display at the Funambules" (Champfleury, "Revue des arts et des ateliers," *Salons, 1846-1851*, in *Oeuvres posthumes de Champfleury*, Paris [Lemerre], 1894, p. 135). The essay is headed: "Silhouette de M. Ingres (en tant que lacrymal)."

[13] Amaury-Duval, *L'Atelier d'Ingres*, Paris, 1878.

[14] Mantz said that Gérôme was deserting the world in favor of archaeology (P. Mantz, "Le Salon de 1859," *Gazette des beaux-arts*, Vol. II, 1859, p. 196). In 1863 he referred to Cabanel's and Baudry's nudes as "mythologies"—a rather diminutive label (Mantz, "Le Salon de 1863," *Gazette des beaux-arts*, Vol. XIV, 1863, p. 483).

[15] This was a very common complaint among all the critics.

[16] Cf. Maxime DuCamp's complaint in 1857 that there was talent everywhere and genius nowhere (DuCamp, *Le Salon de 1857*, Paris, n.d., p. 4). See also Z. Astruc, *Les 14 Stations du Salon—1859*, pp. 12-13: "I extend no felicitations to the painter [Cabanel] for his vapid painting, executed without decision. . . ."

ever, is clear that he, too, felt that he belonged to what had gone before rather than to what was to come after. His sympathies lay with the tradition even though he was quite capable of admiring good painting wherever he saw it. From his journal one gathers that as he approached the end of his career he was frankly worried about the future. He speaks of the abyss to which a passion for change has brought society,[17] laments the rather inferior caliber of the younger men,[18] and decries the poor taste of the day,[19] but when it comes to solutions he is at a loss. The entry "Modern Style" in his projected dictionary says nothing at all about painting,[20] while the one on "Decadence" carries a lengthy paragraph.[21] Although he thought that the painting in Courbet's pictures exhibited in 1853 was superb, he was repelled by the ugliness of the people, especially the *Baigneuses* (Fig. 32).[22] In 1855, he spent almost an hour alone in the artist's private show and admired the *Atelier* (Fig. 38) immensely,[23] but with all his appreciation for painterly skill, he was not willing to consider that "pure" art was the solution:

Read during breakfast the article by Peisse who examines the Salon as a whole and inquires into the contemporary tendency of the arts. He finds it, very properly, in the *picturesque*, which he believes to be an inferior tendency. Yes, if it is only a question of making an effect on the eyes by an arrangement of lines and colors, as much as to say: *arabesque*;[24] but if, to a composition already interesting by the choice of subject, you add a disposition of lines which increases the impression, a chiaroscuro which catches the imagination, a color adapted to the characters, you have resolved a more difficult problem, and, once more, you are superior: it is harmony and its combinations adapted to a song which is unique.[25]

[17] *Journal de Eugène Delacroix* (ed. by André Joubin), Paris, 1932, Vol. I, pp. 289-290. Entry for April 23, 1849.

[18] *Correspondance générale de Eugène Delacroix*, Vol. IV, p. 97.

[19] Delacroix, *Journal,* Vol. III, pp. 61-62. Entry for Feb. 4, 1857.

[20] *Ibid.*, Vol. III, pp. 5-6. Entry for Jan. 25, 1857. "Modern [literary] style," he says flatly, "is bad."

[21] *Ibid.*, Vol. III, pp. 20-21. Entry for Jan. 13, 1857.

[22] *Ibid.*, Vol. II, pp. 18-19. Entry for April 15, 1853.

[23] *Ibid.*, Vol. II, pp. 363-364. Entry for Aug. 3, 1855.

[24] Cf. Denis on the nature of a work of art (Introduction, p. 7; the whole passage is quoted in Goldwater and Treves, *Artists on Art*, p. 380).

[25] Delacroix, *op.cit.*, Vol. II, pp. 55-56. Under the date of March 29, 1860 (*ibid.*, Vol. III, pp. 269ff.) he copies out several quotations from a book by Frederic de Mercey, *Études sur les beaux-arts depuis leur origine jusqu'à nos jours* (Paris, 1855). These deal with the relation of art to religion and contain advice to artists not to wait for the day of a new conception of God and the universe, since if they do, their brushes and chisels may "go to sleep for eternity" (De Mercey, *op.cit.*, Vol. I, pp. 2ff., esp. pp. 17-18). Delacroix leaves this passage without comment which may, perhaps, indicate his agreement with it. [In Joubin's edition of the *Journal*, the last portion of the quotation is printed in different type and without quotation marks, making it appear to have been written by Delacroix rather than De Mercey. W. Pach in his translation makes the same mistake (p. 678).] Delacroix often emphasized technique and originality as prime virtues of an artist and thus, in a way, was not far from the ideas of Zola, Manet, and their friends. With Kant, he rejects the idea that art has a moral duty to "give lessons" (see E. Delacroix, *Oeuvres littéraires*, Paris, 1923, pp. 65-66). But all the same, he wanted it to have thought, to deal with important subjects. De Mercey, who was for a time Director of Fine Arts, takes a conservative view and puts his faith in improved governmental support as a means for bettering the condition of art. He calls on the artist to do his part, however, in the "great movement of social reorganization" (De Mercey, *op.cit.*, Vol. I, p. 28).

This reservation in regard to art for art's sake, the implication that the function of line, color, chiaroscuro, and so forth, is to animate and harmonize an interesting subject is significant, since for him an "interesting subject" was either traditional or exotic. Of all his major works, only one dealt with a strictly modern theme, and even there he not only called upon the past for his personification of liberty, but intended it as a stirring memorial to an important historical moment (Fig. 7).[26] He viewed stylistic originality with a fine eye and an open mind, but the current progress of the over-all concept of a work of art made him apprehensive. The fault, apparently, lay in the subjects then becoming popular.

By virtue of his revolt against the school of David, the tremendous force of his individuality, and the daring nature of his technique, he, more than any other painter of the early nineteenth century, has been associated with the development of the modern movement. But it must be emphasized again that the connection was stylistic, a fact which was grasped by only a few of his contemporaries, most of whom connected his greatness with that of the tradition. In Baudelaire's brilliant estimates of the painter, it was always either the man himself or his artistry which was new; his subjects, at least at their face value, were not. Other critics saw in this artist a modern reincarnation of the revered geniuses of the past, and the qualities which they seemed to admire the most were those which can hardly be ascribed to the art which was to follow.[27] Edmond About said of him that "his genius consists in lending a body to the tales of history and to the fictions of poetry [Fig. 8]. . . . His greatness lies in the fact that he expresses and inspires ideas; that he portrays and produces passion: his painting lives and vivifies. . . ."[28] Zacharie Astruc, a good friend of the "new" school, described him in this manner in 1859:

M. Delacroix is, and will remain, the finest plastic and intellectual figure in contemporary art in that which concerns painting. He lives with the great masters and shares their glory. Twice great, we see him the brother of the poets, the brother of the painters. . . . No one has more valiantly popularized literary ideas, no one has remained more of a painter. . . .[29]

And this from a man who earlier in the same Salon remarked that the great masters "compose for the eye, very little for the brain"![30] In the same year Castagnary wrote: "Victor Hugo is the last classic as Delacroix is the last great painter."[31] Gonzague Privat, whose astonishing perception of the art of Manet has already been mentioned,[32] and who apparently had the keenest of eyes for essentially pictorial effects, remarked: "Eugène Delacroix moves us by thought, by the idea. . . ."[33] Many further instances

[26] See below, Chap. XIII, for a discussion of Couture's *Enrolés*, a similar attempt at an epic treatment of a relatively modern subject.

[27] That is, the noble or dramatic subject expressed with passion and imagination. The matter of "passion" in nineteenth century art might well be studied further.

[28] Edmond About, *Voyage à travers l'Exposition des Beaux-Arts*, Paris, 1855, p. 176.

[29] Z. Astruc, *Les 14 Stations du Salon—1859*, p. 270.

[30] *Ibid.*, p. 219.

[31] Castagnary, *Salons*, p. 69, "Salon de 1859."

[32] In addition, see below, Chap. XVII, pp. 189-190.

[33] Gonzague Privat, *Place aux Jeunes! Causeries critiques sur le Salon de 1865*, Paris, n.d., p. 126.

could be cited to show that to his contemporaries Delacroix stood not for the new, but for a marvelous, belated, unforgettable, final sunset of that greatness in art whose last days they knew were upon them (Fig. 54). In contrast to the rigid classicism of the Davidians, he was a revolutionary—and thus modern; but in a broader aspect, he was the companion of Veronese, Titian, and Rubens. "That which makes Delacroix the greatest artist of the nineteenth century and perhaps the last of the great family is that he reunites all the faculties of painter, poet, and historian by an innate power and a deep knowledge."[34] In short, the critics of the time saw him as the end of a long development rather than the beginning of some new movement, and this, from their point of view, was essentially accurate. More modern times, caring less for his subjects and more for his style, have emphasized his painterly contributions to the work of many of his successors.

Associated with these towering figures were several figure painters who were highly regarded, but usually placed on a somewhat inferior level. Of these, Decamps was probably the most important. He stood preeminent in the field of "orientalists," a section of painting which grew steadily in popularity after 1830, and was often treated as a separate section in Salon reviews. The relation of orientalism to history painting on the one hand, and to the modern scene on the other, not to mention its romantic connections, is a matter of some complexity and need not be entered into here, for it was not particularly influential in any of the developments under consideration. However, the exoticism of Africa and its people exerted a tremendous fascination on the French of the earlier part of the century, and a whole regiment of painters were soon available ready to give the public all it could take on this score.[35] Ingres and Delacroix both dealt with such scenes, as did also Chassériau, Vernet, Isabey, Fromentin, and others of less note, but from 1831, when *La Patrouille turque* (Fig. 6)[36] was first exhibited, Decamps was the leading specialist. Critics with tastes ranging all the way from the conservatism of Delécluze to the subjectivism of the Goncourts (who asserted that he was "le maître moderne")[37] seemed to find his art both moving and technically remarkable, especially in the matter of light effects.[38] But he, too, was firmly established in manner and theme long before 1848, and espoused a type of subject which was neither closely connected with the tradition nor particularly appealing to the newer groups. Duret paired him with Delacroix, but on a lower plane.[39] Today his talents seem modest enough and, taken en masse, his pictures appear repetitious, for they were

[34] Silvestre, *Histoire des artistes vivants* (1856), p. 75.

[35] The orientalists painted the Near East, Spain, and places still farther afield, but Africa was favored, largely on account of the French colonial enterprises there.

[36] The author is not sure whether or not the picture by this title in the Metropolitan Museum, New York, is the same one or not. Identification in these cases is not always easy.

[37] E. and J. de Goncourt, *Études d'art*, p.

202, "La peinture à l'Exposition de 1855."

[38] Rosenthal, in *Du romantisme*, attempts to make Decamps a member of a trio including Ingres and Delacroix. In the end, however, he describes the effectiveness of Decamps' work as "le charme précieux" (p. 145, note 1). He does, however, give an interesting critique of his subject matter: pp. 138ff.

[39] Th. Duret, *Les Peintres français en 1867*, p. 159.

all conceived within a rather narrow range of effects. It would seem, in fact, that he was overpraised.

Horace Vernet (1789-1863), Ary Scheffer (1785-1858), and Paul Delaroche (1797-1855) were all leaders in particular specialties during the doldrums of art which occupied the years from the July revolution to the next one in 1848. Vernet, the latest member of a distinguished family of artists,[40] achieved an initial success in 1822 with his *Combat de la barrière de Clichy* and continued thereafter to exploit the rich vein of popular interest in battle pictures, one of the minor categories in which the remains of history painting were preserved (Fig. 14). His greatest triumph attended the showing of the *Prise de la smalah d'Abd-el Kader* in 1845, a presentation of an incident from the French colonial wars in North Africa, the description of which occupied six pages of small type in the Salon catalogue that year.[41] It was an enormous canvas intended to appeal directly to the public, not by means of its artistry, but through the almost overwhelming vividness of the incident itself. Champfleury noted in the following year that his *Battaille d'Isly* was less successful since it was much smaller![42] There were, of course, other critics who took him more seriously. Gautier, for example, wrote: "The glory of Vernet is in having been the first to paint the 'modern battle.' "[43] But a popular talent such as his was not particularly effective in the transformation of art just then in preparation, and most critics declined to praise him beyond the limits of his specialty.[44]

Ary Scheffer, one of the lesser romantics whom Focillon has aptly described as a "half-temperament,"[45] made his début in 1827 with the *Femmes Souliotes*, and painted most of his life in a rather gentle, sentimental, uncertain vein. There was an undeniable charm to his best work but it was neither vivid nor robust, and was of so personal a sort that it had little influence and commanded no very great respect. By the 'fifties he was classed among those whose talents were already aging.

The perversity of official recognition was made abundantly clear in 1857 when Delacroix was elected to the seat in the Academy left vacant by the death of his former pupil Paul Delaroche. Of all the painters of "historical genre" set forth in a *trompe-œil* realism, Delaroche was undoubtedly the most popular. In an obituary in *L'Artiste* (1858), the ever-agreeable Gautier gave an interesting and sympathetic account of his work in which the immense public interest in his pictures is explained on the grounds

[40] He was the son of the history painter Carle Vernet (1758-1836) and the grandson of Claude-Joseph Vernet (1714-1789), a well-known painter of landscape and marines.

[41] Catalogue, *Salon de 1845*, pp. 196-202.

[42] Champfleury, *Salons*, p. 6, "Salon de 1846."

[43] Th. Gautier in an article on Vernet which appeared in *Moniteur*, Jan. 23, 1863 (here quoted from *Portraits contemporains*, Paris [Charpentier], 1898, p. 314).

[44] Delécluze, for example, called him a "stratographer," i.e. a student of the composition and handling of armies (E. J. Delécluze, *Les Beaux-arts dans les deux mondes en 1855*, p. 234).

[45] H. Focillon, *La Peinture au XIXe siècle. Le Retour à l'antique. Le Romantisme*, Paris, 1927, p. 216. Baudelaire lists him among the "doubters" in his Salon of 1846 and calls him "the ape of feeling" (*le singe du sentiment*) (Baudelaire, *Curiosités* [ed. Lévy], pp. 163ff.). Even Gautier could not put him in the first rank (Gautier, *op.cit.*, pp. 510-511).

that he was interested in subject, not painting, and always gave the observer the fifth act of a melodrama or a tragedy after which the curtain would fall.[46] This is a very just observation, as a glance at *Les Enfants d'Edward IV* (The Princes in the Tower) or *La Mort du Duc de Guise* (Fig. 9) will confirm.[47] But he paid the price for his popularity: most of the critics were very reserved about him, and as conservative a writer as Clément de Ris pointedly failed to include his name among the notables of the "generation of 1830."[48] They knew an almost total absence of painterly ability when they saw it.

One of the characteristic comments made in the Salon reviews of the mid-century was to the effect that it had become very difficult to divide the pictures into the traditional categories.[49] Was the art of Delaroche history painting or genre? Were battle pictures genre? Was a scene like Courbet's *Demoiselles de village* (Fig. 29) genre or landscape? As the ideas which had held the old classifications together became more and more modified and devitalized, pictorial subject matter had to be rearranged into new groups named after the types of scenes which were popular. For instance, peasants shown in their native habitat were regularly described as "paysanneries" (Fig. 46) while more or less poetic themes of nymphs, personifications, and the like, were "fantaisies" (Fig. 17).[50] Artists, particularly those who had achieved a measure of success in one of these more minor subdivisions, tended to stick to one type rather than risk a new departure which might be less popular.

Delaroche, Decamps, and Scheffer were all examples of this trend, but the most famous and prosperous was Meissonier, who was nearly always discussed separately, and with a good deal of deference. His minute compositions, always painted with great care and sometimes with quite brilliant color,[51] were ideally suited to the salons of the prosperous bourgeois, and their tiny perfection brought the highest prices received by any painter of the day (Fig. 40). Not only military scenes, but also costumed smokers and card players were achieved with an attention to detail which attracted an almost hypnotic interest. However, one interesting objection to his work was that he resolutely declined to make studies of contemporary characters, preferring, for reasons which are possibly not too far to seek, to stay in the field of historical genre. So specialized was his talent that he had no serious rivals even many years after the establishment of his reputation in the later 'thirties. He undoubtedly had a great influence on the historical realists generally, and the military painters in particular (Fig. 67),[52] but not beyond them into the more significant aspects of the problem of modernism.

[46] Gautier, *op.cit.*, p. 295.

[47] The whole picture has the air of a stage set, with the climax of the murder just over.

[48] Clément de Ris, *Critiques d'art et de littérature*, Paris, 1862, p. 446, "Les Notabilités de l'art depuis dix ans. 1848-1858."

[49] Felix Jahyer complains of this at the start of his *Deuxième étude sur les beaux-arts. Salon de 1866*, Paris, 1866.

[50] "Fantaisies" with classical themes were never regarded as history paintings. See Chap. II, note 34.

[51] *A General and Adjutant* (1869) in the collection of the Metropolitan Museum, New York, is an excellent example.

[52] This was true of his later years especially when he turned more toward military subjects such as the well-known *Emperor Napoléon III à Solferino*, 1864. Détaille is a fair example of the later painters in this specialty.

The last painter of this older group who requires mention here is Diaz (1807-1876),[53] who was mainly a landscapist but produced a number of dreamy idylls bathed in a soft iridescent light half revealing the graces of his bathers, Venuses, nymphs, and amors (Fig. 17). These charming scenes won him the reputation of being the foremost "fantaisiste" of his time, and from his debut in 1831 onward, he had a marked and lasting success. In works of this kind he was a sort of later Prud'hon, expressing a poetic sensitivity in a charming but quite traditional manner.[54]

There were several other painters of approximately the same generation who had more direct connections with the developments under consideration, but these will be discussed in greater detail in the following chapters. Daumier, Corot, Chassériau, Couture, and Chenavard, were all more or less well known before the beginning of this period, but each had such a significant relationship in one way or another with what was to come after, that they must be considered in relation to the new rather than the old.

[53] Narcisse Virgile Diaz de la Peña.
[54] His influence on Adolphe Monticelli was marked, but his work does not seem to have been otherwise very influential.

XII. THE GENERATION OF 1848
DAUMIER AND COROT

IT is deceptively easy to regard great instants in history as definite turning points, watersheds as it were, on one side of which events flow one way, and on the other, move in quite a different direction. But all such times have their antecedents, which are partial climaxes in themselves, and earlier ideas and systems survive long afterwards to refute the implication of a final and irrevocable change.[1] Such a moment was the year of 1848, whose hundredth anniversary has been recently observed. Politics, social theories, philosophy, even life itself seemed to take on a different aspect after this upheaval, yet its causes lay far back in the past and many of its important effects were not apparent until much later.[2] It was, possibly, the moment when the preparations for the modern world were essentially complete, when all its component elements were finally at hand, albeit in a most confused and incoherent state. Science, new political and social systems, the industrial revolution, and the waning authority of the Church had created problems everywhere that cried for solution. Art, too, was in search of answers to the fundamental difficulty of reorienting itself once more into some sort of reasonable relationship with the world at large. As has been already pointed out, the ideas, the means by which this was to be done, were already at hand, but they needed to be reexamined, sorted out, and assembled into a coordinated system that would have some chance for success under the new conditions in which art was to be carried on. This is what was done in the years after 1848, partly by the critics, but more importantly by the artists.[3]

About the beginning of our period, a number of important artists made alterations in their work which may or may not have been connected with the external events in the social and political spheres.[4] Courbet shifted from a rather marked romanticism

---

[1] A classic example is the French Revolution of 1789. It may be noted that it did not include any really startling change in painting; this occurred a number of years later during the Bourbon restoration.

[2] Cf. Brinkley, *Realism and Naturalism*, *passim*.

[3] This readjustment, while excluding much that was traditional, by no means ended stylistic eclecticism. Cf. Malraux (*Musée imaginaire*), Goldwater (*Primitivism in Modern Art*), and others on the new fields in which such borrowing occurred. Malraux maintains that it was only the antique-Renaissance tradition which they wanted to get rid of, accepting primitive, oriental, and Byzantine sources with enthusiasm. In some cases even primitive ideas as to content were adapted for more modern uses. The majority of this development falls later than our period, but see M. Schapiro,

"Courbet and Popular Imagery," *Journal of the Warburg and Courtauld Institutes*, Vol. IV, 1941, pp. 164-191, for a very interesting discussion of Champfleury's interest in primitive and folk arts: "The idol cut in the trunk of a tree by savages, is nearer to Michelangelo's Moses than most of the statues in the annual salons" (Champfleury, *Histoire de l'imagerie populaire*, 2nd ed., 1869, p. xii; here quoted from Schapiro, *op.cit.*, p. 178).

[4] Any final connection between the two would be hard to establish. Corot and Millet seem to have kept pretty well apart from events. Courbet's ideas on the matter are not too clear, and Chenavard was so wrapped in his own theories that he took no active part, although the revolution did give him his great opportunity and his ideas were certainly connected with republican ideals.

to the objective naturalism which brought him his great notoriety;[5] Daumier took up painting with a new interest and exhibited it for the first time in 1848; Corot began that impressive series of female figure studies which are so admired today but were so little known or appreciated at the time; Millet virtually gave up painting the nudes for which he had previously been best known and turned his attention to his beloved peasants; Chenavard at last found the great mural opportunity for which he had been looking and started on his scheme for the Panthéon, while but a short time before, Chassériau had shown unmistakable signs of shifting his allegiance from Ingres to Delacroix. Whatever may have been the cause for these developments, they help to establish this date as a convenient starting point, and possibly allow the artists involved to be grouped as "the generation of 1848."

Before discussing them, mention must first be made of a group of young academics, appearing at almost the same time, whose work was so traditional and so devitalized that it forms a clear contrast, a sort of backdrop against which the originality of the others may be measured. Cabanel was the first of them to exhibit ('44), followed by Gérôme ('47), Baudry ('52), and Bouguereau ('53). They were the leaders among the current inheritors of the stricter interpretation of the past and the precepts of the École; all of them were popular, and all of them achieved seats in the Academy in the same order as their debuts.[6] Baudry was a great favorite with the imperial family (Fig. 56); Cabanel's *Vénus* (Fig. 57, '63) was one of the most widely-praised nudes of the century; but the outstanding public triumph of them all was achieved by Gérôme with his very first picture, *Le Combat des coqs* (Fig. 11, '47). The critics, however, were not as easily pleased as the people, for most of them saw in such work actual signs of the decadence which was everywhere deplored (Fig. 35).[7] Gautier, of course, said very flattering things about Gérôme's Greek maiden, but Alphonse Karr remarked that she looked like a "terracotta demijohn" to him.[8] The liberal wing naturally attacked them with a venom quite equal to that with which the conservatives condemned Courbet and Manet. A comment by Castagnary will serve as a sufficient example: "M. Gérôme invents clumsily, composes meanly, executes poorly: M. Gérôme is not even a mediocre painter."[9] Most of this opprobrium was, of course, well deserved, for the art in question scarcely formed a monumental valedictory to the great tradition. Champfleury pitilessly described the group as a faded lot who ate veal and never drank wine because it had color. Gérôme, he said, was the boldest because he drank cider, the rest only water.[10] Every one of them possessed a high degree of technical competence, quite perfect of its kind, but this was not enough to relieve the boredom induced by their neat but bloodless forms, and their vapid handling of the subject. They had their defenders among the more popular-minded critics, but the better ones had little good to say of them, and history has confirmed this judgment.

[5] The *Après dînée à Ornans* of 1849 is the picture which shows the change. See Fig. 20.

[6] Cabanel 1863, Gérôme 1865, Baudry 1870, and Bouguereau 1876 (Stranahan, *A History of French Painting*, chart facing p. 134).

[7] Even the conservatives could see the trouble with art of this sort.

[8] A. Karr, *Les Guêpes*, Paris, 1847, p. 57.

[9] Castagnary, *Salons*, p. 94, "Salon de 1859."

[10] Champfleury, *Salons*, pp. 155-156.

There are a variety of reasons why Daumier's exact position in the general development of painting in this period is not easy to establish. Along with Gavarni, he was generally believed to be a very great caricaturist, so remarkable in fact, that he could not be measured by the ordinary standards applied to this form, which was commonly regarded as inferior.[11] Because of his almost miraculous power of raising his characters from the level of the particular to that of the universal—a power possessed by no other artist of the day, with the possible exception of Millet[12]—he was honored as a master by such eminent critics as Baudelaire and the Goncourts. Even so, he was not considered to be a great painter. Baudelaire accurately described him as a "special" artist for the very reason that he transcended the limits of his medium,[13] but his paintings, mostly done in the years after 1848, were known chiefly to his friends and admirers; they were seldom exhibited, and attracted little attention when they were.[14] His now famous entry in the ill-starred competition for the figure of *La République* (Fig. 15), for example, went unnoticed in the account published in *L'Artiste*.[15] The following year he exhibited a painting in the Salon for the first time: the *Meunier son fils et l'âne* (Fig. 21), but the reviewer for this same journal thought it merely "charming if a little brutal" and doubted if La Fontaine would recognize his fable.[16] Albert de la Fizelière noted that he had made a special effort to see the Daumier in the Salon of '61, but when he found it, it was so skeyed that he couldn't even make it out.[17] Most critics left his work unmentioned entirely. In those days, for an artist to have much influence outside of the circle of his associates, it was essential that he exhibit often and that at some time he should have a "success," or failing that, at least a "scandal" at the Salon.[18] Daumier never achieved this, and though his influence on the graphic arts was marked, he made little impression in the major field for the gap between graphic caricature and Salon painting was too wide to be thus bridged.[19] A later age has seen

[11] It is interesting that the great caricaturists of the age were of particular interest to such advanced critics as Baudelaire, the Goncourts, and Champfleury.

[12] Thoré called him "the great Greek" in 1861. "Daumier, who was a great painter with the pencil, has taken to painting on canvas in real earnest with colors and brushes. The figure, the expression, the kind of simple and original grandeur which marked his drawings, above all the precision of his mimicry—these qualities are in his paintings at all times" (Thoré, *Salons de W. Bürger*, Vol. I, p. 116). The picture exhibited that year was a *Blanchisseuse*. The one reproduced (Fig. 53) may or may not be the same as it is difficult to establish which of these was the one actually shown, but in any case it illustrates Thoré's remarks.

[13] See p. 83.

[14] The author has been able to find mentions of works exhibited by him in the Salons of 1849, 1851, 1861, and 1869.

[15] *L'Artiste*, 5e série, Vol. I, 1848, p. 160. No names are given but a number are described and none fits the Daumier. Gautier wrote the notice.

[16] *L'Artiste*, 5e série, Vol. III, 1849, pp. 99, 113. This Salon review is signed "Feu Diderot." Champfleury gave him a short chapter in his review of the same Salon (Champfleury, *Salons*, pp. 176-178).

[17] A. de la Fizelière, *A-Z ou le Salon en miniature*, p. 23. This was the *Blanchisseuse* of Fig. 53.

[18] Arsène Houssaye says of Chintreuil that he never had such a "success" and that it was hard for an artist to get along without some public recognition of that sort (A. Houssaye, *Life in Paris. Letters on Art, Literature, and Society*, Boston, 1875, pp. 120-121).

[19] The rigidity of these boundaries was much more pronounced then than now. Artists were hemmed in by certain unwritten restrictions

that he was one of the very few artists of the whole century who could raise the trivial to the monumental, but he did it in the wrong medium and under the wrong auspices. Gautier, speaking of Gavarni, said that people were not apt to think of these prints as art at all, and underlined the fatal distinction between the two media: ". . . one can say with perfect assurance that neither the men nor the women of the world, nor almost any of the thousand actors of nineteenth century society have left a trace in *the serious art* of the nineteenth century."[20] No one assessing Daumier's position in the critical opinion of the time can afford to ignore this distinction nor the results of it.

Even the reviewers who saw and admired the paintings were inclined to regard them as a sort of continuation of his satiric manner transposed into a different medium. Ernest Hache, speaking of two of his gouaches exhibited at the Salon of 1869, described them as "miracles of animation and wit, two striking bits of that immense satire drawn by Daumier. Firmness and justice of observation have never been pushed farther."[21] When the Goncourts admired his *Silène* they could not see him as anything but the great caricaturist "who has his place marked among that small pleiad of *masters of the pencil [crayon]*."[22]

This modest and unassuming man was not much given to making pronouncements about art; what he thought he set down in his pictures. His political sympathies were Republican (i.e. liberal) and he had a deep affection for people,[23] both of which facts can easily be discovered after a very cursory glance at his cartoons. But his paintings seem to be less pointed, less socially charged; they have a sort of majestic detachment which contrasts with the social insight so characteristic of him otherwise. In some of them he turns to literature—Cervantes or La Fontaine[24]—but even the contemporary subjects like the *Blanchisseuse* (Fig. 53), the *Voiture de 3ᵐᵉ Classe*, or even *L'Émeute*, have a certain impersonality as though the artist were relaxing from the necessity of being significant. They seem to show a delight in painting for its own sake, a retreat into artistry after a lifetime of almost forced labor in a less grateful medium. Champfleury spoke warmly of the sketch for the Republic which, among a group of mediocre efforts, seemed "simple, serious, and modest," and he was, in fact, ready to maintain that Daumier had proved his right to walk with Delacroix, Ingres, and Corot in this

---

the departure from which was usually severely condemned. Large canvases were, for instance, considered reserved for history paintings. Thus the size of Courbet's work was a direct affront.

[20] Th. Gautier, "Gavarni," in *Portraits contemporains*, Paris, 1898, p. 327 (italics mine). Since they came in the paper each day they were not taken seriously as art (*ibid.*, p. 337).

[21] E. Hache, *Les Merveilles de l'art et de l'industrie*, p. 317.

[22] E. and J. de Goncourt, *Pages retrouvées*, Preface by Gustave Geoffroy, Paris (Charpentier), 1886, p. 263. The article first appeared in *Le Temps illustrateur universel*, July 8,

1860.

[23] According to Arsène Alexandre, he hated Napoleon III so much that he could never say his name without trembling; he referred to him as "that deadly man" (*Daumier raconté par lui-même et par ses amis*, Geneva, 1945, p. 104).

[24] He painted an astonishing number of classical subjects. There was something of the great tradition in his style, also. Cf. Balzac's famous remark about him: "This lad has something of Michelangelo under his skin" (*ibid.*, p. 16).

new medium,[25] but only a handful of others were willing to echo this opinion. Thoré, who might have been expected to appreciate him if anyone, mentioned the *Blanchisseuse* in his Salon of 1861, saying that it was among the few pictures which "rediscovered the people of the cities," but made no further comment.[26]

It is interesting to consider what might have happened had Daumier been primarily a painter, if he had devoted his immense genius entirely to achieving in that field what he actually accomplished in the popular medium of caricature. It is unthinkable that a man of such power and insight would have gone unnoticed very long even in the immensity of the Salons, or that he would have failed to attract a following among younger painters. It would also seem likely that some of the developments already discussed in criticism might have begun much earlier than they did, particularly in humanitarian circles, for Proudhon, Thoré, Castagnary, and the others could well have thought they had found in him the man for whom they actually looked in vain.[27] He was the one artist they knew, again with the possible exception of Gavarni, who saw deeply into the mind and spirit of the city-dweller, whose every action he could universalize with such effortless sureness.[28] Even Millet now seems narrow and rather repetitious beside the flexibility of these fine interpretations in black and white. If it was at all possible to paint the epic of the man in the street, Daumier was the one to have done it.

The classifying habit of mind which insisted on seeing in Daumier nothing but a superlative wit was partly responsible for the lack of interest with which the figure painting of Corot was received. When this patient master was finally recognized in the 'fifties, it was as a landscapist, and that remained his claim to public attention. He did not exhibit many of his figure studies, for reasons which are not entirely clear, but when he did, the critics had very little to say of them.[29] Ever since his important painting of *Hagar au desert* (Fig. 3), which attracted favorable notice in the Salon of 1835, he had done a number of scenes in which figures were introduced into the landscape, some of them looking rather Poussinesque in their general appearance (*Homère et les bergers*, Fig. 4), but they were essentially traditional in concept and were judged as such. Furthermore, his characters were usually accessory rather than the chief object of interest.[30] As Venturi has noted, when Corot used his imagination to people the scenes he had observed from nature, the results were usually unimpressive.[31] DuCamp

---

[25] Champfleury, *Salons*, p. 99. He says that the fifteen people in Paris who said that Daumier was a great artist passed for "bizarre creatures" (*ibid.*, p. 98).

[26] Thoré, *Salons de W. Bürger*, Vol. I, p. 39.

[27] See Part One, *passim*. It will be made clear later that Courbet was, in a sense, a second best in comparison to the man they were really looking for, and Millet, of course, stuck to the country people.

[28] Cf. Baudelaire's choice of Guys, a wash and line maker of "sketches."

[29] He showed *La Toilette* in 1867, a picture in which the figures shared honors with the landscape, and the *Liseuse* (Fig. 83) in 1869.

[30] They were, to all intents and purposes, "classical" landscapes in the traditional sense of the term, but largely as regards their content.

[31] L. Venturi, "Corot," in *Corot 1796-1875*, Philadelphia, 1946, pp. 17-18.

complained that the figures in the *Macbeth* and *Dante et Vergile* (Fig. 47) of 1859 all looked the same.[32]

It is evident from the writing of the time that the greatness of the figure studies is a later addition to his fame (Fig. 83). Silvestre scarcely mentions them at all,[33] and Jules Claretie, who knew and loved him, said, "Corot has *even* left some portraits, portraits of a striking vigor and truthfulness enveloped in that eternal cloud which is like the silvery gauze with which the master covers his idylls."[34] He was one of the leaders of the naturalist revolution in landscape, but he was not a force in the development of new ideas about figure painting.[35] It is interesting to note further that his landscapes were not particularly pleasing to the two greatest humanitarian critics. Thoré is quite reserved in his praise of him,[36] and Castagnary, who put the painting of nature at the peak of contemporary art, attacked him vigorously in '59: ". . . no truth in his invention, no variety in his tones and lines: his composition is uniform, his color improbable, his drawing false and invariably careless."[37] The reason for this, of course, was the fact that although nature was the heart of the matter for Corot, he painted it in a "poetic" haze, a type of imagination which had little appeal for these critics.[38]

In a quiet, rather stubborn way, the master was an exponent of art for art's sake, a painter's painter. Art was nearly everything to him; the events of the world of affairs were ignored in favor of a different world where his eye for light, atmosphere, forms, and cool spaces could find delight and satisfaction. Nature was an almost holy thing and was to be treated with reverence; other facts and situations were of little consequence by comparison. His indifference to the revolutions through which he lived is well known, amounting almost to ignorance. He read very little, and in 1848 remarked with a staggering naïveté: "It seems that M. Hugo is a rather famous literary man."[39] Nor did he take any very active part in the artistic controversies raging in the press and Salons, although he did serve on juries quite regularly, and his generous help to distressed artists was one of the finest sides of an endearing character.[40]

Corot must be described as a narrow-minded man: art and nature bounded his world

---

[32] M. DuCamp, *Le Salon de 1859*, Paris, n.d. p. 151. The charge of sameness was leveled at Corot quite frequently.

[33] Th. Silvestre, *Histoire des artistes*, p. 89. This book appeared, of course, in 1856 before the artist had taken very markedly to this type of subject. The majority of them seem to date from the 'sixties.

[34] Jules Claretie, *Peintres et sculpteurs contemporains*, Paris, 1882, Vol. I, p. 112 (italics mine).

[35] His contribution to modern art, which was very considerable, was stylistic. See below.

[36] *Salons de T. Thoré*, p. 320, "Le Salon de 1846." He thinks here that Corot lacks sparkle, his pictures are too pale. In 1863 he said he was "a master but debatable" (*Salons de W. Bürger*, Vol. I, p. 401).

[37] Castagnary, *Salons*, p. 88. He came to like him better later on, however.

[38] Corot was accused of using a sort of impressionism, of painting sketches rather than finished works. A number of critics made this point. Both Castagnary and Thoré preferred Rousseau, possibly because he painted nature more boldly. Chaumelin says that Thoré died looking at his two favorite pictures, one by Rembrandt, the other by Rousseau (*L'Art contemporain*, Paris, 1873, p. 191, "Le Salon de 1869").

[39] *Corot raconté par lui-même et par ses amis*, Geneva, 1946, Vol. I, p. 63.

[40] In 1848 he received the ninth largest number of votes cast for the jury. He came right behind Meissonier. His charming gift of a house for Daumier is well known.

on all sides, and his dogged faithfulness to these two interests was the key to his success and to his isolation. He confessed that it had taken him a very long time to see the greatness in Delacroix, and Millet's *Glaneuses* (Fig. 44) was incomprehensible to him.[41] His outlook was too personal to see that of others very clearly: the academics and history painters were on the wrong track, even though he painted his own versions of "historical" landscape, and the moderns were "spoiling" nature.[42] This single-mindedness allowed him to be true to himself artistically, and the calm results were so perfect in their way that they won him the admiration not only of artists but of such advanced critics as Duret and Zola. Baudelaire praised his work as early as his first Salon, but by 1859 he was inclined to find him rather unexciting. Others, too, complained mildly of the monotony of his crepuscular effects. Zacharie Astruc, however, thought him one of the fathers of modern art, and this was a fair example of the almost universally favorable critical reaction.[43] Even the conservatives found much to praise, for although he was a leader of the naturalists, he was also a most imaginative artist with a strong poetic turn of thought. Émile Cantrel, writing in *L'Artiste* (1859) said of him: "M. Corot is not a landscapist, he is a dreaming Dante who has taken the brush to tell the trees of the old legendary forests about the mystic visions they have seen passing in the night of despair. . . ."[44] There was something for everyone in his painting of nature, but his people were ignored, mainly, it must be admitted, because they were unseen.

In the light of the characteristics previously discussed, Corot's art seems modern in several respects. The fact that what was traditional in it was its least important aspect,[45] combined with his own preoccupation with purely pictorial effects, makes his connection with the modern movement both easy and natural. Landscape, as we have seen, was more easily modified than figure painting; it was regarded as an understandably congenial form for artists passionately devoted to painting as such, but the more revolutionary step which Corot took of applying a similar approach to the human figure unfortunately went relatively unnoticed. By temperamental preference, rather than from any reaction to social problems, extensive reading, or close contact with the world of affairs, he set his models into a position which made them equal, but not superior, to the trees and water he loved so well, an equation of man and nature which is one of the premises of much modern art. He was as placid, or as dreamy, in the presence of a woman, as he was before the soft lights and quiet ponds of the Ville d'Avray, and in exactly the same way; both were objects of his artistic contemplation, both could carry a similar artistic mood.[46] Speaking of these women (Fig. 83) he said:

[41] *Corot raconté*, Vol. I, p. 111.

[42] *Ibid.*, p. 112.

[43] Much of this is available in *Corot raconté, passim.*

[44] *L'Artiste*, 7e série, Vol. VII, p. 69, "Les Paysagistes," a separate section of the Salon review.

[45] It is interesting that his current reputation rests upon the landscapes of his earlier and latest periods plus the figure studies which he was so loath to exhibit. The criticism discussed here, of course, applied to the more feathery and poetic manner of his middle period. The popularity of this style seems to date from about 1855.

[46] In spite of the apparent poetry of these

For the most part they are humble girls, humble women whom I have always represented. I met them in the streets, in their Italian or servant costumes. Or else they have come to my studio asking if I needed models. I never let them go away. In them I saw the beauty of life. This beauty is in every creature, it is in everything which breathes as in everything impregnated with life. I have had as much fun painting these women as in painting my landscapes. On their flesh I have seen the poem of the hours unroll—as beautiful, as enchanting as on the earth, the water, the hills, the leaves. The mysteries of the woods were in their hair, the mystery of the sky and ponds in their eyes. Spring and autumn passed before me when they smiled, joyously or sadly. And their ingenuous words let me see the dance of the nymphs.[47]

He was, of course, not so removed from daily life that he did not feel the sting of harsh criticism or the disappointment that came from the callous rejection of his pictures for many years,[48] just as he felt the warmth of friendship and the elation of final success, but he never was the man to fight for his art in the way that Courbet fought. He was content to gain his ends in the fullness of time by quiet perseverance and a faith in his own creative ability. His art was pitched somewhere between the old and the new so that it eventually appealed, if for somewhat different reasons, to both camps; and in the end the world came to him without his having ever sought it out.

Thus both Daumier and Corot seem to stand a little to the side of the arena where the main ideological struggle was being fought. Their contribution was made more quietly than that of Courbet or Manet, and a fair share of it went unnoticed altogether.

---

scenes, there was a firm underlying naturalism, a fact which did not escape the attention of his contemporaries.

[47] *Corot raconté*, Vol. 1, pp. 24-25.

[48] He took his reverses very philosophically and was sustained by a pride which was quiet but firm: "Any distinction you have to ask for doesn't tempt me, if they want to give me any, they know where to find me: but I'll make no overtures" (*ibid.*, p. 138). He sold his first picture in 1847.

XIII. ORIGINALITY WITHIN THE TRADITION

ALTHOUGH Ingres and Delacroix were regarded as the last great traditional painters, and although it seemed clear to the critics that great painting was in a decline from which it was not likely to recover in the near future, there were artists of the generation of '48 who achieved notable results, quite as closely connected with certain future developments as they were with the past. Chassériau, Couture, and Chenavard may stand as examples, although it is possible that further research into this little-understood portion of nineteenth century art might well uncover more.[1] Chassériau established his connection with modern art through his pupil Gustave Moreau and the influence he exerted on Puvis de Chavannes;[2] the other two might well be classed as failures, but their very lack of success is instructive, and in Chenavard's case it was a fall of such magnitude as to constitute the greatest failure of the entire nineteenth century.[3]

Chassériau, as is well known, was one of the most promising of all Ingres' pupils, entering the master's studio in 1830 at the tender age of twelve. He rapidly became the favorite, for Ingres said to the other students one day, "Come, gentlemen, you will see this child will become the Napoleon of art."[4] By 1836 he had exhibited a *Caïn maudit* and won favorable notices in such journals as the *Revue de Paris* and the *Journal des débats*.[5] But in that year, returning to Paris from Rome, he began to paint romantic subjects taken from Dante, Shakespeare, and English history, an indication of the rift which was developing between himself and Ingres. By 1840 he was writing to his brother: "After a fairly long conversation with M. Ingres, I saw that in many respects we could never agree. He has outlived his prime, and he does not understand the ideas and changes that have taken place in the arts in our time; he is completely ignorant of all the recent poets. It is all very well for him; he will remain as a memory and a repetition of certain periods in the art of the past, having created nothing for the future."[6] The changes referred to were obviously connected with both style and content.

His reputation was growing in certain quarters and Gautier in particular gave him support, complaining bitterly when his *Suzanne* was put in a dark corner of the Salon of 1839.[7] Thoré gave him a favorable notice as well,[8] but in the following year, Gautier made the first of the fatal comparisons between his style and that of Delacroix.[9] Yet there was something quite original in his conceptions, and Bénédite goes so far as to say that by this time "the profound and thoughtful art of Gustave Moreau and Puvis

---

[1] There is a real need for a restudy of this period to make a more accurate appraisal of the art of a number of men who have been largely forgotten.

[2] Léonce Bénédite calls him Chassériau's "heir" (*Théodore Chassériau, sa vie et son oeuvre*, Paris, 1931 [?], Vol. II, p. 467).

[3] Couture's reputation declined steadily after his great success in 1847.

[4] Bénédite, *op.cit.*, p. 58.

[5] *Ibid.*, pp. 70-71. This excellent biography gives many quotations from the critical reactions to the artist's works.

[6] *Ibid.*, pp. 137-138.

[7] *Ibid.*, p. 96. Gautier's article appeared in *La Presse*.

[8] *Ibid.*, p. 97.

[9] *Ibid.*, pp. 108-109.

de Chavannes is already born in these two figures of *Suzanne* and *Vénus*."[10] In one of his letters, the artist said that he wished to make a reputation in portraiture so that he might become independent and be permitted "to accomplish the duties of a history painter,"[11] a statement which was apparently genuine. He had a number of opportunities to fulfill his ambitions, for he decorated several churches, particularly St. Merry and St. Roch, and also did the stairway of the Cour des Comptes.

He was staunchly defended by Gautier and Arsène Houssaye (often under the pseudonym of Lord Pilgrim) during these years, but when his illustrations for Othello appeared in 1844, the cry of a direct plagiarism from Delacroix was raised, and it never entirely subsided thereafter.[12] It was essentially just, for the styles were so close as to be almost deceptive at times, and in one painting of a war scene, the entire central motif is taken from the *Massacre de Scio*.[13] Baudelaire cautioned him on the subject in 1845,[14] and Delécluze, who didn't like Delacroix anyway, was quite savage about it.[15] Clément de Ris and several others took a more charitable view by saying that he was just having difficulty in settling down to a style which was properly his own. In any case, it does not matter greatly whether they thought he was leaning too heavily on his new idol or not, for his real originality was to be found elsewhere.[16]

Its origin lay in the very fact that he, and he alone of the important artists of his time, attempted to move from the camp of Ingres to that of his great rival, a move which was hardly likely to seem admirable to the admirers of either. Even after he had made the change, a portion of his thought remained, as it were, on the other shore. His pencil portraits continue to be stamped with the delicate realism of his master's style in similar works, and toward the end of his life he momentarily reversed his romantic trend and confounded the critics by exhibiting the very "classic" *Tepidarium* in the Salon of 1853.[17] The truth would seem to be that he was never quite able to come to rest between the two polarities of his admiration, and as a result, was tortured by an indecision which his reviewers were quick enough to point out.[18] And yet they missed that very quality in his art which must have particularly endeared him to Moreau and even to Puvis: namely, an elusive inwardness which imparts a mysterious and provocative effect to certain of his pictures, an effect obtained partly by expression and use of detail, and partly by color and light effects. Yet the sensitive Goncourts,

[10] *Ibid.*, p. 103.

[11] Here quoted from Freund, *La Photographie en France*, p. 121.

[12] Bénédite tries to refute this charge, but does not entirely succeed.

[13] Reproduced in Bénédite, *op.cit.*, p. 142.

[14] Baudelaire, *Curiosités* (ed. Lévy), p. 25, "Le Salon de 1845."

[15] Delécluze, *Les Beaux-arts dans les deux mondes en 1855*, p. 212. The idea that any artist could desert Ingres for Delacroix was almost too much to be borne.

[16] Paul de Saint-Victor, in an article on his murals for St. Roch, said, however, that he had an "instinct for style and a taste for strangeness" which suggests that he, at least, saw something of the real essence of his work (P. de Saint-Victor, "Beaux-arts. Peintures murales de Saint-Roch par M. Théodore Chassériau," *L'Artiste*, 5e série, Vol. XIII, 1854, p. 67).

[17] Clément de Ris was enthusiastic about it (*L'Artiste*, 5e série, Vol. X, 1853, pp. 131-132). Even Nadar liked it, which is somewhat more peculiar (*Nadar jury au Salon de 1853*, p. 19).

[18] For example, Ernest Gebaüer, *Les Beaux-arts à l'Exposition Universelle de 1855*, Paris, 1855, p. 91.

quick to feel the same quality in Moreau, failed to see it in him, and made the common accusation of a too heavy imitation of Delacroix.[19] This inwardness is, however, very plain in many of his pictures. An early example, dating from 1841, is the *Esther se parant* (Fig. 1) in which the rich jewelry and elaborately wrought urn impart a somewhat bizarre splendor to the nude woman whose face is cast in an expression of dreamy abstraction. Another striking instance is the painting of Sappho huddled on the Leucadian cliff, clutching her lyre, meditating on her unrequited love (Fig. 22). The theme is classical enough, but the handling is not only romantic, it has a strongly subjective quality. Some of the fragments remaining from the murals for the Cour des Comptes show it too, especially the figure of Silence with her fingers to her lips (Fig. 19). Very much in the vein later exploited by Moreau is the *Baptème de l'eunuque* from the Church of St. Roch, especially the strange oriental chariot and trappings for the horses, the weird light, and the umbrella-shaped object held by the Ethiopian in the background (Fig. 30).

Scenes such as these were traditional enough on the surface, and the style by which they were presented was a strange blend of influences rather conservatively handled, but the total effect was new—a highly personal expression which, in the last analysis, was Chassériau's own. It is not as marked here as it was later in the work of Moreau, but it is present and identifiable, one of a succession of such secret visions to appear in the later nineteenth century. The taste which produced it was, apparently, akin to the one which afterwards conceived the turtle with a shell inlaid with precious stones found in Huysmans' famous novel, *À Rebours*. Moreau, the first artist to make this type of content the basis of his whole creative activity will be considered in a later chapter, and it was here that the critics first recognized it, but it stems from Chassériau and Baudelaire. A more detailed analysis of the reaction to it can be reserved until we reach Moreau himself.

In 1847, while Chassériau was working on the murals for the Cour des Comptes, Thomas Couture exhibited his large canvas, the *Orgie romaine* (Fig. 5). This huge scene, based on similar compositions by Veronese,[20] was one of the greatest Salon successes of the century, and was received with such universal acclaim that Gérôme's *Combat des coqs* (Fig. 11), exhibited along with it, was forced to accept a second place.[21] In the hundred years since, however, it has become something of a horrible example, a sort of final proof of the vacuity of academic nineteenth century art. This may be a more proper judgment, but at the time it was regarded very differently, for

[19] Goncourts, *Études d'art*, p. 99.

[20] Couture's admiration for Veronese was well known. The picture is based on the general scheme of such works as the *Feast in the House of Levi*.

[21] No particular purpose would be served by quoting the eulogies which appeared at the time. Thoré made a reservation to the effect that it lacked a certain originality (*Salons de T. Thoré*, p. 421, "Le Salon de 1847"). Paul Mantz passed a very harsh judgment on it, however: "M. Couture is directly attached to that school of painters who have the talent necessary to cover huge canvases with nothings, to make an uproar but not a style, to declaim but not feel" (Paul Mantz, *Le Salon de 1847*, Paris, 1847, pp. 4off.). Mantz didn't like Gérôme's picture much either (*ibid.*, p. 60).

it seemed to be just such a revitalization of great painting as the critics were seeking, though they may have been somewhat deceived into this belief by its great size.[22] At all events, it established Couture's reputation for the balance of his life, and as the years went by, he gradually became known as a "one picture" artist, a man who never again equaled his first greatness. Certainly in the field of history painting this was true, with one exception to be mentioned presently. Nevertheless, he was at times a better artist than he is commonly considered today, for most moderns remember him only as the irascible antagonist and master of the young Manet, a crusty academician typifying the conservatism against which the *avant-garde* so properly revolted. Even in his own time, his renown was not helped by a reputation he acquired for being insufferably conceited and impressed beyond measure with his own importance. This was doubtless accurate in part, but there was another, and far more agreeable, side to his character which has been largely forgotten today. Many of his students, particularly the American ones, were devoted to him, and his behavior during the trying times of the German occupation seems to have been a fine blend of pride, patriotism, and restraint.[23]

Camille Mauclair, in the introduction to a recent study of the painter's life and works, attempts to show that he was not only a better-than-average artist, but also taught the young Manet rather more than that hot-headed young man was willing to admit,[24] an interesting suggestion which will be discussed later. Couture, the author points out, was caught in that very confusion of ideas about the significance of subject matter which was so fatal to traditional art of the time: "this teaching through pictures was an impulse in conformity with the French habit of mind. We scarcely understand it today"—but the pictures are beautiful and can be enjoyed on that basis without bothering about "the error of intrusive literature."[25] The evidence of the paintings themselves shows how widely Couture vacillated: *L'Amour de l'or*[26] of '44 was a straight piece of symbolic moralizing, while the *Boules de savon* is a scene of pure sentimental genre. Between these two extremes lies a group of works notable for their unevenness of insight. The best portraits are marvels of strong and solid modeling done with a dry brush technique adapted from the Venetians, serious and penetrating studies of the sitters; the worst need not concern anyone. There is no doubt that Couture believed himself to be a history painter in the great tradition, but he was

---

[22] For an interesting defense of this kind of academic art on technical grounds, the reader is referred to I. Gammell, *Twilight of Painting*, N.Y., 1947. Mr. Gammell believes that there are very few, if any, artists alive today who would have the technical ability to design or paint such a picture as this. Whether or not one can agree with the author, he has several interesting points to make. Couture's picture, however, was an enormous anachronism at the best.

[23] The American painter Healy and the German Anselm Feuerbach were among his leading admirers. See *Thomas Couture 1815-1879. Sa vie, son oeuvre, son caractère, ses idées, sa méthode*, by himself and by his grandson, Preface by Camille Mauclair, Paris, 1932. The book is obviously prejudiced in his favor and may not, therefore, give an entirely accurate picture of his character.

[24] *Ibid.*, Preface.   [25] *Ibid.*, Preface.

[26] It may be noted in passing that many of the pictures mentioned had more than one title. This one, for instance, was also called *The Thirst for Gold*. *The Roman Orgy* was also called *The Romans of the Decadence*, etc.

troubled by the need for modern subjects to such an extent that he suggested a loco-motive as a possible motif![27]

In 1848 he was invited by the government to paint *Les Enrôlements volontaires de 1792* (Fig. 16), a commission which apparently called forth his finest powers, but later became the greatest disappointment of his life. He met this challenge to his ability as a history painter with great vigor and achieved at least two fairly complete versions, one of which is now in Colmar, while the other has been recently purchased by the Springfield Museum. Before the task was completed, the work was stopped by order of the Duc de Persigny, who found far too much "liberty" in it, though Couture was paid 12,000 francs for his trouble.[28] In 1856 he was given another commission, a decoration for the Pavillon Denon of the Louvre consisting of two subjects: *Le Baptême du Prince Impériale* and the *Retour des troupes de Crimée*.[29] Neither of these was brought to completion either, partly because the painter was angered by the refusal of the *Enrôlements*.[30]

It should be recorded that the unhappy fate of the latter work was a real tragedy.[31] The composition was genuinely monumental with a fine scale obtained by placing the platform on which the officials are standing as a sort of apex to the design, the foot of which is formed by the forward-sweeping procession of volunteers. Every detail was studied with care, each group skillfully coordinated with the larger mass until the whole built up to a fine climax of feeling and movement. One is tempted to compare it with Delacroix's *Liberté aux barricades* (Fig. 7), and the better known picture does not seem greatly superior. Couture placed a Victory in the center which is less success-ful than the figure of Liberty in Delacroix's picture, but there is a surge of movement coming out at the left, sweeping across in front of the stand where the officials are placed, and moving back and out to the right, which is grander than the disposition of figures in the earlier picture. Such comparisons of value serve very little purpose except to show that at his best Couture could produce a type of history painting that was both moving and honestly emotional, as well as being of first quality artistically. Beside this achievement, the *Orgie romaine* seems to be only a preparatory effort. In this instance, if never before or after, the artist was on the way to joining the ranks of the few who could still handle this outworn type in a fresh and exciting manner. The measure of his inadequacy was provided by the uniqueness of this example of greatness.

Since the picture remained in his studio, it never came before the public eye, but had it been completed, there is little question about the probable increase in the

[27] Thos. Couture, *Méthode et entretiens d'atelier*, pp. 252ff.

[28] *Thomas Couture*, p. 45. This was ap-parently another example of the tight rein kept on artists and writers under the Second Empire.

[29] The former gives a weird impression since the body of Napoleon is complete but there is no head.

[30] *Thomas Couture*, p. 47.

[31] The Goncourts, in their review of the Salon of 1852, remark that there is no use talking seriously about great painting until Couture sends his *Enrôlés volontaires* to the Palais Royal. This would imply that they had seen it in the artist's studio or had talked to those who had. It was never exhibited. Several American efforts were made to purchase the main study for it, but these came to nothing (Goncourts, *Études d'art*, p. 124).

artist's reputation, the more so since no comparable work was then being done. It is interesting to observe that some of the best and most important art of the time went thus unnoticed owing to accidents of temperament or patronage, and by that fact failed to exert their full measure of influence on the times.[32] None of the examples so far mentioned would have altered the general course of events had they been better known, but in view of the caliber of the best contemporary criticism, one must regret that a fuller account of the reaction to them is not available.

It is often said that time has a sure way of weeding out the good from the bad, a generalization which has much merit, but time also has a habit of obscuring certain facts which do not always deserve oblivion. An instance of this is to be found in the extraordinary career of Paul Chenavard.[33] This essay is not the place for an exhaustive account of the work of this peculiar man, but he cannot be passed over in silence even though he was virtually forgotten within a very few years of his death in 1895. His memory might well be kept fresh if for no other reason than the fact that his scheme for the decoration of the Panthéon was probably the most ambitious mural plan ever worked out by one man in the entire history of art, excepting, perhaps, Ghirlandaio's fabled desire to fresco the walls of Florence. But there is another reason for remembering him, and that is the fact that he was the only painter of the century in France who attempted an historical, symbolic analysis of the sweep of history expressed from a peculiar, but essentially modern, point of view.

The stature of the man was, however, appreciated in his own day, and the many references to his work and ideas, fragmentary as they are, show that he was, at the very least, one of the most fascinating intellectual oddities of the century. Born in Lyon in 1808, he entered the École in 1825, studied briefly under Hersent, Ingres, and finally Delacroix.[34] In 1827 he left for Italy where he stayed for two years, studying and reading with an intense but unfocused enthusiasm. He met Hegel and is thought to have picked up his ideas about a cycle of universal history from him, though it seems likely that he got more of them from his fellow Lyonnais, Pierre-Simon Ballanche.[35] The young man traveled about sketching in the churches and gallaries of the whole of Italy, charging his almost photographic memory with an endless store of forms which he

---

[32] Examples: Corot's figure studies, much of Daumier's best painting, this picture, and Chenavard's great scheme for the Panthéon. The cartoons for the latter were exhibited in 1853 and 1855 and did attract a great deal of critical attention. They were only cartoons, though, and should not have had to be seen away from the setting for which they were planned.

[33] Since Chenavard is so little known, a brief account of his career is given here. A full explanation of his ideas must await further study.

[34] The facts about his life have been taken from Thieme-Becker, *Allgemeines Lexicon der*

bildenden Künstler.

[35] For Ballanche see Albert J. George, *Pierre-Simon Ballanche*, Syracuse, N.Y., 1945. The philosopher's works can be found in *Oeuvres de M. Ballanche de l'Académie de Lyon*, Lyon, 4 vols. The two most influential books in the case of Chenavard were *Essais de paligénésie sociale*, Paris, 1830, and *Vision d'Hébal chef d'un clan écossais*, Paris, 1831. See also Herbert J. Hunt, *The Epic of Nineteenth Century France*, Oxford, 1941, Chap. v, and Joseph Buche, *L'École mystique de Lyon. 1776-1847*, Paris, 1935.

used thereafter without further reference to models, by which he gained a reputation for being an eclectic, if not an outright plagiarist.[36] Michelangelo was his chief idol and figures from the Sistine Chapel turn up often throughout his work.[37] Actually he was not eclectic in the usual sense of this term, apparently employing these borrowed motifs as any learned man might use quotations, to express his thought more perfectly than he could do himself. This is, admittedly, a charitable explanation, but the people who knew him mention the fact that in conversation he was always quoting others,[38] and it seems possible that he did the same in his art. Just about the time of the triumph of romanticism[39] he returned to Paris, but his self-education was uninterrupted, and he apparently began work on his great cycle, making a sketch of *Luther devant la diète de Worms*. Two studies of scenes from the French Revolution were exhibited at this time, one of which met the stern disapproval of Louis Philippe for political reasons (Fig. 2).[40]

Returning to Rome, he met Cornelius and Overbeck, whose coldly philosophical approach to art struck a responsive chord in his mind. Throughout his career he was regularly compared to this German group, and his hard colorless style was, indeed, very close to theirs.[41] Whether he learned it from them or not is another question, though it seems likely that he did, since the style of his early *Convention nationale* is broad, shadowy, and romantic, while all his later work has the marked finish and wire-like line which is characteristic of the German school of Rome and Munich.

There is reason to believe that he showed some sort of outline for his historical sequence to his friend the philosopher Ballanche prior to the latter's death in 1847,[42] and the year before he had exhibited a painting of *L'Enfer* which must have been a part of it.[43] By this time his reputation had grown in a somewhat mysterious manner,[44] so that he was well known in the intellectual life of Paris, and though he was ap-

---

[36] See, for example, E. Loudun, *Le Salon de 1855*, p. 131.

[37] In the *Divine tragédie* (Fig. 83), see the group of Apollo and Marsyas in the extreme lower left corner. The figure of Venus on the other side may be taken either from the Eve of the Sistine ceiling or from Correggio's *Antiope*.

[38] For an interesting insight into his character, friendship, etc., see Eugène Vial, "Chenavard et Soulary," in *Mémoires de l'academie des sciences, belles-lettres et arts de Lyon*, 3e série, Vol. XVII, 1921, pp. 95-125.

[39] I.e. 1830.

[40] Silvestre says it was "removed from the galleries of the Louvre by order of King Louis-Philippe who found the familiar conversation . . . between Philippe-Égalité and the tribune Marat insulting to his house" (Silvestre, *Histoire des artistes*, p. 114).

[41] This cold style was intentional, of course. He said much later in answer to the criticism of it: "I conceived the idea of not painting the compositions, of only rendering them by drawing, and, to amuse the eyes, of coloring the architecture after the manner of the ancients in such a way that I would return to their system of framing monochrome pictures by means of columns, capitals, etc., which would be colored and gilded" (from a letter of Chenavard's to his friend Mariéton; Vial, *op. cit.*, pp. 107-108).

[42] Joseph Buche, *L'École mystique de Lyon*, p. 259.

[43] This was presumably the study from which he planned later to create one of the mosaics. Their subjects were: Hell, Paradise, Purgatory, the Crucifixion, and, in the center, the Philosophy of History—"Le Palingénésie sociale."

[44] Mysterious because he had painted so little and exhibited even less. It was probably based mainly on his fame as a conversationalist and intellectual.

parently unable to write his thoughts—even his letters were miserably misspelled[45]—as a conversationalist he seems to have had few peers. Many distinguished people enjoyed hearing his somber views on art, history, and philosophy: Delacroix, Courbet, Charles Blanc, and Gautier, among others,[46] and his ideas exerted a fascination on such assorted minds as Baudelaire, Chennevières, and Théophile Silvestre.[47] His fellow artists did not know him as well, and strenuously protested his being given so important a job as the Panthéon murals when he was only an "unknown."[48] But these objections went unheeded until the time when the building was restored to the Church in 1852.

Charles Blanc was the man responsible for getting him the appointment in 1848. The two called upon M. Ledru-Rollin, the new Minister of the Interior, bringing with them the designs for the whole scheme, and they stayed up all night discussing them. Ledru-Rollin was so impressed that a day or two later the matter was made official, money was allotted, and the final work begun. With the help of assistants[49] Chenavard worked steadily for four years, at the end of which time a group, apparently headed by M. de Montalembert,[50] succeeded in having the edifice once more made into a church. This was the end of the project, but some of the huge cartoons were exhibited in the Salon of 1853, and a great number at the Exposition Universelle of '55. After that they were apparently forgotten until a showing of them was held in Lyon in 1876 where they were discussed in a small pamphlet written by the faithful Blanc.[51] After that they again passed out of the public ken, the majority of them now lying rolled up in the basement of the Museum of Lyon.[52]

[45] E. Vial, "Chenavard et Soulary," p. 100.

[46] Vial, op.cit., pp. 98-99. Silvestre and others mention the high intellectual caliber of his friendships.

[47] Baudelaire was interested in him and went to special pains to mention his friendship with Delacroix: "But the one with whom he liked best to engage in lengthy conversations was the man least like him in talent as well as ideas, in complete antithesis to himself. This man has not yet received his due; and his brain, although misty like the smoke-filled sky of his native city, contains a host of admirable things. I mean Paul Chenavard" (Ch. Baudelaire, Eugène Delacroix [ed. Lear, N.Y.], pp. 78, 80). Chennevières' interest was the stronger because he himself had had so much to do with the decoration of the Panthéon (Ph. de Chennevières-Pointel, "Les Décorations du Panthéon," in Souvenirs d'un Directeur des Beaux-Arts, Paris, 1883). Silvestre obviously thought him one of the more important artists of his time.

[48] A. Houssaye in a notice in L'Artiste, 5e série, Vol. 1, 1848, pp. 106-108. Houssaye defends the choice of Chenavard for the work.

[49] According to Chennevières, the assistants were Papéty, Bézard, Brémond, and Comairas (Chennevières, op.cit., p. 63).

[50] Chas. Blanc, Exposition des cartons de Paul Chenavard pour la décoration du Panthéon, Paris, 1876, p. 41. Blanc gives the name of Montalembert on hearsay. This little volume gives a complete account of the granting of the commission and a list of the subjects. There are several of these lists in existence and a tentative examination shows that there is a considerable variance among them. The artist probably prepared more than he needed, intending to make a final choice later.

[51] Blanc, op.cit.

[52] Vial, "Chenavard et Soulary," p. 104. Vial tells how Chenavard left his cartoons and his money to Lyon. He declined the honor of having a "Chenavard Room" in the Museum, insisting it be called the "Pantheon Room." In spite of protests by Soulary, he did not have it put in his will that the pictures be kept there, and they were placed in the cellar six years later. The cartoons illustrated here are drawings, others were actually painted.

Stylistically they are not of great importance (Fig. 34), painted as they were entirely in grisaille, and in the hard cold contours of the current German fashion. At the time there was much criticism on these very grounds,[53] but the artist's defense was that they were to appeal to the mind not the eye, and furthermore, he felt that the austere grandeur of the Panthéon would best be complemented by similarly grave paintings which were, however, to be set in elaborately colored frames. Outside of their intended setting, as they were when exhibited in the Salon, they look dull and traditional (Fig. 31) though several of them have truly monumental designs (Fig. 36).[54]

It is tempting to wonder what effect they would have had on the observer in the huge structure of the Panthéon. The plan was to fill each of the forty panels around the walls with scenes from the history of man beginning with Adam and Eve (on either side of the entrance) and going around to the left, ending with a representation of Napoleon in the bark of history. At the end of the left transept was to have been a statue of Alexander, the apse was to have contained the Sermon on the Mount, and the right transept the figure of Charlemagne. Above these scenes and figures was to have been a continuous frieze containing a procession of the great men of all times, while on the floor were to have been mosaics of Purgatory, Hell, Paradise, the Crucifixion, and, under the central dome, a culminating composition forming a huge exposition of "Social Rebirth" (Fig. 36). The piers of the nave and the pendentives above were to have had scenes as well, and statues of Moses, Homer, Socrates, and Galileo were to stand against them. There were other variants and additions but these suggest the enormous scope of the enterprise.[55]

Aside from the general idea of presenting the sweep of history to the eyes of the visitor to this national shrine, there were more subtle meanings involved, so subtle, in fact, that they cannot be analyzed here, for the kind of historical evolution expressed in them was recondite and difficult to explain.[56] Chenavard seems to have owed a great deal to Ballanche, who was an exponent of an historical interpretation which saw societies as dying and being reborn in even higher forms, albeit in a sense acceptable to the Catholic Church.[57] Chenavard, however, was not so clerically inclined, and if he placed the Sermon on the Mount in the central position of the apse, it was mostly as a concession to popular feelings. He included such figures as Voltaire, an astonishing anachronism, and the accounts we have of the whole scheme suggest that although he felt that Christianity was possibly the greatest of religions, he did not believe it was the

[53] Cf. Théodore Pelloquet, *Dictionnaire de poche des artistes contemporains*, Paris, 1858, p. 43. The author complains that there is not enough art in the painter's work.

[54] The *Mort de Socrate* is a good example and bears no relation to the scheme of David's picture.

[55] Detailed accounts of the subject matter may be found in Th. Gautier, *L'Art moderne*, pp. 1-94, and Th. Silvestre, *Histoire des artistes vivants*, pp. 124ff.

[56] The description given by Gautier is full of references to such obscure matters as pre-Adamism and the burial of Moses by God. His account shows a very intimate knowledge of this rather mystical philosophy of history.

[57] Space does not permit any discussion of Ballanche's philosophic scheme. For a brief bibliography see above, note 35. A preliminary discussion of the sources of Chenavard's iconography will appear in the near future in an article by the author.

only one to have contributed valuable ideas and beliefs to society in the long years of man's development. The great panel of the *Palingénésie sociale* gives Christ the central position, but many figures are included which could hardly have met with the approval of the Church at Rome.[58] It was, in short, heretical, and therefore condemned when clerical authority over the building was reestablished. What was really celebrated here was the triumphant progress of human reason, the rise of man by his own efforts through a series of trials and errors. One may compare this notion with the words of Castagnary about shutting God out from man's new Eden;[59] the kinship is clear. Although Chenavard was involved in a rather mystical interpretation of events, and though he was a complete pessimist according to the accounts of his contemporaries, he was essentially modern in his thought, and was trying, as it were, to bring history up to date and then teach people what he believed it to be in a most didactic fashion.[60] Any idea that art was essentially a useless creation for the delight of the senses was utterly opposed to his views, which in one sense echoed those of St. Gregory; he wanted those who could not read to see. The cartoons thus represent a paradox. They are modern in their meaning, but they are almost archaic in their intention, for even in the tradition such unabashed didacticism was long past. The philosophy of history which they represented was, unfortunately, far too complex for the average man to have understood even with the help of a guidebook; it was really addressed only to the most advanced minds. Had the work actually been completed, there would surely have been many a puzzled visitor to this shrine of France's glory, though most people would have been simply bored. And yet one cannot help admiring the scope of the concept, the lofty and solemn theories set forth, and the forlorn bravery of the belief that they would really help people toward a higher understanding of life.

The measure of the impression the cartoons made is to be found in the attention paid to them by the very best critics of the time. Whether the ideas were shared or rejected, they had to be mentioned, and there was no other mural work of the time which elicited as much careful discussion.[61] Baudelaire, Thoré, Blanc, Chennevières, Gautier, and Silvestre all gave extended accounts and analyses of them, tacitly admitting by so doing, that they were both unique and stupendous.

Chenavard himself was more prone to think than to paint, and the collapse of this effort left him not only more bitter than ever, but even less inclined to put his ideas in tangible form. He exhibited just once more in the Salon, this time in 1869. The

[58] Gautier maintains that this figure is not really Christ but The Word, a figure which might be considered to signify the divine spark in man (Gautier, *L'Art moderne,* p. 60). In the illustration (Fig. 36) the lower third of the circle which portrayed man's reversion to a state of savagery and anarchy—Chenavard's gloomy forecast of the future—has been destroyed.

[59] See page 69.

[60] Chenavard confessed that his art had always been devoted more to ideas than to their pictorial execution (Vial, "Chenavard et Soulary," p. 109). "The inconvenience of my type of mind is that it makes every idea which comes to me encyclopaedic" (*ibid.,* p. 107).

[61] The reaction in some popular quarters seems to have been a little like that accorded the theories of Dr. Einstein—the cartoons were vastly learned and important even if most people hadn't the remotest idea what they meant.

memory of his earlier efforts was still green enough to cause this to be regarded as an important event,[62] and crowds gathered to look at *La Divine tragédie*, the most discussed picture in the show (Fig. 82). Most people found it bewildering in spite of a long explanation published in the catalogue, and a glance at the illustration shows plainly how this might have been a normal reaction. All they saw was a great mass of figures whose identification was difficult and whose meaning was quite obscure. According to the official, published account,[63] it represented the triumph of Christianity—as represented by the Trinity—and the downfall of all pagan cults in a sort of general *Götterdämmerung*: Maia, Thor, Diana, Hercules, and the rest overwhelmed by the ultimate power of the faith. The Angel of Death swoops down to finish their final agony. Regarded in this light, the critics thought it overingenious, too complicated, and rather artificial.[64] Besides, they thought the colors inharmonious and picked out a number of forms whose origins were only too easy to establish, for Chenavard, as usual, had called heavily on his repertory of Italian and antique forms.[65]

But the fact of the matter was that this was not what the picture meant at all. A few critics, most notably Paul Casimir Perier, pointed out that the picture really was the downfall of *all* cults, including Christianity itself.[66] Perier went so far as to maintain that pressure exerted on the editor of the catalogue had forced a sort of censorship of the picture, and that as a result the more orthodox interpretation had been given out to the public. The clue to his interpretation is given by the figure of the hermaphrodite seated upon the hippocamp at the upper left. This figure was described as the "Great Androgyne," but few cared to say what it meant or why it was both uppermost in the design and the only personage picked out by a radiance behind the head. Perier said it represented reason triumphant when cults, which are not reasonable in this sense, were finally banished and man came into his own. In view of Chenavard's anticlericalism[67] there can be little doubt that this was indeed his meaning. This interpretation is strengthened by a passage from Ballanche's *Vision d'Hebal*, a book with which the painter was unquestionably familiar.[68] In the account of this vision, mention is made of a tearing apart of the sexes—a sort of Platonic notion—which would, in the fullness of time, be reunited.[69] If the *Divine tragédie* actually represented the artist's final

[62] It was mentioned in *L'Artiste* in a kind of preview of what would be forthcoming in the Salon, written by Élie Roy and entitled "Pérégrinations dans les ateliers" (*L'Artiste*, 9e série, Vol. IX, 1869, p. 97).

[63] *Salon de 1869. Explication des ouvrages*, etc., Paris, 1869, p. 65. The picture is here called *Divina tragedia*.

[64] For an example of this criticism, see M. Chaumelin, *L'Art contemporain*, Paris, 1873, pp. 207-208, "Le Salon de 1869": ". . . his picture shows the complete inanity, absurdity, and powerlessness of such systems and devices as he used. . . . His *Divina tragedia* is only a colossal and lugubrious farce."

[65] As, for example, Élie Roy who reviewed the Salon for *L'Artiste* (9e série, Vol. IX, 1869, p. 362). The reader, if he wishes, may get considerable entertainment by picking out the origins of many of the principal figures.

[66] Paul Casimir Perier, *Propos d'art à l'occasion du Salon de 1869. Revue du Salon*, Paris, n.d., p. 47. At the end of the book is a section entitled: "La Commission de l'index à l'exposition" (pp. 297-322), and it is here that he makes his charge of censorship.

[67] This is clearly established by Vial in "Chenavard et Soulary."

[68] See above, note 35.

[69] P.-S. Ballanche, *Vision d'Hebal*, p. 35.

word on the significance of history, if it really dealt with the ultimate moment for which men had waited, then we can be sure that for him the climax would not be the triumph of the faith which he neither believed in nor had any reason to be grateful to,[70] but rather the establishment of man as complete and whole when all false doctrines had been done away with. He was too clever to commit himself plainly to this thesis, and the ambiguity of his presentation was attested by the fact that he had two offers for the purchase of it, one from the Church and the other from a man who seems to have been a Saint-Simonian.[71] Chenavard claimed that he only painted it for the Luxembourg (!), but he had acquired a less disinterested reputation in certain quarters. At the time of the exhibition of the cartoons in '55 he was attacked as an anti-Catholic by at least one reviewer who saw him as the leader of an artistic heresy, a humanitarian opposed to kings and the divinity of Christ and the saints, an accusation which was, doubtless, quite just.[72]

These two significant and esoteric examples of the work of this remarkable man stand forth as unique in the French art of the century. Never was so determined an effort made to paint the modern epic, never was the humanitarian position so laboriously stated, never was a fine mind so oddly misdirected. One of the reviews of 1855 summed the matter up very well (the pairing of Chenavard with Glaize is very peculiar for the latter was considered quite insignificant by comparison):[73]

M. Chenavard and M. Glaize are not painters, they are philosophers, pantheistic philosophers; they do not seek beauty, do not concern themselves with passion, they wish to render an idea; they have imagined a system, instead of writing a book, they paint a canvas. One does not know where to place their works, it is neither historical nor religious painting: a category must be created, as was done for genre, *humanitarian* painting. What M. Chenavard has aspired to represent in the series of cartoons he exhibits, is the History of Humanity.[74]

The artist's connection with humanitarianism is accented by the reaction of Castagnary, who, reviewing the Salon of '69, was very much impressed by *La Divine tragédie* as long as he thought it represented the triumph of human reason, but when he found out from the catalogue that it was the glory of the faith, lost all interest.[75] This oddly quixotic note runs through the whole story of the painter—his life, his work, and the

---

Note especially (p. 36): ". . . the division of the sexes will be the emblem of the division of castes and classes in primitive human institutions"; also: ". . . the identity of man attests his genetic unity, and foretells his final unity" (p. 37).

[70] On his death he wanted no religious rites: ". . . having never practiced any cult, although I have always been profoundly religious before the immense living unity of the universe" (quoted by Vial, *op.cit.*, p. 119). Chenavard's complete pessimism was almost legendary. His distaste for Catholicism must have been intensified by the collapse of the Panthéon scheme.

[71] Vial, *op.cit.*, pp. 104, 106-107.

[72] C. Lavergne, *Exposition Universelle de 1855*, Paris, 1855, pp. 93ff. Chenavard is the leader of the anti-Catholic artists.

[73] It would be interesting to look into Glaize's work for similar philosophical expressions, but the author has not as yet been able to do so.

[74] E. Loudun, *Le Salon de 1855*, p. 130.

[75] Castagnary, *Salons*, pp. 337-339. The critic says that the picture was in the Salon Carré (i.e. the place of honor) but was later ordered removed to a back room. Possibly too many people suspected its real meaning.

ideas people had about him. He was never to be quite understood, yet he exerted a strange fascination on some of the most cultivated minds of the day; modern in much of his thinking, he was so traditional in style as to seem reactionary; full of vast enterprise, he achieved almost nothing; living in the great day of scientific optimism, he preached the immanent collapse of society. Whatever else may be said of him, his position in the artistic history of the last century is unique.

XIV. MILLET

THE critical commentary of both the humanitarians and the objective naturalists centered chiefly about the work of Courbet and Millet, though for purposes of comparison a third name should be added to theirs, that of Jules Breton.[1] All three painted subjects of a similar sort—the life of common people in the country districts.[2] But the resemblance ceased at that point for they were neither admired nor criticized together, nor did they have much use for each other's work. Courbet and Millet were not particularly compatible,[3] and the latter expressed his ideas about Breton in a typically mild way when he remarked: "M. Breton paints girls who are too pretty to stay in a village very long."[4]

Among the critics, the basis of the distinction lay in the belief that Courbet accepted the surface appearance of things, but painted it with unexampled force and vitality; Millet saw the inner person worn by toil and care, and through imagination and a capacity for generalization lifted him to a point bordering on the noble or, conversely, lowered him to the level of an animal; Breton took the same people and by the use of "style" made them proud, handsome, happy, serious, and generally as admirable as the ordinary Parisian could wish (Fig. 42).[5] The honors heaped upon the last-named indicated the direction of popular and official taste, and cast considerable light on contemporary ideas about "realism." The work of these three men posed the problem of how art should deal with contemporary characters of humble station. The fact, well noted at the time, that there was much traditional technique in the art of Millet did not excuse him from the charge in some quarters of reducing noble man to the status of a beast (Fig. 62), any more than Courbet's undeniable genius with a brush saved him from charges of socialism and a worship of the ugly (Fig. 28).[6] Breton, succeeding where the others failed, was entirely acceptable to the extreme right (always admitting that his was, at best, an inferior form in their eyes) and for no other reason than the habit he had of dressing up what might be a painful subject to a point where it was not only agreeable but actually quite grand.[7] France, people thought, could well be proud of his

---

[1] Breton also belongs to the "generation of 1848." He exhibited first in 1849, but his success came later in the mid 'fifties.

[2] These subjects were almost the exclusive concern of Breton and Millet; Courbet did only a few, as will be pointed out later.

[3] Cf. the outline for an article written by Millet to Sensier in which the differences separating them are made very clear (quoted at length in E. Moreau-Nélaton, *Millet reconté par lui-même*, Vol. II, pp. 136-138). In 1871 at the time of the formation of the ill-fated *Fédération des Artistes de Paris*, Millet wrote to Sensier: "What a set of wretches all those people are! Courbet, of course, is their president" (*ibid.*, Vol. III, p. 73).

[4] Ph. Burty, *Maîtres et petits maîtres*, Paris, 1877, p. 292.

[5] As has been mentioned previously, in conservative circles the word "style" was intimately bound up with concepts about subject matter; it was, in their view, an idealizing process of the imagination.

[6] In the years of Courbet's greatest notoriety his technique was not particularly revolutionary. See below, pp. 149ff.

[7] Breton's views on Courbet are interesting for they show the mixture of admiration for his painterly ability and distaste for his egotism and self-glorification which one would expect from a more genteel practitioner (see J. Breton, *Nos peintres du siècle*, Paris, n.d., pp.

peasants, but it was a different matter with the wretches presented by the other two (Figs. 45, 46).

Breton was surely the least of this trio, however much he may have pleased his own times, and except as a foil for the others he need not concern us at great length. The differences between Millet and Courbet, however, go very deep and have a real significance for an understanding of the thought of the times. Leaving aside for the moment the question of their own purposes in painting, and restricting ourselves to the few of Courbet's pictures that caused all the discussion,[8] it is clear that the distinction made by the critics lay in the way the subject, man or woman, was regarded, or rather, seemed to be regarded, by the artist. Courbet's people did not seem to be personalities: the *Baigneuses* (Fig. 32) were only bodies, the *Casseurs de pierres* (Fig. 24) had their faces concealed, even the worthy folk in the *Enterrement à Ornans* (Fig. 23) formed little more than a gallery of types or portraits, for there was little emotional interrelation between them. In short, all of them seemed to be objects rather than actors in any human event. The artist apparently did not see them as anything else, nor was he concerned with their hopes and fears, their private lives and emotions, whether they were beautiful or ugly, but was interested in them only as things seen and of interest to paint. As we have seen, it was this neutrality which led Proudhon to admit that the ideas he attributed to Courbet weren't really there,[9] and kept Thoré from giving him his whole approbation.[10] When Castagnary wrote his first Salon, full of the most intense humanitarian idealism, he was quite reserved about the great man from Ornans;[11] later he made him into the greatest artist of the time, but only by sacrificing some of his theory. Champfleury, and the young Duranty, on the other hand, sought only an acceptance of the world as it was presumed to be; they asked for no brotherhood of man, and so were quite content, at least for a time, with what they got from Courbet. Later, his subjects shifted to more commonplace themes: landscapes, flower pieces, nudes and the like, but by that time the realist movement in art had passed its peak.[12] Thus on the one hand, the humanitarians felt that a lack of imagination prevented Courbet from getting beneath the surface appearance of things, while on the other, the

---

123ff.). His remarks on Millet are also typical. While praising his undeniable powers, he finds his countryside "savage" and his men ugly and overwhelmed by the cruel pressure of nature. "I received," he said, "a profound emotional impression even though I felt myself drawn toward nature by an entirely different feeling, by its abundant and voluptuous attraction" (*ibid.*, pp. 150-152).

[8] The chief ones were: *Les Casseurs de pierres*, *L'Enterrement à Ornans*, *Les Baigneuses*, *L'Atelier*, and *Les Demoiselles au bord de la Seine*. See below.

[9] See the discussion of Proudhon's views in Part One.

[10] Courbet was not deep enough to be entirely satisfactory to Thoré; who in 1861 said of him that he "lacked taste although he had spirit" (*Salons de W. Bürger*, Vol. I, p. 100).

[11] See Castagnary, *Salons*, pp. 26ff., and also the discussion of Castagnary in Part One.

[12] Much later (1882), Castagnary said that this shift was due to the fact that Courbet felt he was using up his energies in a fight that wasn't really worth it (G. Riat, *Gustave Courbet, peintre*, Paris, 1906, p. 144). In 1863 Champfleury condemned the *Retour de la conférence* as being very ill-advised, but by this time the writer had become very much more conservative (see Riat, *op.cit.*, p. 207, and Schapiro, "Courbet and Popular Imagery," pp. 188-190).

objective naturalists were quite satisfied by his bold depiction of new and interesting fragments of the real world.[13]

The case of Millet was quite different. In the contemporary view, he also turned to the real world for his themes, and was "realistic" in choosing to paint poor farm folk, but what he did thereafter was to turn them into symbols for his own deep-seated ideas about man's place in the scheme of things.[14] His people lacked the particularity of Courbet's; the man breaking stones was a specific object, an individual model, but the *Semeur* (Fig. 27) was no one man, nor was he intended to be. Where Courbet seemed merely to observe, it was felt that Millet, in his own way, transformed and idealized. One could hardly tell from the pictures what the great Gustave thought of his characters, but in Millet's case there was no question whatever: he loved, admired, and sympathized with them, ugly or not, clean or dirty, young or old. It was for this reason that the humanitarians found a responsive chord in his art and, since there were no more Millets, virtually nowhere else. The realists—that is, the objective naturalists—did not count him as one of them, for he *transformed* his people into something which, in a strict material sense, they were not, and he used his imagination, which they were inclined to forbid. Théodore Pelloquet (an admirer) said that although some people called Millet a realist, the realists regarded him "as a romantic—or an academician which is the same thing in their eyes."[15] Only the more superficial critics ever attempted to relate the two as exponents of the same ideas.

It might surprise anyone acquainted only with Millet's better-known pictures to discover that in his early years he was a painter of nudes and mythological scenes.[16] His first favorable mention was for a pastel in the Salon of '44, which was noted by Thoré,[17] but his *Oedipe détaché de l'arbre* (Fig. 13) in the Salon of 1847, marked his real debut in the critical press. Thoré said that in spite of its incomprehensible appearance, the artist was "an excellent painter who will soon be a celebrated one."[18]

[13] It is interesting that Duranty, the youthful editor of *Le Réalisme*, later became the most confirmed defender of Degas, in whom he continued to admire an objective naturalism whereas it would seem now that Degas was far more of a pure painter and that his realism was of less importance in the total estimation of his art. In the story "Le Peintre Louis Martin," written after the close of our period (publ. in 1881 in *Le Pays des arts*, pp. 315-350), he makes Courbet out to be something of a poseur who is remarkable mainly for his virtuosity with the brush! The shifts in opinion about "realism" are often very difficult to follow and explain. Duranty continued, however, to name the painter as one of the most important founders of the modern movement (cf. *La Nouvelle peinture*, Paris, 1876, p. 32).

[14] Cf., for example, the following by M. H. Dumesnil (*Le Salon de 1859*, Paris, n.d., p. 34): "Millet is a philosopher painter who wants to make the canvas speak like a book, and his pictures are, in a way, a doctrine. . . ." This author notes in passing that the peasants aren't really as badly off as Millet makes them out to be.

[15] Quoted in Moreau-Nélaton, *Millet*, Vol. II, p. 130.

[16] For example: *L'Offrande à Pan* (1845), *La Madeleine* (1846), *Samson et Dalila* (1848), etc.

[17] Thoré, *Salons de T. Thoré*, p. 47: ". . . M. Millet, the author of a little sketch in the mood of Boucher, and of a large pastel which is most harmonious." The pastel was called *La Leçon d'équitation* and was a highly sentimental study of children.

[18] *Ibid.*, p. 506.

The next year he showed the *Vanneur* (Fig. 18), which indicated very plainly the direction his art was to take thereafter and for which the now famous *Semeur* of 1851 became almost a hallmark.[19] According to Sensier, the *Semeur* was regarded in some quarters as being socialistic,[20] but this criticism could not have been very widespread, for De Ris, reviewing for the moderately conservative *Artiste*, found the picture energetic and full of movement, objecting only that it was done in too heavily loaded an impasto.[21] Delécluze found it unintelligible (!) and took it to pieces as thoroughly as any admirer of Ingres might be expected to, but he didn't find it socially suspect; it was just painted very badly.[22] In fact, the stories about Millet's poverty and lack of official recognition have tended to obscure the fact that for most of his career he was very highly regarded by many of the very best critics of the time. To be sure, they couldn't see to it that he always got medals[23] or sold his pictures for good prices, but what could be done by a sympathetic press was done for him, and that year after year. A rather stupid critic by the name of de Lépinois may be cited as an example of the cheaper kind of adverse criticism (the date is 1859), but the matter need not be pursued much further:

> This artist [Millet] has had the courage to proclaim himself the author of a *Femme faisant pâturer sa vache* [Fig. 46], which surpasses anything that exaggerated realism has ever produced of the most hideous. I doubt if one would find in the insane section of the Salpêtrière a more frightfully vile, degraded, animal type than that of M. Millet's female cowherd: one may ask if the cow isn't herding the woman![24]

It is true that Gautier, in his typically inconsistent way, turned on Millet after his years of earlier praise and described his pictures as "monstrous fantasies" in 1861.[25] Of a picture showing a mother feeding her child he exclaimed "We refuse to recognize a human being in this woman," while in the same review he said, "In the case of M. Breton there is a deep feeling for rustic beauty which separates him from the vulgar makers of peasant scenes (paysanneries)."[26] Even with allowances for differences in time and outlook, such remarks seem silly.

Baudelaire found the underlying symbolism of these rustic characters rather shallow and pretentious,[27] but he was not the sort of person who would have been likely to enjoy so solemn an attempt to make common people into an object almost of worship. He was contemptuous of the run of humanity and disliked naïve simplicity. The

---

[19] The *Homme à la houe* of 1863 eventually became an even more famous symbol. Cf. Markham's poem.

[20] Alfred Sensier, *J.-F. Millet* (de Kay trans.), Boston, 1881, p. 111. See also, Moreau-Nélaton, *Millet*, Vol. I, pp. 86-87.

[21] *L'Artiste*, 5e série, Vol. VI, 1851, p. 6.

[22] E. J. Delécluze, *Exposition des artistes vivants, 1850*, pp. 59-60.

[23] He received a second class medal in 1853, again in 1864. In 1867, at the Exposition Universelle he was awarded a First Class medal,

and the next year received the ribbon of the Legion of Honor.

[24] E. and B. de Lépinois, *L'Art dans la rue et l'art au Salon (1859)*, Paris, n.d., Part II, p. 147. For some reason Arsène Houssaye was willing to write a very laudatory preface to this mediocre work.

[25] Th. Gautier, *Abécédaire du Salon de 1861*, Paris, n.d., p. 283.

[26] *Ibid.*, p. 84.

[27] See his remark quoted on p. 86.

Goncourts also seem to have been uninterested, which is not difficult to explain in view of their rather exquisite natures. More interesting is Champfleury's silence on Millet, for he is never discussed at length and not mentioned in any connection during the long account of Courbet's art which includes the following reference to Breton: "... [he saw in] realism only a motif for anecdotes, the dry study of faces, [he] grappled meanly with modern subjects without the great painterly qualities of the author of the *Enterrement à Ornans*."[28] One can only conclude from this that, as Pelloquet suggested, the realists didn't recognize Millet as one of themselves at all.

The roster of those who appreciated this type of humanitarianism is impressive: About, Astruc, Castagnary, Chesneau (who was converted to a taste for it sometime after 1863),[29] De Ris, Duret, Mantz, Thoré, and Burty. (The latter quotes a letter written to Gautier in 1864 by Théodore Rousseau warning him against getting tangled up in mediocrities after having been a notable and skillful critic for so long: "Already you have yielded to the sway of idle talk by giving a bad reception to the only true painter to appear since 1830. ... I am referring to François Millet."[30]) Not all of them were as interested in Millet's social message as were Thoré and Castagnary, but they saw an artist of real power, genuine feeling, and distinguished technique, a refreshing and vigorous change from the mass of cheap sentiment and meretricious style covering so much of the Salon walls.

The painter was not at all averse to telling his friends what he was trying to do in his pictures; his letters contain the clearest evidence of his attempt to see beyond the surface to a deeper reality, his belief that art was a means of communicating definite ideas to the observer, and his independence of any socialistic intention. He often wrote to the critics who spoke well of him giving fuller explanations of the meaning which he had attached to the paintings they were admiring:

In the *Woman Going to Draw Water* I tried to show that she was not a water carrier, or even a servant, but a woman going to draw water for the house, for soup, for her husband and children; that she should not seem to be carrying any greater or less weight than the buckets fill; that under the sort of grimace which the weight on her shoulders causes, and the closing of her eyes at the sunlight, one should see a kind of homely goodness. I have avoided (as I always do with horror) anything that might verge on the sentimental. I wanted her to do her work good-naturedly and simply—as if it were a part of her daily labor, the habit of her life. I wanted to show the coolness of the well, and its antique form is meant to suggest that many before her had come there to draw water.

I try not to have things look as if chance had brought them together, but as if they had a necessary bond between them. I want the people I represent to look as if they belonged to their station, and as if their imaginations could not conceive of their ever being anything else.[31]

The woman was thus a character extended in time beyond any immediate instance to a longer span, the nature of which she summed up by her action. She implied what

[28] Champfleury, *Grandes figures d'hier et d'aujourd'hui*, Paris, 1861, p. 250.

[29] In his review of the Salon of 1863 (in *L'Art et les artistes modernes*) he has no use for Millet (see p. 176) but in *The Education of the Artist*, he says Millet was the true painter of rustic life and refers to him as a seer (pp. 230-232).

[30] Ph. Burty, *Maîtres et petit maîtres*, pp. 156-157.

[31] Sensier, *Millet* (de Kay trans.), p. 141.

had gone before and indicated what would come after. She also stood for a way of life and a moral attitude toward it, an acceptance of the world as she knew it, coupled with a natural association of herself with the well and the business of getting water. She was, in short, a word in the language the painter was using to tell of the life of the peasant (Fig. 44). He once wrote to Pelloquet: "You are of the excessively small number of those who believe that all art is a language, and that a language is created to express thoughts. Say it, and then say it again."[32] Nothing could have been farther from the basic position of the realists, and Castagnary was quite aware of it, although he did not stop to analyze the inconsistency in his own thinking which led him to praise Courbet for translating his own epoch into artistic terms and yet prevented him from seeing that the Ornans master was not even attempting to set forth the ideas which the critic had established as being of the greatest importance, namely the creation of a new interpretation of man's nobility. In a somewhat narrow sense, this was exactly what Millet was after, and yet Castagnary continued to rank him second. At all events, he saw the difference between the two: "In another order of ideas and at the opposite extremity of art [i.e. from Courbet] the painter François Millet is placed." This was a propos of the *Homme à la houe* (Fig. 62; 1863) whom the critic sees as caught up in the endless cycle of the earth which has "devoured" his father and will do the same for his children forever.[33] This was hardly applicable to Courbet's *Retour de la conférence* (Fig. 58) of the same year.

The latter picture was, as we have already seen, the starting point for Proudhon's notable book on art, and we also noted that the author had to confess that he was reading a good deal into the artist's mind that wasn't there.[34] Apparently the *Homme à la houe* was also considered to have some social intent, a suspicion which might, on the surface, seem more plausible since it was a far more thoughtful canvas and obviously meant more than a simple study of a laborer resting from his hard task. But any such charge was indicative of a misunderstanding of the highly individual and unphilosophical mind of the painter; he was never an adherent to any such organized doctrine. In a letter to Sensier, Millet said of this criticism:

The gossip about my *Man with a Hoe* seems to me all very strange, and I am obliged to you for letting me know it, as it furnishes me with another opportunity to wonder at the ideas which people attribute to me. In what club have my critics ever met me? Socialist? Why, I really might answer, like the Auvergnat *commissionaire*, "They say I'm a Saint-Simonist. It isn't true. I don't know what a 'Saint Simonist' is."[35]

Proudhon's admitted ignorance of this painter's work is unfortunate, since he might have felt happier intellectually had he used him as a model rather than Courbet, although he would not necessarily have been more accurate in his appraisal of the painter's true intentions. Jules Claretie, in his reminiscences, says, however, that Millet did reason somewhat in the same manner as the philosopher, for he wished to "moralize" the masses by his painting, an attitude which Claretie feels was quite

[32] Moreau-Nélaton, *Millet*, Vol. II, pp. 130-131.

[33] Castagnary, *Salons*, p. 151.

[34] See Part One on Proudhon.

[35] Sensier, *op.cit.*, p. 157.

foreign to Courbet.[36] In any event, Millet infused his characters with a distinctly religious spirit; De Ris called them "the priests of work" and their creator "the Michelangelo of the peasants."[37]

The lofty purpose, with roots in the soil of the great tradition, which lay behind these paintings was by no means lost on contemporary observers. In praising and in blaming, there is an almost continuous reference to Millet's connections with the art of the past. Maxime DuCamp saw him as a symbolist (i.e. in the traditional sense),[38] Pelloquet described him as painting in the grand style,[39] and Burty actually prophesied that "Millet will be numbered among the true history painters in the highest and most exact meaning of the term . . . ," although it might be that his art was of only mediocre interest for the "city man."[40] Charles Perrier, in his review of the Salon of 1857, rather awkwardly indicated the same general feeling, although with some violence to the facts:

Absolute realism is so ephemeral that here is M. J.-F. Millet, for whom the whole of criticism has been for years trying to create a colossal reputation as an austere realist,[41] yet whose style still appears to us to be singularly conventional. Did not one of the most enthusiastic partisans of M. Millet say recently that his *Paysan greffant un arbre* in the Salon of 1855 had the air of a Platonic philosopher? Is that then realism? . . . The *Glaneuses* whom M. Millet now exhibits are saints not gleaners. . . .[42]

This interesting excerpt might be used as an object lesson in the dangers of the critic's profession. M. Perrier does well when he uses his own eyes, but he is confused when he attempts to make a realist out of Millet on the basis of what other reviewers have thought, and ends by accusing the critics and the painter on grounds unacceptable to both. But Millet's traditionalism, as seen by a sympathetic eye, was better summed up by his friend Pelloquet: "He imagined, and rightly so, that one could deal with the most habitual scenes of the life of the fields in the grand manner and on the most elevated plane, and he managed to do it, so it seemed to him, just as the great painters of former times had done it."[43]

Thus Millet had a peculiar stature in the estimation of his day, and yet no group formed about him to carry on his work, or to extend it from the fields to the city streets. In later years, artists who had similar interests, like the young Van Gogh or Meunier, got much from him, but there was never a broad humanitarian movement which looked to him as its founder, no great surge of artistic interest in the presentation of the soul and feelings of the common man.[44]

---

[36] Jules Claretie, *Peintres et sculpteurs contemporains*, Vol. 1, pp. 86ff. The author notes that the peasants didn't always understand Millet's meaning. One of them laughed at his picture of *Ruth et Boaz* and said that the *garde champêtre* would arrest the girl for stealing garlic!

[37] Clément de Ris, *Critiques d'art et de littérature*, pp. 463-464.

[38] M. DuCamp, *Le Salon de 1859*, Paris, n.d., pp. 96ff.

[39] See below.

[40] Burty, *Maîtres*, pp. 289, 291. The account of Millet given in this book is good throughout. It was written in 1875.

[41] This, of course, was simply not true.

[42] Chas. Perrier, *L'Art français au Salon de 1857*, Paris, n.d., pp. 98-99.

[43] Th. Pelloquet, *Dictionnaire de poche*, p. 160.

[44] There was, perhaps, a greater interest in this kind of thing in Germany. The later exponents of it in France were men like Bastien LePage and Lhermitte. Cf. also A. Legros.

XV. COURBET

THE reticence of Millet's life stands in sharp contrast to the noisy swath cut by his robust contemporary, Gustave Courbet, the great *tapageur*. This interesting epithet has no exact English counterpart, for the word "rowdy" does not quite catch the essence of it, but it was one frequently attached to the rather overwhelming personality of this unusual painter, and suggests in part why he was easily the most controversial figure in the art world of his time. On the evidence of those who knew him well, Courbet can be said to have enjoyed the excitement which his art stirred up; he might even be suspected of making some of it in order to draw attention to his efforts. His good friend and admirer, Nadar, addressed him directly on this score in his review of the Salon of 1853:

. . . coarseness is not strength any more than brutality is frankness, nor is scandal a reputation. It is no longer necessary to rub your hands together and say: "You can easily see that I am the greatest painter because I am the one most attacked." This is to fall into a platitude which is false and stupid like the commonplace it is. Attacks, especially general and sincere ones, have never helped the man attacked: it was not for having been denied that Delacroix prevailed, it was because he was Delacroix.[1]

He was, in short, the *enfant terrible* of the decade from 1850 to 1860, but there was far more to it than that. A group of his pictures became a focal point in the development of the art of the mid-century, a fact which could neither be ignored nor wittily dismissed as an amusing, but never significant, aberration, On the contrary, it assumed proportions of such magnitude that the government itself took note of it,[2] and in one case, at least, attempted to influence the painter to change his ways for the sake of the honor of French art. This occurred when the great Nieuwerkerke himself took the artist to lunch before the opening of the show in 1855, and suggested that if he would only "water his wine" a little, he could go far.[3] No one who has read much of the criticism of this period can have failed to be impressed by the fact that everyone was talking about this work, either pro or con, and that no other painter attracted anything like a comparable volume of attention. It is plain that there was something unusual in his canvases, something never seen before, and that, whatever it was, it cut to the very heart of the artistic thinking of people of all opinions. It was certainly not his style which was at issue. He was, of course, uneven enough to give comfort to his detractors— there were frequent "errors" of scale and perspective, for instance; but in spite of these defects he was generally regarded as a master craftsman even by those who did not appreciate the rest of his genius. Delécluze may surely stand for at least one of the

accepts "errors" in style

---

[1] Nadar (Félix Tournachon), *Nadar jury au Salon de 1853*, Paris, 1853, pp. 6-7.

[2] Cf. the remarks of Fould quoted in Part One.

[3] See Riat, *Gustave Courbet*, p. 129. After the painter decided to have his own show, both Fould and Nieuwerkerke were apparently delighted. The prefect of police received Courbet very courteously, predicted a brilliant success for him and furnished a police guard to handle the expected crowds (Riat, p. 131). The vagaries of official interest were sometimes a little peculiar.

groups opposed to everything the young artist stood for, and yet he said the *Homme à la pipe* (Fig. 26) in the Salon of 1850 was "at least the best painted bit in the show. . . ."[4] Similar instances could be multiplied among the conservatives without adding any light to the problem of Courbet's originality, but the evidence goes to show that his skill as a painter—a "workman" they often called him—entitled him to much more serious attention than he would have received had he been less proficient technically. There was, in fact, a good deal that was traditional in his use of light, form, color, impasto, and the rest; his earlier works were extremely romantic in their shadowy handling, and even some of the later ones exhibit a careful, finely-wrought surface (Fig. 74). He did not use the newer bright colors and broad palette-knife strokes of his later work until long after the excitement over his realism had died down, so it was not his use of the brush and paint that was responsible for his reputation as a revolutionary; it seems to have conflicted with it, if anything.

Nor was his personal character as a public figure at the center of the matter either. A kind of legend about him grew up, it is true, quite early in his career, but that was a result rather than a cause of his fame. As soon as pictures by unknowns were noticed in the Salon, the artist, hitherto just a name, was looked into to fill out the knowledge of the man and his work, and in this case the results were unusually rewarding. Big, hearty, crude, clever, opinionated, gifted—Courbet was nothing if not a character to set tongues wagging, and the stories ran through the studios and down the boulevards, gaining flavor as they went. How sad it would have been to discover that the author of the *Casseurs de pierres* was a mousy, retiring, character who would never impress anyone for a second; how delightful to find that he was as bizarre and preposterous as his pictures! His forthright nature was responsible for the directness of the challenge he flung down before the other painters and the critics—the one-man show of 1855 outside the main Salon was a direct bid for trouble—but few people came and the excitement had already begun long before when the *Enterrement à Ornans* (Fig. 23) and the *Baigneuses* (Fig. 32) were exhibited. His personality operating through his paintings was far more decisive than the same character directing his public life. Paris was full of unusual and peculiar people, but it was much less crowded with painters who executed huge studies of unimportant people in an almost majestically robust style. What was needed to cause a real sensation was an extraordinary person who could at the same time produce extraordinary pictures.

What sort of a man was he really? What did he mean by his pictures? Was he actually a socialist? Did he wish to shock the bourgeois for the fun of making a public scandal of himself, or was this just a by-product of his natural bent as a painter, an accident of his tremendous vitality and naïve honesty? Was it his personal originality coming out in his work which was so shocking? These questions are not easily answered, but a study of his character may shed some light on them.

He was undeniably a man of great vigor, a hard worker, a bold painter, and a strong talker.[5] There was nothing passive or meek about him, nor was he much given to intro-

---

[4] Delécluze, *Exposition des artistes vivants*, p. 31.   [5] Among his friends, that is.

spection. Baudelaire and others decided he had no imagination, by which they did
not mean that he had no pictorial imagination but that he was apparently incapable of
any intellectual or spiritual transformation of his subjects, a matter to which we shall
return later on. He possessed a natural shrewdness, a flair for knowing fairly often just
what was going on around him,[6] though at times his lack of any deeper penetration
seems to have led him into trouble; at least it would appear that his difficulties with the
affair of the Vendôme Column were heightened by a reputation for socialistic tendencies which he had never done anything to contradict in the days when such suspi-
cions were helping to make him the talk of Paris. He was known to have been a friend
of Proudhon, and even claimed to have been responsible for much of the content of
Du principe de l'art,[7] but this does not fit very well with the extremely unliterary
nature of the rest of his life, or the fact that his friends were probably the authors of
his various comments on the nature of art.[8]

In a complimentary sense of the term, he was a natural man, honest about his work,
if a little showy at times, and with an instinctive dislike for the artificialities of the
more academic painting of his day. His ego was large enough to convince him that his
way was the best, that his own interpretation of the masters was a better guide than
those of the École or the Ministry of Fine Arts. He naturally rejected angels and
goddesses as being outside his experience, but later, when things were going well, he
was not averse to painting a picture at least one of whose titles was: *Vénus poursuivant
Psyché avec sa jalousie*.[9] The title *Allégorie réelle* for the huge picture of his studio
(Fig. 38) may have been intended as a sort of insult to the tradition, but all the same
it was his own version of a history painting, the only difference being that in this
instance, the history in question was his own, and he saw no reason for neglecting to
tell it to the world at large. But this type of painting was not characteristic, for he had
a basic and compelling interest in the evidence of his eyes, and no other artist of the
day displayed a wider range of subjects during this period. Portraits (of himself and
others), genre scenes, landscapes, flower pieces, still-lifes, hunting scenes, nudes, sea-
scapes—all these flowed from his tireless brush in profusion, and about them he was
serious enough.

Furthermore, he was certainly a man of the people and never disowned his provincial origins. In fact, he went back often to Ornans and the other towns he knew and
liked, renewing himself by these repeated contacts with the life from which he ulti-

---

[6] He was wrong about the *Demoiselles de
village*, however. He thought (before it was
shown) that no one could object to it. See
below.

[7] P.-J. Proudhon, *Du principe de l'art*, Int.,
p. 1, note 1. See Part One.

[8] A. Estignard in his *Courbet, sa vie, ses
oeuvres* (Paris, 1896), says that Castagnary
wrote the preface to the catalogue of the show
in 1855. In *Gustave Courbet* (London, 1912,
with an introduction by L. Bénédite and notes
by J. Laran and Ph. Gaston-Dreyfus), Bénédite

suggests (p. x) that it was written by Champfleury, while Laran and Dreyfus think Castagnary helped him with it (p. 55). At all events
his lack of formal intellectual interests was
apparently a marked feature of his character,
and it is unlikely that he ever had a very extensive grasp of the theory and practice of
socialism. It is sometimes difficult to decide
just how serious he was. The real title of his
famous picture was *Tableau historique d'un
enterrement à Ornans*.

[9] Painted in 1864.

mately drew his strength. The landscapes which finally won the crowd were still the ones he had always enjoyed, the same ones that had been thought vulgar and ugly before. He liked uncomplex people like himself (although in his circle in Paris he also knew subtler ones like Chenavard) and he undoubtedly thought that a homely man or woman was just as interesting as a handsome one. All this is true and reveals an honesty which is both obvious and appealing, but there is little in his art to suggest that he thought very much more than that, a point which has been mentioned earlier in comparing him to Millet.[10] He was admired by Castagnary for setting down his age,[11] and claimed himself that "an epoch can be reproduced only by its own artists, I mean the artists who have lived in it."[12] But it would be difficult to maintain that he had reproduced more than a very few disconnected fragments of his own. From Daumier, from Gavarni, and Guys, we can learn much of the age directly; what we learn from Courbet is more about himself than about his subjects.

Looking about with a keen eye, he saw much of interest but he failed, either through lack of interest or an incapacity to see any deeper, to evaluate what he saw. The people of Ornans, what were they like? We know their appearance from the *Enterrement* (Fig. 23), we even can identify the various citizens of the town, but there is nothing more. Who were the men breaking those stones? Did he know them, how they lived, what they thought and believed? There is no suggestion; they are just pounding rocks. We know a good deal about his sisters, but not from their sunny afternoon in the company of those celebrated toy cows of the *Demoiselles de village* (Fig. 29). Even his friends assembled in the *L'Atelier* (Fig. 38) are only stage properties, symbols as he calls them, presented to illustrate his life and interests. M. Bruyas in the *Bonjour, M. Courbet* (*La Rencontre*; Fig. 37) is hardly a real personality, though it must be admitted that many of his other portraits are very fine, especially the ones of himself which actually do reveal much of his character. No particular criticism of the man is implied here. But from the standpoint of interpretation he was uninterested in going below the surface; he was content to exercise his gifts on the outside rather than the inside of the object before him. Max Buchon, one of his lifelong friends, gave this account of his intuitive powers:

As an instrument for education and study Courbet never had anything more than his magnificent power of seeing (*regard*), and that was certainly quite enough.

To *live* a constantly energetic and intent life: to *see* with a piercing and final vision, that was the whole secret of this fine intelligence at the service of a great heart.

Courbet didn't know much history, or science, or many books; but this didn't hinder him from knowing nature and men thoroughly.[13]

The passage speaks for itself. In his careful study, Meyer Schapiro has analyzed the degree to which Courbet's art had any significance beyond its more purely pictorial

---

[10] See above, p. 143.

[11] Castagnary, *Salons*, p. 148, "Le Salon de 1863."

[12] From the open letter to a group of students who wanted to study under him (1861).

Here quoted from Goldwater and Treves, *Artists on Art*, p. 296.

[13] Max Buchon, *Receuil de dissertations sur le réalisme*, Neuchâtel, 1856. Here quoted from Chas. Léger, *Courbet*, Paris, 1929, p. 67.

aspects.[14] He points out that the artist's roots among the people extended to a taste for the crude but effective popular prints of the day, and his premised superiority in the field of painting, combined with his estimate of himself as a man of the masses, made him feel that he was the only artist who could really do them justice.[15] But this was more an instinctive than a rational conclusion on Courbet's part, and does not need to be accepted beyond its face value as one more of the somewhat pompous remarks to which he was addicted. Buchon said that he painted in much the same manner as an apple tree bore apples,[16] from which we may conclude that the act was so natural to him that he had few if any intellectual preoccupations at the time of actual creation.

We may then accept, at least provisionally, a picture of Courbet as a big, rather rough, country man, shrewd in some ways, naïve in others, bluff and full of his own importance, yet at the same time gifted beyond most men with an eye to see and a hand to paint the things in which he took interest and delight. A character supremely interested in himself, and for that reason inclined to accept life entirely on his own terms, he was the ideal person to break the bonds of tradition and plow ahead unhampered by the doubts and fears of a more introspective soul, or the niceties which would be regarded as essential by someone more cultivated and less direct. He was bold to a degree, feared no critic, and was sustained throughout everything that happened, except perhaps the misfortune which led to his disgrace,[17] by his own faith in himself. We may now turn to that rather small group of pictures on which the controversy centered, and see to what extent they appear to bear out this character, and how much we can discover about the intention behind them.

Arranging them in a roughly chronological order, we find that his "realistic" manner was first established in the *Après dînée à Ornans* (Fig. 20),[18] a solidly painted work quite reminiscent of the Le Nain, the seventeenth century masters who were slowly coming into new favor in France.[19] The picture was admired and promptly bought by the government, as a sign of its approval, for the modest sum of 1,500 francs. This was the year after the revolution and there was still a strong sentiment abroad which favored work dealing with the life of the people. Courbet here showed that he was abandoning a romantic attitude essentially foreign to his nature and was turning to

[14] M. Schapiro, "Courbet and Popular Imagery," *passim.*

[15] *Ibid.*, p. 170.

[16] Buchon, *op.cit.* in Leger, *Courbet*, p. 66.

[17] I.e. the affair of the Vendôme Column.

[18] "Feu Diderot" writing the review for *L'Artiste*, (5e série, Vol. III, 1849, p. 98) referred to the artist as "This robust newcomer" and called his picture "the triumph of nature" although he still preferred the art of Valentin, a painter to whom Courbet was occasionally compared.

[19] Champfleury wrote a biography of the Le Nain and Thoré has already been mentioned for his work on Vermeer and the Dutch generally. It is, perhaps, paradoxical that a society which could admire the realism of Brouwer and Ostade was offended by a similarly direct realism applied to the contemporary scene. It is possible that distance lent enchantment. The character and limitations of French bourgeois taste should be very thoroughly studied for it was on this taste that the artists were, in a sense, dependent. It was of a rather low order, but the reasons for that unhappy fact have never been properly analyzed.

Courbet himself was fascinated by Dutch art, and his work always received a favorable welcome in Holland.

subjects he knew from direct experience. The liberal atmosphere of the day may have had something to do with this change, though he was not active in the revolution. The next Salon, that of 1850-51, saw the appearance of the *Casseurs de pierres* (Fig. 24), the *Enterrement à Ornans* (Fig. 23), and the *Paysans de Flagey revenant de la foire* (Fig. 28). All of these were subjects which were entirely natural to a man from the provinces who was in no way ashamed of the fact or overawed by the art world of the capital. His friends had posed for the *Enterrement* and could in many cases be identified, the Flagey peasants were merely a study of the sort of rural life to which he was accustomed, and the stone breakers had first been seen by accident, beside the road.[20] These people were important because they were a part of his own personal world and therefore of interest. He painted them large simply to show how interesting they were to *him*. This, of course, was an affront to Paris, for the representation of these unknown and rather ugly people on a scale customarily reserved for history painting led to the conclusion that the pictures were an attack upon custom by a boorish provincial who was out to wreck art as rapidly as possible. Courbet may or may not have had this in mind when he set out to paint them, but he was soon aware of the fact that he had become overnight the most notorious painter in France merely by doing on a large scale what was natural to him.

"Realism" was not unknown to the public; in one form or another they had seen it practiced for years, in the *trompe-oeil* manner of a Delaroche or the painstaking minuteness of a Meissonier, but in previous cases the works had been of a more polite size and they had been done of subjects less likely to jar the sensibilities of the public. To be suddenly presented with the work of an undeniably powerful artist who cared nothing (apparently) for morality, or beauty, or idealism, or sentiment, or the antique, or Raphael or, worst of all, for the delicate feelings of the Parisian bourgeois; who boldly set down what interested him without any regard for what might interest *them*; who seemed to find definitely homely people quite fit subjects for his brush—all this was too much, and the ensuing storm was of gale proportions.[21] It was, essentially, the choice of subject, combined with an uncompromising and matter-of-fact presentation of it that constituted realism as they thought he practiced it. All the rest of the criticism was merely an embellishment of their fundamental refusal to accept either of these elements in his art. From his side, it was merely the easy and unrehearsed product of his personality, a temperament vastly different from that to which the people and the critics were accustomed.

Very much like a small boy, he next conceived the idea of an urban masterpiece connected with the fire department, and the *Pompiers courant à un incendie* was undertaken,[22] only to be abandoned after his friend the lieutenant in charge was jailed on suspicion of having set a fire so Courbet could have the proper local color. This picture, and the later *Demoiselles au bord de la Seine* (Fig. 41) were the two chief attempts he made at painting "city" subjects.[23]

---

[20] The picture was painted in his studio at Ornans with a road mender named Gagey as the model.

[21] See above, p. 48.

[22] This was done in 1852.

[23] Cf. Castagnary's prediction in 1864 that

In the Salon of 1852 some of the critics came down hard on the *Demoiselles de village faisant l'aumône* (Fig. 29), a really fresh and charming picture of Courbet's sisters against a background of Ornans scenery. It was bought before the show ever opened by the Duc de Morny,[24] but this did not save it from the bitterest of attacks, an enormous astonishment to the artist who was sure he had disarmed all his adversaries by painting a "gracious" picture.[25] He learned that he was not to be forgiven so easily for his performance of the year before, and, unfortunately for him, this was one of the pictures which revealed very clearly one of the most peculiar aspects of his realism: an inability to see the subject as a coordinated whole. In this case the result was an extraordinary discrepancy of scale between the girls and the cows.[26] In many of the artist's pictures, similar passages can be found, as well as many examples where the figures remain unconnected to the settings in which they are placed. This is explained, probably, by the fact that the painter was accustomed to study the landscape and the figure separately, and whereas he could paint the model directly in the studio, in the case of hills and sky he either had to work from sketches painted indoors or put indoor-lighted figures into scenes painted directly from nature.[27] To a man lacking in imagination and synthetic ability, this would pose an immediate and recurrent problem, for any putting of the two together would always and inevitably show the signs of an artificial juncture whose roughness could never be entirely smoothed over. Two different bits of reality seen and painted under different lights could never be fitted together as long as they were painted as seen. The only solution would have been to paint the model and the landscape together, outdoors, and this Courbet did not do. He could not, of course, in the case of the pictures of deer, and in these the effect of awkwardness is unusually marked. Whatever the explanation may be for this peculiarity

---

tomorrow art would enter the cities and paint their social customs (Castagnary, *Salons*, p. 205, "Salon de 1864").

[24] It is quite possible that the painter could have had a very successful official career at this point for the Duc de Morny was very influential. Being of a republican turn of mind, Courbet did not take advantage of it.

[25] The critics had a rare taste in invective. The following is from E. Loudun's review of that Salon: "But the girls! My God! One can easily understand why they have sought this solitary place! They are so ill-favored, so disgraceful. . . . The cows doubtless came from Lilliput. . . . I am neither moved, nor instructed, nor amused" (E. Loudun, *Le Salon de 1852*, p. 8).

[26] The peculiar size of the cows was the source of great merriment, particularly in the caricatural reviews. Louis Esnault even thought the dog was ugly (Riat, *Courbet*, p. 98). The landscape and the portrait of Cuenot which were exhibited along with it received very little

attention, but Alphonse Grün, the editor of the *Moniteur universel*, who was one of the few who liked the *Demoiselles*, said of the portrait that Courbet had "smoked up one of his compatriots in a most horrible manner" and that one could only surmise that the painter had wanted to attract attention by showing a bad portrait in contrast to the good one of the year before—i.e. the *Homme à la pipe* (Alph. Grün, *Le Salon de 1852*, Paris, n.d., p. 56). It seemed that it was impossible to suit everyone.

[27] Leger reproduces a photograph of Courbet painting out of doors under an umbrella, but how much of his work was done in this manner at this time is hard to determine. Many of the landscapes of the 'fifties look as if they were finished indoors (Ch. Leger, *Courbet*, p. 112; cf. also p. 57 for an account of the master's manner of working outdoors at Puits-Noir). The evidence of the famous *Atelier* suggests that at least the final touches were put on in the studio.

of his art, the critics noted it in the *Demoiselles de village*, and they made the very best use of it they could, even though otherwise the canvas was truly delightful and totally inoffensive as to content.[28]

In '53 Courbet exhibited *Les Lutteurs*, a rather turgid study of the male nude (which he had painted over his earlier romantic effort, the *Nuit classique de Walpurgis*), the *Fileuse endormie* and a *Baigneuses* (Fig. 32). Neither of the first two created much excitement, but the *Baigneuses* once more loosed the vials of critical wrath. The Empress was credited with the *bon mot* of the show when she inquired, after looking at Rosa Bonheur's *Marché aux chevaux*, if the two women in Courbet's canvas were not "percheronnes"? The artist, judging from his other nudes, liked big women and was not always delicate in his interest in them, or in his feeling about the way they should be painted.[29] To a society which admired Ingres' Odalisques and was later prepared to go into ecstasies over the Venuses of Henner, Bouguereau, and Cabanel, these two forms must have seemed indescribably vulgar—they certainly did to Delacroix.[30] The artist, with a rougher sensitivity to the female form divine, probably thought they were very fine. The difficulty obviously arose over a variance in taste, but Courbet didn't see why his was not as good as anyone else's, and they were not by any means the last such heavy nudes to come from his brush.

The exhibition of 1855 was to be, as every artist knew, a very special occasion. Courbet submitted twelve pictures for it of which ten were accepted and two were refused. Included in the accepted group was the odd portrait of himself meeting his good patron Bruyas (who had been stout-hearted enough to buy the *Baigneuses* along with several other pictures by his friend) which was variously entitled *La Rencontre, Bonjour, M. Courbet* and *La Fortune saluant le génie* (Fig. 37). The deferential attitude of the servant, the bold and handsome features of the artist, as well as his rather romantic pose in contrast to the simple stance of M. Bruyas, were all the cause for much rude mirth among the adverse critics, and one went so far as to point out that in this piece of homage to genius, only the artist was allowed to cast a shadow![31] At best, it was perhaps not a very good picture, but it certainly gave grounds for the belief that the painter had no mean opinion of his talents or his place in the general scheme of society.

It has been thought occasionally that as a result of the refusal of two pictures, Courbet withdrew them all, or that as a result of his arguments with M. de Nieuwerkerke[32] he was finally excluded entirely and so set up his famous show outside.[33] This is erroneous, for the ten accepted pictures were duly exhibited inside and were seen there

---

[28] Courbet's models often had to suffer along with the painter, but his devoted sisters probably didn't mind being condescended to by the elegants of the capital.

[29] Cf. *Les Dormeuses, La Femme aux bas blancs*, etc. He painted a "special" picture for the Egyptian Khalil-Bey (Leger, *Courbet*, pp. 115-116).

[30] *Journal de Eugène Delacroix*, Vol. II,

pp. 18-19.

[31] Ed. About, *Voyage à travers l'Exposition des Beaux-Arts*, Paris, 1855, p. 205.

[32] This episode is described in L. Bénédite, *Gustave Courbet* (notes by J. Laran and Ph. Gaston-Dreyfus), pp. 47-49.

[33] Cf. *A Loan Exhibition of Gustave Courbet* (Wildenstein Gallery), New York, 1948, p. 16.

by all the critics. The two rejected paintings plus forty-one others (including some drawings) were in the special show. The two works so firmly declined by the jury were the now-famous *Enterrement à Ornans* and a huge new canvas entitled *L'Atelier du peintre, allégorie réelle detérminant une phase de sept années de ma vie artistique* (Fig. 38). In a letter to a friend, he tells how hard he worked on this latter scene, and indicates what great store he set by it.[34] Its refusal was a bitter blow, but to anyone less completely wrapped up in his own affairs it would have been clear at once that it wouldn't, and couldn't, be accepted.

This great picture—great in size as well as in design—was, of course, a sort of monument to the artist's importance after some ten years of life in the public eye, and seven as a figure of some note. It had all the trappings of a history painting: large scale, monumental arrangement, symbolic figures, and even a crowd of witnesses to prove that he, Courbet, really was a master.[35] It was, of course, a piece of unparalleled self-advertisement as well as a direct flouting of all that the conservatives held dear. He knew well enough what a fuss had been made over him, both by his admirers and his enemies; he knew, too, that the form and mood of the picture would seem to be worse than satire, a travesty of the standards of the right wing, and yet at the same time he was unabashed and uncontrite at the thought of celebrating his own progress in this grandiose manner. The entire history of nineteenth century art knows of no other case in which an artist came to his own support in such magnificent fashion. That he submitted the picture at all was clear indication of the extent of the egotism that had already caused so much commotion, and the opposition was even more infuriated because the painting was much better than what currently passed for actual history painting elsewhere. Worst of all, there was no denying the stubborn fact that, conceited though he might be, he was one of the major artists of the time.[36]

The description of the picture has been given so often that it need not be repeated here except to note, perhaps, that the nude model standing by the artist's side as he paints a landscape suggests the truth of the explanation given earlier for the common lack of unity between his figures and their settings.[37] It is also interesting to see that he attempted to fall back on a sort of symbolism in order to explain what was generally regarded as the epitome of antisymbolism, that is, objective naturalism (realism).[38]

[34] For an excellent account of all matters pertaining to this picture, see R. Huyghe, *Courbet, L'Atelier*, Paris, n.d.

[35] Note particularly the couple at the right who represent society paying its respects to the painter.

[36] Even the critics who attacked him most bitterly were inclined to devote whole sections of their reviews to demolishing him, a tacit admission of his importance.

[37] See above, pp. 155-156.

[38] In 1863, Champfleury told Max Buchon that Courbet wasn't cut out for painting symbolism and satire (Riat, *Courbet*, p. 214), and DuCamp said a little later that although he was a fine landscapist he should stay away from great painting (M. DuCamp, *Les Beaux-arts à l'Exposition Universelle et aux Salons de 1863, etc.*, Paris, n.d., p. 222, "Le Salon de 1866"). In a letter to Castagnary, Courbet said that he was working (1864) on a symbolic satire of the miserable state of contemporary poetry. It was to have shown a nude figure spitting into the Spring of Hippocrene and thus poisoning it. The picture was spoiled by an accident (Riat, *op.cit.*, p. 215).

In spite of its size and complexity, it seems today to have an air of curious naïveté about it, something suggestive of a child dressed up in an adult's clothes, a sort of wonderful sham which is a tribute, perhaps, to its power, for it has real strength in spite of its pretentiousness. Scorned in its day, unsold in his lifetime, it was finally bought by subscription for the Louvre in 1919 at a price of 900,000 francs. How Courbet must have laughed in his grave when that sale was consummated!

Two years later he exhibited *Les Demoiselles au bord de la Seine* (Fig. 41), and again the cry of the "worship of the ugly" was raised, along with others concerned with the inadvisability of presenting such obviously immoral females to the public gaze. The girls were, in a sense, the immediate forbears of Manet's *Olympia* (Fig. 70) and the young women in the *Déjeuner sur l'herbe* (Fig. 59). Courbet, who was quite capable of painting really shocking pictures when he wished to, was doubtless again surprised, for although his models were obviously not from "society," they were fully dressed and there was not a man in sight. They were, in all truth, his substitutes for the goddesses he could not see.

Once more his directness and his personal interests had caused a scandal, but the time was not far off when all, or almost all, his indiscretions were to be forgiven him. A few of his pictures only have been mentioned, but the total output of these years was large, and the landscapes (Fig. 25), animal pictures, and still-lifes were beginning to become quite popular. After 1857 the number of controversial pictures declined. Some of his nudes were objected to on moral grounds[39] but they sold well enough,[40] and, except for one year, he had apparently settled down into a state of popularity which was more comfortable, as well as more remunerative, than the earlier one of perpetual battle.

In 1863 he painted the *Retour de la conférence* (Fig. 58),[41] a sort of peasant's joke at the venality of the rural clergy, but it promptly raised a protest from the Church as well as from all those who, even if they thought it amusing enough, regarded it as being in bad taste. Proudhon took it up, blowing it up into something far more, but it is doubtful if the artist had any such intentions as were read into it. Two years afterwards, at the time of his friend's death, Courbet exhibited a portrait of him[42] which elicited a good deal of comment, not so much for itself, as the subject of it, for the

---

[39] *Le Reveil*, for example, was refused for the Salon of 1864 for this reason. (This is probably the *Vénus et Psyché*, under another title.)

[40] There was a great row (on Courbet's part) over the *Femme au perroquet* which he believed Nieuwerkerke had promised to buy. According to Riat (*Courbet*, p. 238) the *Vénus et Psyché* of 1864 was sold for 18,000 francs and the *Femme au perroquet* went in 1869 for 15,000 (*ibid.*, p. 276). These were very respectable prices.

[41] The picture was part of a series eventually published as illustrations for a cheap anticlerical tract entitled *Les Curés en Goguette avec six dessins de Gustave Courbet. Exposition de Gand de 1868*, Brussels, 1868 (Schapiro, "Courbet and Popular Imagery," p. 168, note 3).

[42] Thoré remarked that both men were good in their own fields but that the picture was not good and neither was the book (*Salons de W. Bürger*, Vol. II, pp. 268-270, "Le Salon de 1865"). Thoré, however, had a certain sympathy for Proudhon's views, as might be expected of a man of his humanitarian interests.

famous socialist had been hated and feared by many bourgeois.[43] The *Aumône d'un mendiant* of 1868 may be said to conclude the list of works which aroused any real storm of protest over their content, but by this time the painter had become too well liked for even as rough a presentation of poverty as this to bother many people. They were more inclined to write it off as an unfortunate lapse on the part of an otherwise excellent practitioner. The balance of his paintings were generally well received, or if they were not, it was because of stylistic defects and other technical errors they were felt to contain. Indeed, as the years went by, Courbet experimented more and more boldly with his color and brushwork, exerting a considerable influence on the rising generation of progressives,[44] but the public and the critics received these with comparative equanimity—sometimes even with enthusiasm, as in the case of the fine marine views done at Étretat in the late 'sixties.[45]

What conclusions are to be drawn from this brief account of the key pictures in the controversy over realism? One, certainly, is the fact that they constituted but a small part of the artist's total *oeuvre* in the period so that their importance was not proportional to their numbers but was based on the ideas involved in them. Even after Courbet had given up his apparently rebellious ways, they remained as landmarks to which writers kept referring, exerting a steady influence by their mere existence and occasional exhibition.[46] Why then were they so significant? We have seen that it was not because of the way they were done or even because they were "realistic" in the broad sense of the term. It was because they turned to a kind of subject which had not hitherto been considered acceptable and were painted as though these new subjects were just as important as any other—more so, perhaps. What was more, they seemed to be handled objectively in the sense that they were neither idealized nor emotionalized and it was obvious that the presence of "beauty" in the subject, or the painting of it, was of no consequence whatever to the artist. The result of this, of course, was that the object painted appeared to stand out in a new sort of clarity and reality; it was stark, bold, and, to coin a phrase, emotionally naked. Had Courbet chosen to adopt this attitude toward women who were themselves both beautiful and socially acceptable, or toward events which were in themselves sources of interest and pride to the self-esteem of the Parisians of the day, the answer might have been different. But he did not do this because he didn't care to; he had his own interests—those of a rather

[43] Cf. the review by P. Challemel-Lacour in the *Revue Germanique* (Vol. XXXIV, No. 1, 1865, p. 95) in which he discusses both the picture and Proudhon's book on art. Proudhon is clearly the object of both hate and fear on the part of the author and he thinks that this peaceable picture is a denial of Courbet's vaunted realism; otherwise it would show the man for the ogre he was.

[44] Cf. Marius Chaumelin, *L'Art contemporain*, p. 417, "Le Salon de 1870," who says that Renoir's *Baigneuse* is a "relative of the celebrated *Baigneuse* of M. Courbet."

[45] Chaumelin thought Courbet's marines were the best in the Salon of 1870 (*ibid.*, p. 441). Some of these are indeed very beautiful and of a lightness of palette which seems to anticipate the later Impressionist tonalities. *Low Tide* in the William Rockhill Nelson Gallery of Art, St. Louis, is a fine example. The museum dates it 1865-66.

[46] In 1867 a large part of the more important ones appeared in another one-man show held at the Pont de l'Alma. The *Atelier, Retour de la conférence*, and the *Après-dînée à Ornans* were not there, however.

does not interpret subjects [handwritten margin note]

courbet [handwritten margin note]

simple man raised in the country where life was less refined—and he saw no reason to please anyone but himself in the matter of what he should paint or what he should think about it. The chances are that he didn't think much anyway, because it didn't occur to him to do so; he just put it all down in the joy of an enormously fertile and powerful talent. By doing this without imagination, without any interest in interpreting the people and their natures to a world which did not understand or sympathize with them, he alienated many who might otherwise have admired him even more wholeheartedly. He merely *presented* his cast of characters, and no more. Each of them was different because each of them was a separate fact, separately observed. Millet's people, on the other hand, all looked very much alike because they were not individuals but type figures taking parts in his drama of human significance and destiny. Castagnary was quite right when he said that the two men stood at opposite poles.[47]

criticism [handwritten margin note]

Anyone who is interested in a full account of the specific critical opinions expressed about these pictures can find them set forth at length in Riat's fine study of the painter.[48] But there they are mainly arranged in a simple chronological order divided only according to whether they were more or less favorable, so it may be valuable to arrange them here in accordance with the ideas explained in Part One. Some repetition will be unavoidable, for Courbet's position is so central that it has been necessary to refer to his works continually as examples and contrasts to various theoretical positions. Yet when the opinions are grouped around the painter's actual work, they help to bring him into clearer focus.

Courbet began exhibiting as early as the Salon of 1844, but he did not attract much critical attention until 1848. Haussard, writing in *Le National*, said, "At the last three Salons M. Courbet has remained unnoticed. Is it our fault or his? It is certain that in 1848 he has the quality of an artist, he appears to be a painter."[49] Whether the fault was Courbet's or not, no one was ever likely to worry again about his remaining unnoticed. Haussard admired a *Violoncelliste*, while Champfleury, the artist's future champion, praised *La Nuit classique de Walpurgis*.

As we have already seen, the realists were so satisfied with Courbet that he became not only the object of their admiration, but the basis upon which their pictorial theory was built. And yet it seems that when the more complex mind of a man like Champfleury had once fastened upon his art, it became, through his words, something a little different from what it was when it left the hand of the painter. Notice the description of the *Enterrement à Ornans* (Fig. 23):

M. Courbet can boldly mention three women's heads, the children, the gravedigger, and many other figures as types of modern Beauty, while the beadles will tip the balance and make the *Enterrement à Ornans* be declared as the masterpiece of the ugly. Is it the painter's fault if material interests, the life of a small town, sordid egotisms, provincial shabbiness

---

[47] Castagnary, *Salons*, p. 151, "Le Salon de 1863."

[48] I.e. *Gustave Courbet, peintre.*

[49] *Ibid.*, p. 48.

leave their stamp on the face, quench the eyes, wrinkle the forehead, besot the mouth? Many bourgeois are like that; M. Courbet has painted the bourgeois.[50]

The feelings of the worthy folk of Ornans can well be imagined as they read this harsh praise. But what is significant about the passage is that simple observation has been turned into something else. The materialist attitude which it implies was often described as being positivist, because it expressed a relationship between facts, which in this case were the marks left on people by their environment. To the objective naturalistic critics, much of the fascination in such scenes and such objects lay precisely in this evidence of the effects of environment. In other words, one could know almost everything necessary about a man by observing the way he had been marred or otherwise altered by contact with life.[51] The painter was to exhibit what amounted to a case history based upon externals, and if there was a moral involved at all, it was that people would be improved by an examination of the effect society had on a person's physical appearance. Champfleury called "realism" honesty in art,[52] that is, a frankness in showing us as we are so that we may profit from the sight of it. The assumption was, apparently, that people would not observe these same signs as attentively in real life as they would in a picture. He agreed to a certain extent with Proudhon when he maintained that art should be the conscience of society,[53] but in the art form itself, this was to be made manifest only by the choice of subject and the honesty with which it was handled. The idea was much the same as the more modern one by which people are persuaded to contribute to worthy causes by showing them photographs of destitute children. But this somewhat incidental morality does not seem to have been very central to the theory as a whole; the main interest lay in a new and supposedly uncolored look at nature and man. Champfleury never liked the *Atelier* as well as the *Enterrement*, and the reason is clear.[54] In his review of Courbet's work contained in the "letter" to George Sand in 1855, he rejects the idea that the *Baigneuses*, the *Lutteurs*, and the *Casseurs de pierres* "contain the ideas which people have wanted to put in them afterward," but it was possible that some of his own ideas weren't in them either.[55]

Desnoyers carries the idea forward by asserting that realism (i.e. Courbet's art) is "the true painting of objects," but he does not involve himself in any discussion of how many different kinds of truth one object may exemplify when depicted on a piece of canvas.[56] The term, he says in a good partisan spirit, is used for the purpose of distinguishing the "sincere clairvoyant artist from the being who persists, through good

---

[50] Champfleury, "Courbet," in *Grandes figures d'hier et d'aujourd'hui*, Paris, 1861, p. 242. This is actually from an article entitled "L'Enterrement d'Ornans," written in 1851.

[51] Man was, in short, the complete product of his environment. Cf. Duranty's views discussed below, pp. 162 and 206ff.

[52] Champfleury, *Le Réalisme*, Paris, 1857, pp. 10ff.

[53] *Ibid.*, in a long discussion of *L'Atelier*,

pp. 279ff.

[54] *Ibid.* He objected, of course, to the "real allegory."

[55] Champfleury, "Du réalisme. Lettre à Madame Sand," *L'Artiste*, 5e série, Vol. XVI, 1855, p. 4.

[56] The exact nature of "reality" and "truth" is a thorny philosophical problem. One can see what men like Desnoyers meant, but they did not really attempt to argue the matter out.

faith or bad, in regarding things through colored glasses. . . . Realism, while not being the apology for the ugly or the evil, has the right to represent what exists and what one sees."[57]

Today one can suspect that these men were a little carried away by the heat of battle, for it is hard to see how they could have been content for very long with so materialistic an art, an inventory of existence which was to derive its interest neither from the ideas which it possessed in itself nor from the artistry with which the forms were handled, but solely from the novelty of seeing things in pictures which had not been seen there before, and seeing them with what was imagined to be an unclouded eye.[58] As we have mentioned, the excitement over this kind of art waned when the subjects became the same ones with which art had dealt for many years, and objective naturalism remained rather unmoved by developments in the direction of new kinds of pictorial or painterly handling. But the interest in the world directly experienced remained for a long time, underlying much subsequent art and criticism. Duranty, an early follower of Champfleury, still thought of himself in 1876 as a realist, a "primitive in a great movement of artistic renovation."[59]

His famous brochure on "The New Painting" of 1876 shows that in spite of certain transformations in the original ideas of objective naturalism, much of it remained important for him, in fact it was still at the heart of the matter: "What we need is the special mark of the modern individual, in his clothes, in the midst of his social habits, at home or on the street."[60] The appearance of this person will tell us all we need to know: "A man opens a door, he enters, that is enough: one sees that he has lost his daughter."[61] However true this might be in the drama, it was harder to achieve in painting; on this basis, could one have told if the two stone breakers were father and son? For all of Duranty's skillful pleading, it is hard to see how the external aspect of anything can tell us all; if it could, criminals might well be arrested on sight. That art was now committed to drawing its themes from the contemporary scene was true enough, but that even a superior eye for details could, by noting them, reveal as much as any other kind of art had ever been able to about the nature of the human being, was open to serious question. The realists, fighting for a hearing, were not inclined to see every aspect of the problem; they concentrated on only one side of it.

The attitude expressed by the humanitarians was generally favorable, but, as has already been suggested,[62] they could not regard Courbet as the complete answer to their problem. Art, said Thoré, must help society toward the future brotherhood of man, and any painting which dealt honestly with man and nature as they were, was a

[57] F. Desnoyers, "Du réalisme," *L'Artiste*, 5e série, Vol. xvi, p. 197.

[58] Among the *avant-garde*, the reaction set in in the 'eighties at the time of the beginning of the Symbolist movement. A new kind of subjective symbolic meaning was demanded in order to get away from the spiritual sterility of Impressionism.

[59] E. Duranty, *La Nouvelle peinture*, Paris, 1946, Foreword and notes by Marcel Guérin, pp. 12-13.

[60] *Ibid.*, p. 42.

[61] *Ibid.*, p. 43.

[62] See above, p. 65 and elsewhere.

help toward that end, even though it was as yet impossible to produce the new and greater art of the future while society itself was in a state of flux.[63] This, while favorable to realism, was not a complete endorsement of it. So long as Courbet was putting some emphasis, as Thoré believed, on man in the modern world, the critic admired him, for he was helping the cause along, but when he turned to nudes, streams, and foxes, the brave days were over: "There you are, my friend, embalmed."[64] Castagnary, as we saw, opened his critical career with a great plea for the betterment of man which occupied many pages in his Salon of 1857, and in the section where he dealt with the actual pictures, we find that his theories have colored his views about the art of his future hero. Courbet doesn't get down to considering his forms and groups "as condensations of the universal soul."[65] "He has shown his people in the idealism of their baseness, but never in that of their dignity. . . ."[66] But Courbet is a teacher, apparently, for the young critic thinks he has followed Proudhon's precepts too far, and reproaches him for moralizing too much: moralizing by having the public recognize in his people their own misery. He should, it seems, show them something more admirable.[67] He goes on to say that Courbet started out to paint for the crowd, and when he wasn't understood, took his revenge by exhibiting "a double injury to Paris and the people, the *Demoiselles au bord de la Seine* [Fig. 41] whose jovial title indicates well enough the impertinence of the thought. By thus flouting the major part of his admirers, Courbet condemns himself."[68] In other words, Castagnary is thoroughly confused by the apparent contradictions involved in what the painter's art really was, what some thought it to be, what Proudhon said it was, and what he himself believed it should be.

By 1863 he had steadied down somewhat and apparently decided that the thing for art to do was reflect its times, hold the mirror up to nature, and yet reveal the inner nature of man at the same time. He had also obviously achieved a strong liking for Courbet's pictures which never wavered thereafter. He was quite willing to accept Courbet's statement about his art, "to translate the spirit of my epoch. . . ," and thought it was actually being carried out.[69] He called the master a "socialist painter," by which he meant an artist who devoted himself to the "translation" of his times.[70] Paradoxically enough, at this very time Courbet had virtually stopped doing anything of the kind. The *Retour de la conférence* of that year was, as we have seen, one of the last such "translations" he ever made. Castagnary was enthusiastic over the *Remise des chevreuils* (Fig. 73) and the *Femme au perroquet* (Fig. 74), neither of which could be said to have much of anything to do with either the epoch or society. "I have given everything to Courbet," he said in his excitement at his favorite's success, "because to plead the cause of Courbet is to plead at the same time the cause of those who surround him and all realist and idealist youth (naturalism allows the two terms) who come after him: Millet, Bonvin, Ribot, Vallon, Roybet, (Carolus) Duran, Legros, Fantin, Monet,

---

[63] T. Thoré (signed W. Bürger) "Salon de 1861: de l'avenir de l'art," *Revue germanique*, Vol. xv, No. 2, 1861, pp. 252-253.

[64] Thoré, *Salons de W. Bürger*, Vol. ii, p. 276, "Le Salon de 1866."

[65] Castagnary, *Salons*, p. 26.
[66] *Ibid.*, p. 28.
[67] *Ibid.*, p. 28.   [68] *Ibid.*, p. 29.
[69] *Ibid.*, p. 148, "Le Salon de 1863."
[70] *Ibid.*, pp. 146-148.

Manet, Brigot."[71] This is a somewhat odd group, and the inclusion of Millet's name might be classed as an error, but essentially the statement was true enough. The point is that the grounds of the discussion had now been shifted somewhat, for (with the exception of Millet) few of these men fitted the earlier humanitarian system very well. Certainly Monet, Manet, and Fantin didn't even come near it. Courbet himself wasn't as close as he had been earlier, for art was now off on a new track.[72]

It would be tedious and unnecessary to go over the objections raised by the traditionalists. They quite naturally disliked anything of this sort, and their training and their habits inevitably made them think of this whole group of pictures as a well-painted attempt to annihilate nearly everything that was characteristic of great art, and much that was essential to even good art. The reader will recall that in the main the critics concerned themselves with ideas about *the best possible art*, and so, for that matter, did Courbet, but the nature of such an art was quite different in the two views.[73] Had Courbet not maintained that what he was doing was the best that was being done *in any branch*, the cleavage might not have been quite so violent, but as it was, he was thought to be moving in on sacred ground which was profaned by his very presence. As time wore on and the last traces of good historical painting seemed to be fading away, some critics who had been bitter enough earlier, came to look upon him with a more tolerant eye, the more so since he had apparently calmed down and decided to be less difficult. Henri Delaborde, who in '53 had thought his work the epitome of everything that art should not be,[74] found the *Combat des Cerfs* of '61 (Fig. 51) among the more or less good works of the year,[75] and spoke favorably of the Étretat marines 1870.[76] Gautier and Maxime DuCamp went through similar changes of mind,[77] and even officialdom offered him the Legion of Honor in 1869.[78] But by this time things had changed considerably from the brave days of the *Enterrement* and the *Baigneuses*.

Baudelaire, an early example of the modern concentration on art as an end in itself,

---

[71] *Ibid.*, p. 240, "Le Salon de 1866."

[72] Only in the sense that any art which dealt with the subjects of the world of direct experience was it a "step in the right direction." All hints of humanitarian content had disappeared, granting that they may have actually been present, and not just imagined. Courbet did say that one of his bathers was a "proletarian," but much importance need not be attached to this remark.

[73] See the discussion in the Preface.

[74] H. Delaborde, *Mélanges sur l'art contemporain*, p. 83, "Le Salon de 1853." He declined to even mention him by name.

[75] *Ibid.*, p. 200, "Le Salon de 1861."

[76] *Ibid.*, p. 710, "Le Salon de 1870."

[77] In 1855: ". . . we find that he [Courbet] spoils a true painter's talent" (Th. Gautier, *Les Beaux-arts en Europe 1855*, Paris, 1856,

Vol. ii, pp. 155-156). In 1861 he gave him a very favorable comment, especially for the *Rut de printemps* (Gautier, *Abécédaire du Salon de 1861*, p. 113). (But he didn't like the *Hallali du cerf* of 1869!) DuCamp's change of heart has already been mentioned.

[78] Courbet refused in a lofty letter to Maurice Richard, the Minister of Fine Arts: "Allow me, Mr. Minister, to decline the honor you have thought to do me. I am fifty years old and have always lived a free man; when I am dead they must say of me: that one never belonged to any school, any church, any institution, any academy, above all to any régime, if it is not the régime of freedom." The letter is quoted in full in Chas. Leger, *Courbet*, pp. 153-155. Leger points out that Daumier refused the same honor.

had given up this "realistic" art as early as 1855.[79] Three years earlier, the Goncourts had called Courbet a man of "spirit" (*esprit*) but had simultaneously recorded their opposition to a realism "sought exclusively in the ugly."[80] Later, they had even less use for him.[81] Zola admired him too, not as a realist, apparently, so much as a temperament, or at least so he said in *Mes haines*.[82] And yet the two concepts were tied together, for it was the artist's very vigorous and bold approach to real things which had, in the 'fifties, been the visible expression of his "temperament." By being himself, that is, by obeying the dictates of his own personal interest, he not only had been responsible for the realist movement in painting, he had been the leading artistic individualist of the day. By 1866 he seemed to Zola to have "softened his corners" and "gone over to the enemy" and the fiery critic was losing interest in him.[83] Théodore Duret, the later historian of the *avant-garde*, said of Courbet in 1867 that he was the most instinctive painter who ever lived but that he lacked imagination and "feeling" entirely.[84] His pictures produced in the critic no emotional response whatever. Great painters, he said, bring a judgment, an attitude of scrutiny to their task which enables them to make a judgment of the world and thus achieve a proper disposition of its parts, but this quality Courbet lacks.[85] And yet, in the retrospective show of that year, Duret sees some pictures, including the *Casseurs de pierres* (Fig. 24), which transcend his limitations and make him a master of the modern school.[86] Later, when he wrote of the work of his friends the Impressionists, he placed Courbet as the man to whom, along with Corot, the young revolutionaries turned, first, because he had broken so completely with tradition, and second, because he had gone directly to nature for his inspiration. Duret added that some of them learned a good deal from his style as well, especially Cézanne.[87] Duranty also saw him as one of the founders of modernism, having fought for realism in the 'fifties.[88]

The conclusion, however, seems justified that by the middle of the next decade, the advance of artistic thinking had left Courbet's earlier art behind, along with some of the views which had supported it. Stylistically, his later work was as "modern" as that of Monet at the same time, some of it being even more colorful; but he was older by then, and younger artists were drawing the fire of the conservatives. Although he was admired and studied, he was no longer in the forefront of the struggle currently led by Manet. He had, as it were, already joined the ranks of the masters at a time when a

---

[79] Baudelaire, *Curiosités* (ed. Lévy), p. 227, "Exposition Universelle de 1855." The passage has been quoted already in Part One.

[80] E. and J. de Goncourt, *Études d'art*, p. 8, "Le Salon de 1852" (previously quoted).

[81] For example this entry in the Journal (they have been watching the family of a peasant bride arrive for her wedding): "It was horrible among the greenery: one would have said it was a wedding by Labiche in a genre picture by Courbet" (*Journal*, Vol. II, p. 204; Labiche was a writer of comedies, etc.). In 1867

they thought nothing of Courbet's show (*Journal*, Vol. III, p. 164).

[82] Zola, *Mes haines* (ed. Charpentier), 1895, p. 34, "Proudhon et Courbet."

[83] *Ibid.*, p. 313, in "Mon salon" under the heading, "Les Chutes."

[84] Th. Duret, *Les Peintres français en 1867*, p. 86.

[85] *Ibid.*, p. 91.   [86] *Ibid.*, p. 100.

[87] Th. Duret, *Histoire des peintres impressionistes*, Paris (ed. Floury), 1922, p. 1.

[88] E. Duranty, *La Nouvelle peinture*, p. 32.

new and somewhat different advance was being worked out. After the events of 1870 and 1871 he went into a kind of eclipse. Banished from home, maligned by his artistic inferiors,[89] heartbroken but still painting doggedly and beautifully, he lived his life out in a personal obscurity which cleared almost miraculously after his death in 1877. The two sales of his paintings held in 1881 and 1882 grossed 324,000 francs; the *Combat des cerfs* brought nearly 42,000 francs,[90] a good price for those days. Once the man was gone, the fine artist was appreciated more nearly at his true worth.

[89] His pictures were refused at the Salon of 1872. Meissonier is reported to have said: "We need not look at it (*La Femme de Munich*). It is not a question of art but of dignity; Courbet cannot appear at our exhibitions. He must be considered dead as far as we are concerned" (quoted from Bénédite, *Gustave Courbet*, p. 89).

[90] The figures are taken from Appendix 1 in Leger, *Courbet*, p. 215. Just how accurate these are is perhaps a question. It is certain, however, that his popularity was quickly regained when he was dead.

XVI. THE GENERATION OF 1860
MOREAU, PUVIS DE CHAVANNES, AND REGNAULT

IF certain artists whom we have just discussed can be grouped together as "the generation of 1848," some of their younger contemporaries might be similarly classed as "the generation of 1860." At all events, we must now consider the work of several men who first came into prominence shortly after 1860 and were also, in various ways, intimately connected with the critical and artistic developments of the later years of the period. It will not be surprising to find that only a few of them had much to do with the great tradition, which might be regarded as being even feebler than it had been twelve years before, but there are at least three such painters who deserve mention in any account of contemporary criticism. Gustave Moreau, Puvis de Chavannes, and Henri Regnault all represented different and creative approaches to what was still being stubbornly referred to as *la peinture d'histoire*. The inclusion of Regnault may be questionable, for although he died after the shortest of careers, there were signs that his art was already yielding to a kind of academic dry rot, although this might not have been true had be been able to continue. Certain it is, however, that some of his earlier work was extraordinarily vigorous in spite of the fact that it was well within almost all the confines with which the current traditionalism bounded the field of subject matter.

Both Moreau and Puvis were, in somewhat different ways, the heirs of Chassériau, the former having been a student, the latter a close friend.[1] They saw in this indecisive soul something new and appealing, something arising, perhaps, from that very indecision itself,[2] and which they shared with him. It was a certain reflective inwardness which in the case of Puvis was marked by an almost glacial calm, and in that of Moreau, took the form of a strangely opulent imagination conceiving scenes never seen by mortal eye. Since both of them looked at the classic tradition in a new way, they presented unusual problems to those critics who recognized the forms easily enough, but were baffled by the substance and the way it was suggested. Each relied to a considerable degree on Chassériau's style, which was the key to the expression of his particular form of individuality, and became a similar means in their own art. Puvis was affected very directly by the great murals for the Cour de Comptes,[3] and became the only important painter of his day who was primarily a "decorator," that is to say, a painter of walls rather than easel pictures.[4] Moreau adopted his teacher's taste for rich effect,

---

[1] See above, pp. 129ff.

[2] This would be a natural state of mind for anyone caught between a strong admiration for Ingres and an equally powerful interest and sympathy for Delacroix.

[3] H. Focillon, *La Peinture aux XIXe et XXe siècles, du réalisme à nos jours*, Paris, 1928,

p. 242.

[4] To call a man a "decorator" was very high praise among the conservatives, for it implied the ability to work successfully on a large scale. Much of the mural art of the time was more like easel painting blown up to size.

unusual lights, and exotic forms, all of which he developed further into a highly personal and esoteric manner. Both died in the same year, 1898, and with them the creative part of the conservative tradition in the nineteenth century came to a close, for the "classicism" of Cézanne and Seurat was of a much different kind.

Of one thing there was absolutely no doubt after Puvis' great success in the Salon of 1861 (Fig. 52). This was the fact that he was a history painter in the most exact sense of the term. Whether or not he was a good one was another matter, but the classification was easy.[5] This description seems to be borne out by what is known of the man himself. His biographer, Marius Vachon, who knew him well, observed that "by his temperament and education he belongs directly to those great masters of former times who have covered our country with so many marvels of art which are made more beautiful and glorious by the passing centuries."[6] There would seem to be no evidence in his art to contradict this description and the great succession of mural designs which he left behind are proof enough of the direction taken by his sympathies. In spite of the fact that he professed ignorance of matters intellectual, it seems more plausible to regard him as a man who was both well read and thoughtful.[7] "Je suis un ignorant" he said, but the involved symbolisms of his pictures belie the words. That art was the passion of his life is entirely true, and his mastery of it was gained by hard work, endless study, and an apparently inexhaustible perseverance. It was his interest in style, however, rather than in religion or history which later made him acceptable to the moderns, the reverse being true of the conservatives. To make a somewhat loose generalization, the traditionalists liked his subject matter while they didn't approve of his style; whereas the more advanced "moderns" admired everything *but* his subjects, or at least they didn't do so in the traditional manner.[8]

He showed in the Salon for the first time in 1850, but after being refused at the next one, he dropped out of the public sight until 1859 when he was received again,[9] and in the next exhibition (1861) he scored his first real success with *La Guerre* and *La Paix* (*Concordia*) (Fig. 52). From that time on, through the rest of the decade, he received notices which ranged from the rather harsh attacks of Castagnary, which were quite understandable,[10] to the warm praise of Gautier and Paul de Saint-Victor. Vachon paints a rather pathetic picture of the artist wounded by the outrageous criticism he received,[11] and yet it is scarcely credible that any artist could not have realized that there

---

[5] For an excellent account of the critical reaction to his art, see Robert Goldwater, "Puvis de Chavannes: Some Reasons for a Reputation," *Art Bulletin*, Vol. XXVIII, 1946, pp. 33-43.

[6] Marius Vachon, *Puvis de Chavannes*, Paris, 1895, p. 13.

[7] *Ibid.*, p. 14.

[8] Goldwater, *op.cit.*, pp. 36ff.

[9] He was refused twice more but held a private show at the Galeries Bonne-Nouvelle which, according to Vachon, only made the public laugh (Vachon, *op.cit.*, p. 17). This

show was held in 1854. Vachon says that Puvis returned to the Salon in 1861, but actually he had a *Retour de la chasse* in the Salon of 1859.

[10] Goldwater, *op.cit.*, p. 34. In the sense that this critic abandoned his idealism for an enthusiasm for Courbet in his post-realist years, he might be called a realist of sorts, as Goldwater describes him, but he should not, in the opinion of the present writer, be included with Champfleury and his *confrères* of the brave days of the early 'fifties. Puvis did not stay near enough to nature to suit Castagnary.

[11] Vachon, *op.cit.*, p. 21. "Outside of that,

was a battle in progress, that everyone had to be on one side or the other—or at least on *some* side, for we have seen that it was not only a dispute between the academics and the progressives, but also among a much wider variety of other opinions. The artists who had the larger talents naturally were singled out as champions for the positions which they inevitably represented, and they had to stand the consequences. How any painter in those days could have thought that he could be important and at the same time agreeable to everyone, is hard to understand, unless he was entirely naïve about the general critical situation. Puvis took up his stand with the traditionalists and was duly admired by them, but he could hardly expect the humanitarians to be as enthusiastic. He wasn't painting the men they wanted to see, his people were symbols set down in pale tones in airless, flat landscapes. Castagnary was not one to appreciate the delicacy of his technique or the refinements of his abstractions. We have already seen that this critic was not capable of making a similar shift from his humanitarianism to a more painterly naturalism in the case of Courbet; that is, he was somewhat insensitive to style as such. Thoré, who was a more balanced observer, at first found Puvis' works restful and fine, even if he did not see any reason to make much more of them than that, but later he found much to criticize.[12] Castagnary objected to the extended explanations given in the catalogues for the work of painters like Puvis and Moreau,[13] but the reason was that he wanted not an art where the subject had no meaning beyond itself (which was what the realist critics were after) but one in which the moral and the human ideal would be so perfectly attuned to the real nature of man that the meaning would be self-evident.[14] Thoré's later adverse criticism was based on similar grounds, and shows exactly how he thought Puvis should have gone about making his pictures immediately understandable: "[He] would have been more of his time and more in the tendencies of modern art if he had shown the laborers of Picardy as they

what sadness!" said Puvis, "Absolute and forced stagnation in my artistic affairs. How could it be otherwise, given this wind of inept, savage, cowardly cruelty" (*ibid.*, p. 21).

[12] Thoré, *Salons de W. Bürger*, Vol. I, pp. 41-42, "Le Salon de 1861." As will be seen presently, Thoré was all for meaning, but it had to be phrased in contemporary terms.

[13] Goldwater, *op.cit.*, p. 34.

[14] See the discussion of Castagnary in Part One. This is a difficult point to make clear. Thoré was certainly in hopes that society would produce a new symbolism, and Castagnary's writings in the 'sixties are full of references to the necessity for art to interpret the depths of human nature in modern terms. If such terms were used, explanations would not be necessary, any more than they had been for devout Catholics in ages past when confronted with scenes from the Gospels or the lives of the saints. It should be recalled that Chesneau (*The Education of the Artist*) believed that the trouble was in a lack of education—i.e. these subjects were "literary" only because people now had to read about them to know what they were; in other days they knew them in advance as part of their general cultural stock in trade. This lack of a usable and effective symbolism was one of the great issues in this period. In a previous chapter it was pointed out (p. 140) that Castagnary was very much interested in Chenavard's *Divine tragédie* until he thought it represented the triumph of the Trinity—proof that it was not complex subject matter per se that he objected to. His inability to understand Moreau was absolutely typical: his imagination could not possibly work along such lines, nor did he want to retreat from the world into his fancy. Thoré, too, could not appreciate Moreau.

are, instead of allegorizing them in undressed figures. . . ."[15] The objection was not to a moralizing memorial to the good folk of Picardy, but to the way in which it was done.

If Puvis' manner of painting and the subjects he chose were not particularly agreeable to the humanitarians or those with more directly realist sympathies, how did he fare (Fig. 63) with the conservatives who might have been expected to approve of him? Most of them did approve; some, like Henri Delaborde, even looked to him as a possible deliverer from the evil days on which art had fallen, but there was some criticism even here.[16] Men like Lagrange, Mantz, and Anatole de Montaiglon were often to be found giving the painter advice as to how to improve his style, color, modeling, and so forth.[17] Now a critic like Paul Mantz had been looking at art for so long that he might easily have imagined that he knew just what this kind of thing ought to look like. He had been talking about history painting in one way and another for many years and had also studied the masters on whom it was supposedly based. It is easy to see, therefore, why he felt that he could set the artist straight, but in trying to do so, he missed the point which was, of course, that Puvis was trying to work not in the traditional manner *à la Mantz*, but in his own.[18] The painter felt entirely free to take only what he wanted from the past. Mantz and the others would be unwilling to appreciate this and had to see him as a wayward traditionalist, just as a later day was willing to overlook the traditional side in favor of his mastery of flat tones and design, as well as the personal, rather mystical nature of his subjects. It was in just such ways as this that the shift toward an increasing preoccupation with pictorial style and a more individual vision were at first noticed only as a sort of irritant in works which, without them, would have been entirely pleasing to an academic eye. From the point of view of this study, it is interesting to watch the difficulties the conservatives encountered here, right in the very citadel of the past, when the influence of the modern approach began to assert itself. Most of the artists treating these themes had a "system," a well-rounded body of procedure which covered everything about the picture from its conception to its final appearance. It was, in fact, the very perfection of such systems that was drying traditional art up at its roots. In Puvis, the system seemed askew and the critics wanted to repair it for him.

[15] Goldwater, *op.cit.*, p. 35, note 15.

[16] H. Delaborde, *Mélanges*, p. 183, "Le Salon de 1861." He suggests that he foreshadows a revival of the grand manner.

[17] Goldwater, *op.cit.*, p. 35.

[18] Mantz is an interesting figure among the critics of the day. He was highly individual, and often differed pointedly from others of a more or less conservative persuasion—as for instance his condemnation of Couture's *Orgie romaine*. He admired Millet and professed to have admired Courbet in his earlier years though he disapproved of him regularly in the 'sixties when others were coming around to a guarded praise. He was very hard on the academics because they lacked any real power, and on Moreau because his "system" was wrong, but praised Ribot who, he said, was the best man in the Salon of 1867. Monet got a very laudatory notice in 1865, and Whistler's *Dame blanche* was the best picture in the *Salon des Refusés*, but as late as 1869 he felt that if Manet had anything to say he had not yet said it. After 1859 his views can be followed in the *Gazette des beaux-arts*. Before that he wrote for a number of journals such as *L'Artiste*, *l'Evénement*, *Revue de Paris*, and *Revue française*. His reviews begin as early as 1846 (*L'Artiste*).

Everyone now remembers the famous quarrels which broke out in Couture's studio between the master and Manet about how people should see the model. The pupil insisted that his way was his own and therefore, for him, better than any other.[19] In that very same studio an almost identical episode occurred earlier with Puvis. According to the story told by people present at the time, Couture came along one day, frowned at the young man's effort and demanded his palette. Seating himself at the easel he did the whole thing over, making severe corrections. The thunderstruck youth watched this transformation and then exclaimed, "What! M. Couture, is that how you see the model?" and left the place never to return.[20] The parallel to Manet's experience is both striking and significant, and another one could have been drawn from the evidence of the actual pictures of the two painters, but almost no one saw it at the time.

In a review of the Salon of 1870, however, Camille Lemonnier, an otherwise not very brilliant critic, made the following observations after remarking that M. Puvis de Chavannes apparently lacked a *system*:

M. Manet and you are the two men of art who touch each other most closely at this moment in the matter of system and perhaps detest it the most: I speak only of system. M. Manet does not paint any more than M. Puvis: but I affirm out loud that they are both expressive. M. Puvis refines the ideal, and M. Manet refines reality. No color, mind you, but an idea.[21]

This was a shot very close to the mark, and seems to contain the germ of the belated praise for Puvis' style that came to him so late in his life. As Robert Goldwater has said, "By the 'nineties his triumph was complete,"[22] but this recognition was still far off.

The case of Moreau was somewhat similar, for here again was an artist who was ostensibly painting classical and religious subjects but in a manner which seemed strange to critics accustomed to the more pedestrian conceptions of men like Flandrin or Bouguereau (Fig. 35). It was not that they thought the work of these latter was a fulfillment of their ideals; but at least they thought they understood it and the ideas which lay behind it. It was not so with Moreau. Like Puvis he had begun to exhibit in the early 'fifties, but had retired for a while reappearing in 1864 with an *Oedipe et le Sphinx* (Fig. 68) which attracted immediate and favorable notice.[23] The Goncourts had, it is true, spoken well of his *Pietà* in 1852,[24] but for the most part he was regarded as a *débutant*. It must have taken some courage to start afresh with a theme which had already been so successfully handled by the great Ingres himself fifty-six years before. But his courage was rewarded, for the picture was a great success, "the discussed picture of the Salon" the *Artiste* called it,[25] and Maxime DuCamp gave it his most grandiloquent praise:

---

[19] See below, chapters on Manet.

[20] Vachon, *Puvis de Chavannes*, p. 9.

[21] C. Lemonnier, *Salon de Paris 1870*, Paris, n.d., p. 38.

[22] Goldwater, *op.cit.*, p. 40.

[23] Moreau showed in 1853 and 1855 but attracted little attention.

[24] E. and J. de Goncourt, *Études d'art*, p. 23, "Le Salon de 1852."

[25] Hector de Callias, "Le Salon de 1864," *L'Artiste*, 8e série, Vol. v, 1864, p. 219.

It is to history painting, to grand painting that we must return under penalty of irremediable decadence; any tendency toward this end ought to be encouraged and applauded, and in this connection we find the example given by M. Gustave Moreau is respectable, meritorious, and of good augury, although his picture was not judged worthy of the grand medal which, in every respect, it deserved.[26]

This was an accolade of no small proportions, but in the midst of the general praise there was one note of warning. Several critics, Lagrange among them,[27] saw his style as eclectic, and for reasons which are not entirely clear, decided that it stemmed from Mantegna, or if not Mantegna, then Perugino. This charge of eclecticism was somewhat justified, for these strange visionary scenes recall to the modern observer the Italians of the late fifteenth century and some details are definitely suggestive of Lucas Cranach.[28] But the main source of influence, Chassériau, went almost unmentioned, even though one of the pictures in the Salon of the following year, *Le Jeune homme et la mort* (Fig. 72), was signed: "To the memory of Théodore Chassériau, Gustave Moreau, 1865."[29]

The success which attended the *Oedipe* was apparently somewhat short-lived, for the *Jason et Médée* (Fig. 71) of the next year got a much cooler reception.[30] DuCamp thought it as good as the other,[31] but Paul Mantz was as dissatisfied as he had been with Puvis: "M. Moreau has noble aims; what is vicious about him is his system."[32] Jules Claretie was equally hard on him,[33] and Challemel-Lacour, who had given him a good notice previously, said that he was now headed for a dead end. "Let M. Moreau take care; allegorical painting has two stumbling blocks which are difficult to avoid: subtlety and falsity."[34] Edmond About went into greater detail, likening the artist to a man with good legs who walks on his hands. Moreau's formula, he said, was "to recover the inexperience of the Florentine primitives and apply it to the antique."[35] It was wrong, he felt, to mix borrowed details, to see nature through the eyes of others, to impose this primitivism on himself and "that is why his pictures, while flattering the taste of a small group of dilettantes, offends the great majority of the competent public."[36] About was not as competent as he thought, perhaps, and went on to an error

[26] M. DuCamp, *Les Beaux-arts*, p. 119, "Le Salon de 1864."

[27] L. Lagrange, "Le Salon de 1864," *Gazette des beaux-arts*, Vol. XVI, 1864, p. 506.

[28] See, for example, *Les Licornes* in the Musée Gustave Moreau (*Catalogue sommaire des peintures, dessins, et aquarelles exposés dans les galeries du Musée Gustave Moreau*, Paris, 1904, facing p. 76).

[29] But Paul Mantz noted it, for in his review of the Salon that year he said that in 1853 Moreau had done a *Fuite de Darius aprés la bataille d'Arbèle* which was an imitation of Chassériau ("Le Salon de 1865," *Gazette des beaux-arts*, Vol. XVIII, 1865, p. 491).

[30] It might be noted that the first pictures in the 'sixties were quite smooth and clear; later they became much hazier and more dreamlike.

[31] M. DuCamp, "Le Salon de 1865," *Revue des deux mondes*, 1865, p. 661. One reason he liked it was because its ideal was one strange "to vulgar aptitudes." He did find, however, that Moreau's art was "something of a rebus."

[32] Mantz, *op.cit.*, p. 493.

[33] J. Claretie, "Deux heures au Salon," *L'Artiste*, 8e série, Vol. VII, 1865, p. 227.

[34] P. Challemel-Lacour, "Le Salon de 1865," *Revue germanique*, Vol. XXXIV, No. 1, 1865, pp. 96-97.

[35] This was from the review of 1866. E. About, *Salon de 1866*, Paris, n.d., pp. 136ff.

[36] *Ibid.*, p. 141. Just who might compose the "competent public" he does not say.

which was quite common in criticism of this period: namely the idea that since archae-ology had shown people what the past was really like, the knowledge it provided must be used for contemporary versions of past events, a somewhat naïve theory which had already done a good deal of damage in actual practice.[37] The dilemma which this new "science" had posed for the artist cannot be examined here, but could well be carefully investigated in a separate study.[38] At any rate, this was certainly not the way to under-stand the art of a man like Moreau. His art seemed so difficult and mysterious that apparently few were interested in making the necessary effort or willing to abandon themselves to a purely imaginative reaction to it. By 1869, Gautier said that his vogue was over and people no longer found him anything but strange.[39]

The difficulty, of course, was the same one that affected the criticism of Puvis' work, that is, the fact that a man who was original, and yet gave the appearance of being in the tradition of history painting, was working against a whole set of ideas about that form which were rigid and had been so hallowed by time that changes were regarded as sacrilege. Originality in landscape, or even in genre, was not as difficult to admire. What Moreau had done was to take the outward forms and turn them, as well as the stories themselves, into vehicles for his personal reveries. Some had an apparent moral significance,[40] but most of them were more like visions whose meaning might be akin to the strange emotional reactions to dreams. Salome, Oedipus, Prometheus, Hercules, Moses, and the rest of his characters were presented as the figments of an imagination which did not seem entirely healthy to more rational minds. To them his art presented a symbolism gone astray, a world of the imagination, but not the imagination they were accustomed to. The pontiffs of critical opinion must have felt somewhat thwarted by these subjects which slipped away from their intellectual, or even literary, analysis. They could be felt, if one were so inclined, but they were very hard to explain.[41]

There is little doubt as to the artist's own attitude toward his work for his comments on it are borne out by what is apparent in nearly every one of them. To a friend who wrote asking for some remarks on a picture of the artist's which was in his collection, Moreau answered: "Everything I write you about my picture, to be agreeable to you, does not need to be explained by words; the sense of this painting, for anyone who knows a little about reading a plastic creation, is extremely clear and limpid, all that is necessary is to love, to dream a little, and not be contented, in the case of a work of

---

[37] It was to be found among the Neo-Greeks and also in painting of the *juste milieu*. In military painting, Paul Mantz called it "the religion of the gaiter button" ("Le Salon de 1859," *Gazette des beaux arts*, Vol. II, 1859, p. 140). For About's views, see About, *op.cit.*, p. 142.

[38] There were many who lamented the happy anachronisms of such Renaissance painters as Veronese. Now that people knew better, it was no longer possible to use contemporary dress and settings for such scenes.

[39] Th. Gautier, *Tableaux à la plume* (ed. Charpentier), p. 280, "Le Salon de 1869."

[40] As, for instance, the *Moïse ôtant ses san-dales* (*Cat. Mus. Moreau*, facing p. 20). Many of them had a very complex interpretation, some of which are transcribed in the catalogue.

[41] Cf. Felix Jahyer, *Deuxième étude sur les beaux-arts, Salon de 1866*, Paris, 1866, p. 186. He says that Moreau still won't take advice (*sic*) and gets more "recherché" every year. His pictures are veritable hieroglyphs.

imagination, with a disgustingly simple ba, be, bi, bo, bu, under the pretext of simplicity, clarity, and naïveté."[42] He was an old man when he wrote these words, but they
seem entirely applicable to his work from the beginning. In one of his albums appears
the following description of his aims as an artist:

O noble poetry of living and passionate silence! Beautiful is that art which under a
material envelope, mirror of physical beauties, equally reflects the great transports of the
soul, the spirit, the heart, and the imagination, and replies to those divine needs of the
human being of every age.
It is the language of God! A day will come when the eloquence of this mute art will be
understood; it is this very eloquence, whose character, nature, and power over the spirit
have not been able to be defined, to which I have given all my care and efforts: the evocation
of thought by line, arabesque, and plastic means, that is my aim.[43]

His descriptions of some of his pictures, written near the end of his life, bear ample
witness to the spiritual quality of the meanings he attached to his subjects, but they also
reveal how personal and incomprehensible they were. Here is the passage accompanying a painting of Orpheus (Fig. 90):

The sacred singer is stilled forever. The great voice of beings and things is muffled. The
Poet has fallen prostrate at the foot of the withered Tree with the groaning sorrowful
branches.
The soul is alone, it has lost all that was its splendor, its strength, its sweetness; it weeps
over itself in this renunciation of everything, in its disconsolate solitude. Silence is everywhere, the moon appears above the little building and the sacred pond shut in by walls.
Rosy drops falling from watery flowers alone make their regular discreet sound, this sound
so full of melancholy and sweetness, this sound of life in the silence of death.[44]

It is small wonder that few people understood what he was trying to say.

But there were those who did understand, for it was impossible that a lyric note,
even of this mysterious sort, should not have found an echo anywhere among the
people who looked at his visions. The Goncourts, as has been mentioned, took note of
his *Pietà* of 1852, and other critics had noted his beginnings with some sympathy,
among them Nadar, who called him "a serious painter" in '53,[45] although he cautioned
him on being too preoccupied with Delacroix. The humanitarians could not be expected to appreciate him,[46] but the few critics who had keen eyes for artistry and

[42] From a preface, written in 1897, included
on unnumbered pages in the *Catalogue, Musée
Moreau*. There would seem to be little change
in his ideas over the years.

[43] *Ibid.*

[44] *Ibid.*, p. 45. Unhappily no attempt is made
to date the pictures. There is a distinctly
Baudelairian flavor to this passage.

[45] Nadar (F. Tournachon), *Nadar jury au
Salon de 1853*, Paris, 1853, p. 29.

[46] Cf. Castagnary, *Salons*, p. 196, "Le Salon
de 1864" where he discusses the *Oedipe et le
Sphinx*. The man is going backward, he says,
and doesn't really want to talk about him.

Castagnary considers painting a language and
as such it must be clear: "Art addresses itself
to everybody, to the ignorant as well as to the
literate, to men as well as to little children:
is not the book of nature and of life equally
open to all human creatures?" And on p. 199
we find the plight of such a critic before a
work of pure imagination: "M. Gustave Moreau, in fact, has not seen his subject as in
nature. He has found it in his head in a day
of poetic hallucination ... he is utterly in error.
In his deranged imagination, he has thought
that one could bring a human myth before
the eyes, an eternal thought applicable to every

imagination, and were not too prejudiced in favor of certain other attitudes, could see what he was doing. After their first mention, the Goncourts said little more about him, but his art must have impressed them, for years afterward there was a brief mention of him in the *Journal* as "the goldsmith-poet" whose water colors "gleam with the treasures of the Thousand and One Nights."[47] The most perceptive eye to catch his bizarre charm was that of Gonzague Privat. At the Salon of 1865 he paused for some time before the *Le Jeune homme et la mort* and the *Jason et Médée*. He decided that this was no place for quick judgments since the argument which had arisen over the man's work proved that he was not ordinary. To Privat, his thought was clear, even if personal, so why should there be such a disturbance? He concluded that it must be because of the eclecticism about which nearly everyone but himself agreed (though there was less agreement about just who the artists were from whom he was borrowing). Privat admitted that he took bits here and there—which was entirely true—but denied that his whole style was eclectic, which was also true. "M. Moreau is a poet, a thinker; furthermore, a painter in every sense of the word."[48] After a long study of the two pictures he said: "I came, little by little, to the discovery in them of the work of a serious artist, a draughtsman, a colorist, above all a poet. Ah! I insist on this word for we have them with us no longer: the last one became extinct with Delacroix."[49] This view might be contrasted with that of Thoré who thought the *Oedipe* entirely literary and hardly "painted" at all, at least in the sense of Rembrandt's *Syndics*—a somewhat unusual comparison.[50]

There is certainly a kinship between work of this kind and the poetic strain which stemmed from Baudelaire. Moreau was among the first of that small but important group of artists of the later nineteenth century whose individuality and whose escape from the traditional took a direction almost exactly opposite to that of Manet and the men from the Café Guerbois. Rops and Redon bear comparison, as well as Huysmans and others in literature, but the tendency did not spread very far until the general symbolist reaction after 1880.[51]

In official artistic circles, there was no prize more eagerly sought by aspiring young painters than the Prix de Rome, but for reasons which are clear enough by now, the pictures these young pensioners of the state produced during their tenure of the award

---

moment of time: he has not seen that by its very nature this myth would escape his art." How, Castagnary goes on, can one universalize a theme like this because no clothing (or the lack of it) on Oedipus will free him from being tied to some age or other (p. 201).

In 1865 Thoré took him very severely to task, apparently not liking anything about his work (Thoré, *Salons de W. Bürger*, Vol. II, pp. 203ff., "Le Salon de 1865").

[47] Goncourts, *Journal*, Vol. VI, 1881, pp. 145-

146.

[48] Gonzague Privat, *Place aux jeunes!*, p. 81.

[49] *Ibid.*, p. 81.

[50] Thoré, *Salons de W. Bürger*, Vol. II, p. 14.

[51] Rops was a Belgian and very highly regarded by Baudelaire. Both Rops and Redon were essentially graphic artists at this time. For information on the Symbolist reaction, the author is indebted to an unpublished thesis by Dr. Elizabeth Puckett, *The Symbolist Criticism of Painting. France, 1880-1895*, 1948.

were of a perfection and dullness seldom lightened by any signs of real life. Year by year the artists thus honored sent their work to Paris, where it was duly exhibited and always reviewed by the more conservative critics in measured, if unexcited, tones. In the year 1866, the subject of the competition for the prize was *Thétis apportant les armes d'Achille*, a subject which indicated the general modernity of the École at the time.[52] The winner was Henri Regnault, the son of an academician, and a very unusual young man. He departed in due course for the Holy City and the next year sent back a painting of *Automédon et les chevaux d'Achille* (Fig. 78)[53] which must have caused the academicians in Paris to sit up suddenly and take careful notice. A picture of so much fire and passion had not come from Rome in years, and a sudden hope was born that a man had at last appeared who could redeem the almost lost cause of the great tradition.[54] There was certainly some excuse for this hope, for the picture was indeed a remarkable effort for so young a man brought up in the environment of official art. It had a fine design, great animation, a striking play of tones from fiery red to a rich chestnut brown, and a brush stroke which inevitably led to comparisons with the great Delacroix. Charles Blanc later spoke of him thus, in *Les Artistes de mon temps*:

> But since the name of Delacroix comes up so often and by itself when one speaks of Regnault, one must say in what manner they differ, and how deep these differences are which separate them. What goes on in Regnault is surface, his understanding is all external; his soul is constantly at the window. With Delacroix, on the other hand, the work is accomplished on the inside, in the intimacy of his being, *intus et in cute*.[55]

This was true enough, but since Regnault never had a chance to paint anything after his twenty-eighth year, a comparison with the mature Delacroix may not have been entirely fair.

In Rome, the young artist met the orientalist Fortuny, from whom he gained a love for Spain and Morocco, and thither he went to work in 1868. He arrived in time to paint an equestrian portrait of General Prim (Fig. 86), the leader of the recent successful revolution against the Bourbons.[56] It is clear that the passion which had so enlivened the *Automédon* was still with him, for the entire century saw no more exciting portrait of a man on horseback than this one. The horses of Achilles breathed only a little more fiercely than the huge animal that carried the worried-looking man on his great back. In fact, the horse is the more admirable figure, and one can hardly blame the general for refusing the painting, though the grounds he gave were that it showed "a dirty fellow with an unwashed face."[57] The picture appeared in the Salon

[52] For these and other facts about the artist's career, the author has relied on Stranahan, *A History of French Painting*, pp. 321-325.

[53] Mantz mentions it in his review of the Salon of 1869, though it was never shown in any of these exhibitions: he thought it a little exaggerated.

[54] The reader will recall the similar hopes aroused by Puvis.

[55] Paris, 1876, p. 351.

[56] Blanc says it was "bitten into our memory like an etching by Goya" (*ibid.*, p. 356). He thinks Regnault was under the influence of Velásquez at this time, but this seems a dubious assumption, particularly in the light of the fact that the style is very close to the *Automédon* done before the artist came to Spain.

[57] Stranahan, *History*, p. 322. The phrase is General Prim's.

of '69 and received wide, and mostly favorable attention, all of which it richly deserved.

But this was not the main purpose of Regnault's visit to Spain and he soon turned out a number of "oriental" scenes, among them an *Exécution sans judgment sous les rois Maures* (1870, Fig. 89) in which the bloody head of the victim rolled on the ground with such convincing realism that it has been reported to have made "delicate women" faint away upon sight of it. To the modern eye, this change in style was an unfortunate one, for it deprived the artist's work of the very quality which had made it unusual and exciting before, that is, its bravura and emotional intensity. Regnault would seem to have stood for a while between two styles, for the portrait of the Countess of Barck, dating 1869,[58] shows a breadth of handling and an accentuation of plane in the drapery which is reminiscent of Manet.

The *Salomé* (Fig. 87) of the Salon of '69 was one of the great successes of the year. It was painted in the same tight, careful manner as the slightly later *Exécution*, but in such brilliant colors that everyone was dazzled. Charles Blanc, Jules Claretie, and Camille Lemonnier all praised it practically without stint,[59] and none of them seemed to feel that it represented any decline from the ardor and fine brushwork of the *Automédon* and *Prim*. To them it seemed to combine color and drawing to perfection, to show a sharp eye for the natural combined with a good imagination. Great things might well be expected of the young man. But if it is fair to include a later judgment, one might say that this very praise was indicative of the impoverished state of conservative criticism, for apparently the more Regnault got rid of the dashing quality of his earlier manner in favor of the careful colorism and smooth surfaces of the popular painters, the more he was admired.

But all contemporary speculation was cut off by his tragic death in the war of 1870. Although exempt from military service by virtue of being a pensioner of Rome, he left Spain and enlisted at once. In June of 1871 he was shot and killed in a sortie at the village of Buzenville, having stayed behind the general retreat to "fire my last cartridge." What he might have done had he lived is hard to predict, though the evidence points to a successful career with the conservatives rather than an advance with the new group of progressives. Even so, he left behind at least two pictures, the *Automédon* and the *General Prim*, which showed what might have yet been done with tradition in the hands of a man who had at least some of the spirit that made Delacroix so great.

[58] The difference between this and the *Salomé* is very marked. For a reproduction, see Focillon, *La Peinture aux XIXe et XXe siècles*, p. 99. About this same time he did a study of a Spanish shepherd in the same broad style.

[59] Blanc, *Les Artistes de mon temps*, p. 361; J. Claretie, *Peintres et sculpteurs*, p. 20; C. Lemonnier, *Salon de Paris 1870*, p. 75.

XVII. MANET

THE position in the public eye which Courbet occupied during the 'fifties, was filled in the next decade by Edouard Manet. Just as the powerful painting and obstinate individualism of the former had forced all critics to consider what he was doing and come to some conclusion about his art, so also did the daring and original technique of the younger man claim attention from everyone, and if this usually took the form of attack rather than praise, it was still a sign of his true importance.

Manet's reputation grew slowly, but it eventually achieved such large proportions that it is somewhat difficult to arrive at an objective appreciation of the man or the criticism he received. As it became increasingly apparent that he was really the first great modern, that he had set the stage for many of the performances of his younger contemporaries, and that he had seen clearly the principles on which art could function in the new society, he became a hero, his every canvas a masterpiece. When modern times and modern criticism had finally succeeded in discrediting the conservative position and had shown the hopes of the humanitarians to be impossible of fulfillment, Manet turned into a great master. It is no purpose of this book to refute this claim, but it must, in all fairness, be recorded that there were somewhat reasonable grounds for a part of the adverse comment leveled at him—though not for its ill-tempered and vituperative tone. The words spoken were so harsh on both sides that wounds caused by them healed slowly if at all, and the final victory of the pro-Manet side inevitably made his detractors seem to be stupid, quarrelsome characters whose opinions were no longer worth a sympathetic hearing. But the blame must be laid at the door of the cheaper popular critics to whom the public was only too willing to listen. If the unhappy artist was regarded as almost on the level of a criminal, if he was brought to the edge of insanity by cruel jibes, it was the fault of small minds; the larger ones took a more penetrating look. Just as in the case of Courbet, there were those among the conservatives who saw quite well what Manet was trying to do. A number of them praised his originality and his undeniable command of color and tone; but they couldn't overlook what they considered to be his serious defects. It would certainly be an error from the historical point of view to use his art as a touchstone for criticism in general, assuming that that which was favorable to it is, by that fact alone, worthwhile, and that all unfavorable views are thereby in error. An understanding of his painting is most useful for an appreciation of Impressionism, even certain aspects of post-Impressionism, but it is not all that is needed in the cases of Poussin, Michelangelo, or Delacroix.

The person most responsible for the sharpness of the line which presumably had to divide those who liked Manet from those who did not (there was apparently no middle position at all), seems to have been Théodore Duret, who wrote books on his artist friends which have been so widely and continuously read that they have had an important part in forming the general opinions held about these painters, their times, and their critics. Since he knew them personally, and had begun writing criticism as early as 1867, he was, and is, listened to attentively. This is just and proper so long as it is remembered that he was an ardent partisan in the matter, and thus not particularly objective in his opinions. The following paragraph from his *Histoire des peintres impressionistes* will serve as an example:

It must be remembered that at the moment when Manet came on the scene, Courbet and Corot, who represented the progress made, were always displeasing to the public, that their freedom of manner and procedure were only understood and imitated by a minority of young painters; that Delacroix was still generally considered only as an irregular and incorrect artist, a man who pushed color to extremes. The members of the Institute, the painters moulding the students in the studios, the School at Rome, the men of letters in general, the public remained submissive to the tradition. All honored what was called great art, history painting, the representation of the Greeks and Romans, the nude understood and treated in the manner of formulas derived from the Italian Renaissance.[1]

A more misleading account of the actual state of affairs could hardly be imagined. Since this kind of summary of the time has become fixed in many minds, it will be worthwhile to examine it in some detail. It is true that Courbet and Corot did represent progress, though to many critics it was Rousseau rather than Corot who led the landscapists. If 1863 be taken as the year when Manet really began to make a general impression, Courbet had already begun to become popular, and three years later, when Manet had just done his *Fifre* (Fig. 76), the great "realist" from Ornans sold 123,000 francs worth of pictures,[2] a sum which might represent about $75,000 in purchasing value. During these years the landscapes by Corot had a steady sale at good prices and his followers, men like Chintreuil, were receiving very laudatory reviews. In 1869, as has already been mentioned, Courbet was offered the Legion of Honor. That a majority of young painters should have instantly flocked to the standards raised by these two is almost an impossibility; such things take (or at least used to take) longer than a few years. Everyone who knew anything about art, with the exception of a very few die-hards like Delécluze, proclaimed loudly and often that Delacroix was a great master, easily the peer of Ingres.[3] To say that the majority of the men of letters were "submissive to the tradition" was only a half truth. In the first place, if all of the hundreds of critics be considered, this is overwhelmingly true, but so also is the fact that in any such group there would be only a very small percentage of able men, and most of these were antitraditionalists. In the second place, the assumption is that the critics were submissive to the tradition as it was being practiced, but the facts are that the standard opening to nearly every review was a complaint of the general caliber of what was being done. To lump the members of the Institute, all artists who had studios where students were studying, the School at Rome, men of letters and the public all together as subscribing to the same ideas about art is to confuse the real situation almost hopelessly. The Institute was anathema to most critics; it was also at odds on

[1] Third edition, Paris, 1922, p. 2. The book was first published in 1878.
[2] Riat, *Courbet*, p. 231. The information came from *Liberté*, May 23, 1866.

[3] Duret's error probably came from confusing the antagonism of the Institute and the most extreme right with the general estimate.

more than one occasion with the Ministry of Fine Arts, and so on. Reasoning of this kind makes Couture an academic, although he was not, nor did he ever have a seat among the Immortals—as even the "irregular" Delacroix eventually did. That history painting was supposedly confined to the Greeks and Romans was simply not true.[4]

What Duret and others have done, apparently, has been to take the worst, rather than the best, criticism, join to it the stupidities of an uninformed popular taste and the desperate conservatism of the outmoded (and relatively inconsequential) academicians, in order to achieve the impression of a solid and unrelieved phalanx of opposition to all novelty and originality. This picture has just enough truth in it to obscure its flaws somewhat. We have been led to believe, for instance, that original artists are never understood in their own day, that no one but a few friends and their fellows in painting ever understand what they are doing until long after their deaths. But the facts are that every artist we are considering was understood by some people, and that several of the most original made comfortable sums by their painting. To be sure they did not make them by virtue of their most advanced and rebellious efforts because it was not until rebellion was equated with genius, and criticism had abdicated its former predicated share in the formation of standards, that any large section of the public, critical or more general, was willing to follow the artist to any extreme he might care to explore, and enjoy the process.

So we return to Manet to see, first of all, what sort of a person he was. He came of a prosperous Parisian family headed by a father who was a magistrate, an important position in the bourgeois hierarchy. The boy's early desire to become an artist led to an argument over his father's plans for him to enter the law, an almost perfect case history of that suspicion of art as a career which Chesneau dealt with at such length. Manet appears to have been hot-headed and impulsive, but finally offered to undertake a career at sea as a compromise. This plan was put into effect, but without permanent success, for on his return from a voyage to Brazil he was as determined as ever to paint, and was at last allowed to go where he wished. This was to the studio of the somewhat opinionated Thomas Couture. Couture's earlier difficulties with Puvis have been mentioned;[5] there were even greater ones in store for him with Manet. During the latter's years in his studio the relations between the two were apparently anything but cordial. Antonin Proust was there at the time, and to his famous recollections, published long after, we owe most of our knowledge of what the young painter was like. These memoires were printed in the *Revue blanche* for 1897[6] after a lapse of about forty-five years and they may have been colored somewhat by later events, but they are at least vivid and seem to agree with what others thought who had known Manet well.

Couture, while not of the Academy, was certainly a traditionalist; what is more, he was convinced that his own methods were good, otherwise he would not have followed

[4] The matter could be pursued still farther, but no useful purpose would be gained.

[5] See above, p. 171.

[6] Vol. XII, under the title "Edouard Manet, souvenirs."

them. He may also be pardoned for thinking that if a young man wished to study under him, it was because that man believed that the artist whose studio he was entering was someone from whom he wished to learn. There were a number of places in Paris where other masters held forth, and there were also "free" studios where for a small fee artists could work from the model and paint as they pleased without criticism.[7] Duret says that Manet chose Couture himself,[8] and it is a fact that he stayed there for six years, although he was presumably quite free to leave at any time. If we are to believe Proust, this period was marked by a mounting tension broken by a series of sharp exchanges (in all of which Manet came off the better) which were the delight of the more retiring students. In view of the fact that the two were apparently so utterly opposed in their approach to painting, why did Manet stay so long? Puvis de Chavannes left almost at once.

It may be that in spite of the quarrels over how the model should be posed and how one should see form, Manet was really learning something. Camille Mauclair asserts that Manet did indeed get much from his master, not, of course, in the way of an interest in history painting (which actually formed a very small part of Couture's total *oeuvre*) but in the matter of style.[9] There seems to be more than a hint of Manet's use of flat surfaces and abrupt transitions of tone in a number of Couture's pictures. Should this influence be actual, even if disowned, there is a good reason for Manet's long stay. At all events, it was the only formal training he had, and was obviously highly selective on Manet's part. As a result, when Manet began to exhibit in public he was frequently accused of not having mastered his art sufficiently, of wanting to run, so to speak, before he could walk properly. That he acquired a profound distaste for certain aspects of traditionalism during these years is, however, open to no doubt whatsoever. He worked hard on the styles of the masters he admired, especially the Spaniards, but academic artificiality and thoughts of art as an idealizing medium for the elevation of the human soul were ruled out. Henceforth his models would be of his own choosing and his ideas would be his own reactions to things as he knew and saw them.

It was clear from the start that Manet intended to be modern: ". . . one must be of one's time, do what one sees without worrying about the fashion."[10] He also insisted that the models behave in a natural manner: "Can't you be natural? Is that the way you stand when you go to buy a box of radishes at your grocer's?"[11] This did not, however, prevent him from copying Raphael's design outright, poses and all, for the famous *Déjeuner sur l'herbe* (Fig. 59). When Couture reproached him for not painting what he saw, by which the master meant what he, Couture, saw; Manet replied,

[7] For an extended study of Parisian art life in this period, see A. Tabarant, *La Vie artistique au temps de Baudelaire*, Paris, 1942. This book contains a vast amount of material but the absence of any index or any footnote references makes it extremely difficult to use.

[8] Th. Duret, *Manet and the French Impressionists*, Philadelphia, 1910, p. 6.

[9] *Thomas Couture 1815-1879*, from the unnumbered introduction.

[10] A. Proust, *op.cit.*, p. 125.

[11] *Ibid.*, p. 127. The date of the incident is 1850.

"I paint what I see and not what it pleases others to see, I paint what is and not what does not exist."[12] He also felt that this painting had to be direct and as rapid as possible: "There is only one true thing. Bring out what you see the very first time. When that's it, that's it. When that isn't it, begin again. All the rest is a joke."[13] These quotations are familiar enough to any student of the painter's life and could be augmented by many more, but only one more need here be added to the evidence of the pictures themselves. In May of 1867, the unhappy artist appealed directly to the public by holding a one-man show at the Pont de l'Alma. Courbet had tried the same experiment in 1855, including in the catalogue a statement of what he was trying to do,[14] and Manet followed his example:

From 1861 on, M. Manet has exhibited or tried to exhibit.

This year he has decided to put the whole of his works directly before the public.

When he first exhibited in the Salon, M. Manet obtained an honorable mention. But afterwards, the repeated rejection of his works by the jury convinced him that, if the first phase of an artist's career is inevitably a kind of warfare, it is at least necessary to fight on equal terms—that is to say, to be able to secure publicity for what he has produced.

Without that, the painter too easily suffers an isolation from which egress is difficult. He is compelled to stack his canvases, or roll them up in a garret.

It is said that official encouragement, recognition, and rewards are, for a certain section of the public, a guarantee of talent; they are informed what to admire and what to avoid, according as the works are accepted or rejected. But, at the same time, the artist is assured that it is the spontaneous impression which his works create upon this same public that is responsible for the hostility of various juries.

Under these circumstances the artist has been advised to wait.

To wait for what? Until there are no more juries?

The artist does not say today, "Come and see faultless works," but, "come and see sincere works."

The effect of sincerity is to give to works a character that makes them resemble a protest, when the only concern of the painter has been to render his impression.

M. Manet has never wished to protest. On the contrary, the protest, quite unexpected on his part, has been directed against himself, because there exists a traditional teaching as to form, methods, modes of painting, and because those who have been brought up in this tradition refuse to admit any other. It renders them childishly intolerant. Any work not done according to their formulas they consider worthless; it provokes not only their criticism but their active hostility.

The matter of vital concern, the *sine qua non*, for the artist, is to exhibit; for it happens, after some looking at a thing, that one becomes familiar with what is surprising, or, if you will, shocking. Little by little it becomes understood and accepted. . . .

By exhibiting, an artist finds friends and supporters who encourage him in his struggle.

M. Manet has always recognized talent where he has met with it, and he has no pretensions either to overthrow an established mode of painting or to create a new one. He has simply tried to be himself and not another.

Further, M. Manet has received valued encouragement, and recognizes that the opinion of men of real ability is daily becoming more favorable to him.

The public has been schooled into hostility towards him, and it only remains for the artist to gain its good will.[15]

[12] *Ibid.*, p. 131.
[13] *Ibid.*, pp. 132-133.
[14] Courbet had another one in this same year,

near the same spot. See above, Chap. xv, note 47.

[15] Duret, *Manet*, pp. 39-40.

As Duret says,[16] this was a fair enough statement of what Manet believed, and a natural reaction to the very harsh treatment he had been getting. It is also significant as a partial explanation of why the *avant-garde* finally gave up trying to show in the Salons—they had to get to the public somehow, and the badly prejudiced juries rendered this uncertain and difficult. In the future, dealers, one-man shows of their own, and group exhibitions which they controlled had to furnish an outlet to public opinion. Most criticism remained unfavorable for many years, but patrons were gradually attracted and a clientèle eventually established.

Manet suffered, as he said, from the jury system, which was certainly pernicious and thoroughly out of date, although it was amazing how few genuinely good painters could be found in the famous Salon des Refusés of 1863.[17] Not every artist rejected by the juries was, by that very fact, a good painter. The problem of exhibitions and the way they should be managed occupied the attention of many intelligent people throughout this period, but no system was discovered, even in theory, which would always assure admission to all artists destined for future greatness while excluding those later to be condemned to oblivion.[18] The democratic method had been tried once in 1848, and no one seemed particularly anxious to repeat the experiment, at least not in the same way.[19] As long as the official Salons remained as the gateway to recognition, artists of all persuasions had to try to exhibit in them, and the controlling conservative majority naturally tried to exclude examples which they thought were either threatening to their supremacy or just plain bad art. When other avenues were opened, the rebels could, and did, leave their adversaries in possession of the field, making their reputations in other ways and in other quarters.

The path of the innovator is bound to be difficult, a fact which, unhappily, attends the later glory of having shown the way, and Manet was no exception. What made it particularly trying in his case was a certain naïveté which apparently prevented him from foreseeing the manner in which his paintings would inevitably be received. He was apparently just as astonished as he says he was in his introduction when he discovered that people found his work harsh, crude, or sketchy; when he learned that his painting of a nude girl on the grass with some fully-dressed young Parisians was shocking as was also his picture of a hard, thin demimondaine with her black cat at her feet.[20] He saw nothing wrong in either of these subjects; they were unexceptional

---

[16] *Ibid.*, p. 39.

[17] The list would hardly include more than the following names: Manet, Fantin-Latour, Whistler, Pissarro, Jongkind, Legros, Harpignies, and Chintreuil—these, from among many exhibitors. There was another Salon des Refusés the following year but almost no one of account was in it. As one critic said, they were all in the main show.

[18] A bibliography of the articles on this subject would be reasonably lengthy. It was also a frequent subject for discussion at the start of Salon reviews.

[19] There had been a great flood of pictures, many of which were so bad that everyone was agreed about them. Also, an exhibition of that size was too unwieldy. It would appear that the problem of jury injustice has not yet been solved. It is interesting to speculate what might have happened had the progressives been in control.

[20] The cat was particularly objectionable for some reason. Duret says (*Manet*, p. 26) that the cat was there for the simple reason that the painter liked them.

in any artist's life, and he painted them, as Duret says, by instinct.[21] In other words, what was true of Courbet in this respect was, in a sense, true of Manet as well. In a highly organized and rather artificial society such as that of the Second Empire, anyone who behaved in public according to his instincts was very likely to cause something of an uproar. The idea that Manet intended to shock people by these pictures is apparently refuted by the evidence of those who knew him.[22] That he was thought of as being in any way immoral, or that his art was a direct challenge to artistic tradition, was as much of a surprise to him as to anyone. He thought that he had only to be himself and others would soon see that he was an interesting person and that his own means of expression were as good as anyone else's.[23] As it turned out, his methods were actually better than almost all the others, but this was naturally apparent to only a few people at the time. The break was too sharp and radical to be easily understood, let alone admired.

The distance which separated his rather direct individualism from that of a painter of the more imaginative type, is made clear in a comment he made on Moreau: "I have a lively sympathy for him, but he walks in the wrong direction; men of the world swoon before *Jacob et l'ange* [1878]. Gustave Moreau is a man of conviction who will have a deplorable influence on our times. He leads us to the incomprehensible, we who wish everything to be understood. . . ."[24] To Manet, dreams were of no particular interest, the passing show was the thing to look at. It was, indeed, the only thing of interest to a painter: "An artist must be spontaneous. There is the exact term. But to have spontaneity one must be master of one's art. Groping about never leads to anything. One must translate what one experiences, but translate it instantaneously, as it were. . . . Invariably, in fact, one discovers that what one did the day before is not in harmony with what one will do tomorrow."[25]

To sum up, it appears that Manet was a man who was extraordinarily gifted in the direction of artistic, pictorial vision. In this respect he is quite similar to Courbet, but where Courbet was a hearty, rough product of the country, Manet was city born and bred, something of a dandy in his appearance, and emotionally far more thin-skinned. He, too, was passionately devoted to his art and, partially as a result of this devotion, lacked the objectivity which would have explained to him why his work was so bitterly criticized.[26] It is doubtless fortunate for art that this was the case, for otherwise he

---

[21] *Ibid.*, p. 17 and elsewhere. This is precisely the picture of him that Zola gives at this time (*Mes haines*, pp. 334-335).

[22] Zola confirms this (*ibid.*, p. 355).

[23] Duret, *op.cit.*, p. 41.

[24] Proust, "Edouard Manet," p. 205.

[25] *Ibid.*, p. 427.

[26] This is not to imply that Manet was a pure creature of instinct. On the contrary, within the limits of his interests and his prejudices, and in spite of a certain naïveté about his place in the scheme of things, he had a keen mind.

His studies of the masters, his work on his own style, the effort he made to achieve a satisfying expression of his own manner of seeing, all attest the fact. He had a circle of interesting friends and was very much the Parisian. But like many people, there was more than one side to his nature, and it was the tender naïve side which was so wounded by the criticisms he could not honestly understand. Just like Delacroix and Cézanne, he wished for recognition from the very quarters where he was sure not to get it. A free-thinker would hardly

might have given in, adjusted his effort to something which he could have seen would be more acceptable, and been far less of a master as a result. The gods bestowed the gift of an original style upon him, and to protect it, they deprived him of the fore-knowledge of what this would mean to others. The outcome, as might be expected, was a great gain for art at a terrible price of personal suffering and bitter unhappiness. He was sustained in his tragedy by the stubborn belief in his own rightness and the encouragement of the few who saw and appreciated what was driving him forward. He could not change without being false to himself. But it was unfortunate for him that his gift was of such a kind as to seem, and indeed to be, a threat to the modes of painting then in vogue among those who more or less controlled the art world. It did him no good to disclaim any "pretensions to overthrow an established mode of paint-ing"[27] because that was what he was doing in spite of anything he could say, nor was it of any avail to appeal to the example of such masters as Giorgione, for the analogy could not possibly be accepted by his opponents.[28] He was, so to speak, born too soon; he gave his world an art appropriate to it, but at a time when it was not prepared to accept it.

The critical opinions about Manet's art have been so carefully gathered and set forth in Tabarant's treatise on the painter, that the reader is referred to his book for a more complete quotation of them than will be attempted here.[29] But M. Tabarant is so ardent a defender of Manet that he does not attempt to analyze these opinions to any great extent beyond showing which were for, and which against, this new art form. Some of the comments made at the time have been repeated so often as to have become almost commonplace, such as the passage of Gautier's about the *Guitarrero* (*Chanteur espagnol*) (Fig. 55) of the Salon of 1861 ("Caramba! there is a guitarist who doesn't come from the Opera Comique . . .").[30] Others are less well known and may, therefore, bear repetition along with certain observations on the general tenor of the reaction.

Gautier's initial praise was not an isolated example, for Edmond About remarked that "Ugliness has its charm and frankness, and more than one talented painter lets himself be taken with it in his youth. Look, preferably, at M. Manet, a bold, spirited colorist."[31] This is an interesting passage for it shows that Manet's talents were recog-

---

expect to be the darling of a strict Calvinist, and yet the analogy is not far-fetched.

[27] See the statement from his show of 1867 previously quoted.

[28] This was a propos of the *Déjeuner sur l'herbe*. Unless one is quite familiar with the critical climate of the time, the utter folly of this attempted defense will not be apparent, for it was, after all, entirely right in one sense. But to take a hallowed Italian master, dead and glorified for hundreds of years, as a defense for a picture which was technically antitradi-tional, and in the process assume that both painters were masters together, was merely add-

ing insult to injury. It has already been men-tioned that the French were willing to admire certain things in the art of the past which they rejected hotly in contemporary painting. Manet should have known this.

[29] Adolphe Tabarant, *Manet et ses oeuvres*, Paris, 1947.

[30] Gautier, *Abécédaire du Salon de 1861*, pp. 264-265 (also quoted in Tabarant, p. 42). The picture was also called *Chanteur espagnol*.

[31] E. About, "Le Salon de 1861" in *Derniers lettres d'un bon jeune homme à sa cousine Madeleine*, Paris, 1863, p. 270.

nized at once for what they were, i.e. those of a daring colorist, and also shows that the critic believed the ugliness of the picture, that is, its lack of ideality and finish, was a youthful indiscretion which was permissible since it would be outgrown. It was because it wasn't ever outgrown that the artist experienced such great trouble. The favorable opinion expressed by these two critics (and others) extended to the jury as well, for the young artist was encouraged by an honorable mention. As is well known, however, this was a false dawn.[32]

The next year he was refused along with many others and had to wait his chance for critical appraisal until after the Salon des Refusés had opened. The auspices were hardly of the best, for all the painters were automatically suspected by their very presence in this kind of a rump exposition.[33] Most of the critics went to see it, however, and Manet was at least generally listed as one of the ones whose exclusion from the regular exhibition was unwarranted. The worthy Thoré saw a general effect of rough strength in the show as a whole: "They strive to render the effect in its striking unity without care for the correction of lines nor the minutiae of accessories." If he was referring to Manet, which seems possible, he was not too far from the mark.[34] This critic said that Whistler had caused the most comment and after him, Manet, who was "a true painter too" even though his three pictures, the *Bain* (i.e. *Le Déjeuner sur l'herbe* [Fig. 59]), the *Majo*, and the portrait of *Mlle. Victorine* (Fig. 60) seemed to be "provocations" of the public. This, as we have seen, was an erroneous suggestion, for Manet had no such intention, but only appearances counted, and Thoré found the *Déjeuner* in bad taste.[35] At the same time he saw virtue in the light and color, especially in the body of the woman.

Castagnary, as might have been expected, missed the point more than once in his estimate of this show.[36] Whistler's *Dame blanche* (Fig. 61) is, incredibly enough, considered only as a subject: a young woman on the morning following her bridal night.[37]

---

[32] About himself can serve as an example of just how false it was. In his Salon of 1864 he said: "We will not speak of the two damp firecrackers which M. Manet has not been able to set off. This young man, who paints with ink and lets his escritoire fall every minute, will end by not even exasperating the bourgeois. It will be in vain for him to draw a caricature of angels or paint a wooden torero killed by a horned rat, the public will go on its way saying: 'It's just M. Manet amusing himself again, let's go see the pictures'" (E. About, *Salon de 1864*, Paris, 1864, pp. 156-157). The reference is to *Le Torero mort* (Fig. 66) and *Le Christ et les anges* (Fig. 65).

[33] Castagnary tells the legend of the Refusés: It seems that when the news that it would be held was first announced, there was great joy followed by doubts as to the reception the pictures would get in an exhibition of this kind. One night an angel visited Harpignies and by banging his head on the floor taught him to read the divine book. In this volume the painter read the one word "Exhibit," and then the angel sent him out to preach the word to the others (Castagnary, "Le Salon des refusés," *Salons*, p. 156).

[34] Thoré, *Salons de W. Bürger*, Vol. i, p. 414, "Le Salon de 1863."

[35] *Ibid.*, pp. 424-425.

[36] Castagnary, *Salons*, pp. 154ff.

[37] *Ibid.*, p. 179. This passage gives an interesting view of Castagnary's talents as a critic, and therefore it may be quoted at some length: "M. JAMES WHISTLER.—I have proposed an interpretation of the *Dame blanche* which has had no success except with me, so true is it that one is loath to grant painters ideas. 'What have you wanted to do?' I asked the strange painter whose fantastic etchings I alone had previously admired. 'A *tour de force* of your craft as painter, consisting of dashing off whites

He was too devoted to people as themes for art in their human aspects to imagine that an artist could be largely indifferent to this side of the matter and see the form mainly for its more aesthetic possibilities. He agrees that the three Manet pictures are "good sketches" and that there is a certain life in the tones and freedom in the brushwork which are uncommon, but the rest of it is bad—the bodies lack structure, the forms are inadequately defined. The limitations of this critic in matters of style are clear enough, and even later when he came to admire the painter, as he said he did in 1868 after the shocking refusal of Manet's pictures along with others by Monet, Degas, Renoir, and Bazille, he praised him as a character rather than a painter (Fig. 80). Associating himself with the progressive artists he wrote:

A certain token of our triumph is the fact that our battalions are reinforced each day and that youth comes to us, a youth which will not be unseated again because it is now certain of its aspirations. Do you think M. deGas will not rise again from the setback he has received? Do you think that M. Renoir will not hold a grudge for the injury which has been done him? . . . The strong always resist. Didn't Courbet resist? Hasn't Manet resisted? Manet! I was going to forget to speak of him. This year he deserved a true success. His *Portrait de Zola* is one of the best in the Salon. The accessories, table, books, prints—everything which is still-life is done with a masterly hand.[38] The principal figure is less happily done except for the hand, which is very beautiful, and the velvet of the trousers which is stunning.[39]

He hasn't yet completely understood the style, even though he is all for the advance of art and the courage of youth. The next year he is still worried about the lack of human interest in Manet's *Déjeuner* (Fig. 85) and *Balcon* (Fig. 84). Why has the young man got his back turned to the table? Who are the two ladies on the balcony? Art should say something *about* life; it is not enough to see it as an excuse for a picture. You can say what you like, "but the feeling for function, the feeling for suitability are indispensable."[40] This was the point he could never understand, namely that function, in the sense of the subject's nature, needs, life, etc., was just exactly what could be dispensed with, since the interest in these things was now to be that of the artist's reaction to them, not their own quality as human attributes.

Marius Chaumelin, a firm admirer of Thoré and the ideals he stood for, had the same difficulty. Art, according to him, was a "free reproduction of moral and physical beauty, an elevated language of the soul interpreting for other souls the poetry of nature, that sensible expression of the ideal. . . ."[41] He admired Regnault's *Général Prim* (Fig. 86), but thought that the two Manet pictures of that year lacked expression,

---

on whites? Permit me not to believe it. Let me see in your work something loftier, *The Bride's Tomorrow*, that troubling moment when the young woman questions herself and is astonished at no longer recognizing in herself the virginity of the night before.'" He then compares the picture to Greuze's *Cruche cassée* and interprets it as an "allegory." For Whistler's views on art, see *The Gentle Art of Making Enemies*, N.Y., 1893.

[38] Manet's skill with still-life details was noted by a number of critics, including Privat and Zola.

[39] Castagnary, *Salons*, p. 313, "Le Salon de 1868."

[40] *Ibid.*, p. 365, "Le Salon de 1869."

[41] M. Chaumelin, *L'Art contemporain*, p. 201, "Le Salon de 1869." This Salon contains an account of Thoré's death, at which Chaumelin was present.

feeling, and composition. The tones were wonderful, but the artist was to be blamed for painting "subjects of a repulsive vulgarity, types without character, scenes deprived of all interest."[42] To be sure, the subjects were scarcely of a "repulsive vulgarity," but he was right in saying that the scenes had no interest in the sense in which he meant interest—that is, that there was nothing happening in them of interest and the character of the people involved was largely ignored. It was not a fault in the painter that this was so, any more than it was a fault in the critic to wish for something that he, but not the artist, was interested in. It was only a difference of opinion set down as a judgment. A more modern observer would say that the critic had no right to criticize the picture on any grounds other than those of the artist's intention, which, in this case, was certainly not concerned with character or dramatic meaning. In those days, however, the critics still felt that such matters were integral to good painting and felt free to say so. In a second review of the same Salon, Chaumelin said of the *Déjeuner* (Fig. 85) that it was painted by the hand of a master.[43] Because he did not like all of it, he was not barred from praising very warmly what he did like, which might seem to be his privilege. Unfortunately, he seems to have been wavering in his admiration, for the next year he turned on the unfortunate painter with a savagery which seems quite out of proportion to its object. The critics, apparently, were just as uncertain about this rapid change going on before their eyes as they might be expected to have been.[44]

It is not necessary to call the roll of critics for each year, since that has already been done by M. Tabarant, but among the less well-known there was one who seemed to see the essence of Manet's art very clearly. This was Gonzague Privat, who may also be mentioned in connection with the prejudice which has clouded the statements made about Manet as the hero of modern art. In Laran and Le Bas' book the critic is quoted as follows on the *Olympia* (Fig. 70):

"Ignorance!" said Privat. "The proof of this artist's lack of knowledge lies in the fact that he always does well when he paints still-life, while it is much less difficult to paint a saucepan or a lobster than a nude woman."[45]

He is also listed among the adverse critics in Michel Florisoone's recent study.[46] Most other biographers do not even mention him, but his actual remarks were both pertinent and laudatory.

He called his review of the Salon of 1865, "Place aux Jeunes!" referring to the painters who seemed original; the others he called "neutrals" (i.e. Gérôme, Bougue-

---

[42] *Ibid.*, p. 235. Chaumelin wrote two Salons for this year, one in *La Presse*, the other for *L'Indépendance belge*; the reference is to the latter.

[43] *Ibid.*, p. 332. This is from *La Presse*.

[44] *Ibid.*, p. 377, "Le Salon de 1870." It must have been very trying for Manet to continually receive these contradictory criticisms from people who seemed to be on his side one year and violently opposed the next.

[45] *Edouard Manet*, int. by Louis Hourticq, and notes by J. Laran and G. LeBas, Philadelphia, 1912, p. 23. The word "ignorance" is an interpolation and the passage is not correctly translated. See a more correct version given below.

[46] Michel Florisoone, *Manet* (Les Documents d'art), Monaco, 1947, with an appendix summarizing the critical comment.

reau, etc.), or else did not discuss them at all.[47] He has words of praise for Ribot, Chaplin, Baudry and a few others whom we would scarcely include, but he also picked out Puvis de Chavannes, Courbet, Whistler, Manet, Chintreuil, Moreau, and Berthe Morisot. At the time, this was unusual, the mention (at some length) of Morisot being particularly so;[48] but most important is his estimate of the *Olympia* and its author:

Do not be displeased; in the *Olympia* of M. Manet there is more than something good; solid and rare painterly qualities predominate in it. The young girl is done in a flat tone, her flesh is of an exquisite delicacy, a nicety, a perfect relationship to the white draperies. The background is charming, the green curtains which enclose the bed are of a light and airy color. But the public, the crude public that finds it easier to laugh than to look, understands nothing at all of this art which is too abstract for its intelligence.

I confess that M. Manet is wrong in exhibiting the works he produces each year; they are full of interest for artists and special men who see beyond the ends of their noses; but how can he believe that this painting, so outside of everything well-known, will ever be admitted to be a success?[49]

It is hard to imagine a more accurate appraisal of the dilemma in which Manet found himself. Privat says frankly that he admires the painter and has for years, and the day he paints something everyone can understand he will be a success; no one will say he is crazy then:

If these brave characters who make such coarse fun of M. Manet could know how little it would take to make this too-artistic painting readable; if they knew how rare originality, color finesse, and harmony are, they would not kill a sincere man with vulgar jibes, a man whom they irritate by presumptuous disdain.[50]

The artists know his brilliant qualities and they know, too, that what he has done are but impetuous trials, "full of audacity."[51]

Well! . . . I, for one, do not hesitate to say it: M. Manet has a painter's temperament, poetic inspiration, the charm of naïveté, tones, delicacies, and a living side to his art which few artists possess. . . . You don't have to believe me.[52]

After discussing several other painters, Privat returns to his favorite whose work seems to have an irresistible attraction for him:

Since concerning himself with art he has had but a single aim, to find a harmony of gentle strength, a subtlety of color.

M. Manet has sought *the picture* without concerning himself enough with form and detail. In short, he has arrived at one of these results.[53] Suppose the *Olympia* well drawn,

---

[47] All references are from this one review. Apparently he did not write much on art. Privat should be studied more exhaustively than the author has been able to thus far.

[48] *Ibid.*, pp. 146-147. "Under the modest name of 'studies,' Mademoiselle Berthe Morisot shows a *Jeune femme* clad in a white dress and dreaming on the green and flowery edge of a stream. This canvas is very luminous, the white material which covers the body of the young woman is very delicate and warmly

colored, the landscape, like the young thinker, is true of tone and painted with much energy. . . . I sincerely congratulate you."

[49] *Ibid.*, pp. 63-64.

[50] *Ibid.*, p. 65.

[51] This, of course, was not entirely true. The works in question were entirely mature.

[52] *Ibid.*, p. 66.

[53] That is, he has achieved a picture even though it may not have form and detail.

even in this understanding of form, suppose it to be more skillfully modeled, and you would have a charming picture, because it has in it the great seed: life, because it has been conceived and painted by a sincere man.

What then does M. Manet lack? Science [i.e. technique] it is true. But one learns to paint and not to feel. The proof that only technique is lacking in M. Manet's case is that when he does still-life he does a very pretty picture, though it is understood that it is less difficult to paint a casserole or a lobster than a naked woman.

If M. Manet was not a true artist with the right temperament for it, would his *Olympia live?* Why have certain people been frightened by the appearance of the young woman? Why has she made others laugh? Because she is alive, because everyone can sense that life; because one feels that she could move, this woman whom people find, not without some reason, ugly and ill-made. But finally, in actual fact, this picture is a hundred times better than the yellow, coarse *(pandouillarde) Odalisque* which swells up on the opposite wall.

One knows that M. Manet experiments, that he is seeking, that he can and wants to make progress. At the point where he now is, one learns to make an academy in twelve months, and M. Manet has the structure of an artist, whereas one feels that the author of the *Odalisque* in question has arrived at the peak of his talent, at the last degree of perfection of which he is capable.[54]

Privat, who was an artist himself, makes the mistake of thinking that Manet will tidy up his art to a point sufficient to make it more easily understood, and then he will have the success which he so rightly deserves. He sees the great pictorial power of the artist applied eventually to a more conservative and familiar statement of form. This was, of course, incorrect, for Manet was in full possession of his powers at the time the *Olympia* was done. He was not working his way along, he was there already, a fact which the critic could not, or did not care, to see. But even with this reservation, it must be admitted that under the circumstances, this description reveals a brilliant insight into his artistic purpose. His concentration on the picture, his skill with flat tones of charmingly harmonious tints, his mastery of still-life, his naïve belief that people would accept his work when they obviously would not do so—all this, and more, is set down in tones of warm admiration. Although it appeared a year earlier that Zola's more booming defense (which had no reservations at all), it seems to have had little effect.

The modern reader's reaction to Privat's remarks will vary, of course, depending on what he himself thinks of the painter. Was his drawing weak or was it entirely adequate to his purpose? Is the roughness of his handling *in itself* one of the virtues of his style? Again we come to the difference between the attitudes of that period and our own. Sketchiness, if it may be so described, was to men of an earlier day a sign of incompleteness, an indication that the artist hadn't filled out his thought about the picture, and was considered, consequently, a defect as long as the picture was offered as a finished product.[55] Today it is commonly believed that a lack of finish is often desirable in order to enliven the picture and make it more personal. This difficult and complex question cannot be examined here, but it is noteworthy that it was one which

[54] *Ibid.,* pp. 136-137.
[55] We have already seen that Courbet was attacked on this score (Chap. x, note 2).

came up over and over again in the criticism of the period as more and more artists exhibited pictures whose brushwork was an important part of the final effect.

A significant aspect of Privat's review is the fact that he never reproaches the artist for any lack of human significance in his art. He says the *Olympia* has life, which it certainly has, but he doesn't worry as the others did about the cat or the negro servant, or the girl herself as a person. All of these are omitted and the concentration is on exactly the same things which interested the artist, that is, the forms as artistic, and not social, phenomena. The picture, he says, is too abstract for public comprehension, an abstraction which he understands and admires, even if he finds it a little extreme. In fact, he has put his finger very neatly on the whole point of this new kind of art, and instead of finding it repulsive, he is interested and appreciative.[56] Manet's work was painter's painting, and Privat was only too well aware of the reasons why the people couldn't like it: they didn't have the eyes to see anything as artistically novel, to appreciate a type of painting in which, from the spectator's point of view, the subject was the least important thing in the picture. Since the crowd and most of the critics were used to pictures about things rather than about painting, Privat could suggest only that Manet make it a little easier for them, and the problem of recognition and reputation would resolve itself. But Manet was too proud and too whole-souled an artist to trim his sails to catch the breeze of popular favor. Long afterward he was victorious, and it may not be out of place to quote here what one of the best of a much later generation of painters had to say of him. The words are Matisse's:

Manet was the first painter who accomplished the immediate translation of his sensations by thus liberating instinct. He was the first to act through his reflexes and thus simplify the painter's profession. To do it he had to eliminate everything which his education had given him only keeping that which came from himself. . . . A great painter is the one who finds the personal durable signs for the plastic expression of the object of his vision. Manet found his.[57]

[56] There is a slight note of reservation, however, as though he were not quite convinced.
[57] Quoted from Florisoone, *Manet*, p. 122.

XVIII. MANET (CONTINUED)

DURING the earlier years of Manet's professional life, a very few gave the young painter encouragement. In a charming picture, *La Musique aux Tuileries* (1860, Fig. 48), Manet included the portraits of some of them: Gautier, Baudelaire, Champfleury, and Zacharie Astruc, along with other friends of the time.[1] Gautier turned against him later, but Baudelaire and Astruc remained firm. In 1863 the latter came directly to his defense in a little paper published during the life of the Salon:

Manet! One of the greatest artistic characters of the day. I will not say that he has had triumphs at this Salon, where so many valiant ones meet—to use an expression which his modesty would disavow; but he has brilliance, inspiration, powerful knowledge, the ability to astonish. The injustice committed in his case is so flagrant that it confuses; and for anyone who wishes to stop before his canvases, examining them with the attention which such spontaneous harmonious works deserve, works done with such life and vigor that they seem to have leaped from nature at a single bound, for such a person it is impossible not to recognize their merits and not praise them with the justice that beautiful works demand.[2]

Astruc goes on to a very competent analysis of the style with its bold use of tone, its Spanish effects, and its direct connection with nature.

The year before, Baudelaire had published an article in *Le Boulevard* in which he spoke warmly of the *Guitarrero* of 1861 (Fig. 55), and went on to say: "At the next Salon one will see several of his pictures with a strong Spanish flavor which lead to the belief that the Spanish genius has taken refuge in France. MM. Manet and Legros unite to a decided taste for reality, modern reality—which is already a good sign—that lively and ample, sensitive, audacious imagination without which, it must be said, all the best faculties are only servants without a master, agents without a government."[3] The use of the word imagination to refer to a form of spontaneous artistic vision rather than an image conjured up out of the mind is an interesting distinction, both with reference to the poet's own use of his imagination and the meaning more commonly attached to the word by others, for it was precisely a lack of "imagination" which troubled so many of Manet's opponents.[4] Baudelaire came to the support of his friend a number of times thereafter, a particularly well-known example being the letter to Thoré refuting the latter's statement (in an otherwise laudatory review of *Le Christ et les anges* of the Salon of 1864, Fig. 65) that Manet was imitating Goya and Greco. These artists were not known to Manet at the time, Baudelaire said, although he was somehow familiar with Velasquez by virtue of one of those "astonishing parallelisms" by which the poet himself had supposedly imitated Edgar Allan Poe before he really knew his work. He and the American "resembled" each other, just as did Manet and Velasquez.[5] Both

---

[1] Champfleury was a friend but apparently took no public part in his defense.

[2] Quoted in E. Moreau-Nélaton, *Manet raconté par lui-même*, Paris, 1926, Vol. I, p. 51.

[3] Quoted in Florisoone, *Manet*, p. 113. The article appeared in the issue of Sept. 14, 1862.

[4] Cf. Gautier in 1869: "For M. Manet in his character of realist scorns imagination" (Gautier, *Tableaux à la plume*, pp. 244-245, "Le Salon de 1869").

[5] Baudelaire, *Lettres 1841-1866* (ed. Soc. du Mercure de France), Paris, 1907, pp. 361-362.

Astruc and Baudelaire, like Privat and Zola, were willing to admire Manet's interest and skill in painting as painting without requiring anything more in the way of subject matter. The following account of the origin of one of his pictures casts some light on what his attitude in this direction actually was.

In 1864 there occurred off the coast of France the famous naval engagement between the Confederate cruiser *Alabama* and the Northern ship *Kearsarge*, whose name is invariably misspelled as "Kearsage" by all Frenchmen including Manet himself. In this exciting battle the *Alabama* was sunk in full view of a crowd of persons on shore at the port of Cherbourg. There is some question as to whether or not Manet actually saw the action,[6] but at all events he painted a picture of it at once (Fig. 64). As Moreau-Nélaton puts it: "The sailor sleeping in the heart of Manet throbbed with emotion. He threw himself on his brushes and, less than a month after the sinister combat, one might see in Cadart's window in the Rue de Richelieu, a painting of his manufacture, retracing the pitiless cannonade under which the *Alabama* went down."[7] Philippe Burty pointed the picture out to the readers of *La Presse*, promising that there would be several paintings of the celebrated event in the next Salon but that meanwhile one could see it at Cadart's, painted by M. Manet "with a rare power of realization, or at least life-likeness."[8]

Whether or not the picture was the result of an actual experience of the event is relatively immaterial, for our purpose is to see what Manet did with it. The finished product can scarcely be described as the work of one who is "throbbing with emotion" for the entire foreground, which occupies two-thirds of the canvas, is taken up by open water with a small sailboat towing a dinghy and steered by a gentleman in shirt sleeves and a top hat. This small craft, headed out presumably to pick up survivors, is the

---

[6] Proust says he was there, but most authorities believe he was at Boulogne, the more so since a letter to Burty thanking him for his praise of the picture says that the artist went to visit the *Kearsarge* when she anchored in the harbor of Boulogne (see Moreau-Nélaton, *Manet*, p. 61). The picture he painted of her there (No. 75 in Tabarant's list) was sometimes incorrectly called *The Alabama*, an obvious absurdity since, as Tabarant points out, the *Alabama* was at the bottom of the sea. There is, however, one bit of evidence to support the theory that Manet was *not* there which, to the author's knowledge, has been overlooked.

It is well known that Manet went to sea as a young man on the school-ship *Havre et Guadalupe*, leaving in December 1848. He spent six months on board and may be presumed to have picked up a certain amount of naval training and experience. In the painting of the battle, the ship nearest the spectator is the sinking *Alabama*, her stern already beneath the waves. Her rigging is, however, plainly

visible and shows a foremast, mainmast, then a stack, and then a mizzenmast, i.e. three masts with the stack between the second and third, counting from the bow. It would appear that this rigging was incorrect, for a picture of the *Alabama* in an old print (prints of this sort were very careful about such details) shows that the stack was placed between the fore and mainmasts, that is, between the first and second, counting from the bow. This appears to have been the standard rig for "steamers" of this class. (For all these details see Francis J. Reynolds, *The United States Navy from the Revolution to Date*, New York, 1918, pp. 43, 52, 53, 55.)

It would seem very hard to believe that had Manet been present, with his knowledge of such matters, he would have made such an obvious mistake. If, on the other hand, he was relying on hearsay, the mistake could easily have occurred.

[7] Moreau-Nélaton, *op.cit.*, p. 60.

[8] *Ibid.*, p. 60.

principal object of interest in the picture. The luckless *Alabama* is shown half concealed by smoke with her stern already settling beneath the waves, while the victorious *Kearsarge* is hardly visible at all behind her sinking victim. At the right is the English yacht which stood by to rescue the men in the water.[9] The composition is virtually identical to the painting of the *Kearsarge* at anchor in the harbor of Boulogne, including the small sailboat (which in this picture is on the opposite side of the composition), and the sense of excitement, or lack of it, is not greatly different in the two. The treatment of the episode, in short, is undramatic in the extreme. It is difficult enough to make battles seem convincing in art, but the impression here is that of a rather pleasant marine with the almost accidental inclusion of a sinking ship in the far middle distance. The fight, the attempt to take off survivors, the victorious ship— all the elements of the drama have been toned down and the emphasis placed upon the little boat, which has no integral part in the action but a highly important one in the composition. It is a good picture, but a very unexciting portrayal of an event filled with such unusual excitement for the hundreds who watched it on shore.

This discussion of one of Manet's good, but not superior, pictures is not intended to cast any reflection upon the artistry involved, but to show, if possible, that he was uninterested in dramatic content to such an extent that he could take a thrilling subject and reduce it to a point where it does not raise the observer's pulse rate by a single beat. The same might be said of all his pictures of similar types of subject. The *Torero mort* (Fig. 66) is a study of an unusually foreshortened body, but it does not arouse any emotion of horror, pity, or anything connected with one's possible feelings attendant upon the sight of a dead bullfighter.[10] In his pictures of horse races there is never concern about the possible winner.

Most outstanding in this sense is surely the famous *Exécution de Maximilien* of 1867 (Fig. 79). The picture went through a number of vicissitudes which prevented it from being exhibited in any Salon. Even the lithograph of it did not appear, according to Tabarant, until after the painter's death, but Manet's reaction to his subject here is again the point to be observed.[11]

Maximilian, the Hapsburg brother of the Emperor Francis Joseph of Austria, had been set upon the shaky throne of Mexico largely through the efforts of Louis Napoleon, who dreamed of extending French influence in the western hemisphere. But the plan miscarried, the revolutionary element under the leadership of Juarez grew stronger instead of weaker, and finally the French troops were withdrawn, leaving Maximilian helpless. His handsome wife Charlotte went mad after vainly trying to get help for him, and finally his tragic career came to an end at the hands of a firing squad

[9] Several accounts of the battle mention this yacht.

[10] A similar impression is given by his other scenes of the bull ring. The dramatic intensity of Goya's etchings and lithographs of similar subjects is in sharp contrast. Note also the use of a bull fight as a sort of backdrop for the very artificial arrangement of *Mlle. Victorine en costume d'espada* (Fig. 60).

[11] For the history of this picture see Tabarant, *Manet*, Chap. XIV, pp. 140-142, and particularly Kurt Martin, *Edouard Manet, Die Erschiessung Kaiser Maximiliens von Mexico,* Berlin, 1948.

194

on June 19, 1867. History probably can tell of no more reluctant ruler than this un-happy man who found himself the victim of imperial ambition and power politics without being able to resist his fate or make a success out of a task which was hopeless from the start. He was a mild, pleasant man who would doubtless have liked nothing better than to be allowed to go home and leave Mexico to the rebels, but he was caught by circumstance. The tragedy of his life was almost Greek in its scope and motivation.[12]

Manet resolved to paint a picture of his death even though the subject was politically very dangerous. His first version was denied exhibition on order of the government,[13] but he tried again, using a squad of French soldiers as models. The two versions were not vastly dissimilar, and in both any sense of drama is virtually absent. It has been thought that Manet had Goya's famous night scene, the *Massacre of the Second of May*, in mind, but if so, he did not choose to take over its terrible emotional content. From the point of view of the actual event, Manet's picture is a strange one: the Emperor of Mexico and his two fellow victims are placed in an impossible position a foot or two from the ends of the long muskets, their faces are barely sketched in, the grouping of the squad is determined not by any military order but entirely by the design, and the group of spectators surmounting the wall introduces a note of odd informality to the proceedings. The whole picture has an extraordinary air of total detachment; no attempt whatever is made to give it significance in any moral or human sense. It may be claimed that the political issues involved made it unwise to do so, but one can hardly suppose that Manet, or anyone else, would have been inclined to distinguish one kind of a presentation from another. Furthermore, to have used French soldiers as models was, in itself, rather hazardous.[14] As in the *Kearsarge* picture, one is struck by the essentially pictorial treatment. The soldiers' uniforms with their pipeclayed belts and gaiters are decorative; the design is extremely effective; the coloring restrained but delicate. If one wished to make the point that in the best painting the subject does not

[12] For the facts involved the reader is re-ferred to any good history of Mexico. E. Regi-nald Enock, *Mexico*, London, 1909, stresses the tragedy of Maximilian's life and the rather shameful part played by Napoleon III. Ironi-cally enough, Maximilian seems to have been quite a connoisseur of the arts himself. See P. Dax, "Maximilien, critique d'art," *L'Ar-tiste*, 9e série, Vol. IX, pp. 357-381.

[13] Tabarant, *op.cit.*, p. 141. He presumably made up the scene from newspaper accounts of the execution. Later he obtained photo-graphs of the firing squad, etc. See Max Lieber-mann, "Ein Beitrag zur Arbeitsweise Manets," *Kunst und Künstler*, VIII, 1910, pp. 483ff.

[14] The matter of the French uniforms and the use of French soldiers as models is very curious indeed. In view of the part played in the affair by the Emperor of the French, any representation of the event would seem to have been almost a political attack in itself, the sort of thing that Manet was most unlikely to do. Then to change the costume of the execu-tioners from Mexican to French would seem to have made the point more obvious still. It is hard to believe that Manet had no idea of the political interpretation which could be put on such a scene, and yet it was certainly pro-vocative enough. The publication of a litho-graph was apparently forbidden as well as the display of the picture. Both Tabarant and Moreau-Nélaton give quite extended accounts of the episode but apparently see nothing peculiar about it. The latter says that Manet hoped to have a success with it based on the popular sympathy for the death of the un-happy man (Moreau-Nélaton, *Manet*, p. 93). For a very different interpretation from the one offered here, see K. Martin, *op.cit., passim.*

intrude upon the enjoyment of formal values, this would seem a most excellent example to use as illustration. It is odd, however, that Manet should have chosen this particular subject for such treatment. Why did he pick one of the saddest and most disgraceful episodes of nineteenth century French politics, only to turn it into an essentially charming picture? It is possible that he himself thought the picture far more moving than it is, but if so, he would not appear to have been very successful in carrying out his intention. At the time of the War of 1870 he did several scenes, mostly sketches, of the fighting in Paris and in one of them, *La Barricade* (Scene of the Commune, May 1871), the same firing squad appears as the principal element. It was, apparently, a motif which could be used in more than one context.[15]

From a traditional point of view, therefore, Manet's greatest gift, his innate artistic vision, which turned the humblest object into a thing of pictorial beauty, was at the same time a defect, for it seemed to prevent him from seeing anything more than what his specialized sight allowed. The models before him were interesting colored forms, but they were not, essentially, human beings with passions, thoughts, and complicated characters. His realism was strong enough to give the *Olympia* an impression of life,[16] of truth to nature, sufficient to make her shocking to the public, but we do not feel that the artist penetrated her character very far. Mlle. Victorine (Fig. 60), Lola di Valencia,[17] Zola (Fig. 80), and others were all presented from the outside without much interest in them as people. The artist was too immersed in his own sensations to project himself into the personality and life of someone else, nor could he be really dramatic in a scene where action was involved, because it remained a pictorial, rather than an emotional, problem for him. It has even been suggested that his famous portrait of Zola is less a picture of that fiery man of letters than a sort of self-portrait of the artist himself, and the idea seems highly plausible.[18] Where Courbet savored the subject for what it actually was, ugly or not, Manet saw it only as a stimulus to his, rather than the observer's, reactions.

It is clear that an attitude such as this one puts an entirely different value on any possible theme for a painting. In the traditional position there was a hierarchy of subjects based on considerations as to their worth in moral and spiritual terms, i.e. some subjects were better than others because they were more important to mankind in the general scheme of things. A hero was higher in such a scale than a banker or a street sweeper, and this was a fact which the artist was supposed to bear in mind in his painting. In objective naturalism this was done away with; all objects were theoretically of equal interest as facts with which people had to deal in life. But although they were equalized, their interest still lay largely in *them*, in their appearance, their

[15] This picture is a water color known to the author from the reproduction in the Platt Collection, Princeton University. It was No. 137 in the Manet Sale of 1884, now in Majorsky Collection, Budapest. There is a lithograph of the same subject (M. Guérin, *L'Oeuvre gravé de Manet*, Paris, 1944, No. 76).

[16] Cf. Privat, quoted above, pp. 189-190.

[17] Baudelaire's charming quatrain written on seeing this picture is quoted in Tabarant, *op.cit.*, p. 53.

[18] This suggestion was put forward in an article by S. L. Faison in *Magazine of Art*, May 1949, pp. 162-168.

existence itself, even though no further analysis might be attempted or even desirable. As we have seen, the humanitarians asked for something more than this; they required that these real objects, above all man himself, be studied not only with attention but also with imagination and insight so that a new morality and a new ideal might be made visible to everyone. Manet shifted the focus of interest again, and turned it, so to speak, from the object *as object*, to his appreciation of that object, which was quite a different matter. He did not do this with conscious intent but because, by his very nature, he could not do otherwise. Duret is very emphatic on this point: "Manet's special quality of vision was not acquired by study, by an effort of the will, or by a process of reasoning. It was simply a fact of his physical being. It was given him. . . . He saw the world in a brilliance of light to which other eyes were blind; he transfixed on canvas the sensations which were flashed upon his eye. The process was an unconscious one, since what he saw depended simply upon his physical organism."[19] It is no great wonder that, in an age when ninety-nine painters out of a hundred were made and not born, natural gifts such as his should have seemed quite "out of line," as the phrase went.

Whether a man so gifted by nature was, in a sense, incomplete by having little or no rational thought to bring to bear on his art, is a point which might be reflected upon. Rationality and training without the gifts of a natural painter admittedly produce sterile results, but what shall be said of a painter who has the natural gift but is given to little or no intellectual interests? The answer which most of his contemporaries gave was only too plain, just as the modern answer has often been to raise this natural simplicity to the level of the greatest of artistic qualities.

The question now arises, did the critics of the day notice this lack of interest in people as people? Did they sense the new neutrality toward the subject? From the fact that his defenders like Astruc and Privat scarcely mention this matter, it would seem that they felt it was quite fitting and proper that he should paint as he did. But there are more direct statements. Gilbert Hamerton, the English critic who was so devoted a student of contemporary French art, wrote of Manet in 1869:

The artist paints for some artistic purpose, as the line, or the patch, and[20] the people go to his pictures for the subject alone, which may be insignificant or even repulsive. Manet's aims are exclusively technical, anything suits him as a subject, if only it presents a suitable arrangement of patches.

. . . it is curious . . . how at last all we ask of a picture is that it present to us some side of art with skill and power. Thus, after sixty years of servitude to the line, Ingres drew *The Spring* and it may be that Manet will ultimately do something wonderful and admirable after long servitude to the patch.[21]

Hamerton expressed some interesting ideas here,[22] but his taste was weak; it is hard to see how he could have thought that Manet had yet to do something good with "the

[19] Th. Duret, *Manet and the Impressionists*, p. 42.

[20] This sentence would read more clearly if the word "but" were used in place of "and."

[21] P. G. Hamerton, *Painting in France after the Decline of Classicism*, London, 1869, p. 21.

[22] As, for instance, the idea that a picture should emphasize some aspect of art rather

patch," when he had already painted *Olympia, Le Fifre* (Fig. 76), and *Le Déjeuner sur l'herbe.*

Thoré, too, was well aware of this aspect of Manet's art for he said in 1868 that Manet saw light and color very well, but after that, nothing:

> When he has made his spot of color on the canvas, a spot which makes a person or an object on[23] the nature surrounding it, he calls it quits. . . . But he will get out of his difficulty later when he thinks to give their relative value to the essential parts of beings. His real vice is a sort of pantheism which values a head no more than a slipper; which sometimes even grants a greater importance to a bouquet of flowers than to the face of a woman, for example in his famous *Black Cat* [i.e. the *Olympia*]; which paints everything almost the same way; furniture, drapery, books, costumes, flesh, facial accents—for example in his portrait of M. Émile Zola exhibited in the present Salon.[24]

It is hard to deny that this is what Manet was doing; the point is rather to decide whether this procedure was, or was not, a proper one. It was certainly adopted by the Impressionist group generally and has since received the most sympathetic attention from many modern critics who are inclined to the belief that artistic form is an end rather than a means. If the glory of modern art has been its extraordinarily ambitious and daring exploration of almost all possible means of pictorial expression, and if in the process it has had less regard for the meaning of the subject in its own right than for its effect upon the artist (often, but not always, visual), then Manet may well be regarded as the first great modern in the field of figure painting. In his art, well before the close of our period, are to be found a majority of the attributes pertaining to content that separate modern art from what preceded it.[25] The subjective, imaginative strain which led from Baudelaire to Moreau, Redon, Munch, and later to surrealism was not congenial to him, but he was justly regarded as the father of the Impressionists with all which that implies for later movements down into the present century. If we are correct in seeing him, along with Courbet, as an essentially naïve individual, he can also be connected with those later forms of painting which were variously influenced by the primitive arts of different regions and times, arts whose appeal lay very largely in their own natural simplicity and childlike directness of expression.[26]

With Manet, the shift to an essentially modern approach to subject and style was virtually complete. It was a rather sudden step which he took so unwittingly, and it carried him well beyond the point reached by Courbet in the previous decade. It also, as we have seen, carried him past the great majority of the critics. But although there

---

than attempt a more balanced presentation, and that spontaneity (i.e. sketchiness) is a desirable trait in a painting. Though Hamerton was opposed to realism he admitted readily that it had value and that it had achieved some amazing results. Manet, he felt, was a realist.

[23] The use of "on" is interesting (the French word is *sur* here) for it would seem that for Thoré the figures remained in front of their setting rather than in it. The *Fifre* would certainly be an example.

[24] Thoré, *Salons de W. Bürger*, Vol. II, p. 531.

[25] See the discussion on these points at the end of Chap. VIII.

[26] Cf. Goldwater, *Primitivism in Modern Painting* (N.Y., 1938), and also Malraux, *Le Musée imaginaire.*

were those like Astruc, Privat, and Baudelaire who spoke up in his behalf, the appearance of Zola's commentary in 1866 must really mark the date of the first total and whole-hearted approval. No passing mention, no quiet analysis, no reasoned comparison would do for Manet's impetuous friend; he launched into an attack upon the opposition with a fury which was designed to level it at a single charge.

"Mon Salon" was dedicated to Cézanne, Zola's good friend with whom he had so often discussed the progress of art, the stupidity of the crowd, and the true basis for art—which was life, "powerful and individual, beyond which there is only falsehood and stupidity."[27] As has already been mentioned, Zola felt that since nature was, relatively speaking, a constant, the variable must be the temperament of the artist and the seat of artistic value.[28] For this reason it was a changeable quality which could never be tied down by rules or epitomized by ideals: "The work of tomorrow will not be that of today; you must bravely abandon yourself to your nature and not try to deceive yourself."[29] In the future, therefore, the only thing was to be yourself and, as far as art went, pay no attention to anyone else. For the artist, this meant a complete absorption in personal reactions; for the critic, it meant that all that should be done was to try to understand as best one could what the artist was up to, but never oppose it since one did not have the right.[30] It was, in short, proper to look through the artist's eyes, but not through one's own as a nonartist observer. With the statement of ideas such as these, the scene was well set for a discussion of the instinctive art of Manet.

In the year that Zola wrote, the painter had suffered one of his periodic rejections at the Salon,[31] so Zola began with him, a procedure guaranteed to infuriate innumerable people before they read another word, though it must also have caught the attention of others by its sheer audacity. He started out at once by saying that Manet was not trying to be eccentric, he was just obeying his own nature—a fact the author must have known very well from his acquaintance with the artist.[32] Zola explained very clearly why he was interested, and at the same time why he was able to understand Manet: "It was in this studio that I understood M. Manet completely. I liked him by instinct; afterwards, I penetrated his talent, this talent which I am going to try to analyze."[33] If the artist's work was instinctive, so also was the critic's understanding of it. The creative method is described in these terms: "He put himself bravely before a subject, he saw it in the form of large patches (taches), and he painted everything just as he saw it. Who dares to speak here of shabby scheming, who dares accuse a conscientious artist of making fun of art and himself? . . ."[34] A little later, while discussing the Fifre (which had just been refused), he says of the painter: "His whole being leads him to see by patches, by simple energetic bits. One can say of him that he is content to seek proper tones and then juxtapose them on a canvas. It happens

[27] Zola, "Mon salon," Mes haines (ed. Charpentier), p. 258. All the same, the critic was disappointed at his friend's slow progress.

[28] See the discussion of Zola's views in Part One.

[29] Zola, op.cit., p. 282.

[30] By what standard does one criticize the vision or dreams of another?

[31] The Fifre and an Acteur tragique were refused.

[32] Zola, op.cit., p. 290.

[33] Ibid., p. 293.   [34] Ibid., p. 293.

that the canvas is thus covered with a strong solid painting. I rediscover in the picture a man who has the curiosity for the true and who draws from it a world alive with a particular and powerful life."[35] The last sentence is particularly revealing. The critic, in a work of this sort, not only finds marvelously painted bits which make a painting—one is reminded of Denis' famous phrase[36]—but the artist himself reflected in it. The fifer boy *himself* is a nonentity.

Toward the beginning of the chapter, Zola says that if he had the money he would buy up all Manet's work, for "in fifty years they will sell for fifteen or twenty times more than now, and then certain pictures now valued at forty thousand francs will not be worth forty."[37] "Manet's place is marked in the Louvre like that of Courbet, like that of every artist with a strong original temperament. In other respects there is not the least resemblance between Courbet and Manet, and these artists, if they are logical, ought to deny each other. It is exactly because they have nothing in common, that each can live a separate life."[38] The modern reader can only marvel at a prophecy so true and an insight so exact. Zola made it clear that although a vivid naturalism was essential and an important part of the art of his favorite, pure realism was of little interest since if the artist was too concerned with the statement of the real for its own sake, there would be little room for temperament.[39] Whatever his views may have been later on, however "scientific" or analytic he may have been in his novels, it was not this quality which first drew him to Manet. What he admired in 1866 was the transformation of that reality by a highly personal manner of seeing and painting. Fernand Doucet, in his study of Zola's aesthetic,[40] sees "Mon salon" as a great cry for *vérité* in art, and includes his discussion of it under the heading "To what extent he remained scientific," but the reasoning is not entirely convincing, at least not as it applies to his art criticism. *Thérèse Raquin* may have been "a work of reality and truthfulness," but if the art of Manet was "truthful" it was in a highly personal and non-scientific sense. Zola admired Corot (except for the nymphs)[41] and yet the art of that poetic painter was certainly not wholly "truthful" in this meaning of the word. He gave Courbet up, not because he was less of a realist, but because he was less of a personality. "My Courbet, for me, is simply a personality" he said in answer to Proudhon.[42]

It was, in fact, this matter of the fascination of individuality which he felt so strongly in Manet that caused him to part company with Taine whose mind and theories he admired immensely. In an interesting passage in "M. H. Taine, artiste," he suspects that Taine is being too quick for him, that he is being led to support views to which he can't honestly subscribe. "Yes," he says, "these remarks are just, these interpreta-

---

[35] *Ibid.*, p. 295.

[36] "Remember that a picture—before being a battle horse, a nude woman, or some anecdote—is essentially a plane surface covered with colors assembled in a certain order" (Goldwater and Treves, *Artists on Art*, p. 380).

[37] Zola, *op.cit.*, p. 290.

[38] *Ibid.*, p. 296.

[39] *Ibid.*, p. 300.

[40] Fernand Doucet, *L'Esthétique d'Émile Zola et son application à la critique*, The Hague, 1923, p. 117.

[41] Zola, *op.cit.*, p. 319.

[42] *Ibid.*, p. 34, "Courbet et Proudhon."

tions are true, and one must conclude from them that the artist cannot live outside his times, and that his works reflect his age. . . . But we are not at that degree of dryness of the problem by which, in any case at all, one can deduce the work from the simple knowledge of certain given factors. . . . As a man I only say to M. Taine: 'You walk in the truth, but you come so close to the edge of the false that sometimes you must certainly encroach on it. I don't dare follow you.' "[43] He goes on to say that there is an intentional omission from Taine's system: he "avoids speaking of personality."[44] This was certainly not a scientific voice, in spite of the fact that he occasionally expressed himself in terms which have the flavor of the physiologist: "Like everything else, art is a human product, a human secretion; it is our body which sweats the beauty of our works. Our body changes according to the climate and custom, and the secretion changes equally."[45]

Such a sentence is exceptional in his criticism; he thought of Manet as a natural artist, but on a loftier plane than that of human perspiration, and his admiration for Corot and the unknown Pissarro was more spiritual by far.[46] But be that as it may, Zola seems, at this moment at least, to have been gifted with an insight into the art of Manet which was almost exactly equal to the gift the painter had for setting down his visual impressions of things seen in beautiful artistic form. As a pair, they may well stand for the true beginnings of the modern movement in its creative as well as its critical aspects.

[43] *Ibid.*, pp. 221-223.   [44] *Ibid.*, p. 224.
[45] *Ibid.*, p. 282, "Mon salon."
[46] Speaking of a picture by that unappreciated master he said: " An austere and sober manner of painting, an extreme concern for truth and rightness (*justesse*), a hard strong will. You are a great blunderer, Sir—you are an artist whom I love" (*ibid.*, p. 320).

XIX. THE GROUP AROUND MANET. DEGAS

THE growing influence excited by Manet's art did not pass unnoticed by the critics. Marius Chaumelin, for example, was not only aware of the charm of his art, but also saw that it was furnishing an example to several younger men. In his review of the Salon of 1868 he described the painter as a "master" because he now had followers like Renoir, whose *Lise* (Fig. 81) "catches the attention of the connoisseurs as much by the strangeness of the effect as by the precision of the tone. It is what is called in realist language, a handsome spot of color."[1] In the same year Castagnary also gave Renoir a short but favorable mention.[2] However, aside from rather scattered notices, the younger group did not receive anything like the attention which was lavished on their unhappy and notorious leader. Some did not exhibit very often, others were refused admission to the Salons, and when they did, their styles seemed so similar to that of Manet, that they were not singled out, since he could be used as a whipping boy for them all. Monet's *Camille* (Fig. 77) was quite well received in 1866; even the reviewer for *L'Artiste* gave it a sort of back-handed compliment: "In the manner of M. Manet who makes a whole picture for a piece of rag, M. Monet makes a portrait for a piece of green silk with black stripes."[3] The result, he says, is a dress but no body, though the dress is certainly the work of a painter; better, in fact, than Manet's.

The story of the critical reaction to Impressionism and the mature work of Degas, Renoir, and the others does not belong within the limits of this study, but one extraordinary appreciation of the "new" art must be quoted. This came from a rather unexpected quarter, namely, the busy pen of Arsène Houssaye, long one of the leading figures on *L'Artiste* and a lifelong amateur of the arts. He had written many pieces for this paper—Salon reviews, discussions of individual painters, notes on events in the world of art as well as many other articles and poems—but in all of them he had been very reserved about the changes taking place, and had seemed something less than enthusiastic about the greater innovators.[4] It is astonishing, therefore, to find him writing to M. Bertrand, the reviewer for the Salon of 1870, as follows:

The two true masters of this school [i.e. of Manet] who, instead of saying "art for art's sake," say "nature for nature's sake" are Messieurs Monet (do not confuse with M. Manet) and Renoir; two true masters, like the Courbet of Ornans, by virtue of the brutal frankness of their brush. They tell me the jury has refused M. Monet, it had the good sense to receive

---

[1] M. Chaumelin, *L'Art contemporain*, p. 137, "Le Salon de 1868." The picture by Renoir attracted the favorable attention of several critics, among them, Thoré: "The effect is so natural and true that one ought to find it false for one is accustomed to imagine nature in the conventional colors of bad painting" (Thoré, *Salons de W. Bürger*, Vol. II, p. 531).

[2] Castagnary, *Salons*, p. 313, "Le Salon de 1868."

[3] Chas. Beaurin, "Le Salon de 1866," *L'Artiste*, 8e série, Vol. XII, 1866, p. 136. Thoré also

thought it better than Manet; in fact, he went into an almost lyrical praise of it: "*Camille* is immortal and is called *The Woman in the Green Dress*" (Thoré, *op.cit.*, Vol. II, p. 286, "Le Salon de 1866"). This picture was bought by Arsène Houssaye; see below.

[4] The general conservative tone of this journal has already been described, and Houssaye seemed generally to agree with it. He liked to express his own ideas, however, and often contributed a short appreciation of the current Salon in addition to the regular account.

M. Renoir. One can study the proud painterly temperament which appears with such brilliance in a *Femme d'Algers* which Delacroix would have signed (Fig. 88).

Gleyre, his master, must be thoroughly surprised to have formed such a "prodigal son" who makes fun of all the laws of grammar because he dares to make one of his own. But Gleyre is too fine an artist not to recognize art whatever its expressions are.

Remember well, then, the name of M. Renoir and the name of M. Monet. I have in my own collection the *Femme à la robe vert* [Fig. 77] by M. Monet and an early *Baigneuse* by Renoir which, one day, I will give to the Luxembourg Museum when the Luxembourg Museum will open its doors to all the opinions of the brush.

In the meantime they arouse admiration, I will not say among the French, who scarcely see anything except through convention, but the Spanish and the English who salute a painting where there is one, that is to say, truth under the light.[5]

M. Bertrand merely passed this along for what it was worth, though he couldn't resist saying that even so it was a shame these painters *didn't* obey the laws of grammar. Coming from a man like Houssaye, this was an unusual endorsement of the new form painting was taking, and must have seemed to the harried artists like a real step toward more general recognition. In passing, it might be noted that the reference to the flexibility of English and Spanish taste in comparison to the stiffness of the French is most refreshing. The chauvinism of Parisian criticism in this perod, which has already been referred to, is so blatant as to be quite painful; the reader almost blushes at the extravagant claims made for the work of the French School even though justified in comparison to the art of the rest of Europe.[6] It is, of course, well known that Courbet had a strong following in Germany, Belgium, and Holland at the very time his countrymen were trying to discredit his most important pictures.

It would be interesting to examine the critical comments made upon the work of some of the less famous members of this younger group, like Legros, Stevens, and Fantin-Latour who painted rather unusual group portraits of his friends in a style which must surely owe a great deal to the camera,[7] but not a great deal of further insight into the developments we are considering would be gained. Much research remains to be done in this field, and these painters may, perhaps, be left to a later and less general study than this one. The case of Degas, however, must be examined briefly, for he had a very direct connection with the great tradition in his early years, and his reaction to it—as evidenced by his pictures—is an interesting example of its inadequacy for a truly original artist with a strong interest in contemporary life.

Reference has already been made to Edmond Duranty's story, "The Painter Louis Martin," which concerns the life of a young artist in the 'sixties and his love affair with the daughter of an old classical painter named Richard.[8] In it, there is an incident relating to a commission for a copy of a Poussin, which has been obtained for Martin by Richard. The youthful painter goes to the Louvre to get to work and finds Degas

[5] See Karl Bertrand, "Le Salon de 1870," *L'Artiste*, 9e série, Vol. XIII, 1870, pp. 319-320.

[6] The following letter from Arsène Houssaye to the Salon reviewer of *L'Artiste* in 1869 will illustrate: "Today France has the honor to contain the capital of the arts, as it does the capital of letters and the political capital" (*L'Artiste*, 9e série, Vol. IX, 1869, p. 234).

[7] Cf. the *Hommage a Delacroix* (1864) and other similar pictures.

[8] E. Duranty, *Le Pays des arts*, pp. 315-350.

already installed in front of the picture. He is described as follows: "an artist of rare intelligence, preoccupied with ideas, which seemed strange to the majority of his companions."[9] This was an interesting description, for Degas was often grouped with the Impressionists in spite of the fact that he was really quite independent, and never employed the technique which is associated with this movement. What is more interesting for our purposes, however, is the fact that he was copying a Poussin: the *Enlèvement des femmes Sabines*.[10] The fact of the matter is that Degas was the only one of the group from the Café Guerbois who started out his career as a genuine history painter.

Whether or not he was an intellectual, it seems clear that he did very well in school[11] —particularly in the study of literature—and as a young man, does not seem to have been an instinctive artist like Manet, though he showed real talent at an early age. He entered the École des Beaux-Arts in 1855, spending much time in the Louvre and in the studio of Louis Lamothe who was a pupil of Flandrin's, but more obviously a follower of Ingres. It was here that Degas acquired the admiration for the great master of line which remained with him for the rest of his life. But he did not stay long. Unlike Manet, who set himself up as a full-fledged painter as soon as he had separated himself from the evil influence of Couture, Degas seems to have been filled with a strong desire to get closer to the fountainhead of tradition, and went off to Italy. He studied in Rome, Florence, Orvieto, and elsewhere, learning what he could from a wide variety of masters but apparently with complete independence.[12] After 1860 he settled in Paris more or less for good, but continued to work after the masters, even studying the recently acquired Niké of Samothrace. Holbein, Poussin, Ingres were copied and analyzed, yet in all this there is little or no revolt against the past, no general distaste for anything which could be associated in any way with academism.[13] On the contrary, it would seem that he was associating himself with it voluntarily.

In 1860 he painted the *Jeunes filles spartiates provoquant des garçons* (Fig. 49), and this was followed at somewhat uncertain dates, by *Alexandre et Bucéphale*, *Sémiramis construisant une ville*, *La Fille de Jephté* (Fig. 75), and finally *Les Malheurs d'Orléans* (Fig. 69) which was his first Salon picture, shown in 1865. The dates of these paintings have not been too firmly fixed,[14] but it is sure that the *Orléans* was the only

[9] *Ibid.*, p. 335.

[10] The date of this copy is not certain. Meier-Graefe dates it as late as 1870, but possibly it was earlier, since Degas was much less interested in such themes by that time. However, this biographer thinks he did many of his copies in the 'seventies (J. Meier-Graefe, *Degas*, N.Y., 1923, pls. VIII, IX, X).

[11] The facts of his life have been taken from Hans Graber, *Edgar Degas nach eigenen und fremden Zeugnissen*, Basel, 1942, pp. 7ff. (p. 29).

[12] That is, he was not connected with official art schools or instruction.

[13] Manet, of course, copied many old masters

too, but it would seem that he was interested only in style as previously indicated.

[14] Cf. Eleanor Mitchell, "*La Fille de Jephté par Degas*," *Gazette des Beaux-arts*, 6me période, Vol. XVIII, 1937, pp. 175-189. The author dates the *Sémiramis* and the *Alexandre et Bucéphale* in 1861. She also finds certain similarities with the *Sabines* which would suggest that that copy was done earlier than 1870. However, the date of the *Fille de Jephté* remains uncertain. A comparison with the *Mademoiselle Fiocre dans le Ballet de la Source*, suggests that the *Jephté* is earlier, but if so, it may have been retouched somewhat at a later date, for some of the coloring is brighter than that employed by the

one of this type he exhibited publicly at this time, for the others seem never to have left his studio. From 1866 to the interruption of the war he exhibited portraits and one racing scene ('66).[15] After 1870 he never showed in the Salon again.

The five major pictures mentioned above were not done for any other purposes than his own,[16] and must, therefore be considered as representing an important interest during about five years following his intensive studies in Italy. In size and theme, they agree with traditional ideas about what history painting should be, and so they would have seemed to the people of the time, if the quiet reception accorded the *Malheurs d'Orléans* (Fig. 69) can be regarded as a typical reaction. Almost none of the critics even mentioned it, since it was apparently just another conservative work by a virtually unknown painter.

And yet actually these pictures were unlike any other history painting then being done, for although the subjects were of the proper kind, and the size adequate, the attitude toward the subject was most unusual. Two of the most important requirements for this kind of art were that it should represent the ideal in some form, and that its meaning should be both significant and elevating.[17] If these be applied to the *Filles spartiates* (Fig. 49), the earliest of the group, the difference between Degas' ideas and those in common practice become clear at once. Far from being idealized, the adolescent boys with their tough faces and strange haircuts are obviously straight off the streets of Paris or Naples, just as the pug nose of the leading girl is anything but classic.[18] To anyone familiar with the later art of Degas, the impression of the general setting of the picture is almost identical to that of the airy scenes of country horse races;[19] there is little here beyond nudity and the title to suggest antiquity. Nor is there any real emphasis upon meaning in the traditional sense of the term, the groups are arranged for design, for pattern, while the expressions are quite devoid of any coordinated emotional suggestion. The same lack of interest in meaning can be discerned in the *La Fille de Jephté* (Fig. 75). The scene is confused dramatically, and neither Jephthah nor his daughter are easily discovered among other figures of no particular significance to the story. The tragedy which was so heavily emphasized in Le Brun's painting of the subject[20] is hardly understandable in the Degas version, though the design is interesting and the general treatment harmonious. It is well known that

---

artist in the early 'sixties. The *Mademoiselle Fiocre* is sometimes included in this group, but it seems to have a different, more romantic, air.

[15] Graber, *Degas*, p. 35. They did not receive much attention. Castagnary noted the *Deux soeurs* in 1867, mentioning the artist as "a *débutant* who shows remarkable aptitudes" (Castagnary, *Salons*, p. 246, "Le Salon de 1867").

[16] That is, they were not done for any official competitions with set titles.

[17] A comparison with Puvis is illuminating. The Degas paintings seem less assured and controlled; also, the naturalism of the Spartan picture is very different from the mood of abstraction prevailing in Puvis' art.

[18] For Degas' own views on this matter (undated, however) see the letter quoted by Duranty in *La Nouvelle peinture*, pp. 28-29: "The turned up nose which delights them [i.e. the artists of the Greek persuasion] in the evening is betrayed in the morning and made straight."

[19] Cf., for example, *Courses en Province* (1873; Meier-Graefe, *Degas*, pl. XXI).

[20] The picture is now in Florence. The towering figure of the unhappy father actually holding the sacrificial knife dominates the composition.

Degas made many studies for this work (in itself a traditional procedure) using motifs from several sources in Italian art, but his interest apparently did not extend to any emotional interpretation of the drama involved in the subject.

The *Malheurs d'Orléans* (Fig. 69) is probably the least successful of the group[21] and there is little in it which would have aroused the interest of even a conservative critic except for one rather lovely nude figure standing by the tree at the left.[22] The forms are all disposed around the edges of the canvas leaving a large void in the center which nullifies the cruel gesture of the man with the bow. The horseman on the right is having great and awkward difficulty with the woman he is holding on his saddle, and the action of the whole scene lacks both compositional and emotional motivation.

These remarks are not intended as any infringement upon Degas' reputation as a modern master, but they do show what were the results of an apparent attempt on the part of the young painter to do something in which he was intellectually interested but for which he was temperamentally unsuited. His heart was not in it, only his intelligence, and the final effect was one in which the formal qualities seem to struggle against the traditional quality of the theme chosen.[23] It was the more real world of dancers, horse races, ballet, and washerwomen that properly suited his mind as well as his talent. With a few exceptions, such as the remarkable enigmatic "Interior" of the McIlhenny Collection,[24] he gave up dramatic or "meaningful" scenes even of contemporary life in favor of superb studies of pose and design executed with a draughtsmanship which was as accomplished as any the century produced. The neutral subject was a necessity for him as it was for Manet.

Duranty, his most notable defender, saw him as a "realist," and his description illustrates some of the difficulties attendant upon the use of this term.[25] The author of *La Nouvelle peinture* was a literary realist himself and considered that he was one of the earliest champions of it, a claim which had some justification.[26] It was natural that,

---

[21] By some error the picture was listed as a pastel in the catalogue of the Salon.

[22] Graber says that the notice quoted from Castagnary (note 15, above) is the first he received (Graber, *Degas*, p. 201). The author has found no mention to date of this picture in any review.

[23] This seems particularly true of the *Sémiramis*.

[24] Whatever this picture actually means, it cannot represent the aftermath of a rape as described by Camille Mauclair (*Degas*, N.Y., 1941, pp. 47-48). There is no convincing evidence of a struggle and the bed has not been touched. The author of the present work would suggest "The Rendezvous" as coming closer to its meaning. At all events it is a picture of a singularly haunting quality and quite unusual in contrast to the rest of the painter's work.

[25] Cf. particularly the interesting preface by Marcel Guérin to the new edition (pp. 11-12).

[26] He was an early admirer of Champfleury and one of the editors of *Le Réaliste*. His attack on Fromentin, with which the essay opens, is interesting. There was a great deal of truth in the ideas that worthy painter had put forth, but Duranty chose to ignore them and harp only on the nefarious influence of the new generation coming out of the École and the fact that Fromentin himself painted contemporary Arabs. Once again the tragic disparity between theory and practice was made plain, and once again the ideas which had had a real validity for centuries were held up to scorn because the art which was supposed to express them was so obviously bad. It would be hard to disagree with Fromentin when he said that the new group was only interested in a part of the truth, that "the choice of subjects, drawing,

as a result, he should emphasize this quality in his friend's work whereas later criticism was inclined to make it rather secondary to its formal power of line and design. Duranty traces the origins of "realism" back to Courbet, Ingres, and Millet, and includes in his pantheon such diverse figures as Corot, Jongkind, Boudin, Legros, Whistler, Fantin-Latour, Alfred Stevens, and even Joseph de Nittis.[27] The common bond between them was the fact that they "grappled with the tradition, admired it and wished to destroy it; they recognized that it was great and strong and for that very reason attacked it."[28] Why then, the author goes on, should they be bothered with, especially when they often produced only sketches and summary abridgements?[29] The answer, of course, was that, at a time when everyone else thought there was nothing else to be discovered or learned about art, they had produced something quite new: "a way of coloring a design, and a series of original views."[30] It was these latter which seemed most important to Duranty: "The idea, the first idea, was to remove the partition which separated the studio from common life. . . . It was necessary to make the painter get out of his snuffbox, his cloister, where he was in contact only with heaven, and lead him back among people, into the world."[31] Once this had been accomplished, the telltale appearance of reality would tell the observer all about the subject: a window is a fascinating guide to the world.[32] But this wasn't an accurate guide to the art of Degas, who admittedly drew his art directly from life (once he had gotten history painting out of his system), but did not stop there, preferring to go on to something far more personal.

Rivière, in his book on the painter, ascribes the novelist's views to the artist himself, a point which is well refuted by Marcel Guérin in the preface to the new edition of this important little volume.[33] The ideas expressed by Duranty are akin to what his friend believed, but the emphasis is in the wrong place. Not reality, but the practice of painting and pastel was the focus of Degas' interest. Indeed, Duranty seems not to have

---

palette, everything participates in this impersonal manner of seeing and dealing with things" (p. 22). He was right, too, when he said that the tradition was "brilliantly defended and very little followed." But no criticism could be tolerated. Duranty even turned on Lecoq de Boisbaudran, whose system of memory education for artists had a considerable effect on some of the moderns. (Lecoq de Boisbaudran, *Éducation de la mémoire pittoresque*, Paris, 1862. There were other books by him on this same theme. For his influence see H. Focillon, *La Peinture au XIXe et XXe siècles*, pp. 161ff.) Boisbaudran wanted to help free the student from his reliance on the model and thus help him to make use of his imagination, but Duranty can't get away from the horrid fact that he was a teacher in the hated École des Beaux-Arts. Thus it was that, little

by little, the entire traditional position was discredited.

[27] Duranty, *La Nouvelle peinture*, pp. 33-37.
[28] *Ibid.*, p. 38.
[29] *Ibid.*, p. 38. The reader will recall the conservative objections to "sketchism."
[30] *Ibid.*, p. 38.
[31] *Ibid.*, p. 43.
[32] *Ibid.*, p. 46. Baudelaire criticized the landscapists for doing just that—a window frame did not, he felt, make a poem (Baudelaire, *Curiosités* [ed. Lévy] p. 326, "Le Salon de 1859").
[33] Georges Rivière, *Mr. Degas (Bourgeois de Paris)*, Paris, 1935, p. 67: "What did Degas say about realism through the pen of his friend Duranty?" For Guérin's views, see *La Nouvelle peinture*, pp. 10-11.

understood clearly the general change which had occurred in naturalist art from the objective days of Courbet's early fame to the subjective form, developed by the naïve and immensely gifted Manet, and practiced by Degas and others. The analysis of the influence of Japanese prints shows that this misunderstanding was well established in his mind.[34] He tries to make them (and the Chinese) into Impressionists, instead of believing that it was simply their sense of design and pattern which influenced the formal pictorial interests of a group of men interested in art as an end in itself. But for all of the errors in his presentation of the case for this particular group of moderns,[35] he was essentially right when he described their contribution as a new look at the world expressed in a new coloration and a new design. They did want to destroy the old ways so that they could be free from the oppression which weighed so heavily on them.[36] They also wanted to break up the hard shell which habit had put around the great art of the past so that they could take from it what they needed and be justified in ignoring the rest. More than that, they wanted to be able to look anywhere at all for inspiration, an opportunity of which they made full use very shortly. The tendency to look with fresh eyes at the scenes of the country and city was only one phase; others looked at the arts of the Orient, of Oceania, of Byzantium, and elsewhere, and the results were far from the "realism" of which Duranty spoke. The Symbolists, who followed so fast on the heels of the Impressionists, looked into their imaginations, their subconscious selves, and sought for all manner of sensations of which the hard world of actual fact knew nothing. Gustave Moreau, for whom Duranty had little use, was in his way just as modern as Degas, yet the gap which divided the two in his mind was very wide. He discusses the painter Fromentin's interest in Moreau:

. . . a tormented spirit, often delicate, nourished on poetry and ancient symbology, the greatest friend of myths which there has been here below, spending his life asking questions of the Sphinx, and both of them [i.e. Fromentin and Moreau] have succeeded in inspiring new groups of those young people who are brought up on the nursing bottle of official traditional art, with a strange system of painting bounded on the south by Algeria, on the east by mythology, on the west by ancient history, on the north by archaeology: true painting muddied by an epoch of criticism, curio collecting, and eclecticisms.[37]

The sin Fromentin had committed here was to dare to admire the poetic and symbolic art of a man who could never say anything to a mind like Duranty's which professed to be able to tell all about a man's age, temperament, and social status from a look at

[34] Duranty, op.cit., p. 34. He seems to make realists out of the Japanese. Their coloring comes from "the instinct of the people of Asia who live in the perpetually dazzling light of the sun, [which] has led them to reproduce the constant sensation by which they have been impressed, that is to say, that of clear flat tones. . . ." Surely Degas could have kept him from statements like that. Indeed, the proof that Degas did not dictate this book lies in the fact that for all its admiration for his work it does not understand it properly.

[35] As Guérin points out, he didn't approve of all of them, or at least his omission of Renoir, Monet, et al. is decidedly peculiar (ibid., p. 10 of Foreword). Duranty made amends to Monet and Pissarro in a little article published in Chronique des arts in 1879: "La Quatrième exposition faite par un groupe d'artistes independants" (La Nouvelle peinture, pp. 56-59).

[36] As, for instance, their frequent rejection by conservative juries.

[37] Duranty, op.cit., pp. 23-24.

his back.[38] It may have been that Fromentin was really looking for a revival of some form of old-fashioned history painting and thought that the art of Moreau was the nearest thing to it he could find, but in this particular instance, he was actually defending a kind of painting which Duranty and his friends were excluding, but which was, nevertheless, modern also. Only a few years later this imaginative approach was expressed in a variety of novel ways by the Symbolists and others.

The art of Degas and his fellow independents was not as opposed to the subjective and imaginative classicism of Puvis and Moreau as Duranty was inclined to think. The question would seem to be whether, if the former were "modern," the latter, being different, were not; or whether they were all modern, being separated only by the differences in their originality. It was true, of course, that there was a real gap between them in the matter of subject, for one group used themes drawn from contemporary life while the other did not, but this was not in itself decisive, for "classical" subjects abound in the art of Cézanne, Picasso, Chirico, and many more. What is important is the fact that these classical themes were treated in a manner essentially the same as that used for landscape, genre, and still-life.

The crux of the matter lies in what might be called the status of the object as it exists in the artist's pictorial world. In both of the cases cited above, the thing painted had lost importance from the traditional point of view, for the purpose was no longer to present *its* meaning or significance, but to use it as a basis on which to create effects of line, form, color, and design, or else suggest mental states which were to be felt rather than understood. The painter's attitude was alike in each type, for it was his own individualism which was embodied in the final effect rather than a creative rephrasing of the traditional conception of the object studied. Puvis stayed closer to the past than did Moreau, but he was still highly individual in his handling of religious and antique material.

It was only too easy for the critics to be aware of the originality of Manet's art, for it was quite unlike any of the old forms, but the problem was subtler in the case of the two more classical painters, and Duranty seems to have been misled by the label. We have already seen that the conservative critics were disturbed by elements in their art for which they were at a loss to account, and which they put down to an improper application of "system" or some other rather academic defect, whereas in reality the cause lay in the fact that they were taking a modern view of old themes. This imaginative attitude was no more of a sport in the artistic development of the century than pure painting based on an underlying naturalism, for it had a direct and important influence upon younger painters of undeniable excellence. Both concepts of subject matter remained noticeable in the later fabric of modern art.

[38] *Ibid.*, p. 42.

XX. CONCLUSION

THE history of art during the years after 1848 has here been examined from the point of view of the role of subject matter. The discussion has been centered on this particular aspect of the total artistic expression of the age because it was in relation to content that the arguments about an emergent "modernism" seem to have been most vigorously carried on, and in them the newer views as to the nature and function of painting were vividly apparent. The break which was to separate the present from the past was sharper here than in the domain of style, where earlier modes continued to exert a steady and powerful influence right down to the present, while traditional ideas about content became virtually anathema to the *avant-garde*.

What has concerned us was a broad complex of artistic thought, somewhat variously derived, but considered as a whole. Evidence was drawn from the works themselves, from the painters' own views both spoken and written, from the critical accounts of men of widely divergent backgrounds, and from the characteristics of the age itself. Since we saw that the main ideas were shared or attacked by artists and nonartists alike, and on the same grounds, this treatment seems justified both as an approach to a better understanding of the painting itself, and as a means of assessing the temper of the period in general. Conservatism, humanitarianism, objective naturalism, and pure painting were all concepts which can be profitably studied from the side not only of the creator, but of the observer. The former tells more about why the painters acted as they did, while the latter shows the reactions to the rather startling developments which accompanied the reorientation of art in historically novel directions. If the opinions of critics and like forms of commentary were to be ruled out of the account of the total artistic activity of any age on the grounds of irrelevance, they would, of course, immediately assume a purely historical and rather incidental interest which could well be largely ignored. But such an account would be in danger of misinterpreting that epoch and the effect it may have had upon the artists, and also of missing certain important elements in the art itself which were more easily noted and intelligently described at the time than later. As long as one believes that art is intended for the contemplation of someone other than the man who produces it, just so long will contemporary evaluations of it have interest: if they are well done, they may increase our own pleasure and insight in a picture and will help to reveal the details of the environment in which it was produced. Most of the great periods of art history are singularly lacking in such material—it either was not written at all or has since been lost—but such is not the case with the nineteenth century, where the evidence is almost too plentiful. Art scholarship has been developed almost to a science, but it has not been able to fill in many vital details about the circumstances originally surrounding the appearance of interesting pictures or statues created centuries ago, circumstances which, if known, might cast an altogether fresh light on their meaning or significance. But in the case of the art of Delacroix, Chenavard, or Manet, we can easily learn what not one or two, but a great many, people thought and the opportunity should be thoroughly exploited.

So many of these critics were men of affairs, active in fields other than those of art history or criticism, that there is a striking connection between their interest in painting and their interest in literature, science, politics, music, social movements, and many other elements that, together, made up the larger structure of society. This connection is the source of much valuable comment that set art in a wider perspective than an exclusive concern with its special history and particular characteristics would have done. And this material, taken together with the evidence of the art itself, provides a picture of the artistic times which, while lacking detail in some places, gives a clear impression of the larger issues affecting painting as such. Combining thus all types of evidence, certain conclusions concerning the relation of art to society can be drawn.

The most important of these is concerned with the idea of the place of man in the scheme of existence. According to the conservative view he was a creature with ideals, a glamorous past, and an uncertain future. Though imperfect and often frail, he was conceived as possessing a capacity for nobility which could, under certain circumstances, be called forth; in short, on occasion he was capable of both high thoughts and high actions. When these were actually operative, he was at the peak of his nature and little lower than the angels, and even in disaster and disappointment, he derived a certain grandeur from the very fact of being the superior individual among all living things. To this predicated nobility, art had a definite relation, for part of its function was to celebrate examples of nobility and also to evoke it in the beholder. Christian and classical literature were thought of as supplying the archetypes which, by their long history, were considered permanently valid as precepts and examples applicable to all ages.

This was the attitude challenged in various ways by all other schools of thought. For the objective naturalist a human being was an object not essentially different from other objects, the most interesting, perhaps, but still something to be considered quantitatively or descriptively rather than qualitatively or ideally. He did not embody something beyond himself nor show the traces of any divine origin; he was just what he was, a man with the imprint of life upon him.

To the humanitarians he was noble, not in the sense that the conservatives knew, but rather because he belonged to the great brotherhood of humanity in whose hands lay the future of the race. The power had been taken from the kings and priests and given to him, and he was to use that power to free the world of its ills. For this reason he had a new majesty which made him the fitting object of the artist's highest effort. It was the task of the painter to examine him in this new collective nature and see wherein its greatness lay. Once this essence had been distilled into an appropriate symbolism, the art which would follow would be understandable to all and universally moving.

For the pure painters and their supporters, man was really none of these things, for the reason that *in the picture world* he counted for little in any direction. His character was not to be studied nor was his appearance to be minutely portrayed; he was not to take part in dramatic events nor was his superiority, real or imagined, over the rest of nature to be set forth. What, then, was he to be? It was his lot to arouse the artist to creation just as did the fields or flowers or fish or sky, and then to be the vehicle by which the results of the artist's reaction were to be made manifest. The important man for this group was not the one on the canvas but the one in front of it. Since the painter put no store by the old notions of man's nobility, the figures he painted didn't either, though at the beginning they often reflected their creator's own humanity with startling and even touching vividness. Later everything was put more entirely at the artist's disposal so that the picture world—man and all—became fragmentary or broadly distorted or photographically accurate entirely at will. And there was no reason why this should not be so, for the autonomy of the object had been surrendered to the desire for individual expressiveness. The world of art, the world behind the picture plane, was entirely under the painter's control, and for what went on there, he was not responsible to standards established in the past nor to any claims which might be put forth by contemporary social requirements. A priori norms and ideals were to be excluded henceforth; the individual now made all the decisions. This view, with certain later additions and modifications, finally prevailed over the others and became basic in a large section of modern art, a development which was, under the circumstances, both natural and inevitable.

It is permissible to inquire whether this triumphant position was justified beyond this fact, what value it had beyond its suitability to the time in which it was formed. To put it a little differently, was the artist "wrong" in excluding moral considerations, in avoiding traditional judgments of value and the themes which presumably embodied them in favor of his own personal conclusions and individual reactions? Or was the conservative critic or painter "wrong" in claiming that such values had to be preserved even though they seemed to be discredited and the art which set them forth was dull and inept? It must be remembered that in this latter view what was at stake was not painting as such, but "great art," i.e. the highest form to which it might be brought, a challenge which did not trouble the progressives since they had lost faith in this kind of greatness and also since the concept involved the idea of norms of comparison among human actions in which they were not interested.

Yet between these opposed concepts of the function of art lay a larger issue whose existence was revealed by both of them, but which actually transcended the limits of purely artistic controversy, for it was to be found elsewhere in many other fields of human activity and speculation. Similar questions could, for example, be raised in regard to philosophy, where it might be inquired whether or no certain of its historically precious doctrines should be abandoned in favor of a more materialistic and neutral view of the universe. Should not literature make a firm break with *its* past, paying more attention to its inner structure and the personal sensitivity of the author without much more thought for universal intelligibility? Might it not be wise for families to give up the old habits of behavior hitherto held sacrosanct and launch forth bravely into new ones more perfectly adapted to the new social stresses of life? Should not Christianity itself be done away with pending the discovery of some more applicable faith? Once the need for sweeping change is postulated in one field, it may seem required in others as well.

The more advanced painters answered this question in the affirmative as far as subject matter was concerned, and in thus snapping some of the bonds which held them to the past they were not altogether alone. People generally seemed to be sloughing off their faith in many of the old values, for materialism did not fit comfortably with idealism, and science seemed to be showing the way to a world where things would be better without much concern over the old Christian ethics. There were many who thought that a new era was at hand and should be prepared for by getting rid of a lot of excess baggage inherited from a past which seemed to become more remote every day. This is not to say that western civilization drifted rapidly into moral anarchy, but the principles by which it professed to be living, most of which were still Christian or classic in origin, became harder to discern as they became less public and more private in nature. More important than this from the artist's point of view was the fact that these moral principles were gradually divorced from the contexts in which they had hitherto been preserved, and the knowledge of these contexts—the Bible and classical lore—became the honest property of fewer and fewer people, and were no longer readily recognized in their various epic expressions. As a result the epics came to seem strange and out of date, and the principles themselves to appear less and less applicable to current problems because the situations in which they were framed had no visible connection with the world outside the front door.

But these epics had been the painter's means of externalizing moral values, which could only be presented by means of previously known events in which they figured prominently. No modern symbolism carried by a new epic cycle had appeared to reclothe them in popular form, and so as subjects they were doomed with the outworn scenes to which they were connected. They could reappear as themes for great art only when a form had evolved capable of carrying them to the minds of a whole people, and such a form had not been found, nor were the old ones sufficiently revived. As Chesneau said, it was time for prose, not epics.

One might say that progress, democracy, evolution, and scientific truth were concepts as noble as those set forth by the Greeks, or even maintain that their moral potential compared favorably with that of Christianity. But these too were unusable for the artist since they had never been cast in any generally familiar symbolic mould. The collapse of humanitarianism as an artistic credo bore witness to the difficulty inherent in any attempt to create such a symbolism too rapidly. The hundred years which have passed since the beginning of our period have given little indication that any solution is even now in preparation.

Morally speaking, a good part of society has come to live in a partial vacuum, its "philosophy of life" little more than a pragmatic set of customs whose precepts are obeyed for the ease they impart to existence rather than because of any inner compulsion to do right before God or in the light of some ideals higher than comfort and security. The members of such a society are not aware of the vacuum, since they have never known anything else. But this absence of ultimate purpose, of final ends, is revealed in a sort of short-term benevolence directed at the alleviation of immediate ills but ignoring the necessity for long-range cures. The artist, if he is concerned over evil and tragedy, is hampered in his efforts to deal with them by the general social lack of a sense of the nature of a final perfection toward which we should be moving. The chief defect of the concept of progress is its failure to supply a valid and inspiring goal.

What, then, is the painter to do? If he has willingly cast aside the traditional human values as subjects for his art along with the scenes in which they were historically set forth, he can create according to the dictates of his own conscience and his individual impulse. Like any true artist he will derive a measure of deep satisfaction from the result when it seems to him to exhibit those qualities of order, harmony, and feeling for which he was looking. Since he did not set out to deal with the problems of human existence, he is not disappointed by being unable to do so, and the nonartist of like mind is as charmed and moved as he. The problems of a work of art conceived on this individual level can be solved there by those possessing the requisite genius, and in the solving, much beauty is brought into the world.

But if the artist feels that he must speak of man's social condition, if he wants to get at the human spiritual crisis which has been developing inexorably over the last hundred years or more, his problem is more difficult. He can, if he wishes, paint angry pictures revealing the all-too-obvious defects of society and hope that by calling attention to them, someone will be moved to find solutions. In this case he functions solely as a social critic, a spur to conscience, a pleader for action, and when his message is expressed with formal power, as it not infrequently is, the results are fine enough to mask the tragic lack of any suggested solution, the absence of any higher authority to which men might turn in their extremity. The highest form of such critical art is reached when, as in the case of Daumier's lithographs, the wrongs and inadequacies of life are universalized and lifted to a point of real majesty which, in itself, has a moral power lacking in a mere particular complaint. But art of this kind is rare, and for all its true symbolism, it still lacks any positive assurance of something better than itself.

When the artist attempts to turn from criticism to something more positive, toward an ideal that, if followed, would help to change evil to good, the problem becomes most acute. He may wish to seek some guide to indicate the difference between right and wrong, but to what higher order can he appeal and be listened to? Progress can scarcely be the answer, since there is little agreement as to its final aim and the present indications are that if such a goal were to be voted on by the people generally, it might turn out to be twin ideals of comfort and security, neither of which would seem to furnish the artist with much usable material, since neither involves the nobler aspects of the human soul. Nor would a political faith appear to solve the difficulty. Democracy, the finest political form yet evolved in the west, is too loose and ill-defined to supply an iconography or even a clear set of moral values. This very lack of definition makes it difficult to grasp even as a concept. As a source of artistic subject matter it would have to be made far more concrete and related in some definite way to events capable of pictorial interpretation. The various totalitarian systems have attempted to create legends and symbols for their artists, but with sterile results since the symbolizing has been done under duress and the treatment of the symbols determined by the coldest kind of political expediency.

Science holds little hope either, for by its very nature it is opposed to artistic manipulation and its aims are not those of ethics. It demands the greatest possible exactness and the greatest possible objectivity. But art is neither exact nor objective in this sense, and in the past three hundred years it has found itself powerless to celebrate the wonders of a staggeringly effective method of arriving at certain parts of the truth. Galileo, Newton, Harvey, Faraday, Pasteur, Darwin and a host of others have lived and worked and died to the everlasting glory of the human mind, but they have inspired no art to celebrate their deeds to compare with the simpler but more human achievements of St. Francis of Assisi. He could found a legend which cast much light on the nature of human conduct, but legends can cast little light on the true movements of the planets or the circulation of the blood.

Religion remains a guide for some, but it has lost much of its hold on the imagination of humanity, and Catholic art, which was for centuries the glory of western civilization, has fallen on evil days indeed. This is not the place to analyze the reasons for the decline of the power of Christianity or even to discuss the possibilities of some greater revival of it; but this much can be said: if it should ever again assume the spiritual leadership of society, its art would achieve a corresponding renaissance. It is possible, too, that some new faith may be born; but until it is, the search for moral values must continue.

But what has such a search to do with art? Is not art better off unpreoccupied with things outside its own particular formal nature? Some influential modern criticism has maintained that art has no business commenting on human affairs, that the work of art is a unique thing, complete in itself, and is to be admired or condemned for itself alone without reference to other, nonaesthetic, considerations. Much logic has been brought to bear in support of this contention and many artists have asserted it to be the basis of their creative effort. Admittedly, this may be a perfectly valid approach to painting, but it excludes, perhaps not entirely justifiably, the whole question of "great" art.

As has already been mentioned in the preface, to subtract the moral content from many of the finest paintings of the past is to reduce their total effectiveness. But the attitude described above would sense no loss at all, but rather a gain, for what is discarded would be regarded as hampering a true appreciation of the formal qualities present. It is only the person who honestly believes that painting can and should carry a profound, and at the same time intelligible, spiritual message who will feel that such an approach does violence to his idea of what the greatest art really is. He comes to it for spiritual revelation and that is what he receives, in a form impossible to obtain from literature, music, or any other kind of art.

Turning now to the art of the last hundred years, those making no moral demands on art will find in it formal achievement surely the equal of that of any previous age. But the seeker after moral value, the searcher for the noble in man's humanity will be disappointed. Can we say that we have no right to look for such meanings in the art of our time? The answer will, of course, depend on the individual's requirements, but it is certainly true that the artist cannot be blamed for the lack; we cannot expect him to find what may not exist; he cannot speak effectively in symbols if we don't bring those very symbols to the contemplation of what he has done. A common moral awareness will have to be established between the two before any effective communication can take place, and this awareness on any universal level is not abroad in the world today, although it may be that already, somewhere, some artist has already found what the rest of us may discover later. If so, and if he is now ignored, he will exemplify again the recurrent tragedy of seeing too clearly before the rest of mankind has seen at all.

If in the last hundred years a new moral system had grown up to restore the balance between the scientific and the ethical, if, in short, we had received some fresh and mastering insight into our own natures to match the blinding view we have had into the workings of the material world, would it not be logical to suppose that we would soon have a new form of great art, a new classification to describe those paintings which honestly tried to use the power of art to reveal these profound human truths? In ages past, art had a manner of dealing with such matters which was unique and stirring, and it has that power still—once it can be given the proper substance to deal with. The painters will not be lacking, and with the enormously expanded public for whom they would work, their achievement would be magnificent indeed. The solution to the problem lies with men everywhere: if, out of the welter of the modern world, they can find and establish consistent moral attitudes to fit their experience, or if they are fortunate enough to receive a fresh revelation, art will come forward to celebrate the fact in fitting and beautiful terms.

APPENDIX

TO assist the reader in identifying the authors cited in the text, the following brief notices have been prepared. The list includes only those whose writings may be considered source material for the period; in the cases of well-known figures, little more than an identification has been given since an extended account can be obtained easily elsewhere. Unfortunately, in spite of careful search, a few of the critics cited remain unidentified. Their names have been included in the hope that any reader who may happen to know more about them will be kind enough to communicate with the author. Except where a different listing seemed more natural, all names containing the preposition *de* have been placed under the letter D.

ABOUT, Edmond-François-Valentin. 1828-1885. Man of letters, who tried his hand at a number of literary forms including novels, short stories, plays, and essays. As a journalist he wrote for several periodicals including *Le Figaro*, *Le Moniteur universel*, and *Le Constitutionnel*, contributing articles on politics, economics, literature, and art. A well-known figure, of anticlerical sentiments, he became a Republican in 1870. In 1884 he was elected to the Academy but died before his formal reception.

AMAURY-DUVAL, Eugène Emmanuel-Pineux. 1808-1885. Portrait and history painter, a pupil of Ingres and a nephew of Alexandre Dumas. His chief works in the great tradition were the murals executed for such churches as St. Merri, St. Germain-l'Auxerrois, and St. Germain-en-Laye.

ASSELINEAU, Charles. 1821-1874. Man of letters and novelist, for many years connected with the Bibliothèque Impériale. In addition to several novels, he wrote a study of Baudelaire and several books on artistic subjects such as *André Boulle, ébéniste de Louis XIV* (1855) and *Notice sur Lazare Bruandet, peintre de l'école française* (1855).

ASTRUC, Zacharie. 1835-1907. Painter, sculptor, and man of letters. He was a friend of many of the literary and artistic men of the *avant-garde*, first trying journalism and later turning to painting and sculpture. In 1859 he helped to found *Le Quart d'heure, gazette des gens demi-sérieux*, and in the same year published *Les 14 stations du Salon—1859* which attracted favorable mention among other critics. From 1869 on, he exhibited in a number of Salons, his works including a relief bust of Barbey d'Aurevilly (1870) and a bronze head of Manet (1881).

AUVRAY, Louis. 1810- (?). Sculptor and art critic, for a time director of *La Revue artistique et littéraire*, and a contributor to *La Revue des beaux-arts*, and *L'Europe artiste* among others. At one time (1867?), he was president of the *Comité central des artistes*.

BALLANCHE, Pierre-Simon. 1776-1847. Philosopher and writer on social reform, one of a quite distinguished group of mystical philosophers centered in the city of Lyon during the first half of the nineteenth century. He was a friend of Chateaubriand, Mme. Récamier, Nodier, and other well-known figures in the literary world, and was prominent in the movement which tended to to regard social development as a series of rebirths.

BANVILLE, Théodore Faullain de. 1823-1891. Poet, essayist, and writer of *contes* and romances. Possibly his best-known work is the *Odes funambulesques*, published in 1857. He knew many of the artists of his day, and had a particularly warm admiration for Daumier.

BARBEY D'AUREVILLY, Jules. 1808-1889. Novelist, journalist, and critic. His literary debut occurred in 1841 with the publication of the novel *L'Amour impossible*. This work was followed by a number of others of which, according to Maurice Tourneux, the best was *L'Ensorcelée* (1854). In 1851 he became literary critic for *Le Pays*, and in addition wrote many articles on religion, philosophy, art, and kindred subjects.

BAUDELAIRE, Charles. 1821-1867. Poet, critic, and translator of the works of Edgar Allan Poe. He is most famous for the *Fleurs du mal*, but was unquestionably one of the most brilliant art critics of the century. Possibly his best works in this field were his essays on the art of Delacroix.

BEAURIN, Charles. Known only as the reviewer of the Salon of 1866 in *L'Artiste*.

BERTRAND, Karl. Known only as the reviewer of the Salon of 1870 in *L'Artiste*.

BESLAY, François. 1835- (?). Lawyer and journalist. In 1862 he published a life of Lacordaire, and the year before a book entitled *Du Style et des formes de la plaidoirie*. At one time he was editor of the daily political paper *Le Français*. Alfred PAISANT, the co-author of *La Peinture au Salon de 1857*, was for many years President of the civil court of Versailles.

BLANC, Charles. 1813-1882. Brother of the journalist Louis Blanc, art historian, critic, and graphic artist. After his arrival in Paris in 1830, he studied engraving under Calmatta. His Salon reviews were first published in *Bon sens*, and later in *La Revue de progrès, Courrier français*, and *L'Artiste*. In the early 'forties he edited several republican journals, and in 1845 brought out the first (and only) volume of an intended two-volume work on artists of the nineteenth century. In 1848 he was made Director of Fine Arts, but after the *coup d'état*, he returned to private life. In 1859 he founded the famous *Gazette des beaux-arts*, and nine years later was elected to the Academy. In 1870 he was again made Director of Fine Arts, a post he held for three years. He later became professor of aesthetics and art history at the Collège de France. His most important book, the great collaborative history of painting, was completed in 1875. Blanc was one of the best known and influential of the conservative critics.

BONNARDOT, A. 1808-1884. A rather obscure man of letters who wrote books on such widely diverse topics as Parisian archaeology, book and print restoring, dogs, and telescopes.

BOUGOT, A. 1842-1892. Critic and man of letters. His *Étude sur "Iliade d'Homère"* appeared in 1888.

BOYELDIEU-D'AUVIGNY, Mme. Louise. Woman of letters and writer on social questions. In 1846 she published *Les Droits du travailleur. Essais sur les devoirs des maîtres envers leurs subordonnés*, and later, *Petit-Jean, ou le bonheur dans le devoir* (1851).

BRETON, Jules-Adolphe. 1827-1905. A highly successful painter of rural subjects. His first master was Félix de Vigne, whose daughter he married in 1858. Success came to him with the exhibition of *Le Retour des moissoneurs* in 1853. Two years later he received a Third Class Medal, and from there he rose steadily through all the grades of honor, receiving the Legion of Honor in 1872, and was elected to the Academy in 1885.

BUCHON, Maximin. 1818-1869. Poet, specializing in rural themes: *En Province. Scènes franc-comtoises* (1858), *Noëls et chants populaires de la Franche-Comté* (1863), etc. A great friend of Gustave Courbet.

BURTY, Philippe. 1830-1890. Art critic and collector. As a young man he worked as an "ornamental" painter at the Gobelin works. His debut as an art critic was made in *L'Art du XIXe siècle*, and later, in 1859, he joined the staff of the *Gazette des beaux-arts* as editor of sales and "curiosités." He also wrote articles and reviews dealing with photography. An interest in prints and Japanese art led to excellent collections in both fields, as well as published catalogues of the work of Meryon and his own Japanese material. In 1861 he published catalogues of the lithographs of Charlet, Vernet, and Géricault, and was one of the cataloguers of Delacroix's drawings. He took on the section of *La Presse* which dealt with art matters, and later did the same on the staff of *La Liberté*. In 1876 he published a volume of the etchings of Jules de Goncourt, and nine years before his death was made an Inspector of Fine Arts.

CANTREL, Émile. Known only as a contributor to *L'Artiste* (1859).

CASTAGNARY, Jules Antoine. 1830-1888. Art critic and journalist. At first destined for a legal career, he turned to an interest in the arts and made his debut with a review of the Salon of 1857 in *Le Présent* which attracted immediate attention. Following somewhat in the path of Thoré and influenced at first by Proudhon, he became a strong opponent of academism and the staunchest of Courbet's admirers in the 'sixties. He contributed articles to *L'Audience, Le Courrier du dimanche, Le Nain jaune*, and *Le Siècle* of which he became one of the chief editors. Turning to politics, he was elected to the municipal council of Paris in 1874 and re-elected in 1877, becoming president in 1879. The year before his death he was made a Director of Fine Arts.

CHALLEMEL-LACOUR, Paul-Armand. 1827-(after 1885). Man of letters, teacher, and politician. After a short career as a teacher in the Lycées of Pau and Limoges, he was exiled for his political views in 1851, going to Belgium and Switzerland. At the time of the general amnesty of 1859 he returned to France and began contributing articles to a number of journals including *Le Temps*, *La Revue nationale*, and *La Revue des deux mondes*. In 1870 he was prefect of Rhone, and two years later was elected to the General Assembly. In later years he was ambassador to Berne and London and even held the portfolio of External Affairs for a brief time. Outside of his political career he seems to have been interested in art and philosophy, in which latter field he wrote and translated several books.

CHAMPFLEURY. Pseudonym of Jules HUSSON, called FLEURY. 1828-1889. Novelist and critic. He was the undisputed leader of the so-called realist movement and was, for a time, an ardent supporter of Courbet. Aside from his novels, he contributed to a number of periodicals including *Le Corsaire Satan* and *L'Artiste*. His pseudonym seems to have been assumed on the suggestion of Arsène Houssaye. He apparently became more conservative in the later 'fifties and turned increasingly to art history, publishing a history of caricature in five volumes (1865-1880), the *Histoire de l'imagerie populaire*, 1869; *Les Frères Le Nain* (1862); etc.

CHAUMELIN, Jean-Marie-Marius. 1833-(?). Man of letters and journalist. After studying law, he entered the Ministry of Finance and was sent to Marseilles where he wrote a series of sketches of picturesque spots about the city. He was later associated with a whole series of journals published in the south of France including one called *La Tribune artistique et littéraire du midi*. He was much interested in matters pertaining to the arts, was a collaborator in Blanc's famous history of painting, and also in the publication of the enormous *Grande dictionnaire universel du XIXe siècle*, for which he contributed many of the artistic notices.

CHENNEVIÈRES-POINTEL, Charles Philippe, Marquis de. 1820-1899. Administrator and art historian. In the government service he was successively an inspector of museums, curator of the Luxembourg, and Director of Fine Arts, in the last capacity being charged with the final scheme for the decoration of the Panthéon. He wrote a number of books including *Essais sur l'organisation des arts en province* (1852) and *Portraits inédits d'artistes français* (1853). He occasionally used the pseudonym Jean de FALAISE.

CHESNEAU, Ernest. 1833-1890. Critic and scholar. He contributed many articles to a variety of journals including *Le Constitutionnel*, *Le Pays*, *La Revue des deux mondes*, *L'Art*, and *Le Gazette des beaux-arts*. In 1869 he was made an Inspector of Fine Arts. His particular interest was the general relationship of the arts to society, and he published a number of works on this theme, such as *Les Interêts populaires dans l'art, la verité sur le Louvre, le musée de Napoléon III et les artistes industriels* (1862). For a number of years he was on the staff of the Louvre and appears to have been somewhat of a protégé of Nieuwerkerke.

CLARETIE, Jules. Pseudonym for Jules Arsène ARNAUD. 1840-1913. Novelist, historian, and journalist. His career as a contributor to the Parisian press began about 1860 while his first novel appeared in 1862 (*Un Drôlesse*). In addition to his writing on art, he was much interested in the theater and was made administrator of the *Comédie française* in 1885. Three years afterward he was elected to the Academy.

CLÉMENT, Charles. 1821-(?). Journalist, administrator, and art historian. From 1850 to 1863 he was Editor of *La Revue des deux mondes* and then went on the staff of *Le Journal des débats*. In 1857 he published *De la peinture religieuse en Italie jusqu'à Fra Angelico de Fiesole*, which was followed in 1861 by *Michel-Ange, Léonard de Vinci, Raphael*. For a time he was attached to the Napoleon III Museum.

CLÉMENT DE RIS, L. 1820-1882. Museologist, essayist, and critic. He was for some time attached to the staff of the imperial museums, and in 1877 was curator of the museum at Versailles.

COMTE, Auguste. 1798-1857. The famous positivist philosopher, later professor at the École Polytechnique.

COUTURE, Thomas. 1815-1879. History and genre painter. He won the Prix de Rome in 1837 and scored his great triumph in the Salon of 1847 with the *Orgie romaine*. His book on method appeared in 1867 (?); another volume on landscape came out two years later.

DAX, P. Pseudonym for Éva GATOUIL. Dramatist and woman of letters.

DE BELLOY, Auguste, Marquis de. 1815- (?). Poet and man of letters. He was the author of *La Mal'aria; drame en un acte et en verse* (1853); *Légendes fleuries* (1855); *Les Toqués* (1860); etc.

DE CALLIAS, Hector. Journalist. He published a book called *Le Livre de la vie* in 1862 and seems to have been a somewhat occasional contributor to *Le Figaro, L'Artiste*, and possibly other journals.

DECAMPS, Alexandre. 1803-1860. Painter. A pupil of Bouchot and Abel de Pujol, he became the famous "orientalist" of his day. In spite of his success in this field he seems to have always wanted to be a history painter.

DELABORDE, Henri, Vicomte de. 1811-1899. Painter, administrator, and critic. At first he intended to follow a diplomatic career but soon gave it up to enter the studio of Delaroche. He made his Salon debut in 1836 with a *Hagar au desert*, and finally achieved a first medal in 1847. In 1855 he was appointed associate curator of the *Cabinet d'estampes*, later becoming curator. Articles by him appeared in *La Revue des deux mondes*, and *Le Gazette des beaux-arts* as well as other journals. Several volumes of his collected essays on art were published as well as a book on Ingres, etc. In 1868 he was elected to the Academy. His book, *Maintien du goût public par la direction des arts* attracted much interest at the time of its serial publication (1857) in *La Revue universelle des arts*.

DELACROIX, Eugène. 1798-1863. Painter. The most famous of the "romantic" painters and author of numerous articles on the arts as well as his famous *Journal* and a large correspondence.

DE LA FIZELIÈRE, Albert. 1819- (?). Critic and man of letters. He reviewed Salons and critical articles for such journals as *L'Artiste, Journal de Paris, La Patrie, Le Courrier français*, etc. In addition to these he published books on political subjects, a study of Baudelaire, and another one on the landscape painter Chintreuil (1874).

DE LA ROCHENOIRE, Émile-Charles-Julien. 1825-1899. Landscape painter, *animalier*, and etcher. He studied under Cogniet, Gleyre, and Troyon, after which he exhibited regularly in the Salons from 1857 to 1878. He was the author of two books on the technique of painting: *La Couleur et le dessin appris seul* (1857) and *Le Dessin et la peinture des fleurs appris seul* (1858), as well as other books on art.

DE LASTEYRIE DU SAILLANT, Ferdinand, Comte. 1810-1879. Archaeologist and art critic. A graduate of the School of Mines, he served in 1830 as aide-de-camp to Lafayette. In 1842 he was elected deputy from Seine and held several offices in the revolutionary government of 1848. After protesting against the *coup d'etat* in 1851, he retired to private life and the study of art. His writings in this field cover works on enamels, architecture, stained glass, etc.

DELAUNAY, A. H. Journalist and art critic. In 1846 he was editor-in-chief of *Le Journal des artistes*. If this is the same man as Aimable Delaunay, he was also a painter who exhibited in the Salons from about 1830 to 1850, dying in Paris in 1856.

DELÉCLUZE, E.-J. 1781-1863. Man of letters, painter, and art critic. He was Ingres' staunchest defender and wrote on art for *Le Journal des débats* and *Le Moniteur*. In 1841 he wrote a book on Rabelais, and four years later his two-volume work, *Roland ou la chevalerie*, appeared. For all his conservatism he was intelligent and honest, enjoying a very considerable reputation throughout most of his life.

DE LEPINOIS, Ernest de Buchère de. 1797- (?). He was referred to as a former *sous-préfet* and was the author of a two-volume history of Chartrés (1854-1858) and a history of the city of Coucy (1859).

DE MERCEY, Frédéric. 1803-1860. According to Tourneux he also used the pseudonym of F. de la FALOISE. Painter, lithographer, and art historian. He exhibited in the Salons from 1831 to 1857, mostly landscapes. In 1840 he entered the Ministry of the Interior, and at the time of his death was Chief of the Division of Fine Arts in the Ministry of State as well as member of the *Institut*. He wrote a novel or two, but his chief work was the *Études sur les beaux-arts* which appeared in 1857.

DE MEZIN, B (ernard?). No information available.

DE MONTAIGLON, Anatole. *Ancien élève de l'École de Chartres*. An art historian, he published a catalogue raisonné of the work of Claude Mellan in 1858, but most important of all was his *Mémoires pour servir à l'histoire de l'académie royale de peinture et de sculpture depuis 1648 juqu'en 1664* (2 vols., 1853).

DE MONTIFAUD, Marc. Pseudonym for Mme. Léon Quivogne de MONTIFAUD. 1850 (?)- (?). Art critic and woman of letters. She wrote Salons for *L'Artiste* and later published *Les Courtisanes de l'antiquité; Marie-Magdeleine* (1875), *Histoire d'Héloise et d'Abelard* (1873), etc.

DE SAULT, C. Pseudonym for Mme. Guy de CHARNACÉ. She was apparently a critic and her husband a man of letters, but no other information is available.

DESCHAMPS, Émile. 1791-1871. Poet and man of letters. An ardent romantic who did much to forward that movement in literature, particularly in acquainting France with foreign literatures through translation. With Victor Hugo he founded *La Muse française*. The preface to his *Études françaises et étrangères* is an excellent statement of the romantic position (1828).

DESNOYERS, Fernand. 1828-1869. Journalist and man of letters. He left a few volumes of prose and verse, including one on the subject of Courbet: *Le Bras noir* (1856), and wrote for the *Almanach parisien* for several years along with Duranty, Théodore de Banville, and others. He is reported to have been a frequenter of the cafés and restaurants where the young literary men of the Second Empire gathered.

DE STAËL, Mme. (Anne Louise Germaine NECKER). 1766-1817. The famous woman of letters, friend of Schlegel, Mme. Récamier, and many others. Her greatest work, *De l'Allemagne*, appeared in 1810.

DOLENT, Jean. Pseudonym for Antoine FOURNIER. 1835-1909. Novelist and man of letters. He made his debut in 1862 with a group of literary portraits entitled, *Une Volée de merles*.

DOLLFUSS, Charles. 1827-1910. Philosopher and man of letters. He began life as a lawyer but later turned to journalism. In 1857 he founded *La Revue germanique* with Nefftzer, a journal which was later called *La Revue moderne*. Later he was editor of *Le Temps*. His books include the following: *Le Calvaire* (1855), *Essai sur la philosophie sociale* (1856), *Liberté et centralization* (1859), and others.

DUBOS, Jean Baptiste (L'Abbé). 1660-1742. Lawyer, diplomat, and writer on art. His history of the League of Cambrai appeared in 1712 and his *Réflexions critiques sur la poésie et sur la peinture* in 1719. Admitted to the Academy in 1720 he was made perpetual secretary in 1722.

DUCAMP, Maxime. 1822-1894. Journalist, critic, and historian. As a young man he was a good friend of Flaubert's with whom he traveled to Egypt and the Near East. In 1851 he founded the *Revue de Paris*, and from time to time wrote for other journals including *La Revue des deux mondes*. In 1853 he was decorated with the Legion of Honor and in 1880 was elected to the Academy.

DUMAS, Alexandre (*père*). 1802-1870. Novelist. In spite of his enormous productivity in this field, he seems to have found time to write somewhat on the arts.

DUMESNIL, M. H. 1823- (?). Man of letters. In 1872 he published *La Guerre, étude philosophique*, but his other work seems to have been in the field of the arts. *Corot, souvenirs intimes* appeared in 1875, and a similar volume on Troyon came out in 1888.

DURANTY, Louis-Emile-Edmond. 1833-1880. Man of letters. His debut occurred in 1856 with the founding of *Le Réalisme*, a short-lived journal which suspended publication after six issues. Thereafter he wrote novels and short stories as well as many articles in favor of the new school in painting, especially in defense of his friend Degas. A study of caricature appeared in the *Gazette des beaux-arts* in 1870-1871.

DURET, Théodore. 1838-1927. Journalist and art critic. The great defender of Manet and the Impressionist group, he began life with political ambitions, even serving as mayor of the fourth arrondissement of Paris during the Commune. In 1867 he published *Les Peintures français en 1867*, and thereafter was a lifelong student of art, particularly that of the Orient (to which he traveled with the famous economist Henri Cernuschi) and that of the modern movement.

FOURNEL, Victor. 1829-1894. Man of letters and journalist. He wrote on a wide variety of subjects including the theater, old Paris, seventeenth century literature, and the arts.

GALIMARD, Nicolas-Auguste. 1813-1880. Landscape and history painter, specializing in church decoration and glass painting. A nephew and pupil of Auguste Hesse, he also studied under Ingres and later exhibited quite regularly at the Salons from 1835 until his death. His writings on art included Salon reviews and monographs on individual artists such as Aubry-Lecomte and Hippolyte Flandrin.

GAUTIER, Théophile. 1810-1872. Novelist and critic. He was for many years the drama and art critic for *La Presse* and later, after 1854, for *Le Moniteur*. He was possibly the most widely read and popularly respected art critic of his day.

GEBAUER, Ernest. 1828- (?). Journalist and playwright. At one time he was editor of *L'Echo des Orphéous*, and in 1855 he published a play: *Peut-on aimer sa femme! Comédie en un acte et en vers.*

GIGOUX, Jean. 1806-1894. Draughtsman, lithographer, and collector. His illustrations for *Gil Blas* were quite well known.

GILL. Pseudonym for Louis-Alexandre Gosset de GUIGNES. 1840-1885. Painter and critic. He exhibited in the Salons of the mid-'seventies, and did semiserious Salon reviews for a number of journals: *La Lune, L'Eclipse, Journal pour rire*, etc.

GIRARDIN, Marie-Alfred-Jules. 1832-1888. Man of letters and professor at the Lycée of Versailles(?). This identification with the author of the article quoted on photography may not be correct, however. If it is, his only other work on art is a translation of Schliemann's book on Mycenae which appeared in 1879.

GONCOURT, Edmond de (1822-1896) and Jules de (1830-1873). The famous literary brothers who were so influential in reestablishing a taste for the art of the eighteenth century and in making Japanese art popular in France.

GOUJON, J. No information available. Possibly a pseudonym.

GRANGEDOR, J. Pseudonym for Jules JOLY. (?)-1870. Apparently well known as a chemist and lecturer. A notice on him appeared in the *Chronique des arts* for Dec. 10, 1871, but the author has not been able to consult it.

GRÜN, Alphonse. 1801-1866. Lawyer, editor, archivist. He was for a time chief of the legislative and judicial section of the Archives de l'Empire and was also editor of *Le Moniteur universel*. He wrote numerous works on the law, legislation, socialism, etc., but his account of the Salon of 1852 is the only writing on art which the author has been able to find.

GUEULLETTE, Charles. 1834-1892. Art critic and historian. Author of *Les Ateliers de peintre en 1864, Études historiques sur la dynastie des Bourbons d'Espagne* (1862), *Les Peintres espagnols* (1863), etc. For many years he was deputy head clerk in the Ministry of Finance.

GUIZOT, François-Pierre-Guillaume. 1787-1874. The famous political figure. At various times he was Minister of the Interior, of Public Instruction, and of Foreign Affairs. He was a noted historian but wrote very little on the fine arts.

HACHE, Ernest. No information available.

HAMERTON, Philip Gilbert. 1834-1894. Artist and critic. He studied to be a painter, but being unsuccessful, turned largely to criticism. Athough an Englishman, his interest seems to have centered very largely on French art, of which he was a keen and informed observer.

HORSIN-DÉON, Simon. 1812-1882. Painter and restorer. He entered the École des Beaux-Arts in 1831, and exhibited at the Salon for the first time two years later. Though he continued to paint, his interest turned to the restoration of pictures and he eventually became the chief restorer for the national museums. In 1851 he published a book on the subject entitled: *De la conservation et de la restauration des tableaux.*

HOUSSAYE, Arsène. 1815-1896. Man of letters. He was probably the outstanding literary jack-of-all trades of his time, for his published work included novels, plays, poetry, history, and criticism of all the arts. At various times he was director of the Comédie Française, Inspector-General of the Provincial Museums, and Inspector-General of Fine Arts. In 1846 he wrote a book on Dutch and Flemish painting, and in 1860, *L'Histoire de l'art français*. He contributed articles and other pieces to *La Revue des deux mondes, La Revue de Paris*, and *L'Artiste*, of which he was for many years a director.

JAHYER, Félix. No information is available except that in 1866 he published a book called *Pauvretés du coeur.*

JOURDAN, Louis. 1810- (?). Economist and journalist. At one time he was an editor of *Le Siècle*, and was a prolific author of books on political and other subjects.

KARR, Jean-Baptiste-Alphonse. 1808-1890. Novelist and man of letters. His chief work as a novelist was *Sous les tilleuls,* published in 1832. About 1837 he was an editor of *Le Figaro* and was later one of the founders of *Le Journal.* One of his best-known works appeared in 1845: *Voyage autour de mon jardin.* The celebrated *Guêpes* began to appear monthly in 1839. Following the *coup d'etat* in 1851 he retired to private life in Nice.

LACROIX, Paul. 1806-1884. Bibliophile, man of letters, and writer on art. His literary output was both large and varied, including a history of Napoleon III, translations of *Héloise and Abélard,* the works of Aretino, etc., and many articles on the fine arts. A contributor to such journals as *Le Mercure de XIXe siècle, Figaro,* and *Gastronome,* he was also a director of *La Revue universelle des arts* and *L'Annuaire des artistes et des amateurs.*

LAFENESTRE, Georges. 1837-1919. Poet, art historian, and administrator. He made a career out of service in the Ministry of Fine Arts, rising in time to the rank of inspector. In 1888 he was made curator of the Louvre, and was also a professor in the École du Louvre. In 1892 he was received into the Academy. His Salon reviews begin in 1868, a number of them being published later in book form. His books include works on Titian, paintings in the Louvre, Florence, etc.

LA FONT DE ST. YENNE. (?-?). One of the leading French critics and amateurs of the arts of the eighteenth century. A staunch defender of history painting, he published a number of critical works in addition to the one cited. These include: *Réflexions sur quelques causes de l'état présent de la peinture en France* (1747), and *Sentiments sur quelques ouvrages de peinture* (1754).

LAGRANGE, Léon-Marius. 1828-1868. Critic and art historian. In addition to the reviews published in *Le Gazette des beaux-arts,* he wrote a book on the family of the Vernet (1863) and another on Pierre Puget (1868).

LAURENT-PICHAT, Léon. 1823-(?). Man of letters and poet. From 1854 to 1858 he was editor of *La Revue de Paris.* His books include: *L'Art et les artistes en France* (1859), *Chroniques rimées* (1856), *La Païenne* (1857), and others.

LAVERDANT, Désiré Gabriel. 1809-(?). Historian, dramatist, and critic. From the fact that he wrote for *La Phalange,* it may be assumed that he was a Fourierist. His books include,

among others, studies of colonial matters, the relation between pope and emperor in the Middle Ages, and a moral history of the French theater.

LAVERGNE, Claudius. 1814-1887. Painter and critic. A student of the École and a pupil of Ingres, he was also the author of a number of books on the arts including a study of Flandrin's murals at Saint-Vincent-de-Paul and an analysis of historical realism in painting.

LECOQ DE BOISBAUDRAN, Horace. 1802-1897. Painter and teacher. From 1831 to 1859 he exhibited in the Salons, but after that he seems to have been more occupied in teaching in the free school of drawing in the École, becoming director of the school in 1866. The teaching methods explained in the books cited in the bibliography (*L'Éducation de la mémoire pittoresque*) were considered remarkable and won the approval of artists of both the left and right.

LEMONNIER, Antoine-Louis-Camille. 1844-1913. A Belgian man of letters. His works include: *Nos flamands* (1869), *Contes flamands et wallons* (1873), *Gustave Courbet et son oeuvre* (1878), *Peintres de la vie* (1888), etc.

LORENTZ, Alcide-Joseph. 1813-(?). Artist and man of letters. As an artist, he preferred "history painting," i.e. such subjects as *Chasseur de la garde impériale,* but he also appears to have worked in woodcuts and lithography. His work appeared in the Salons during the 'forties. In 1848 appeared a book entitled *Polichinelle, ex-roi des marionettes, devenu philosophe,* and in 1854, *Lettre à l'empéreur de Russie.*

LOUDUN, Eugène. Pseudonym for Eugène BALLEYGUIER. 1818-(?). Man of letters and librarian. After a brief career as a teacher and also a lawyer, he turned to letters making his debut in *Le Correspondent,* for which he wrote articles on history, philosophy, and criticism. In 1848 he became attached to the staff of the Bibliothèque de l'Arsenal, but served in a variety of other capacities during his lifetime, including a position as inspector of railroads. He was a contributor to *L'Union, Journal de l'instruction publique,* and *Le Journal des instituteurs,* and was political editor of the latter in 1858.

MALPERTUY, Étienne. No information available beyond the titles of some of his books such as *La France en 1850, Les Montagnes: poème* (1846), *La Vérité à tous les partis* (1850), etc.

MANTZ, Paul. 1821-1895. Man of letters, critic, and administrator. As a public servant he served in the Ministry of the Interior and was eventually made "Sous-Directeur des affaires départmentales et communales." He contributed numerous articles on art and reviews of Salons to a wide variety of journals including *L'Artiste, L'Evènement, Revue de Paris*, and *Le Temps*. He collaborated with Charles Blanc on the latter's great *Histoire des peintres*, and wrote books on Holbein and Boucher. At one time he was Director-General of Fine Arts.

MÉNARD, Réné. 1827-1887. Journalist and art historian. At one time he was an editor of *L'Art* and later editor-in-chief of the *Gazette des beaux-arts*. He was the author of a three-volume history of the fine arts (1870-1874), *L'Art en Alsace-Lorraine* (1875), and *Entretiens sur la peinture* (1875).

MILSAND, Joseph Antoine. 1817-1886. Critic and man of letters. A man of varied interests and talents, he apparently wished first to be a painter, but gave it up and turned to writing. He had lived both in Italy and England and in the latter probably acquired his interest in Ruskin to whom most Frenchmen were indifferent. His writings cover such diverse topics as *Le Code et la liberté* (1865), *Le Protestantisme et sa mission politique* (1872), and *La Psychologie et la morale du Christianisme* (1880).

MUNTZ, Eugène. 1845-1902. Art historian. An authority on Renaissance art, he was the author of several books and articles including the *Histoire de l'art pendant la Renaissance* (1890-1895).

NADAR. Pseudonym for Felix TOURNACHON. 1820-1910. Photographer, balloonist, critic, and man of letters. He was one of the most colorful of all the artistic figures of the mid-nineteenth century. In his studio were photographed a number of the important authors and painters of his day, many of whom were his close personal friends. A considerable personal fortune made through his camera was spent on balloon ascents, an activity to which he was passionately devoted.

PEISSE, Jean-Louis-Hippolyte. 1803-1880. Man of letters. Coming to Paris in 1826, he collaborated for a while on various liberal journals. At one time he was "Conservateur des collections de l'École des Beaux-Arts," and in 1877 was made a member of the Academy of Moral Sciences, having translated a number of philosophical works from the English, including John Stuart Mill's logic.

PELLOQUET, Théodore. (?)-1867. Critic and man of letters. Little information is available about him, but his writings include a guide to the Louvre, a book on Henry Murger, and the *Galerie des hommes du jour* (1861-1863).

PÉRIER, Paul-Pierre-Casimir. (?-?). Apparently a member of the famous Périer family so prominent in French nineteenth century political life. He seems to have been at one time a member of the Chamber of Deputies, several of his speeches having been printed in the *Journal officiel*.

PERRIER, Charles. 1835-1860. Man of letters. He studied for a time in Germany, knew Liszt and several German artists, and reviewed German exhibitions for *L'Artiste* in the 'fifties. He also studied law and was at one time ('59) attached to the French Embassy in Rome.

PERRIN, Émile-César-Victor. 1814-1885. Painter, critic, and administrator. He came from a family of magistrates but turned to the world of art, exhibiting as a painter in the Salons from 1840 to 1848. Later he turned to music and the stage, becoming Director of the Opera in 1862, and nine years later, Administrator of the Comédie Française.

PETROZ, Pierre. 1819- (?). Man of letters. He wrote on art and letters, translated some of Macaulay's works, and was for a time editor of a journal called *La Philosophie positive*. Joubin says that he was a staunch admirer of Delacroix.

POTÉMONT, Adolphe Martial. Wrote under the pseudonym of AP MARTIAL. 1828-1883. Landscape painter and etcher. He was a pupil of Léon Cogniet and specialized in scenes of Paris and Parisian life. In 1873 he published *Nouveau traité de la gravure à l'eau-forte pour les peintres et les dessinateurs*.

PRIVAT, Gonzague. 1843- (?). Painter and journalist. According to Thieme-Becker he was a pupil of Barrias and Dauzats; Singer says he studied under Dehodencq and Lazergue. Portraits, landscape, and genre were his specialties, but he later turned to criticism and, in 1873, founded the journal *L'Art français*.

PROUDHON, Pierre-Joseph. 1809-1865. Socialist and political writer. The most important French socialist of his day, he was the author of many books on politics and society, and from time to time editor of liberal journals.

PROUST, Antonin. 1832-1905. Journalist, politician, and historian. His active political career included election as a deputy five times between 1876 and 1889. He published a number of books on history, was for a time a correspondent on *Le Temps*, and in 1881 was made Minister of Fine Arts by Gambetta. His history of French art was published in 1890, and the following year appeared *L'Art sous la République*.

QUATREMÈRE DE QUINCY, Antoine-Chrysostome. 1755-1849. Archaeologist and art critic. During the Revolution he took an active part in the government, being elected to the Assembly in 1791. In 1815 he was made Superintendent of Arts and Public Monuments, and the following year was elected Perpetual Secretary of the Academy. In 1824 he became professor of archaeology in the Cabinet des Antiques of the Bibliothèque Nationale. He was the author of a number of books on the fine arts (see bibliography).

RÉGAMEY, Félix-Élie. 1844-1907. Painter. The son of the miniaturist L. P. G. Régamey, he worked for a while under Lecoq de Boisbaudran, and then later became a teacher himself, first at the École des Arts Décoratifs and later at the École d'Architecture. In 1873 he left France, traveling in England, the United States, and Japan. He was the author of the illustrations for Guimet's *Promenades japonaises*.

RENAN, Ernest. 1822-1890. Writer, critic, orientalist, and teacher. He was a great popularizer of the history of religion and the author of the celebrated *Life of Jesus*. He also wrote a history of the Semitic languages and a five-volume account of the people of Israel. His son was the painter Ary Renan, and his wife was the niece of Ary Scheffer.

ROY, Elie. No information available.

SAINTE-BEUVE, Charles-Augustin. 1804-1869. Poet and critic. One of the most distinguished critics of his age, he was a friend of

Hugo and Vigny and a member of the Cénacle. His best-known works are the *Causeries* which began in 1849 in *Le Constitutionnel*.

SAINT-VICTOR, Paul Bins, Comte de. 1827-1881. Journalist and critic. His debut as an art critic was made in *Le Correspondent* and *La Semaine*. By 1851 he was in charge of the dramatic section of *Le Pays*, and in 1855 he succeeded Gautier as theater and art critic of *La Presse*. In later years he contributed to *La Liberté* and *Le Journal officiel*. His very conservative turn of mind rendered him most acceptable to the government of the Empire, which rewarded him with an Inspector-Generalship in the Ministry of Fine Arts. He was both well known and influential in his day.

SILVESTRE, Théophile. 1823-1876. Journalist and author. A strong republican in 1848, he later became far more conservative and went over completely to the side of the Emperor who sent him on missions for the Ministry of State and made him an Inspector-General of Fine Arts. He wrote for *Le Figaro*, and later bought and edited *Le Nain jaune* through which he ardently supported Napoleon III. His writings on art were largely confined to the work of his times, the most famous being the *Histoire des artistes vivants*.

STENDHAL. Pseudonym for Henri BEYLE. 1783-1842. Novelist, art historian, and man of letters. Author of *Le Rouge et le noir* (1831) and *La Chartreuse de Parme* (1839).

STEVENS, Arthur. 1825-1899. Journalist. He was the brother of the Belgian painters Joseph and Alfred Stevens, defending the latter particularly against the attacks of other critics. His articles appeared in *Le Figaro*, sometimes under the pseudonym of J. Graham and usually in defense of the modern school in Belgium.

TAINE, Hippolyte. 1828-1898. Philosopher, critic, and historian. He was probably the most distinguished historian of the later nineteenth century in France. His interest ranged widely from English and French literature to art and history and was marked by a strong tendency toward a scientific interpretation of the evidence.

THORÉ, Étienne Joseph Théophile. 1807-1869. Pseudonym: W. BÜRGER. Lawyer, critic, and art historian. After taking an active part in the revolution of 1830, Thoré became ardently involved with the democratic movement, supporting it through a variety of journalistic efforts including the founding of his own paper, *La Democratie*. After the failure of the Second Republic, he was banished but returned under the general amnesty of 1859. His Salon reviews began in the 'thirties and continued intermittently for the rest of his life, some under his own name and some under his pseudonym. Principally during his years of exile, he became an art historian, one of the most brilliant of his time, especially in the field of Dutch art.

TÖPFFER, Rodolphe. 1799-1846. Swiss artist, teacher, and man of letters. Having been forced to give up painting because of trouble with his eyesight, Töpffer became a most charming essayist and amateur philosopher whose views on life and art were a pleasant, if somewhat rambling, mixture of wit and common sense.

VÉRON, Eugène. 1825-1889. Teacher and journalist. He was at various times editor-in-chief of *Liberté*, later of *Progrès* (a Lyonnais journal) and director of *L'Art*. His interest seems to have centered on the affairs of the working class and the general concept of progress.

VITET, Ludovic. 1802-1873. Politician, art historian, and man of letters. He was associated with the official world of art throughout much of his life except during a period of retirement under the Second Empire. In 1845 he was elected to the Academy and in 1871 returned to an active career in politics as a deputy to the National Assembly. His published works included a study of the Royal Academy, a life of Eustache Lesueur, and a financial history of the government of July 1848.

WHISTLER, James Abbott McNeill. 1834-1903. Painter, of the English school; for a time the friend and associate of the Parisian *avant-garde*, exhibiting in the *Salon des Refusés* in 1863.

ZOLA, Émile. 1840-1902. Novelist and man of letters. He was probably the leading figure in the naturalist movement in French letters, the author of the *Rougon-Macquart* series, and one of the earliest spokesmen for what was, essentially, the modern artist's attitude.

BIBLIOGRAPHY

About, Edmond, "Le Salon de 1861," *Derniers lettres d'un bon jeune homme à sa cousine Madeleine*, Paris, 1863.

———— *Nos artistes au Salon de 1857*, Paris, n.d.

———— *Salon de 1864*, Paris, 1864.

———— *Salon de 1866*, Paris, n.d.

———— *Voyage à travers l'Exposition des Beaux-Arts* (Peinture et sculpture), Paris, 1855.

Amaury-Duval, *L'Atelier d'Ingres*, Paris, 1878.

Anonymous, "Salon de 1849. Critique de la critique," *L'Artiste*, 5e série, Vol. III, 1849, pp. 176-177.

Asselineau, Charles, Review of Castagnary's Salon of 1857, *L'Artiste*, 7e série, Vol. IV, 1858, pp. 247ff.

Astruc, Zacharie, *Le Salon Intime. Exposition au Boulevard des Italiens*, Paris, 1860.

———— *Les 14 stations du Salon - 1859*, preface by George Sand, Paris, 1859.

Aubert, Francis, "De l'art dans la photographie," *L'Artiste*, 7e série, Vol. X, 1860, pp. 155-156.

L'Autographe au Salon de 1864, Paris, n.d.

Auvray, Louis, *Exposition des Beaux-Arts, Salon de 1857*, Paris, n.d.

Avanel, Henri, *Histoire de la presse française depuis 1789 jusqu'à nos jours*, Paris, 1900.

Ballanche, P. S., *Oeuvres de M. Ballanche de l'Académie de Lyon*, 4 Vols., Paris, 1830 et seq.
    Essais de paligénésie sociale (1830)
    Vision d'Hebal chef d'un clan écossais (1831)

Banville, Théodore de, "Honoré Daumier," in *Mes souvenirs*, Paris, 1883.

Barbey d'Aurevilly, J., *Les Oeuvres et les hommes. Sensations d'art*, Paris, 1887.

Baschet, Robert E.-J. *Delécluze, témoin de son temps*, Paris, 1942.

Baudelaire, Charles, *L'Art romantique*, Paris (Lévy), 1885.
    "L'Oeuvre et la vie d'Eugène Delacroix"
    "L'Art philosophique"
    "Le Peintre de la vie moderne"

———— *Oeuvres complètes: Curiosités esthétiques*, Paris (ed. Crépet), 1923 (also: ed. Lévy, 1885; ed. Aubry, 1946).
    "Salon de 1845"
    "Salon de 1846"
    "Exposition Universelle -1855-Beaux-Arts"
    "Salon de 1859"

———— *Eugène Delacroix. His Life and Work*, N.Y. (Lear), 1947.

———— *Juvenilia*, Paris (ed. Crépet), 1939.

———— "Le Peintre de la vie moderne," translated into English in *The Painter of Victorian Life*, by P. G. Konody, N.Y., 1930.

———— *Lettres. 1841-1866*, Paris (ed. Soc. du Mercure de France), 1907.

Beaurin, Charles, "Le Salon de 1866," *L'Artiste (La Revue du XIXe siècle)*, 8e série, Vol. XI, 1866, pp. 451ff.; Vol. XII, pp. 124ff.

Bénédite, L. (ed.), *Gustave Courbet*, notes by J. Laran and Ph. Gaston-Dreyfus, London, 1912.

———— *Théodore Chassériau, sa vie et son oeuvre*, Paris, 1931, 2 Vols.

Bertrand, Karl, "Salon de 1870," *L'Artiste*, 9e série, Vol. XIII, 1870, pp. 319ff.

Beslay, F. and Paisant, A., *La Peinture au Salon de 1857. Causeries à deux sur le Salon de 1857*, Paris, n.d.

Binkley, Robert C., *Realism and Nationalism. 1852-1871*, N.Y., 1935.

Blanc, Charles, *Les Artistes de mon temps*, Paris, 1876.

———— *Exposition des cartons de Paul Chenavard pour la décoration du Panthéon*, Paris, 1876.

———— "Salon de 1866," *Gazette des beaux-arts*, Vol. XX, pp. 497-523; Vol. XXI, pp. 28-71.

Boas, George (ed.), *Courbet and the Naturalistic Movement*, Baltimore, 1938.

———— "Il faut être de son temps," *Journal of Aesthetics and Art Criticism*, Vol. I, 1941, pp. 52-65.

Bonnardot, A., "La Photographie et l'art," *Revue universelle des arts*, Vol. II, 1855, pp. 35-47.

Borgerhoff, E. B. O., "*Réalisme* and Kindred Words: Their Use as Terms of Literary Criticism in the First Half of the Nineteenth Century," *P.M.L.A.*, Vol. LIII, 1938, pp. 837-843.

Bougot, A., *Essai sur la critique d'art*, Paris, 1875.

Bouvier, Émile, *La Bataille réaliste*, Paris, n.d.

Boyeldieu-d'Auvigny, *Salon de 1853 (Guide aux menus plaisirs)*, Paris, n.d.

Breton, Jules, *Nos peintres du siècle*, Paris, n.d.

Brunetière, F., *Discours de combat*, Paris, 1916.

Buche, Joseph, *L'École mystique de Lyon. 1776-1847*, Paris, 1935.

Buchon, Max, *Receuil de dissertations sur le réalisme*, Neuchâtel, 1856.

Burty, Ph., "La Gravure et la photographie," *Gazette des beaux-arts*, Vol. XXIII, 1867, pp. 252-271.

———— "La Gravure, la lithographie, et la photographie au Salon de 1865," *Gazette des beaux-arts*, Vol. XIX, 1865, pp. 80-95.

———— *Maîtres et petit maîtres*, Paris, 1877.

Bury, John Bagnell, *The Idea of Progress*, London, 1921.

Butler, Samuel, *Erewhon*, London, 1910.

Cantrel, Émile, "Salon de 1859. Les Paysagistes," *L'Artiste*, 7e série, Vol. VII, 1859, pp. 33ff.

Cassagne, A. *La Théorie de l'art pour l'art en France chez les derniers romantiques et les premiers réalistes*, Paris, 1906.

Castagnary, Jules Antoine, *Grand album des expositions de peinture et de sculpture. 69 Tableaux et statues gravés par H. Linton*, text by Castagnary, Paris, 1863.

———— *Salons, 1857-1870*, 2 Vols. (only Vol. I used for the present study), preface by Eugène Spuller, Paris, 1892.

———— "Salon de 1868," under *L'Art* in *Le Bilan de l'année 1868*, Paris, 1868.

Catalogue des ouvrages de peinture, sculpture, gravure, lithographie, et architecture refusés par le jury de 1863, et exposés par décision de S.M. l'Empéreur au Salon Annexe, le 15 Mai, 1863.

Challemel-Lacour, P. "Le Salon de 1864," *Revue germanique*, Vol. XXIX, No. 3, 1864, pp. 528-547

———— "Le Salon de 1865," *Revue germanique*, Vol. XXXIV, No. 1, 1865, pp. 91-110.

Champfleury (Jules Husson called Fleury), "Du réalisme. Lettre à Madame Sand," *L'Artiste*, 5e série, Vol. XVI, 1855-56, pp. 1-5.

———— *Grandes figures d'hier et d'aujourd'hui*, Paris, 1861.
"L'Enterrement à Ornans"
"Courbet en 1860"
"Courbet. 1851"

———— *Histoire de l'imagerie populaire*, 2nd ed., Paris, 1869.

———— *Le Réalisme*, Paris, 1857.

———— *Salons. 1846-1851, Oeuvres posthumes*, Paris (ed. Lemerre), 1894.
"Salon de 1846"
"Revue des arts et des ateliers: Silhouette de M. Ingres"
"Salon de 1849"

Chaumelin, Marius, *L'Art contemporain* (La peinture à l'Exposition Universelle de 1867. Salons de 1868, 1869, 1872. Envois de Rome, concours, etc.), introduction by W. Bürger, Paris, 1873.

Chennevières-Pointel, Ph. de, *Souvenirs d'un Directeur des Beaux-Arts*, Paris, 1883.
"Les Décorations du Panthéon"

Chesneau, Ernest, *L'Art et les artistes modernes en France et en Angleterre*, Paris, 1864.

———— *Les Chefs d'école. Louis David, Gros, Géricault, Decamps, Ingres, Eugène Delacroix*, 3rd ed., Paris, 1883 (1st ed. 1862).

———— *The Education of the Artist*, trans. by Clara Bell, London, 1886.

———— "Le Mouvement moderne en peinture," *Revue européenne*, Vols. XIII, XV, XVII, XVIII.

———— *Les Nations rivales dans l'art. L'Art japonais. De l'influence des expositions internationales sur l'avenir de l'art*, Paris, 1869.

Cingria, Alex., *La Décadence de l'art sacré*, Lausanne, 1917.

Claretie, Jules, *Peintres et sculpteurs contemporains*, Paris, 1882, 2 Vols.

———— "Salon de 1864: Le Salon des Refusés," *L'Artiste*, 8e série, Vol. VI, 1864, pp. 3ff.

Clément, Chas., *Artistes anciens et modernes*, Paris, 1876.
"Études sur les beaux-arts en France" (1865)

Clément de Ris, L., "Les Notabilités de l'art depuis dix ans: 1848-1858," in *Critiques d'art et de littérature*, Paris, 1862.

———— "Mouvement des arts.—Cartons de M. Chenavard," *L'Artiste*, 5e série, Vol XI, 1853, pp. 76-78.

———— "Le Salon de 1847," *L'Artiste*, 4e série, Vol. IX, 1847, pp. 75ff.

———— "Le Salon de 1848," *L'Artiste*, 5e série, Vol. I, 1848, pp. 35ff.

———— "Le Salon de 1851," *L'Artiste*, 5e série, Vol. V, 1850-1851, pp. 225ff.; Vol. VI, 1851, pp. 3ff.

———— "Le Salon de 1852," *L'Artiste*, 5e série, Vol. VIII, 1852, pp. 65ff.

———— "Le Salon de 1853," *L'Artiste*, 5e série, Vol. X, 1853, pp. 129ff.

Comte, Auguste, *Cours de philosophie positive*, Paris, 1842, Vol. VI.

———— *The Positive Philosophy of Auguste Comte*, trans. by Harriet Martineau, London, 1896, 3 Vols.

(Corot), *Corot raconté par lui-même et par ses amis*, Geneva, 1946, 2 Vols.

Couture, Thomas, *Méthode et entretiens d'atelier*, Paris, 1868.

———— *Thomas Couture 1815-1879. Sa vie, son oeuvre, son caractère, ses idées, sa méthode, par lui-même et son petit-fils*, preface by Camille Mauclair, Paris, 1932.

(Daumier), *Daumier raconté par lui-même et par ses amis*, Geneva, 1945.

Dax, P., "Maximilien, critique d'art," *L'Artiste*, 9e série, Vol. VIII, 1869, pp. 357-381.

De Belloy, A., "Salon de 1859," *L'Artiste*, 7e série, Vol. VI, 1859, pp. 241ff.

———— "Préface au Salon de 1870," *L'Artiste*, 9e série, Vol. XIII, 1870, pp. 167ff., 294ff.

De Callias, H., "Le Salon de 1861," *L'Artiste*, 7e série, 1861, Vol. XI, pp. 217ff.; Vol. XII, pp. 1ff.

———— "Salon de 1864," *L'Artiste*, 8e série, Vol. V, 1864, pp. 195ff.

Decamps, Alexandre, "Les Arts au XIXe siècle," *L'Artiste*, 9e série, Vol. III, 1867, pp. 208-218.

Delaborde, Le Vicomte Henri, *Articles de Henri Delaborde pour servir à l'histoire de l'art au 19e siècle*. Extracts from *La Revue des deux mondes*, 1864-1874, Paris, n.d.
   "Salon de 1870"

———— *Mélanges sur l'art contemporain*, Paris, 1866.
   "Le Salon de 1853"
   "Le Salon de 1859"
   "Le Salon de 1861"

Delacroix, Eugène, *Correspondance générale de Eugène Delacroix*, ed. by André Joubin, Paris, 1936.

———— *Journal de Eugène Delacroix*, ed. by André Joubin, Paris, 1932.

———— *Journal of Eugène Delacroix*, trans. by W. Pach, N.Y. (?), 1937.

———— *Oeuvres littéraires*, Paris, 1923.

De La Faloise, M. F., "Salon de 1844," *Revue de Paris*, Vol. XXVII, 1844, pp. 349-361; Vol. XXVIII, pp. 198-213.

De La Fizelière, Albert, *A-Z ou le Salon en miniature*, Paris, 1861.

———— "Un coup d'oeil au Salon de 1861," *L'Artiste*, 7e série, Vol. XI, 1861, pp. 249ff.

De La Rochenoire, J., *Le Salon de 1855 apprécié à sa juste valeur pour un franc*, Paris, 1855.

De Lasteyrie, Ferdinand, *La Peinture à l'Exposition Universelle (Londres). Étude sur l'art contemporain*, Paris, 1863.

Delaunay, A. H., *Catalogue complet du Salon 1846 annoté par A. H. Delaunay*, Paris, n.d.

———— *Catalogue complet du Salon de 1847 annoté par A. H. Delaunay*, Paris, n.d.

Delécluze, E.-J., *Les Beaux-arts dans les deux mondes en 1855*, Paris, 1856.

———— *Exposition des artistes vivants. 1850*, Paris, 1851.

———— *Louis David, son école et son temps*, Paris, 1885.

De Lépinois, E. de B., *L'Art dans la rue et l'art au Salon (1859)*, preface by Arsène Houssaye, Paris, n.d.

Delzons, Louis, *La Famille française et son évolution*, Paris, 1913.

De Mercey, Frédéric B., *Études sur les beaux-arts*, Paris, 1855, 3 Vols.

De Mezin, B., *Promenades en long et en large au Salon de 1870*, Paris, n.d.

De Montaiglon, Anatole, "Salon de 1857," *Revue universelle des arts*, Vol. V, 1857, pp. 533-558.

De Montifaud, Marc, "Salon de 1865," *L'Artiste*, 8e série, Vol. VII, 1865, pp. 193ff.

———— "Salon de 1866," *L'Artiste*, 8e série, Vol. IX, 1866, pp. 169ff.

———— "Le Salon de 1867 et l'Exposition Universelle," *L'Artiste*, 9e série, Vol. I, 1867, pp. 244ff.; Vol. II, pp. 101ff.

———— "Salon de 1868," *L'Artiste*, 9e série, Vol. V, 1868, pp. 250ff.; Vol. VI, pp. 41ff.

Denis, Maurice, *Histoire de l'art religieux*, Paris, 1939.

Déon, Horsin (Horsin-Déon), *Rapport sur le Salon de 1853*, Paris, n.d.

———— *Rapport sur l'Exposition Universelle des Beaux-Arts (1855)*, Paris, n.d.

De Sault, C. (Mme. Guy de Charnacé), *Essais de critique d'art*, Paris, 1864.
   "Salon de 1863"

Deschamps, Émile, *La Préface des études françaises et étrangères (1828)*, Paris, 1923, ed. by Henri Giraud.

Desnoyers, Fernand, "Du réalisme," *L'Artiste*, 5e série, Vol. XVI, 1855-56, pp. 197-200.

———— *Salon des Refusés, La Peinture en 1863*, Paris, 1863.

De Staël, Mme., *De l'Allemagne (1813)*, Paris (ed. Charpentier), 1886.

Dolent, Jean, "Notes sur le Salon de 1869" in *Avant le déluge*, Paris, n.d.

Dollfuss, Chas., "L'Art moderne," *Revue germanique*, Vol. XXXI, No. 2, 1864, pp. 244-262.

Dorbec, Prosper, "La peinture française sous le Second Empire jugée par le factum, le chanson, et la caricature," *Gazette des beaux-arts*, Vol. XIV, 1918, pp. 409-427.

Doucet, Fernand, *L'Esthétique d'Émile Zola et son application à la critique*, The Hague, 1923.

Du Bos, l'Abbé, *Réflexions critiques sur la poésie et sur la peinture*, Dresden, 1760.

DuCamp, Maxime, *Les Beaux-arts à l'Exposition Universelle et aux Salons de 1863, 1864, 1865, 1866, 1867*, Paris, n.d.

———— *Les Beaux-arts à l'Exposition Universelle de 1855. Peinture-sculpture*, Paris, 1855.

———— *Le Salon de 1857*, Paris, n.d.

———— *Le Salon de 1859*, Paris, n.d.

———— *Le Salon de 1861*, Paris, 1861.

———— "Le Salon de 1865," excerpt from *Revue des deux mondes*, 1865, pp. 648-679.

Dumas, Alexandre, *L'Art et les artistes contemporains au Salon de 1859*, Paris, 1859.

Dumesnil, M. H., *Le Salon de 1859*, Paris, n.d.

Du Noüy, Lecomte, *The Road to Reason*, N.Y., 1949.

Duranty, Edmond, *La Nouvelle peinture. À propos du groupe d'artistes qui expose dans les Galeries Durand-Ruel* (1876), new ed., with foreword and notes by Marcel Guérin, Paris, 1946.

———— *Le Pays des Arts*, Paris (ed. Charpentier), 1881.

"Le Peintre Louis Martin"

Duret, Théodore, *Critique d'avant-garde*, Paris, 1885.

"Salon de 1870"

———— *Histoire des peintres impressionistes*, Paris (ed. Floury), 1922.

———— *Manet and the French Impressionists*, trans. by J. Crawford Flitch, Phila., 1910.

———— *Les Peintres français en 1867*, Paris, 1867.

Du Val, Thaddeus E., Jr., *The Subject of Realism in the Revue des Deux-Mondes*, Phila., 1936.

Enock, E. Reginald, *Mexico*, London, 1909.

Estignard, A., *Courbet, sa vie, ses oeuvres*, Paris, 1896.

Explication des ouvrages de peinture, sculpture, gravure, etc. (These are the Salon catalogues and were consulted for the following years: 1844, 1845, 1846, 1847, 1848, 1849, 1850-51, 1852, 1853, 1855, 1857, 1859, 1861, 1863, 1864, 1865, 1866, 1867, 1868, 1869, 1870.)

Faison, S. L., "Manet's Portrait of Zola," *Magazine of Art*, Vol. XLII, No. 5, 1949, pp. 162-168.

"Feu Diderot," "Salon de 1849," *L'Artiste*, 5e série, Vol. III, 1849, pp. 81ff.

Florisoone, Michel, *Manet* (Documents d'art), Monaco, 1947.

Focillon, Henri, *La Peinture au XIXe siècle. Le Retour à l'antique. Le Romantisme*, Paris, 1927.

———— *La Peinture aux XIXe et XXe siècles, de réalisme à nos jours*, Paris, 1928.

Fournel, Victor, *Les Artistes français contemporains. Peintres-sculpteurs*, 2nd ed., Tours, 1885.

Freund, Gisèle, *La Photographie en France au dix-neuvième siècle*, Paris, 1936.

Galimard, Auguste, *Examen de Salon de 1849*, Paris, n.d.

Gammell, I., *Twilight of Painting*, N.Y., 1947.

Gauss, Chas. E., *The Aesthetic Theories of French Artists*, Baltimore, 1949.

Gautier, Théophile, *Abécédaire du Salon de 1861*, Paris, n.d.

———— "L'Art en 1848," *L'Artiste*, 5e série, Vol. I, 1848, pp. 113ff.

———— *L'Art moderne*, Paris (ed. Lévy), 1856. "Le Panthéon—Peintures murales"

———— *Les Beaux-arts en Europe. 1855*, Paris, 1856, 2 Vols.

———— *Critique artistique et littéraire*, introduction by Ferdinand Gohin and Roger Tisserand, Paris, 1929.

———— "De l'art moderne," *L'Artiste*, 5e série, Vol. X, 1853, pp. 135-136.

———— *Mademoiselle de Maupin*, trans. by F. C. De Sumichrast, N.Y., 1900.

———— Notice about the competition for *La République*, *L'Artiste*, 5e série, Vol. I, 1848, pp. 160-161.

———— Notice about the Salon awards for 1851, *L'Artiste*, 5e série, Vol. VI, 1851, p. 118.

———— Opening remarks to Vol. III, 6e série of *L'Artiste* (1856-1857), p. 4.

———— "Paul Delaroche," "Gavarni," etc. in *Portraits contemporains*, Paris (ed. Charpentier), 1898.

———— *Salon de 1847*, Paris, n.d.

———— "Salon de 1857," *L'Artiste*, 7e série, Vol. I, 1857, pp. 189ff.; Vol. II, pp. 1ff.

———— *Souvenirs de théâter, d'art, et de critique*, Paris (ed. Charpentier), 1883. "Gavarni"

———— *Tableaux à la plume*, Paris (ed. Charpentier), 1880. "Le Salon de 1869" "Exposition de tableaux modernes"

Gebaüer, Ernest, *Les Beaux-arts à l'Exposition Universelle de 1855*, Paris, 1855.

George, Albert J., *Pierre-Simon Ballanche*, Syracuse (N.Y.), 1945.

Gigoux, Jean, *Causeries sur les artistes de mon temps*, Paris, 1885.

Gilbert, K. E. and Kuhn, H., *A History of Aesthetics*, N.Y., 1939.

Gill, *Salon pour rire. 1864*, Paris, n.d.

———— *Salon pour rire. 1868*, Paris, n.d.

Gilman, Margaret, "Baudelaire and Stendhal," *P.M.L.A.*, Vol. LIV, 1939, pp. 288-296.

———— *Baudelaire the Critic*, N.Y., 1943.

Girardin, Jules, "La Photographie et la peinture," *Revue européenne*, Vol. XIV, 1861, pp. 348-358.

Giraud, Victor, *Essai sur Taine*, Paris, 1909.

Goldwater, Robert, *Primitivism in Modern Painting*, N.Y., 1938.

———— "Some Reasons for a Reputation," *Art Bulletin*, Vol. XXVIII, 1946, pp. 33-43.

Goldwater, Robert and Treves, M., *Artists on Art*, N.Y., 1945.

Goncourt, Edmond and Jules de, *Études d'art*, preface by Roger Marx, Paris, n.d.

    "Le Salon de 1852"

    "La Peinture à l'Exposition de 1855"

———— *Journal*, Paris (ed. Charpentier), 1891.

———— *Manette Salomon*, Paris (ed. Charpentier), 1910.

———— *Pages retrouvées*, preface by Gustave Geffroy, Paris, 1886.

    "Decamps"

    "L'Ivresse de Silène par Daumier"

———— *Préfaces et manifestes littéraires*, Paris (ed. Charpentier), 1888.

Goujon, J., *Salon de 1870. Propos en l'air*, Paris, 1870.

Graber, Hans, *Edgar Degas nach eigenen und fremden Zeugnissen*, Basel, 1942.

Grangedor, J., "Le Salon de 1868," *Gazette des beaux-arts*, Vol. XXIV, 1868, pp. 509-524; Vol. XXV, pp. 5-30.

Grün, Alphonse, *Salon de 1852*, Paris, n.d.

Guérard, Albert, *Art for Art's Sake*, N.Y., 1936.

———— *French Civilization in the Nineteenth Century*, N.Y., 1918.

Guérin, Marcel, "Avant-propos et notes" in E. Duranty, *La Nouvelle peinture*, Paris, 1946.

———— *L'Oeuvre gravé de Manet*, Paris, 1944.

Gueullette, Charles, *Les Peintres de genre au Salon de 1863*, Paris, 1863.

Guizot, M., *Études sur les beaux-arts en général*, Paris, 1860.

    "De l'état des Beaux-Arts en France et au Salon de 1810"

    "Essai sur les limites qui séparent et les liens qui unissent les beaux-arts" (1816)

———— *The Fine Arts. Their Nature and Relations*, trans. by George Grove, London, 1853.

Hache, Ernest, *Les Merveilles de l'art et de l'industrie. Antiquité, moyen-age, renaissance, temps modernes. Salon de 1869*, Paris, n.d.

Hamerton, Philip G., *Painting in France after the Decline of Classicism*, London, 1869.

Hegel, G. W. F., *The Philosophy of Fine Art*, trans. by F. P. B. Osmaston, London, 1920, 4. Vols.

Holt, E. G., *Literary Sources of Art History*, Princeton, 1947.

Hourticq, Louis, *Edouard Manet*, introduction by L. Hourticq, notes by J. Laran and G. LeBas, Phila., 1912.

Houssaye, Arsène, Notice about Chenavard's cartoons for the Panthéon, *L'Artiste*, 5e série, Vol. I, 1848, pp. 106-108.

———— Letter to Karl Bertrand, *L'Artiste*, 9e série, Vol. XIII, 1870, pp. 319-320.

———— *Life in Paris. Letters on Art, Literature, and Society*, Boston, 1875.

———— *Revue du Salon de 1844*, Paris, 1844.

———— "Le Salon de 1845" (with Paul Mantz), *L'Artiste*, 4e série, Vol. III, 1845, pp. 161ff.

———— "Le Salon de 1846" (with Paul Mantz and others), *L'Artiste*, 4e série, Vol. VI, 1846, pp. 37ff.

———— "Salon de 1847. À M. Chenavard à Rome," *L'Artiste*, 4e série, Vol. IX, 1847, pp. 33-35.

———— "Salon de 1848," *L'Artiste*, 5e série, Vol. I, 1848, pp. 1ff.

———— "Salon de 1861. Introduction," *L'Artiste*, 7e série, Vol. XI, 1861, pp. 193ff.

———— "Introduction au Salon de 1868," *L'Artiste*, 9e série, Vol. V, 1868, pp. 239-246.

Hunt, Herbert J., *The Epic in Nineteenth Century France*, Oxford, 1941.

Huyghe, R., *Courbet. L'Atelier* (Monographies des peintures du Musée du Louvre), Paris, n.d.

(Ingres), *Ingres. Écrits sur l'art*, preface by Raymond Cogniat, Paris (?), 1947.

Jahyer, Félix, *Deuxième étude sur les beaux-arts. Salon de 1866*, Paris, 1866.

Janssens, René, *Les Maitres de la critique d'art*, Brussels, 1935.

Jourdan, Louis, *Les Peintres français. Salon de 1859*, Paris, 1859.

Karr, Alphonse, *Les Guêpes*, Paris, 1847.
Kirstein, Lincoln, "The State of Modern Painting," *Harper's*, Oct. 1948, pp. 47-53.
Konody, P. G., *The Painter of Victorian Life*, N.Y., 1930.

Lacroix, Paul, *Annuaire des artistes et des amateurs*, Paris, Vol. I, 1860; Vol. II, 1861; Vol. III, 1862.
Lafenestre, Georges, *Artistes et amateurs*, Paris, n.d.
    "Gautier"
La Font de St. Yenne, *L'Ombre du grand Colbert, le Louvre, et la ville de Paris, dialogue. Réflexions sur quelques causes de l'état présent de la peinture en France*, Paris, 1752.
LaGrange, Léon, "Salon de 1861," *Gazette des beaux-arts*, Vol. X, 1861; pp. 193ff.; Vol. XI, pp. 135ff.
———— "Salon de 1864," *Gazette des beaux-arts*, Vol. XVI, pp. 501-536; Vol. XVII, pp. 5-44.
Lassaigne, Jules, *Daumier*, trans. by Eveline Byam Shaw, N.Y., 1947.
Laurent-Pichat, L., *Notes sur le Salon de 1861*, Lyon, n.d.
Laverdant, D., *La Mission de l'art et du rôle des artistes. Salon de 1845*, Paris, n.d. (extracts from Nos. 2 and 3 of *La Phalange, Revue de la science sociale*).
Lavergne, Claudius, *Exposition Universelle de 1855*, Paris, 1855.
Le Chartier, Marcel, *L'Intervention de l'État dans les arts plastiques*, Thèse pour le doctorat, Paris(?), 1913.
Lecomte, Georges, "Les Goncourts critiques d'art," *Revue de Paris*, Vol. IV, 1894, pp. 201-224.
Lecoq de Boisbaudran, Horace, *L'Éducation de la mémoire pittoresque et la formation de l'artiste*, Paris, 1920.
    "Education de la mémoire pittoresque" (1862)
    "Coup d'oeil sur l'enseignement des beaux-arts" (1872)
    "Lettres à un jeune professeur" (1876)
Léger, Charles, *Courbet*, Paris, 1929.
———— *Courbet selon les caricatures et les images*, preface by Théodore Duret, Paris, 1920.
Lemonnier, Camille, *Salon de Paris. 1870*, Paris, n.d.

Lessing, G. E., *Laocoön or Concerning the Limits of Painting, and Poetry*, trans. by E. Frothingham, Boston, 1863.
Liebermann, Max, "Ein Beitrag zur Arbeitsweise Manets," *Kunst und Künstler*, Vol. VIII, 1910, pp. 483ff.
Locquin, Jean, *La Peinture d'histoire en France de 1747 à 1785*, Paris, 1912.
Lorentz, A.-J., *Dernier jour de l'Exposition de 1865. Revue galopante du Salon*, Paris, n.d.
Lossier, Jean-G., *Le Rôle sociale de l'art selon Proudhon*, Paris, 1937.
Loudun, Eugène, *Le Salon de 1852*, Paris, n.d.
———— (*Exposition Universelle des Beaux-Arts*) *Le Salon de 1855*, Paris, n.d.
———— *Le Salon de 1857*, Paris, n.d.

Malpertuy, Étienne, *Histoire de la société française au XIXe siècle*, Paris, 1854.
Malraux, André, *Le Musée imaginaire* (Vol. I of *Psychologie de l'art*), Geneva, 1947.
Mantz, Paul, "Le Salon de 1845" (with A. Houssaye), *L'Artiste*, 4e série, Vol. III, 1845, pp. 161ff.
———— "Salon de 1846" (with A. Houssaye and others), *L'Artiste*, 4e série, Vol. VI, 1846, pp. 37ff.
———— *Salon de 1847*, Paris, n.d.
———— "Salon de 1859," *Gazette des beaux-arts*, Vol. II, 1859, pp. 129ff.; Vol. III, pp. 21-39.
———— "Salon de 1863," *Gazette des beaux-arts*, Vol. XIV, 1863, pp. 481-506; Vol. XV, pp. 32-64.
———— "Salon de 1865," *Gazette des beaux-arts*, Vol. XVIII, 1865, pp. 489-523; Vol. XIX, pp. 5-42.
———— "Salon de 1867," *Gazette des beaux-arts*, Vol. XXII, 1867, pp. 513-548.
———— "Les Beaux-arts à l'Exposition Universelle," *Gazette des beaux-arts*, Vol. XXIII, 1867, pp. 319-345.
———— "Salon de 1869," *Gazette des beaux-arts*, Vol. I, 2me per., 1869, pp. 489-511; Vol. II, pp. 5-23.
Marguery, H., "Un Pionnier de l'histoire de l'art: Thoré-Bürger," *Gazette des beaux-arts*, 5me série, Vol. XI, 1925, pp. 229-245; Vol. XII, pp. 295-311, 367-380.
Martial, AP (Martial Potémont), *Lettre illustré sur le Salon* (1865), Paris, n.d.
———— *Salon de 1866*, Paris, n.d.
Martin, Kurt, *Edouard Manet, Die Erschiessung Kaiser Maximiliens von Mexico*, Berlin, 1948.
Mauclair, Camille, *Degas*, N.Y., 1941.

Meier-Graefe, J., *Degas*, N.Y., 1923.

Ménard, Réné, "Salon de 1870," *Gazette des beaux-arts*, Vol. III, 1870, pp. 489-514; Vol. IV, pp. 38-71.

———— "Les Théoriciens de l'art," *L'Artiste*, 9e série, Vol. IV, 1868, pp. 385-414.

Milsand, J. *L'Esthétique anglaise. Étude sur M. John Ruskin*, Paris, 1864.

Mitchell, Eleanor, "La Fille de Jephté par Degas," *Gazette des beaux-arts*, 6ᵐᵉ série, Vol. XVIII, 1937, pp. 175-189.

Moreau-Nélaton, Étienne, *Manet raconté par lui-même*, Paris, 1926, 2 Vols.

———— *Millet raconté par lui-même*, Paris, 1921, 3 Vols.

Mott, Lewis Freeman, *Ernest Renan*, N.Y., 1921.

Muntz, Eugène, "Exposition Internationale de Munich," *Gazette des beaux-arts*, Vol. II, 1869, pp. 301ff.

Musée Moreau, *Catalogue sommaire des peintures, dessins, et aquarelles exposés dans les galeries du Musée Gustave Moreau*, Paris, 1904.

Nadar (Félix Tournachon), *Nadar jury au Salon de 1853*, Paris, 1853.

———— *Nadar jury au Salon de 1857*, Paris, n.d.

Pach, Walter, *Ingres*, N.Y., 1939.

Peisse, L., "À propos du Salon" (1852), *L'Artiste*, 5e série, Vol. VIII, 1852, pp. 149-150.

Pelloquet, Théodore, *Dictionnaire de poche des artistes contemporains*, Paris, 1858.

———— "L'École moderne," *L'Artiste*, 8e série, Vol. II, 1862, pp. 260-261.

Périer, Paul C., *Un Chercheur au Salon. 1868. Peinture. Les Inconnus, les trop peu connus, les méconnus, les nouveaux et les jeunes*, Paris, 1868.

———— *Propos d'art à l'occasion du Salon de 1869. Revue du Salon*, Paris, n.d. "La Commission de l'Index à l'exposition"

Perrier, Chas., "L'Art à l'Exposition Universelle," *L'Artiste*, 5e série, Vol. XV, 1855, pp. 15ff.

———— *L'Art français au Salon de 1857*, Paris, n.d.

———— "Du réalisme. Lettre à M. Le Directeur de *L'Artiste*," *L'Artiste*, 5e série, Vol. XVI, 1855-56, pp. 85-90.

Perrin, Émile, "Salon de 1859," *Revue européenne*, Vol. II, 1859, pp. 86off.; Vol. III, pp. 408ff.

———— "Salon de 1861," *Revue européenne*, Vol. XV, 1861, pp. 363ff.; Vol. XVI, pp. 164ff.

Petroz, Pierre, *L'Art et la critique en France depuis 1822*, Paris, 1875.

Peyrouton, Abel, *Paul Chenavard et son oeuvre*, Lyon (F. Armbruster), 1887, 4 Vols.

Privat, Gonzague, *Place aux jeunes! Causeries critiques sur le Salon de 1865*, Paris, n.d.

Proudhon, Pierre-Joseph, *Du principe de l'art et de sa destination sociale, Oeuvres complètes de P.-J. Proudhon*, new ed. by Bouglé and Moysset, introduction and notes by Jules L. Puech, Paris, 1939.

Proust, Antonin, "Edouard Manet, souvenirs," *Revue blanche*, Vol. XII, 1897.

Puckett, Elizabeth, *The Symbolist Criticism of Painting. France, 1880-1895*, 1948 (unpublished).

Quatremère de Quincy, *Considérations morales sur la destination des ouvrages de l'art*, Paris, 1815.

———— *Essai sur l'idéal dans ses applications pratiques aux oeuvres de l'imitation propre des arts de dessin*, Paris, 1837.

———— *Imitation in the Fine Arts*, trans. by J. C. Kent, London, 1837.

Randall, John H., Jr., *The Making of the Modern Mind*, N.Y., 1940.

Raymond, Marcel, *De Baudelaire au Surréalisme*, Paris, 1933.

Régamey, Félix, *Horace Lecoq de Boisbaudran et ses élèves. Notes et souvenirs*, Paris, 1903.

Renan, Ernest, *L'Avenir de la science*, Paris (ed. Lévy), 1890.

Rewald, John, *Cézanne et Zola*, Paris, 1936.

———— *History of Impressionism*, N.Y., 1946.

Riat, Georges, *Gustave Courbet, peintre*, Paris, 1906.

Rivière, Georges, *Mr. Degas (Bourgeois de Paris)*, Paris, 1935.

Rocheblave, S. *Le Goût en France. Les arts et les lettres de 1600 à 1900*, Paris, 1914.

Rosca, D. D., *L'Influence de Hegel sur Taine théoricien de la connaissance et de l'art*, Paris, 1928.

Rosenthal, Léon, *Du romantisme au réalisme. Essai sur l'évolution de la peinture en France de 1830 à 1848*, Paris, 1914.

———— *La Peinture romantique*, Paris, 1900.

Roy, Élie, "Salon de 1869," *L'Artiste*, 9e série, Vol. IX, 1869, pp. 235ff. (con't in Vol. X).

———— "Salon de 1869. Pérégrinations dans les ateliers," *L'Artiste*, 9e série, Vol. IX, 1869, p. 97.

Sabatier, Pierre, *L'Esthétique des Goncourt*, Paris, 1920.

Sainte-Beuve, C.-A., *Correspondance*, Paris (ed. Lévy), 1877.

———— "Horace Vernet," *Revue universelle des arts*, Vol. XVII, 1863, pp 145-174, 217-254.

———— *Nouveaux lundis*, 2nd ed. rev., Paris (ed. Lévy), 1870-1872, Vols. III, IV.

Saint-Victor, Paul de, "Beaux-arts. Peintures murales de Saint-Roch par M. Théodore Chassériau," *L'Artiste*, 5e série, Vol. XIII, 1854, pp. 67ff.

Schapiro, Meyer, "Courbet and Popular Imagery," *Journal of the Warburg and Courtauld Institutes*, Vol. IV, 1941, pp. 164-191.

Sée, Henri, *Esquisse d'une histoire economique et sociale de la France depuis les origines jusqu'à la guerre mondiale*, Paris, 1929.

Sensier, Alfred, *J.-F. Millet*, trans. by Helena de Kay, Boston, 1881.

Silvestre, Théophile, *Histoire des artistes vivants, français et étrangers. Études d'après nature*, Paris (1856).

Sloane, J. C., "The Tradition of Figure Painting and Concepts of Modern Art in France from 1845 to 1870," *The Journal of Aesthetics and Art Criticism*, Vol. VII, Sept. 1948, pp. 1-29.

Spencer, Eleanor, "The Academic Point of View in the Second Empire," in *Courbet and the Naturalist Movement*, ed. by G. Boas, Baltimore, 1938.

Spuller, Eugène, "Préface" in J. A. Castagnary, *Salons 1857-1870*, Vol. I, Paris, 1892.

Stendhal (Henri Beyle), *Histoire de la peinture en Italie*, Paris (ed. Arbelet), 1924, 2 Vols.

Stenger, Erich, *The History of Photography*, trans. by E. Epstean, Easton, Pa., 1939.

Stevens, Arthur, *Le Salon de 1863, suivie d'une étude sur Eugène Delacroix et d'une notice biographique sur le Prince Gortschakow*, Paris, 1866.

Stranahan, C. H., *A History of French Painting*, N.Y., 1888.

Tabarant, Adolphe, *Manet et ses oeuvres*, Paris, 1947.

———— *La Vie artistique au temps de Baudelaire*, Paris, 1942.

Taine, Hippolyte, *Lectures on Art*, trans. by John Durand, N.Y., 1875.

Taylor, Francis Henry, "Modern Art and the Dignity of Man," *Atlantic Monthly*, Dec. 1948, pp. 30-36.

Thoré, Théophile (W. Bürger, pseudonym), "De la beauté dans les arts," *Revue universelle des arts*, Vol. III, 1856, pp. 193-202 (signed: W. Bürger).

———— "Des tendencies de l'art au XIXe siècle," *Revue universelle des arts*, Vol. I, 1855, pp. 77-85 (signed: W. Bürger).

———— "Salon de 1861: De l'avenir de l'art," *Revue germanique*, Vol. XV, No. 2, 1861, pp. 248-259 (signed: W. Bürger).

———— *Salons de T. Thoré. 1844, 1845, 1846, 1847, 1848*, preface by W. Bürger, Paris, 1868.

———— *Salons de W. Bürger*, preface by T. Thoré (actually written by Marius Chaumelin), Paris, 1870, 2 Vols.

Töpffer Rodolphe, *Réflexions et menus propos d'un peintre Genevois*, Paris, 1853.

Tourneux, Maurice, *Salons et expositions d'art à Paris. Essai bibliographique*, Paris, 1919.

Vachon, Marius, *Puvis de Chavannes*, Paris, 1895.

Venturi, Lionello, *Les Archives de l'Impressionisme*, Paris, 1939.

———— "Corot," in *Corot. 1796-1875* (Philadelphia Museum of Art), Phila., 1946.

———— *History of Art Criticism*, N.Y., 1936.

Véron, Eugène, *Supériorité des arts modernes sur les arts anciens*, Paris, 1862.

Vial, Eugène, "Chenavard et Soulary," *Mémoires de l'académie des sciences, belles-lettres, et arts de Lyon*, 3me série, Vol. XVII, 1921.

Vitet, Ludovic, *Études sur l'histoire de l'art, Oeuvres complètes*, Paris (ed. Lévy), 1864, Vol. III.

Vollard, A., *Paul Cézanne, his Life and Art*, N.Y, 1926.

"Wallon," "De la symbolique des arts," *L'Artiste*, 4e série, Vol. VIII, 1847, p. 226.

Webster, J. Carson, "The Technique of Impressionism: A Reappraisal," *College Art Journal*, Vol. IV, 1944, pp. 3-22.

Weinberg, Bernard, *French Realism: The Critical Reaction, 1830-1870*, N.Y., 1937.

Whistler, James McN., *The Gentle Art of Making Enemies*, N.Y., 1893.

(Wildenstein Gallery), *A Loan Exhibition of Gustave Courbet*, N.Y., 1948.

Winckelmann, J. J., *Gedanken über die Nachahmung der griechischen Werke in der Malerei und Bildhauerkunst*, Dresden, 1755.

Wolterstorff, Hermann, *"Essai sur la vie et les oeuvres de Rodolphe Töpffer," Jahresbericht über das Realgymnasium zu Magdeburg*, Magdeburg, 1895.

Zola, Émile, *Mes haines, Oeuvres complètes,* Paris (ed. LeBlond), n.d.; also Paris (ed. Charpentier), 1895.
"Proudhon et Courbet"
"M. H. Taine, artiste"
"Mon Salon"
"Edouard Manet"

ACKNOWLEDGMENTS

Alinari, Florence: 5, 7, 10, 44, 45, 67, 73, 86

Arts Graphiques de la Cité, Paris. (Agraci): 43, 53

Bibliothèque Nationale, Paris: 82

Bruckmann, F., Munich: 85

Bulloz, Paris: 1, 2, 4, 8, 9, 11, 12, 14, 15, 17, 18, 20, 22, 23, 26, 28, 32, 33, 37, 38, 41, 42, 46, 52, 54, 59, 63, 69, 70, 71, 72, 76, 79, 80, 81, 84, 90

Burrell Collection, Glasgow Art Gallery and Museum: 21

California Palace of the Legion of Honor, San Francisco: 62

Camponogara, J., Lyon: 31 (by permission of Musée des Beaux Arts, Lyon)

Cooper, A. C., London: 40 (by permission of H. M. Queen Elizabeth)

Fogg Art Museum, Cambridge, Mass.: 50

Foto Marburg: 24, 77

Giraudon, Paris: 51

John G. Johnson Collection, Philadelphia: 64

Metropolitan Museum of Art, New York: 3, 29, 55, 60, 65, 68, 74, 83, 87

Museum of Fine Arts, Boston: 27, 47, 78

Museum of Fine Arts, Springfield, Mass.: 16

National Gallery of Art, Washington, D.C.: 61, 66, 88

Pennsylvania Academy of the Fine Arts, Philadelphia: 57

Phillips Collection, Washington, D.C.: 25

Services de Documentation Photographique, Paris: 19, 39, 58, 89

Smith College of Museum of Art, Northampton, Mass.: 75

Trustees of the National Gallery, London: 48, 49

INDEX

Since they have little relevance to the argument, proper names of places and locations have, for the sake of brevity, been omitted. For the same reason, not all uses of the word "Salon" have been listed as the number would have been excessive without contributing to the usefulness of the Index.

PLATES

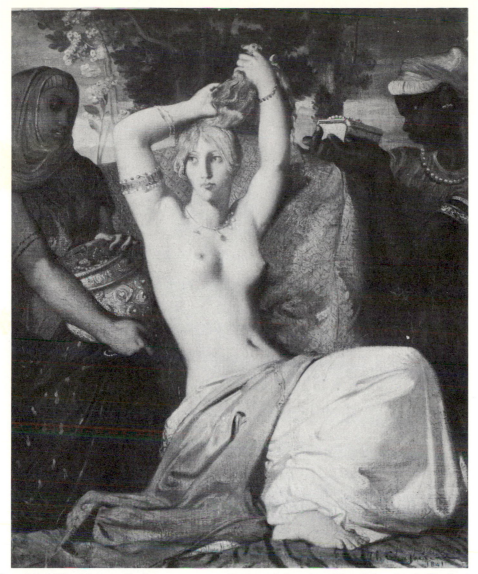

1. Theodore Chassériau. *Esther se parant* (Esther Adorning Herself). 1841*. Paris, Louvre

2. Paul Marc Joseph Chenavard. *Convention Nationale*. 1832*. Lyon, Musée des Beaux Arts

3. Camille Corot. *Hagar au desert* (Hagar in the Wilderness). 1835*. New York, The Metropolitan
Musuem of Art, Rogers Fund, 1938

4. Camille Corot. *Homère et les bergers* (Homer and the Shepherds). 1845*. Musée de St. Lô

5. Thomas Couture. *Orgie romaine* (Romans of the Decadence). Paris, Louvre

6. Alexandre Decamps. *La Patrouille turque* (The Turkish Patrol). 1831*.
London, The Wallace Collection

7. Eugène Delacroix. *La Liberté aux barricades* (Liberty Leading the People). 1831*. Paris, Louvre

8. Eugène Delacroix. *La Mort de Marc Aurèle* (The Death of Marcus Aurelius). 1845*. Lyon, Musée des Beaux Arts

9. Paul Delaroche. *La Mort de Duc de Guise* (The Death of the Duc de Guise). 1835*. Chantilly, Musée Condé

10. Théodore Géricault. *Le Radeau de la Méduse* (The Raft of the Medusa). 1819*. Paris, Louvre

11. Léon Gérôme. *Le Combat des coqs* (The Cock Fight). 1847*. Paris, Louvre (formerly in the Luxembourg Museum)

12. J.A.D. Ingres. *Stratonice*. 1840*. Chantilly, Musée Condé

14. Horace Vernet. *La Prise de Constantine* (The Taking of Constantine). 1838* Versailles

13. Jean François Millet. *Oedipe détaché de l'arbre* (Oedipus Taken Down from the Tree). Etching after a lost (?) original. 1847*

15. Honoré Daumier. *La République*. Exhibited but not in the Salon. 1848. Paris, Louvre

16. Thomas Couture. *Enrôlements volontaires de 1792* (Voluntary Enlistments, 1792). Begun, 1848. Springfield Mass., Museum of Fine Arts, The James Philip Gray Collection

18. Jean François Millet. *Le Vanneur* (The Winnower). Paris, Louvre

17. Narcisse-Virgile de la Pena. *Vénus et Adonis*. Paris, Louvre

19. Théodore Chassériau. *Le Silence* (detail). 1849. (From the Cour des Comptes) Paris, Louvre

20. Gustave Courbet. *L'Après dinée à Ornans* (After Dinner at Ornans). 1849*. Musée de Lille

21. Honoré Daumier. *Le Meunier, son fils et l'âne* (The Miller, his Son, and the Ass). 1849*.
Glasgow Art Gallery, the Burrell Collection

22. Théodore Chassériau. *Sapho* 1850-1851*. Paris, Louvre

23. Gustave Courbet. *L'Enterrement à Ornans* (The Burial at Ornans). 1850-1851*. Paris, Louvre

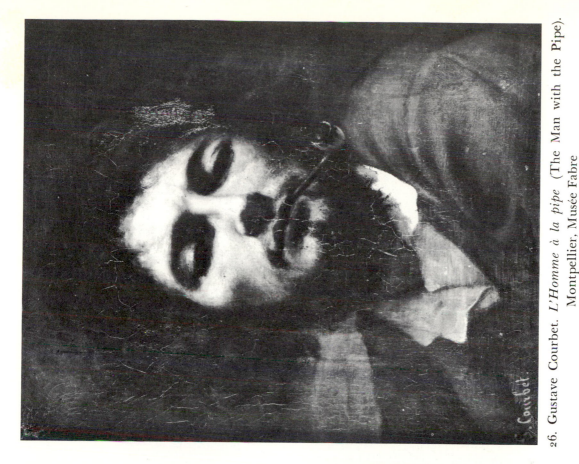

26. Gustave Courbet. *L'Homme à la pipe* (The Man with the Pipe). Montpellier, Musée Fabre

24. Gustave Courbet. *Les Casseurs de pierres* (The Stonebreakers). 1850-1851*. (Destroyed. Formerly in Dresden, Gemäldegalerie)

25. Gustave Courbet. *Les Rochers d'Ornans* (Rocks at Mouthiers). 1850-1851 (*?). Washington, D.C., The Phillips Collection

27. Jean François Millet. *Le Semeur* (The Sower). 1850-1851*.
Boston, The Museum of Fine Arts, Shaw Collection

28. Gustave Courbet. *Les Paysans de Flagey revenant d'une foire* (The Peasants of
Flagey Returning from a Fair). 1850-1851*. Private collection

29. Gustave Courbet. *Les Demoiselles de village* (The Village Maidens). 1852*. New York, The Metropolitan Museum of Art, Gift of Harry Payne Bingham, 1940

31. Paul Marc Joseph Chenavard. *Romulus et Rémus* (cartoon). 1853. Musée des Beaux Arts, Lyon

30. Théodore Chassériau. *Le Baptême de l'eunuque* (The Baptism of the Eunuch). 1853. Paris, St. Roch

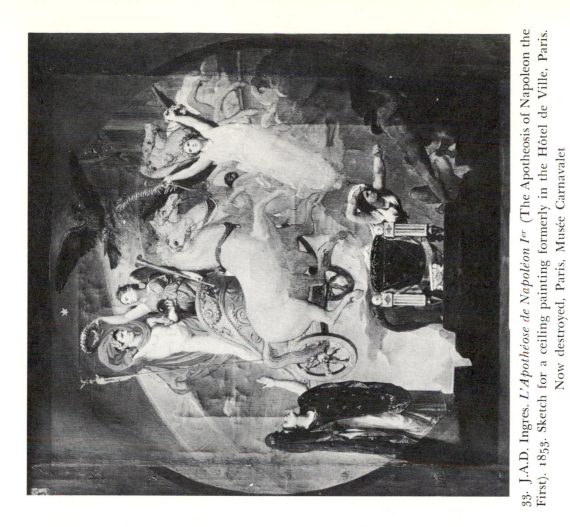

33. J.A.D. Ingres. *L'Apothéose de Napoléon Ier* (The Apotheosis of Napoleon the First). 1853. Sketch for a ceiling painting formerly in the Hôtel de Ville, Paris. Now destroyed, Paris, Musée Carnavalet

32. Gustave Courbet. *Les Baigneuses* (The Bathers). 1853*. Montpellier, Musée Fabre

34. Paul Marc Joseph Chenavard. *Le Déluge* (The Flood). 1855*. Lithograph by
Armbruster after cartoon in Musée des Beaux-Arts, Lyon

35. Adolphe Bouguereau. *Le Triomphe du martyre* (The Martyr's Triumph). 1855*.
Present location unknown.

36. Paul March Joseph Chenavard. *Palingénésie sociale* (Social Rebirth). 1855. Lithograph by Armbruster after cartoon in Musée des Beaux-Arts, Lyon

37. Gustave Courbet. *La Rencontre* (The Meeting, or "Good Day, M. Courbet"). 1855*. Montpellier, Musée Fabre

38. Gustave Courbet. *L'Atelier* (The Studio). 1855. Paris, Louvre

39. Théodore Rousseau. *Paysage: La Mare* (The Pond). 1855*. Reims, Musée St. Denis

40. Ernest Meissonier. *La Rixe* (The Brawl). 1855*. Collection of H.M. the Queen of England

41. Gustave Courbet. *Les Demoiselles au bord de la Seine* (Young Women at the Edge of the Seine). 1857*. Paris, Musée du Petit Palais

42. Jules Breton. *La Bénédiction des blés* (Blessing the Wheat). 1857*. Paris, formerly Musée du Luxembourg

43. Camille Corot. *La Ronde des nymphes* (Dance of the Nymphs). 1857 (*?). Paris, Louvre

44. Jean François Millet, *Les Glaneuses* (The Gleaners). 1857*. Paris, Louvre

45. Jules Breton. *Le Rappel des glaneuses* (Recall of the Gleaners).
1859*. Musée d'Arras (?). Formerly Paris, Musée du Luxembourg

46. Jean François Millet. *Femme faisant pâturer sa vache*
(Woman Grazing her Cow). 1859*. Musée de Bourg

47. Camille Corot. *Dante et Virgile* (Dante and Virgil
Entering the Inferno). 1859*. Boston, The Museum
of Fine Arts (gift of Quincy A. Shaw)

48. Edouard Manet. *Musique aux Tuileries* (Music in the Tuileries). 1860. London, Reproduced by permission of the Trustees of the National Gallery

49. Edgar Degas. *Les Jeunes filles spartiates*. (The Young Spartan Girls). 1860. London, Reproduced by permission of the Trustees of the National Gallery

50. Constatin Guys. *En Carrosse* (Coaching). Ca. 1860. Cambridge, Mass., courtesy of the Fogg Art Museum, Harvard University, Grenville L. Winthrop Bequest

51. Gustave Courbet. *Combat des cerfs* (Fighting Stags). 1861*. Paris, Louvre

52. Puvis de Chavannes. *Concordia* (Peace). 1861*. Musée d'Amiens

54. Eugène **D**elacroix. *Héliodore*. 1861. Paris, S. Sulpice

53. Honoré Daumier. *Une Blanchisseuse* (A Laundress). 1861*. Paris, Louvre

55. Edouard Manet. *Chanteur espagnol* (The Guitar Player). 1861*. New York,
The Metropolitan Museum of Art

56. Paul Baudry. *La Perle et la vague* (The Pearl and the Wave). 1863*. Location unknown

57. Alexandre Cabanel. *La Naissance de Vénus* (The Birth of Venus). 1863*. Philadelphia,
Pennsylvania Academy of the Fine Arts

58. Gustave Courbet. *Le Retour de la conférence* (The Return from the Meeting). 1863. Picture destroyed

59. Edouard Manet. *Le Déjeuner sur l'herbe* (The Luncheon on the Grass). 1863. Salon des Refusés. Paris, Musée de l'Impressionisme (Louvre)

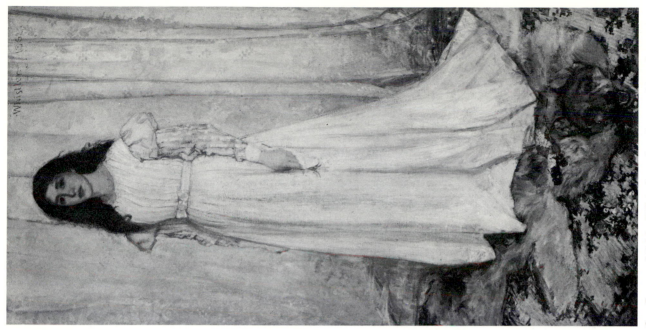

61. James McN. Whistler. *La Dame blanche* (The White Girl). 1863. Salon des Refusés. Washington, D.C., The National Gallery of Art, Harris Whittemore Collection

60. Edouard Manet. Mlle. *Victorine en costume d'espada.* 1863. Salon des Refusés. New York, The Metropolitan Museum of Art, Bequest of Mrs. H. O. Havemeyer, 1929, The H. O. Havemeyer Collection

62. Jean François Millet. *L'Homme à la houe* (The Man with the Hoe). 1863*.
San Francisco, Private collection

63. Puvis de Chavannes. *Repos* (Rest). 1863*. Amiens, Musée de Picardie

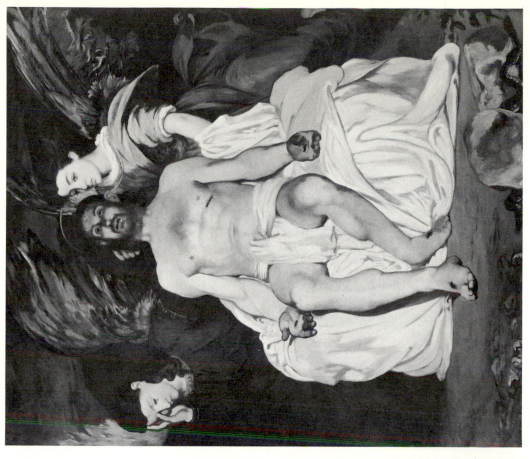

65. Edouard Manet. *Le Christ et les anges* (Christ with Angels). 1864*. New York, The Metropolitan Museum of Art, Bequest of H. O. Havemeyer, 1929, The H. O. Havemeyer Collection

64*. Edouard Manet. *Le Kearsarge et l'Alabama*. 1864. Courtesy John G. Johnson Collection, Philadelphia

68. Gustave Moreau. *Oedipe et le Sphinx*. 1864*. New York, The Metropolitan Museum of Art, Bequest of William H. Herriman, 1921

66. Edouard Manet. *Le Torero mort* (fragment). 1864*. Washington, D.C., The National Gallery of Art, Widener Collection, 1942

67. Ernest Meissonier. *Napoléon III à Solferino*. 1864*. Paris, Louvre

69. Edgar Degas. *Les Malheurs d'Orléans* (The Misfortunes of Orléans). 1865*. Paris, Louvre

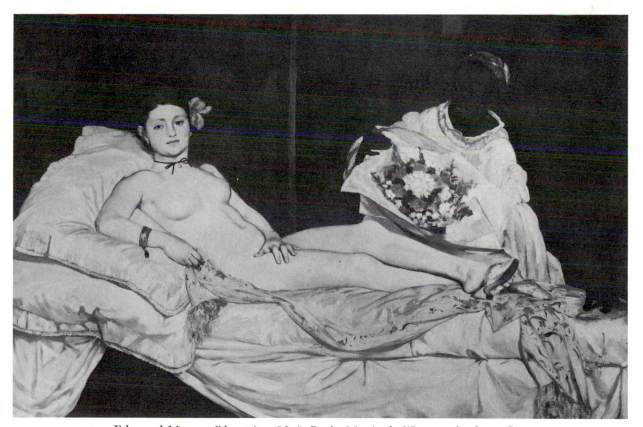

70. Edouard Manet. *Olympia*. 1865*. Paris, Musée de l'Impressionisme, Louvre

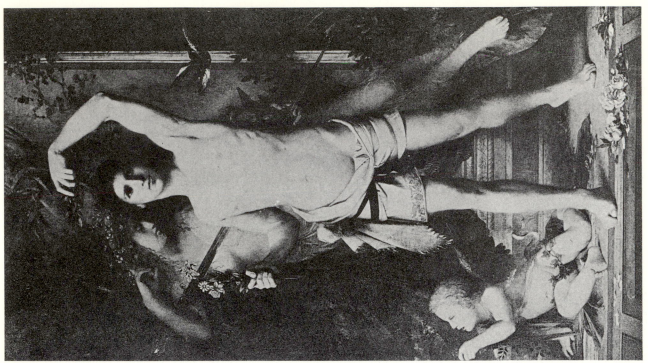

72. Gustave Moreau. *Le Jeune homme et la mort* (The Young Man and Death). 1865*. Paris, Musée du Luxembourg (?), Louvre (?)

71. Gustave Moreau. *Jason et Medée*. 1865*. Paris, Louvre

73. Gustave Courbet. *Le Remise des chevreuils* (The Cover of the Roe Deer). 1866*. Paris, Louvre

74. Gustave Courbet. *La Femme au perroquet* (The Woman with a Parrot). 1866*. New York,
The Metropolitan Museum of Art, Bequest of Mrs. H. O. Havemeyer, 1929,
The H. O. Havemeyer Collection

75. Edgar Degas. *La Fille de Jephté* (Jephthah's Daughter). About 1866. Northampton, Mass., courtesy The Smith College Museum of Art

76. Edouard Manet. *Le Fifre* (The Fifer Boy). 1866. Paris, Louvre

77. Claude Monet. *Camille*. 1866*. Bremen, Kunsthalle

78. Henri Regnault. *Automédon et les chevaux d'Achille* (Automedon and the Horse of Achilles).
1867. Boston, Mass., The Museum of Fine Arts (gift by subscription)

79. Edouard Manet. *Exécution de Maximilien*. 1867. Mannheim, Kunsthalle

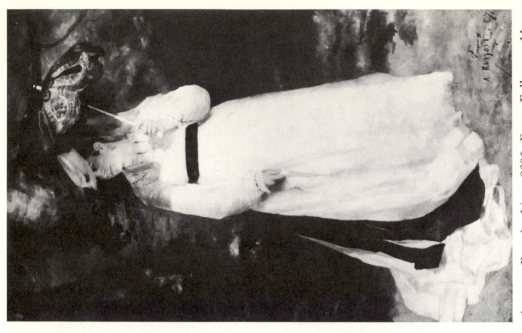

81. Auguste Renoir. *Lise*. 1868*. Essen, Folkwang Museum

80. Edouard Manet. *Portrait d'Émile Zola*. 1868*. Paris, Musée de l'Impressionisme, Louvre

82. Paul Marc Joseph Chenavard. *La Divine tragédie*. 1869*. Paris, Palais du Luxembourg

83. Camille Corot. *La Liseuse* (A Woman Reading). 1869*. New York, The Metropolitan Museum of Art, gift of Louise Senff Cameron, in memory of Charles H. Senff, 1928

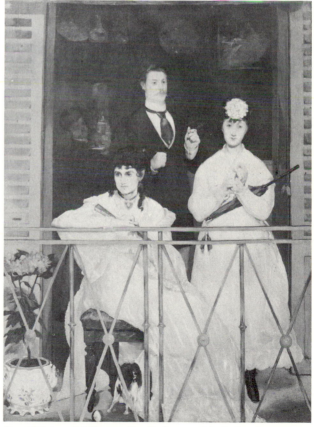

84. Edouard Manet. *Le Balcon*. 1869*. Paris, Louvre

85. Edouard Manet.
Le Déjeuner. 1869*.
Munich, Bayerische
Staatsgemalde Sammlung

86. Henri Regnault. *Général
Prim.* 1869*. Paris, Louvre

87. Henri Regnault. *Salomé*. 1870*. New York, The Metropolitan
Museum of Art, gift of George F. Baker, 1916

88. Auguste Renoir. *La Femme d'Algers*. 1870*. Washington, D.C., The National Gallery of Art,
Chester Dale Collection, 1962

90. Gustave Moreau. *Orphée* (Orpheus at the Tomb of Euridice). About 1870. Paris, Musée Gustave Moreau

89. Henri Regnault. *Exécution sans jugement sous les rois maures* (Execution without Trial under the Moorish Kings). 1870*. Paris, Louvre